EVALUATION
AND EMPLOYMENT
IN ORGANIZATIONS

EVALUATION AND EMPLOYMENT IN ORGANIZATIONS

Edited by

BARRY M. STAW
University of California, Berkeley

L.L. CUMMINGS
University of Minnesota

JAI PRESS INC.
Greenwich, Connecticut   **London, England**

Library of Congress Cataloging-in-Publication Data

Evaluation and employment in organizations / edited by L.L. Cummings,
    Barry M. Staw.
            p.   cm.
        ISBN 1-55938-219-8
        1. Employees—Rating of. 2. Assessment centers (Personnel management
    procedure) I. Cummings, Larry L. II. Staw, Barry M.
    HF5549.5.R3E93   1990
    658.3'125—dc20   90-4533
                                                                        CIP

Copyright © 1990 JAI PRESS INC.
55 Old Post Road, No. 2
Greenwich, Connecticut 06836

JAI PRESS LTD.
118 Pentonville Road
London N1 9JN
England

Manufactured in the United States of America

CONTENTS

LIST OF CONTRIBUTORS

Susan J. Ashford
Dartmouth College

Joel Brockner
Columbia University

Jack M. Feldman
Georgia Institute of Technology

Madeline E. Heilman
New York University

Daniel R. Ilgen
Michigan State University

Gary Johns
Concordia University

Thomas A. Mahoney
Vanderbilt University

Richard T. Mowday
University of Oregon

Nigel Nicholson
University of Sheffield

Richard M. Steers
University of Oregon

Sheldon Zedeck
University of California, Berkeley

PREFACE

The entry of humans into organizations, their evaluations by that organization, and the methods and consequences of adjustment to their organizational roles have long been the interest of scholars in organizational behavior and in industrial-organizational psychology. In this volume we bring together eight selections from *Research in Organizational Behavior* that have emphasized and significantly advanced these topics. The underlying themes are the complexity and dynamic nature of processes of evaluation and employment in contemporary organizations.

The first three chapters focus on the assessment and evaluation of organizational participants. Both of these processes play key roles in the socialization of newcomers into organizations and in the compliance, commitment, and performance of participants within their organizational roles.

Daniel Ilgen and Jack Feldman offer a formal model of the processes underlying the appraisal and evaluation of human performance. This chapter presents a major integration of theories both from personality and from social psychology into the study of performance assessment. The central theme is that the application of performance appraisal should beviewed as a *process*. This process is influenced by three *interacting* forces; the context of the organization (its culture, its reward systems, its history), the abilities and motivations of the appraiser as these relate to conducting appraisals, and the cognitive processing and behavior of the appraisee. The functioning of each force needs to be assessed when predicting the effects produced by any systems of appraisal. Each contains the potential to add distortion and bias to the appraisal process. A program of research is suggested and prescriptions are offered for overcoming these possibilities.

Susan Ashford focuses on the role of self-assessments, not only of performance but of adjustment and attachment to the organization as well. She presents a model of the issues and problems associated with self-assessments in the organizational context. While her analysis focuses on the self-assessment of feelings, it goes beyond to address issues involving the self-assessment of behavior and performance. Ego protection, positive self-esteem, and self-justification and each important needs in organizational life. They provide simultaneously the basis for tension with the need to obtain and interpret valid information about oneself. Ashford offers a dynamic model of the development of these tensions and provides suggestions which would extend theory and research on self-assessment.

Sheldon Zedeck traces the development of one of the most popular of assessment strategies used by organizations—the assessment center. He explores the processes underlying such centers. His claim is that better understanding and improvement of the processes underlying assessment techniques will improve both the validity and the acceptability of assessment outcomes. Basic psychological processes, e.g., cognitions and behavioral schema, are used to explain how assessors typically collect, recall, and integrate information into assessment judgments. Critical commentary is offered about typical assessment center methods based upon this knowledge from cognitive psychology.

One of the most important topics in current psychological and performance assessment centers is the role of sexual bias in performance and selection judgments. Madeline Heilman argues for the theoretical utility of a congruence model in understanding and predicting the occurrence and consequences of sex bias in organizational settings. She encourages systematic scholarship on the processes that underlie such biases both in selection and in evaluation. She also offers tentative recommendations, based on such scholarship to date, for preventing such biasing tendencies.

Thomas Mahoney addresses what was one of the most controversial topics in employee evaluation and compensation in the 1980s, i.e., comparable worth. He does this in a novel manner by emphasizing both the social and the political nature of the comparable worth phenomenon. He traces several important implications of his analysis for human resources policies and for political, economic, and societal organizations. Mahoney's analysis is centered on the assumption that comparable worth is embedded in and defined by a conflictual relation among competing ethical values and differing psychological utility preferences. While the current emphasis on comparable worth has subsided a bit, Mahoney's emphasis on the social and political nature of human resources issues can be applied with equal validity to many controversial topics in personnel administration (e.g., career development, internal labor markets, executive succession planning, and organizational design).

Absence (and turnover) from work have long been topics of central interest to scholars in industrial/organizational psychology and organizational behavior, as well as industrial relations. Gary Johns and Nigel Nicholson provide a welcome, fresh approach to the definition of absenteeism. Their analysis reopens the subject to new, fresh research. They offer propositions about absence behavior that challenge the received wisdom among researchers and practitioners alike. Several new research issues are advocated, focusing on absence as a process with multiple meanings as a function of the time frames applied and the organizational norms and cultures within which absence behavior occurs.

Richard Steers and Richard Mowday present a theoretical model and a review of the literature describing the processes that lead to voluntary employee turnover. Their analysis extends beyond turnover behavior, however, by focusing on the psychological and behavioral mechanisms used by employees to adjust to their decisions to remain in or leave an organization. Thus, the typical time frame for understanding turnover behavior is extended to the post-decision period. Steers and Mowday make creative use of attributional analyses in discussing these post-decision accommodations.

Finally, Joel Brockner presents a creative essay on the adjustment processes that survivors (remainers) make as they assess the meaning of their peers voluntarily or nonvoluntarily leaving the work setting. The key theoretical constructs used in this analysis are drawn from the research on stress and interpersonal equity. Evidence from several studies is offered to help us understand the motivational and affective reactions of those who survive a layoff. Futurer esearch agenda are also suggested.

L.L. CUMMINGS
Minneapolis, Minnesota

BARRY M. BAETZ
Berkeley, California

PERFORMANCE APPRAISAL:
A PROCESS FOCUS

Daniel R. Ilgen and Jack M. Feldman

ABSTRACT

The performance appraisal process is construed as a function of three interacting systems: the organizational context within which the appraisal takes place, the appraiser's information processing system, and the behavioral system of the appraisee. It is argued that aspects of each system constrain the ability of the appraisal process to produce accurate, unbiased, and reliable appraisals of individual behavior and performance in organizations. Most of the previous literature on performance appraisal has tended to focus upon one or at most two of the three systems, ignoring many possible interactions between systems. Furthermore, these earlier approaches have failed to consider performance as a process. As a result, attempts to increase the validity of appraisal ratings have oversimplified the validity problems and/or required standards for appraisal precision and accuracy that were beyond the capabilities of any performance appraisal system. This essay discusses each of the three subsystems just mentioned and its effects on performance appraisal. It concludes by offering suggestions for designing performance appraisal systems that may be better able to deal with the interactive effects of the three subsystems.

1

INTRODUCTION

No organization can function well over the long run without some means of distinguishing between good and poor performance by its members. Even if the standard of "goodness" is arbitrary or is based upon some changing standard (e.g., fashion design), at some point a distinction between satisfactory and unsatisfactory performance must be made.

Pressure to evaluate develops both at the organizational and the individual level. Those concerned with organization design stress the development of performance appraisal systems for control purposes (Lawler, 1976). Employees also desire information about the effectiveness of their performance. As a result of these organizational and individual interests, considerable attention has been paid to the development of performance appraisal systems.

Despite the effort devoted to the construction and evaluation of such systems, there is considerable dissatisfaction with progress in this area (Borman, 1978; Kane & Lawler, 1979; Landy & Farr, 1980). Defined as "the criterion problem" (Campbell, Dunnette, Lawler & Weick, 1970; Smith, 1976) early research on performance appraisal was confined almost exclusively to psychometric issues. While these problems are critical, a focus on the psychometric characteristics of rating forms (e.g., Bernardin, Alvarez & Kelley, 1976; Borman & Dunnette, 1975; Burnsaka & Hollman, 1974; Dickinson & Zellinger, 1980; Latham & Wexley, 1977; for a review, see Landy & Farr, 1980), the effects of rater training (e.g., Bernardin & Pence, 1980; Bernardin & Walter, 1977; Borman, 1975; Brown, 1968; Latham, Wexley & Pursell, 1975; Warmke & Billings, 1979), and the limits of observer validity (e.g., Borman, 1978) overlooks the equally important issue of precisely how real-world observations of behavior are translated into decisions about and evaluations of employees. That is, prior research has tended to overlook the process of appraising performance, concentrating instead upon some of the most severe problems of performance appraisal measures themselves. Those studies that have considered the process have tended to focus upon the use of performance appraisal systems rather than upon the process by which the performance of others is judged (Borman, 1978; Bazerman & Atkin, 1978; Green & Mitchell, 1979; and Stone & Slusher, 1975, are exceptions.) For example, management by objectives, goal-setting and behavior modification represent motivational techniques involving performance appraisal information and practices. Performance appraisal processes, while critical to each of these approaches, are not the primary focus of any of them.

In this chapter, we propose a multilevel, multiprocess conception of performance appraisal and its role in organizations. We are assuming that some individuals are required by their organizational roles to evaluate others in an organization and to share that evaluation with the person appraised and with selected others within the system. Furthermore we are assuming that this evaluation takes place on some relatively regular basis and that the individual being evaluated has at least some interest in the evaluation that he or she receives.

It is our contention that, to understand the determinants and effects of performance appraisals at both an individual and an organizational level, one must begin with realistic conception of the evaluator as an information gatherer and processor, operating in a complex environment. One must then consider the interpersonal relationship existing between the evaluator and the one being evaluated. Finally, all this must be imbedded in an organizational context which serves to promote and constrain behavior in various ways. Psychometric issues, training, and motivational processes related to performance appraisal must be considered in this overall context. Our view of these contiguous and interacting processes owes much to Weick, who pictures organizational processes as "multiple, heterogeneous flows of diverse viscosity moving at variable rates" (1979, p. 42).

Of course, the task of understanding performance appraisal in all its complexity is enormous; in fact, it is impossible to complete, given the current state of theory and the practical limits of space. We hope to make a reasonable beginning in this chapter, integrating present knowledge into a conceptual map for ourselves and others to follow. We shall begin by describing the context within which performance appraisal occurs.

PERFORMANCE APPRAISAL IN CONTEXT

Personnel managers, industrial psychologists, and others who have primary responsibility for the design of performance appraisal systems often unintentionally overlook important features of the work context in which the system must operate. Those responsible for the design and implementation of such systems have very specific expectations for them. These expectations often limit the contextual features of appraising performance and, as a result, lead to ignoring subtle features that may be critical to effective functioning of the system. It is our intention here to highlight some of the most salient features of organizations and to outline their probable impact on performance appraisal.

In our discussion of contextual features, we shall consider four general sets of conditions that influence the effectiveness of performance appraisal systems. We realize that the topics within these areas are not exhaustive. Yet they do appear to us to be some of the major characteristics of the work environment that must be considered in the design of any performance appraisal system. The four topics are: *Systemic Issues, Observational Opportunities, Continuous Work Groups,* and *Reward Opportunities.*

Systemic Issues

Function. Perhaps the most basic potential conflict in performance appraisal is internal, stemming from the primary functions it serves. These are the "controlling" and the "coaching" functions.

Performance appraisal systems serve controlling functions to the extent that they are used to determine rewards or punishments. Controls may be the result of explicit organizational policies, such as the basing of merit pay or promotion on evaluation ratings. They may be relatively informal control mechanisms as well, as when a supervisor uses his or her impression of performance to determine subordinates' job assignments.

The coaching function employs performance appraisals to provide feedback on the quality of an employee's performance and to serve as a vehicle through which the supervisor can contribute to employee development. Some claim that conflict between coaching and control functions may arise because coaching, to be maximally effective, should provide feedback in a nonthreatening manner. If negative feedback implies punishment, goes the argument, the resulting apprehension and possible resentment can interfere with the free exchange of information necessary to successful coaching (McCall & DeVries, 1976; Meyer, Kay & French, 1965).

Alternative arguments are worth considering. Some employees may prefer performance appraisals designed for coaching to have direct implications for reward, because such appraisals serve to clarify both organizational roles and reward systems. Perhaps, when, role requirements are adequately specified a priori, or when a positive reinforcement system tied to specific objectives is used, no conflict arises. When inequities in reward systems do exist, when punishment contingencies (either formal or informal) are used to control behavior, or when feedback is vague, resentment may easily occur. It is doubtful whether an individual who is charged with evaluating another's performance and also charged with determining that same person's future in the organization can, or should, ever completely separate the two functions. Moreover, it is unlikely that employees can (or should) separate the coaching and controlling function of their superiors, since employees who do not respond to coaching may not remain long with the organization. It is the responsibility of the organization to design reward and promotion systems that complement performance appraisals, so that supervisors and employees see the appraisal systems as benefiting both their own interests and the organization's. Lawler's (1971, 1981) review of pay systems provides useful guidance in this regard.

Expectations. Once a performance appraisal system has been in effect for some time, expectations or norms develop as to what constitutes an acceptable performance rating. These norms can be valuable because they may provide standards of judgment. They may also, however, be detrimental to appraisal validity if they lead to distortions of ratings. By distortion we mean the systematic introduction of inaccuracy to the appraisal so that the appraisal reflects what the appraiser believes is necessary for the system rather than the appraiser's actual beliefs about the performance of the appraisee.

A common distortion effect in many organizations is inflation (Fisher, 1979). Often, after only a few repetitions of a new evaluation system, the vast majority of appraisees are rated at or near the top of the scale. This has been common in military evaluation systems and recently has been a concern in academic institutions, where grade inflation has threatened the meaning of grade point averages. Once a system inflates, an appraiser has very little freedom to use the entire scale; receiving a lower than excellent rating has extremely negative consequences for the appraisee.

Lawler (1976) describes several factors that cause distortion in performance appraisal systems. Those most strongly promoting inflation are the subjectivity of the data required by the system and the consequences of the appraisal for the appraisees. Subjective ratings are more easily inflated than objective criteria, and inflation is heightened when the appraisal has important consequences for the persons appraised. For example, grade inflation in colleges and universities increased when failure in school meant the loss of draft exempt status and an increased likelihood of serving in an unpopular war.

Kane and Lawler (1979) propose a statistical approach to rating scale construction—distributional measurement—to deal with the problem of inflation. This approach forces the rater to differentiate more among ratees and therefore uses a wider range of responses on the scale. Although this approach has many positive features, it treats symptoms rather than causes. In many situations the causes of inflation cannot be removed without changing the organization itself and/or the nature of the people who populate it.

Although to the authors' knowledge, no research has been done on the causes of appraisal inflation, it seems most likely that, in addition to the factors mentioned above, it is due to certain organizational policies and to a desire of appraisers (who are also supervisors) to supervise competent employees. In the first case, the norm in many organizations is to stress that employees should perform well or be dropped by the organization. Therefore, ratings of employees over time may tend to improve even when the employee does not, simply because the employee has not performed poorly enough to be dismissed; given the up-or-out policy, his or her continuing presence in the organization suggests a need for higher ratings. In the second case, supervisors appraising their subordinates may inflate ratings either consciously or unconsciously to give the impression that the supervisor is performing the employee development function well. Regardless of the cause, any attempt to develop a performance appraisal system must take account of the fact that expectations about the system itself and about what is a "proper" rating will influence the ratings obtained, biasing both the mean and the variance of the ratings.

Observational Opportunities

Psychometrically oriented approaches to performance appraisal generally assume that the appraiser possesses adequate information about the appraisee's job performance at the time the appraisal is made. Given this assumption, attempts to remove systematic or random error in appraisals focus on the nature of the appraisal instrument and/or the rater's ability to properly use the instrument. In many settings, however, a sufficient knowledge base on which to construct valid appraisals may not be present due to the variety and number of supervisory responsibilities (Borman, 1978; Dowell & Wexley, 1978; McCall & DeVries, 1976; Mintzberg, 1973). The appraisee's job may require work that simply is not observable to the appraiser. Furthermore, in some cases, even if the appraiser were able to observe all of the relevant behaviors of the appraisee, the former may not possess sufficient knowledge about all of the outlooks of the latter's job to accurately assess the quality of performance.

Another cause of limited observational opportunities is the possible lack of synchronization between the time needed to complete one or more cycles of the appraisee's job and the time period covered by an appraisal. For some, the natural job cycle may be measured in minutes and seconds (e.g., an assembly line task or customer service at a fast-food emporium). Academic, professional, or retail merchandising jobs may cycle on an annual basis. Other jobs (e.g., major corporate executives) may require even longer cycles. It is important that the length of the cycle be carefully considered when appraisal practices are established. Although for jobs with extremely long cycles some intermediate criteria may be necessary, for other jobs, the appraisal time should be matched to the nature of the job requirements. This point may seem obvious, yet it is often ignored. It is not an uncommon company policy to require reviews of all new employees after 60 or 90 days on the job, regardless of the nature of the jobs.

Continuous Work Groups

Rarely does the appraiser judge the performance of a single individual on a single occasion. Usually he or she is faced with working and judging several individuals over extended periods of time. Thus, for any given individual at any given time, it is quite likely that a history of appraisals exists, as well as the expectation of future appraisals. These conditions promote comparative judgments. The presence of others on jobs similar to that of a particular appraisee makes it nearly impossible for the appraiser to evaluate any individual's performance without being influenced by the performance levels of others in the work group. The comparison process should be a major factor in evaluation in almost all cases in which an evaluator must deal with several individuals, unless that evaluator is highly experienced and possesses a clear-cut objective standard for performance on the job in question.

Likewise, when the same appraisee remains with an evaluator for more than one appraisal period, the individual's past performance and/or expected future performance may also influence the judgment process. This happens to the extent that the evaluator uses past and/or projected performance as standards against which present performance is compared.

The comparison process is described well by Tversky and Kahneman (1974) in their discussion of adjustment and anchoring effects. An evaluation at one time may be based, at least in part, on an evaluation conducted in a previous period, or on some estimate of the work group's mean performance. Perceptual contrast and assimilation effects may also occur, as they do in attitude change research (e.g., Fishbein & Ajzen, 1975).

Comparison effects can also occur as a result of deliberate policies of the appraiser. In particular, the evaluator may attempt to "manage" the pattern of performance appraisal ratings over time. That is, he or she may inflate or deflate ratings in order to obtain some desired effect, such as showing a performance improvement in a new employee for purposes of positive reinforcement. Appraisals may also be manipulated in order to protect a worker with personal problems whose performance has dropped over one appraisal period.

Appraisers may also manage the pattern of ratings among all the individuals appraised. Frequently, the appraiser is a supervisor or manager of a work group, and his or her primary responsibility is maintaining the effectiveness of that group. Under some conditions, especially those in which work group members are likely to discuss their appraisals with others, the long-term effectiveness of the work group may seem to be better served by a pattern of ratings that does not reflect the actual performance differences among persons. Thus, the appraisers may complete appraisal forms for each individual in order to construct the pattern across the group that they think will create the best overall response from their group, rather than the pattern of appraisals that reflects their best judgment about how each individual is performing his or her particular task. The purpose of the appraisal can become preserving work relationships rather than producing accurate ratings, when a conflict between the two exists (McCall & DeVries, 1976). An example of such a condition could be a case in which a supervisor has two subordinates working closely together on a job. If one of them has more experience but less skill than the other, who had just recently been hired, the older, more experienced person may perform less well than the other. In such a case, it might be advantageous not to emphasize differences between the two by creating a large discrepancy between the two appraisals, when it is known that the two will discuss their appraisals among themselves. In such a case, an evaluation may be somewhat more beneficial to work group harmony and overall performance in the long run. Such an effect would be most likely to occur when the standards for effective performances were relatively subjective.

The overall effect of such comparison processes may be either positive or negative. If the effectiveness of the work group must be preserved by the manipulation of ratings, it could be argued that the appraisal or reward system of an organization is in serious need of overhaul. It may, however, be the case that standards of judgment for the task in question are so ill-defined that overall comparative judgments are the only ones possible.

Strictly speaking, if an objective standard of performance is available, comparative judgments may correlate highly with actual performance but distort the intervals between employees. Being second-best may be either praiseworthy or unfortunate, depending on the actual levels of performance, but purely comparative ratings will not reveal which is the case. Finally, the effect of comparative ratings is to standardize appraisals within work groups. This renders across-group comparisons among employees meaningless, a serious problem when, for example, one person from any of several groups must be selected for promotion, special training, or extra recognition.

It is doubtful that any official policies or new appraisal forms can eliminate the effects that occur when those who appraise the performance of several others must work with these same people on a day-to-day basis, and must provide several evaluations of these individuals over an extended period of time. The forced choice scale is a classic case of the failure of an instrument to eliminate such problems (McCormick & Ilgen, 1980). This rating format was developed to reduce halo and leniency errors by presenting empirically keyed rating alternatives. The rater chooses the one of two alternatives that best describes the ratee, but which alternative is scored more favorably is not known to the rater. The scale does reduce rating errors, but, because it can interfere with the rater's ability to "manage" appraisal ratings, it met with such resistance that the format was abandoned.

In conclusion, we must emphasize that the use of data from performance appraisal systems should be tempered by the quality of the data that goes into the system. Quality will be influenced by the fact that the rating may serve different purposes for the appraiser than it does for the system as a whole.

Reward Opportunities

Information gained from performance appraisals is often used for administrative purposes. Decisions about pay rates, promotions, job requirements, opportunities for training, special awards, and other types of formal recognition (as well as negative sanctions) can be heavily influenced by appraisals. Organizations differ greatly in the explicitness with which appraisals are tied to outcomes. In some cases, outcomes such as pay, promotion/demotion, and dismissal are related to appraisal via some well-known function. In others, appraisals have only the most tenuous relationship to outcomes. In the former case, pressures may exist that force distortions in appraisals in order to justify decisions already made on extraneous grounds. In the latter, appraisals may be carried out in a careless fashion, since they serve only to meet the letter of a regulation. Only where appraisals are reliably related to outcomes, and where extraneous influences are either absent or made an explicit part of a parallel compensation system, would attention to appraisal processes and techniques be expected to have its greatest benefit for the organization and the employee.

The simple availability of resources may also influence patterns of appraisals (McCall & DeVries, 1976). The availability of positions into which employees may be promoted changes as a function of age of the work force, the growth of the organization, turnover, and many other factors. In times of slow growth and general economic malaise, organizations often must alter the degree of association between appraisals and the receipt of outcomes. Do appraisers alter their evaluation of others when the resources become scarce? To our knowledge, no data are available on this question. However, it seems likely that if rewards associated with evaluations are restricted for extended periods of time, morale and motivational problems will arise. Anticipating such circumstances, appraisers may shift their evaluations downward. Likewise, when resources are plentiful, there may be a tendency for evaluations to become more lenient.

Conclusions: Context Effects on Appraisals

The topics discussed above were not meant to be exhaustive. The discussion, rather, was intended to demonstrate that the accuracy of appraisal data is affected by several circumstances present in the organizations in which appraisals take place. Most earlier work on performance appraisal has paid little attention to these and other contextual issues (McCall & DeVries, 1976). In our opinion, these issues cannot be ignored.

It must also be stressed that there are few simple solutions for dealing with them. The immediate response is to try to eliminate their effects through control of the context. In some cases this may be reasonable; in many cases, however, such a solution is too simplistic. In the latter cases, a more realistic strategy is to attempt to understand the extent to which the context affects appraisals and to estimate the magnitude and direction of these effects. In the discussion that follows we shall continue to consider contextual effects and how to deal with them.

APPRAISERS

The typical performance appraisal system requires appraisers to record, on some standard form, their beliefs and feelings about other individuals. How these beliefs and feelings are developed has only recently been considered in depth by those interested in performance appraisal. Much of the work has borrowed from other areas concerned with the information processing capabilities of human beings in general and their ability to process information about other individuals in particular. For example, one line of research has to do with potential biasing factors in appraisals, such as employee sex or race (i. e., Bigoness, 1976; Feldman & Hilterman, 1977; Schmitt & Lappin, 1980; Terborg & Ilgen, 1975). A second line has to do with attribution theory as it is applied to an understanding of the cognitive processes engendered by various evaluation forms (Newtson, 1979; Schneier, 1977; Stone & Slusher, 1975).

These kinds of studies, while useful, are directly focused on what have been called *stimulus-based* judgments, in which all relevant information is immediately available to the appraiser at the time of judgment. However, in actual employment settings, the situation is different. As noted earlier, appraisers have a number of responsibilities demanding their time; some may interfere with their observation of subordinates (see, for example, Dowell & Wexley, 1978; Mintzberg, 1973). Appraisals are made at widely separated periods (e.g., every six months or once a year), while many other tasks compete for time and attention.

The appraisal task is often better characterized as a *memory-based* judgment process rather than as a stimulus-based one. A memory-based judgment focuses on what the supervisor has attended to in the past, the manner in which the information is organized and stored in memory, and other factors influencing the recall of some or all of the relevant information. The reasons for which the information is being recalled also play a part. It will be seen that different judgment tasks and contexts may strongly influence the recall and organization of information (Hamilton, Katz & Leirer, 1980).

We attempt to describe in the following pages a complex and cyclical set of processes. There is no easy place to begin, for the processes at any one point are influenced by the state of the system of every other point. Additionally, there are gaps in our knowledge which, for purposes of the present exposition, are bridged by discussions of an admittedly speculative nature. There are also theoretical controversies and ambiguities which must be appreciated by the practitioner if premature and overconfident application is to be avoided.

To help the reader penetrate the thicket of information that follows, Table 1 presents a brief glossary. In addition, later in this section we shall summarize our discussion using a series of flow charts. Familiarization with all these will show the place of each sub-process in the overall appraisal context. Thus, the issues raised in the following pages will be put in proper perspective and, with the help of the glossary in Table 1, can be understood with minimal confusion.

If there is one concept of central and overriding importance to this section, it is "categorization." We regard the process by which stimuli are grouped into like clusters, and the structure and interrelationships of those clusters, to be the key concept linking processes of attention, perception, memory storage, retrieval, and information integration. In the pages that follow, the concepts of category, category system, schema, and prototype will appear in many contexts. Some redundancy is unavoidable, because the system we are describing is a recursive one. We hope that our discussion will reward the reader's efforts with greater insight and understanding.[1]

Table 1.   Definitions of Terms Commonly used in Social Cognition

	Definition
Attribution	The process by which perceivers assign specific causes to observed events. *Causal* attribution is the assignment of causal responsibility for an event to some aspect of an actor or to an environmental feature; *trait* attribution is a categorization of the causal agent in terms of groups of agents sharing similar characteristics (e.g., *hostile* people or *difficult* tasks).
Automatic process	A cognitive or behavioral process occuring without conscious monitoring or awareness (Kimble & Perlmuter, 1970; Langer, 1978; Nisbett & Wilson, 1977; Shevrin & Dickman, 1980; Schneider & Shiffrin, 1977; Shiffrin & Schneider, 1977; Thorngate, 1976).
Category	A "fuzzy set" of objects considered equivalent, in which membership in the set is defined by family resemblence rather than by the possession of all attributes considered to be critical (Cantor & Mischel, 1979; Rosch, Mervis, Gray, Johnson & Boyes-Braem, 1976). Categorization is considered basic to perception, information storage, and organization (Bruner, 1958).
Controlled process	A cognitive or behavioral process that proceeds under conscious control, about which the person is continuously aware.
Implicit personality theory/Personal constructs	The set of categories and their associated prototypes/schemata used by an individual to represent, evaluate, and predict the behavior of others.
Information integration	The combination of two or more separate items of information into a summary judgment or evaluation (Anderson, 1974; 1976).
Prototype	An abstract *analog*, or *image*, summarizing "central tendencies" or resemblances among category members (Cohen, 1979; Rosch, et al., 1976, Rosch, 1977). A prototype is the cognitive representation of a typical category member, and examplifies the category in memory (see also *Schema*).
Salience	*Prominence* of a stimulus in the perceptual field. In memory it is the availability of a cognition of a memory trace (Taylor & Fiske, 1978).
Schema	Verbal or propositional memory structures representing categories of a more complex nature than prototypes but serving the same function in perceptual organization and memory. Schemata are used to represent the self (Markus, 1977) and well-known other people as well as familiar situations and objects.
Stereotype	A subtype of implicit personality theory, specifically one based on racial, sexual, ethnic, or occupational categories rather than trait categories.

Attention

Before appraisal-related information about a person can be processed, it must be attended to and recognized as information. Two attentional mechanisms, automatic and controlled, are thought to operate, depending on the informational context (Schneider and Shiffrin, 1977; Shiffrin and Schneider, 1977).

The Automatic Process in Attention. The automatic process takes place under "consistent mapping" conditions, where a given stimulus type must be detected in a field of different stimuli (e.g., numbers in a field of letters). The controlled process, in contrast, is activated under "variable mapping" conditions, where a given stimulus type may be either a distractor (field) or a target. The process that emerges under these more problematic circumstances requires conscious direction and decision making.

The extention of similar processes to interperonal behavior is straightforward. Langer (1975) and Nisbett and Wilson (1977) show that people often act in a "thoughtless" or "mindless" fashion and are often unable to verbalize the cues governing their response. The notion of "script processing" (Abelson, 1976; Shank & Abelson, 1976) is consistent with such thoughtlessness, suggesting that in the performance of well-learned sequences of behavior, there is plentiful opportunity for thought to be directed away from one's current behavior (Gibb, 1979). As Langer (1978) shows, only when interaction becomes in some way effortful or problematic may it engage consciousness.

Thus, just as one can drive without being aware of the movements involved (Kimble & Perlmuter, 1970), one can learn to attend to attributes of people and situations with minimal awareness. Attention to such properties as "tree-ness" and "females-ness" is taken to be automatic, based on overlearned attentional responses exactly like those involved in the perception of optical illusions.

The automatic process may direct attention to people and their attributes. Which people and which attributes are attended to, is a function of their salience, which in turn is a function of both individual differences and the environmental context. Taylor and Fiske (1978) show that novelty (i.e., a solo black in an all-white group) and various props or arrangements such as lighting, cameras, seating positions, and so on, may make particular individuals salient. Further when an individual is salient because of some feature (e.g., race, sex, dress, height, etc.), that *feature* itself becomes more salient.

Individual differences in implicit theories of people and situations may also influence the salience of people and their attributes. Markus (1977),

Kelley, (1955), and others have shown that people differ in their category systems. Rosch, et al. (1976) point out that experience in an area of knowledge results in a more highly differentiated category system. Such differentiation requires the development of detailed prototypes representing the more finely developed categories in the system. Since "laymen" do not possess such a category system, it follows that, for the person with a degree of expertise, stimulus features unnoticed by the layman will be habitually salient. The football coach for example, will notice aspects of a player's performance that the spectator misses.

Tajfel (1969) makes a similar point about the affect associated with given categories—more intense affect produces cateogry salience (see also Quanty, Keats, & Harkins, 1975). Both this point and the preceding one are consistent with cross-cultural studies of visual perception showing experience-based differences in susceptibility to optical illusions (Segall, Campbell, & Herskovitz, 1966). While not dealing directly with performance appraisal, these studies imply that the learned category system used to interpret and store information also influences attention to different aspects of the stimulus environment.

Zajonc (1980) has raised an interesting possibility with regard to automatic *affective* responses that may occur in conjunction with automatic attentional processes. He argues that evaluation may be separate from cognition in many cases, and that affective responses to cues, once formed, may be experienced without the prior occurrence of cognition. This is compatible with Anderson's (1974) concept of separate storage for evaluative impressions of people and objects, impressions that must be integrated with any new information.

Although an automatic affective response (if it occurs) cannot be said to *depend* in any way on the attentional process discussed above, it would be surprising if at least some of the same cues were not involved. Thus, when attention is automatically focused on a person or some aspect of a person, it is possible that a nearly simultaneous feeling of liking or disliking occurs as well.

The Controlled Process in Attention.   The processes governing attention under conscious mediation are likewise influenced by the salience of cues in the environment. The controlled process, however, takes place when the individual must first define the dimension on which "target" stimuli differ from distractors and then process the necessary cues allowing such differentiation. Such controlled processing takes place because of the way the task is presented (Enzle & Schopflocher, 1978), the effortful demands the stimuli present to the perceiver (Langer, 1978), or because of some above-threshold deviation of observed observations from those expected (Pyszczynski & Greenberg, 1981).

Under controlled processing condition, attributes of people, tasks, and situations regarded as more informative (novel or evaluatively extreme) receive greater attention. The context in which the process occurs may make certain cues more or less informative and therefore more salient (Tversky, 1977); for example, in a context of male and female professionals, the "laborer" aspect of a male laborer would be informative; in a context of female professionals and laborers, cues of "masculinity" would be most salient.

Finally, the interactive nature of the automatic and controlled processes must be noted. It is entirely possible for some aspects of persons or situations to be attended to automatically—race, sex, or height, for example—and for these characteristics to direct controlled attention to cues that would otherwise pass unnoticed. In a sense, the automatic process sets the baseline against which departures from expectation are assessed.

Implications for Performance Appraisal. Automatic attentional processes are presumed to exist to promote "cognitive economy," the processing of information with a minimal expenditure of time and energy. The fact that attention often is not under volitional control means that irrelevant information about employees is almost certain to be obtained despite the intentions of the appraiser. The controlled attentional process similarly is subject to influence by unintended and uncontrollable factors, such as a stimulus person's "novelty," or how close to the supervisor he or she works, as well as by the perceiver's habits of attention. The nature of the attentional process may explain some variance in "first impressions biases" (see Campbell, et al., 1970, p. 112-113).

The possibility of automatic affective response has obvious and direct implications for performance appraisal. Those adept at "creating a good impression," for example, may have learned to manipulate affectively relevant cues. How these processes influence and are influenced by others will be discussed later.

Categorization and Memory.

Categorization is necessary to cognitive economy; it reduces the amount of information that must be processed and stored (see Smith, Adams & Schorr, 1978; Behling, Gifford & Tolliver, 1980). Categorization and perception are here considered to be one and the same, after Bruner (1958). Perception can be considered the process by which meaning is given to stimuli, and this meaning or "sense-making" is accomplished via the relationship of that stimulus to others, both similar and different. In other words, perception implies the placement of a stimulus in a category along with similar stimuli that share certain of its features; the structure of an individual's category system then determines what a particular stimulus is seen as like and unlike. Evidence indicates that two processes of categorization exist, and that these operate interactively. Newtson (1981) has termed these the "perceptual" and "inferential," but since these are very similar to those processes we have been discussing, we will continue to use the terms "automatic" and "controlled" for categorization.

The Automatic Process in Categorization.   Studies cited in the preceding section are relevant to automatic categorization. Attention to "tree-ness" or "female-ness" implies nearly stimultaneous categorization; the perception of an optical illusion, a "friendly" behavior, or unthinking compliance with an essentially senseless request (Langer, 1978) likewise implies an automatic categorization response. Categorization of a person, behavior, situation, or object is thought to be the outcome of a feature-matching process, in which the stimulus is compared with the feature of a category prototype (or schema); a category assignment is made when satisfactory fit is achieved (Tversky, 1977; see also McCloskey & Glucksberg, 1978, 1979; Medin & Schaffer, 1978; Smith & Medin, Note 6). In the case of the automatic process, it is argued that the categorization response to particular cues (e.g., skin color, the size/weight illusion, etc.) is so highly overlearned that no monitoring is required (cf. Neisser, 1980).

The Controlled Process in Categorization.   An automatic process is insufficient to encompass all categorizations. In the first place, the automatic process is not inborn; cateogry systems must be developed by observation and tuition (Rosch, et al., 1976) which implies a controlled, consciously monitored process. Furthermore, people and situations change, and unique examples of both are enountered. Some process for revising category systems and category placement must exist.

A "switching mechanism" is necessary to bring the controlled process into play. We have noted that "effortful or problematic" situations call for controlled attentional process, and such control would seem to be useful only in conjunction with controlled categorization. Thus, we will assume that the same mechanism elicits both controlled attention and controlled categorization.

For a categorization to be problematic and thus require controlled processing, one of three conditions should hold: (1) No salient cateogry exists into which to place a stimulus. This requires a search of memory for relevant categories as well as more detailed attention to the stimulus. (2) Information is received which is inconsistent with a previous category placement. (3) A single stimulus possesses cues which imply, if not contradictory, then at least negatively correlated categorizations. The first condition probably does not often apply to the perception of people, since a completely unfamiliar and exotic person can always be placed in a "stranger" or "foreigner" category. It could apply to situations or objects, however, for example, when (as is sometimes the case in large organizations) a new management trainee is placed for "on the job training" in an entirely unfamiliar setting.[2] An example of the second case would be the discovery that a seemingly ordinary factory worker was also a nationally ranked chess master,[3] while the third type of situation is exemplified by the studies of Feldman (1972) and Feldman and Hilterman (1975) in which subjects were asked to attribute traits to black stimulus persons who had attained professional occupations. In all three cases, the lack of an immediately salient prototype/schema or the disconfirmation of a previous categorization by new information is thought to trigger the controlled process. We may postulate a hypothetical comparison mechanism that matches incoming information with an available prototype/schema. If no prototype is available, or the "threshold of discrepancy" if exceeded, the mechanism calls for a controlled categorization.

Direct evidence for such a mechanism is minimal. Studies cited earlier have shown that information consistent with a categorization is better recalled (or falsely recalled) than inconsistent information. Other studies, however, (Hastie, 1978) show just the opposite—inconsistent information is better recalled. If a comparison mechanism does operate as discussed above, in the latter case the results can be explained by the elicitation of the controlled process. Langer's (1978) date, the research of Newtson (1976), who showed that the units of perceptual organization become smaller under problematic or uncertain conditions, Ebbesen and Allen's (1979) support of a two-stage trait inference process, and Enzle and Schopflocher's (1978) demonstration that attribution-like (controlled) processes may not occur unless proper questions asked, make plausible the idea of two separate categorization processes.

To date, the most complete exposition of a controlled categorization process in the domain of person perception goes under the label of "attribution theory." While it is true that attribution theory may be modeled via Anderson's (1974) cognitive algebra and may be representable by a feature-matching model as cited above, at present, verbal representations of the process are well worth consideration (see Mitchell, Green, & Wood, 1981).

As described by Kelley (1971a, b), Jones (1979), Jones and Davis (1965), Jones and McGillis (1976), and others, attribution is a rational process in which people act as "naive scientists" when making inferences about others. Two principles are fundamental. The first, *covariation,* states that the perceived cause of an event is found among the conditions varying with the occurrence of the event rather than among those that are unchanging (see Shaver, 1975). Kelley's (1971a) "naive analysis of variance" contains three dimensions over which events or behaviors may vary: (a) *entities,* or things acted toward, such as tasks; (b) *situations or contexts* of behavior, such as stressful work settings, the golf course, or a training program; and (c) *other people*—that is, in what ways does the behavior of the person in question depart from the base rate of behavior across situations and entities? The second principle, *discounting,* states that observers will discount a single causal explanation for a behavior when more than one plausible cause exists (see Kruglanski, 1970; Strickland, 1958). Its counterpart, augmentation, is the complementary increase in the attribution to facilitating causes found, when an inhibiting factor is present in the environment (e.g., the results of Feldman, 1972).

The first stage in controlled categorization is *causal attribution:* perceivers must decide if an event or behavior is caused by the person in question or is due to the situation or entity involved. If the person covaries with the behavior or event, he is seen as the cause. For example, an employee who regularly fails to complete assigned tasks when other employees complete theirs will be seen as the cause of the failure. If only a particular kind of task is not completed, however, and many other employees also fail on that kind of task, the task will be categorized as "difficult" and will be seen as the cause of the failure. Only in the former case would failure be expected to reduce the employee's evaluation. An example of the discounting principle would be a case in which an employee, previously categorized as a member of a low ability group, failed at some new task. The failure would be seen as "caused" by the employee's lack of skill rather than by the difficult task.

Smith and Miller (1979) argue that causal attribution is subtractive; that is, people begin with complex explanations for behavior and eliminate potential causes as the evidence warrants. They also suggest that the set of potential causes with which perceivers begin is determined by the salience of those causes (as discussed by Taylor & Fiske, 1978; see also Fergeson & Wells, 1980) or the cause's presence in a script (Shank & Abelson, 1977). This is consistent with the idea that the controlled attribution processes are influenced by previous automatic attention and categorization.

Once causality has been determined, a *trait* or *dispositional* attribution (categorization) is necessary. Cantor and Mischel (1979) have shown that judgments of "prototypicality" are made as attribution theory predicts, supporting the idea of dispositional attribution as a categorization process.

Besides covariation and discounting principles, attribution theory includes a number of ad hoc "biases" or moderating factors. Ross (1977) has discussed these biases, some of which can be understood as consequences of automatic attention and categorization processes.

First, the "fundamental error" is a tendency to underestimate the importance of situational factors and overestimate that of dispositional factors as causes of behavior. People are seen as causes too frequently, and situations too seldom. This can be explained by noting that situational prototypes and scripts of behavior settings tend to contain features describing the behavior and dispositions of the people in them (Bem & Funder, 1978; Cantor, Note 3; Shank & Abelson, 1977). Parties, for example, are characterized by people dancing and talking. Thus, one's mere *presence* in a situation has dispositional connotations.

Second, actors and observers differ in causal attributions: actors emphasize situational factors; observers, the actor's personal dispositions. This tendency is largely due to the differential salience of situational and personal information to the actor and observer, respectively.

These first two biases can be interactive, in that observed behavior is interpreted in terms of a salient situational prototype. Given a particular definition of a situation, "appropriate" dispositions are readily inferred and/or behavior interpreted dispositionally "in light of" the setting (Snyder & Frankel, 1976).

The third bias, already discussed, is the tendency to see as causal the most salient features of the environment, including "novel" individuals (McArthur & Solomon, 1978; Pryor & Kriss, 1977; Taylor & Fiske, 1978; Tversky & Kahneman, 1974).

The fourth is called "hedonic relevance" (Jones & Davis, 1965): the tendency to see actions having positive or negative consequences for the observer as more dispositional than other actions. Coupled with this is the tendency to see people as more responsible for acts with serious, as opposed to trivial, consequences. This, too, may stem from the consequent salience of the actor.

Fifth, actors are attributed greater responsibility for acts leading to gains (reward) than those preventing losses. Also noted is the tendency for people to pay insufficient attention to base rate information (the degree to which a behavior is common) and the complementary tendency to use one's *own* behavior as a basis for judging the typicality of an actor's (the "false consensus effect"; see Ross, Greene, & House, 1977). This may be another reflection of the "law of small numbers" (Tversky & Kahneman, 1971), reflecting a general tendency to end the search for causes when the first prototype providing a satisfactory explanation for the behavior is found.

A last bias, not considered by Ross, is for attributions to follow affect: good actions by liked people are attributed to the person and bad actions to the situation, while attributions for actions of disliked people follow the opposite pattern (good actions—external attribution, bad actions—internal; Regan, Strauss, & Fazio, 1974). Taylor and Jaggi (1974) have shown that the same pattern exists in the perception of ethnic groups (see also Duncan, 1976). This bias may also explain attributions influenced by physical appearance (Berscheid & Walster, 1974; Cash, Gillen & Burns, 1977), as well as explanations for the success of women (Garland & Price, 1977). The effect of this bias may depend on the initial categorization of the person (Srull & Wyer, 1979) and the operation of the discounting principle (see also Brewer, 1979, and Lindville & Jones, 1980).

Consequences of Categorization for Memory. Once categorization has occurred, the stimulus person (or object or situation) is assimilated to the relevant category, prototype/schema. Subsequent inferences about the individual are made in terms of the cognitive representation of his or her category; unique features of the stimulus person are henceforth unavailable (Wyer & Srull, 1979). Further, free recall or recognition (for example, on a checklist scale) of an individual's behavior or other characteristics is colored by the prototype/schema, such that people recall information that was never actually presented (Cantor & Mischel, 1977; 1979; Lingle, Geva, Ostrom, Lieppe & Baumgardner, 1979; Sentis & Burnstein, 1979; Spiro, 1977; Tsujimoto, 1978; Tsujimoto, Wilde & Robertson, 1978; Wyer and Srull, 1980). These impressions also may be relatively resistant to later disconfirmation (Fleming & Arrowood, 1979). The process is identical to stereotyping of individuals, in that, if a person is categorized as member of a group, the features of the group's prototype come to characterize that individual (Ashmore & DelBoca, 1979; Taylor, Fiske, Etcoff & Rudderman, 1978). It is important to note that the perceiver does not choose to stereotype; this effect is the outcome of basic perceptual and memory processes. Also, the categories used may not be only the common racial, ethnic, or sexual groupings, but may be groupings unique to the person or situation; multiple categorizations are also possible.

Category Selection. In either the controlled or automatic categorization process, the selection of a category is an important consideration. Most behaviors, and most people, are amenable to multiple categorizations. Some aspects of this problem have already been discussed under the topic of automatic attentional processes. The salience of particular cues (as discussed earlier) is important insofar as those cues are associated with category prototypes or schemata. The salience of a particular cue or set of cues implies corresponding salience for the category or set of categories to which those cues are relevant. Other factors also require attention. Srull and Wyer (1979, 1980) have shown that categories more recently used are more salient or accessible, increasing the probability that that category will be used to encode behavior. Individual differences, either transient (such as mood or an automatic affective response to some cue) or enduring (dispositions such as prejudice or depressiveness) also render certain categories more accessible than others (Cantor, 1976; Tajfel, 1969; Teasdale & Fogarty, 1979). In short, any event or condition making a particular category more salient increases its probability of use in encoding information. Considered across time or across observers, different salience effects may drastically change the way an individual with specific characteristics is represented in memory (Wyer & Srull, 1980).

The information processing task itself also influences category selection. Zajonc (1960) in his studies of "cognitive tuning," showed differences in the representation of information depending on whether the purpose was to recall or transmit information. Harvey, Harkins, and Kagehiro (1976) found also that observers tended to make causal attributions more frequently under a "transmission" set than under a "reception" set, suggesting that people use causal attribution-based categorizations as an aid in communication. More recently, Cohen and Ebbesen (1979) and Hoffman and Mischel (1980) have found that information is categorized differently depending on whether one's purpose is to *memorize* behavior or "form an impression" of a person. Recall is most accurate when the intent is to memorize, and most schematically biased when "impressions" are to be formed. This may well be a result of the use of different types of categories under each set (i.e., Hoffman and Mischel found that "actor's goal" categories were used when people's set was to memorize or emphasize, whereas "trait" categories were used when impression or behavioral prediction was the processing objective). Hamilton, Katz, and Leirer (1980) found, however, that impression instructions aided recall as compared to "memory task" instructions, suggesting that the nature of the material to be remembered is an important consideration.

The observer's own behavior can also determine the categories used to code others' behavior. Strickland (1958) and Kruglanski (1970) both showed that a more closely supervised employee was seen as less "trustworthy" and less "internally motivated," despite the fact that the degree of surveillance was not determined by the observer and despite equal performance of the "employee" under both close and general supervision. These studies can be understood as examples of the discounting principle, whose operation would tend to make "external" causal explanations more salient to the obeserver.

Category Formation. Rosch and her colleagues (Rosch, et al., 1976) maintain that categories are formed by observation of covariation in the world, and prototypes represent the central tendencies of those categories. Thus, a prototypical "executive" has some features in common with a broad sample of executives, but given executives vary widely in their "prototypicality." For example, the hard-hatted male vice-president of a construction firm differs in many ways from his counterparts in the auto or fashion industries.

It must be remembered, though, that because these correlations are perceived, they are likely to differ in systematic ways from those existing in nature. Tversky and Kahneman (1974) discuss two judgment heuristics relevant to this issue, "availability" and "representativeness." Briefly, the availability heuristic operates such that the most available event in memory is seen as most likely to occur—that is, salient, striking behaviors and characteristics are seen as most probable. The boisterous, colorful ethnic group member's behavior is noticed and recalled more easily than the quiet one's, and is more likely to be used to represent the category.

The "representativeness" heuristic operates such that "similar" events are seen as associated, so that (for example) a shy person is expected to be a librarian with a greater probability than is justified by the actual joint frequency of shyness and librarianship. Events and characteristics may be associated on the basis of perceived similarity, with little regard for the actual frequency of co-occurence.

In addition to the heuritics discussed above, a number of other biasing factors exist: the tendency to draw too firm a conclusion from a small amount of evidence (the "law of small numbers"; Tversky & Kahneman, 1971); the tendency to focus on consistency of information regardless of its actual predictive utility; and the tendency to attend to only "positive hits," ignoring alternative hypotheses (Einhorn & Hogarth, 1978; Langer & Roth, 1975). The operation of these factors makes the occurence of "illusory correlations" (Hamilton, 1979) understandable. Associations between categories of people and classes of events, good and bad, may be perceived because the categories are equally available in memory, and not because of actual association. A new stereotype, or an additional facet to an old one, is thus created. These stereotypes are difficult to disconfirm, as they are seemingly based on "real-world experience." For example, "everyone knows" that Jews are excellent businessmen, and those holding this belief can provide many examples on request.

Implications for Performance Appraisal. The distortion of recall associated with categorization has a severe impact on trait-type rating scales, because traits are part of any category prototype. It is possible that a person is recalled as "conscientious" or "uncooperative" not because relevant behavior has been observed but because these traits are part of the prototype characterizing that person. Likewise, a behaviorally anchored rating scale, a forced-choice scale, or a behavioral checklist scale is subject to prototype-based distortion, since the "expected" or "recalled" behavior may be reconstructed on the basis of the selected prototype. Halo effects are virtually unavoidable in any type of rating scale since the prototype contains a number of "traits" and their behavioral referents. These traits co-occur in ratings because they are recalled *as a group,* and naturally will be correlated regardless of their actual co-occurrence (see also Berman & Kenney, 1976; Cooper, 1981). Leniency-stringency biases can be understood as a consequence of individual differences (mood, personality factors) influencing the content and salience of positive and negative categories (as well as standards of judgment). The greater the "prototypicality" of the ratee, the stronger these effects will be. Purely evaluative responses (either global ratings of "goodness" or "value" or rankings) are thought to be based on stored evaluative impressions associated with category prototypes/schemata. They may be either "automatically elicited" or based on an evaluative integration.

Even in a new job situation, categories and associated prototypes are not long in forming. These prototypes may contain systematic biases, and categorization of one's coworkers could distort recall as seriously with the new as with one's old category system.

The evaluation effects of categorization carry over to personnel decisions in organizations. Formal decisions (e.g., work assignments, time-span of discretion) and formal decisions (e.g., termination, promotion, transfer) are based in part on some prediction of behavior. The effects of categorization are similar to those noted for behaviorally anchored and trait rating scales. "Expected behavior" tends to be preferred for decision making in familiar situations, "trait" information for unfamiliar situations (Mischel, Jeffrey & Patterson, 1974). Given the category prototype, the availability and representativeness heuristics should determine the matching of people to (the prototypes of) situations they are expected to perform best in, via Tversky's (1977) feature-matching process (Wyer & Srull, 1979; Cantor, Note 2; Bem & Funder, 1978). Other things being equal, the person recalled as tall and confident will be given the sales job, and the person recalled as nonassertive and "bookish" will keep the accounts.

Recall, Information Search, Recategorization, and Integration

Recall. Many of the necessary elements for a discussion of recall have already been presented. The "storage-bin" model of memory proposed by Wyer and Srull (1979) is adopted provisionally, because it fits well with our present orientation.[4] Long-term memory is construed as a set of storage bins, each containing particular kinds of information. These correspond to categories, as we have defined them. Each "bin" has an accompanying "label" (prototype) exemplifying its contents. (Bins may also pertain to particular people, objects events, schemas, scripts, and so on.) A "work space" is also postulated, in which "raw data" for processing by various mechanisms, and the output of such processing, is held. The work space is strictly short-term storage; it is cleared when there is no further use for the material it holds. the implication, as noted earlier, is that any unique behavioral information about a person is eventually lost, and only categorical information remains. Thus, even if a belief about a person is later disconfirmed, the original categorization will continue to affect the peceiver's behavior because the disconfirmation may not be stored with the original categorization (Fleming & Arrowood, 1979; Anderson, Lepper & Ross, 1980).

Information is stored in bins in the order of receipt, so that the most recent information is the most accessible (salient). Information about a person may be stored in more than one "bin." The most recently used bin (as determined by individual differences, contextual and task factors) is the most accessible for subsequent use.

Thus, all the factors governing category salience should also operate to influence recall. An evaluative rating form may elicit stored impressions independent of behavioral recall (Dreben, Fiske, & Hastie, 1979). The positive or negative content of these impressions may make confirming behavioral evidence more salient. A good or bad mood may likewise make positive or negative events ("bins") more salient for all employees being considered (implying validity to the advice: "Catch the boss on a good day." Isen, Shalker, Clark & Karp, 1978; Teasdale & Fogarty, 1978). Only if new information has been recently processed and is available on the "workspace" will relevant behavior unfiltered by memory be influential. (This supports the wisdom of saving some unusually good work for presentation close to evaluation time). Of course, such information is subject to the attention and categorization processes previously discussed.

Information Search. If an appraiser is conscientious, or if contradictory information is obtained about an employee, additional information may be sought. Typically, the appraiser is not in a condition of complete uncertainty. Rather, he or she will be seeking to "test" some hypothesis about the employee in question—character, ability, or motivation.

Under these conditions, two sorts of biases appear. First, people tend to seek confirmation of their hypotheses and frame questions aimed at eliciting positive instances of hypothesized traits (Einhorn & Hogarth, 1978; Snyder & Cantor, in press; Snyder & Swann, 1978a).[5] They also tend to notice and recall hypothesis-confirming behaviors more than disconfirming ones (Zadny & Gerard, 1974). Thus, if an employee is suspected of "laziness," instances of "lazy" behavior will be more readily noted and searched for, while instances of working hard will be less salient.

A second biasing factor exists in interpersonal situations. People holding expectations about another's behavior are likely to elicit the expected behavior in interaction (Snyder & Swann, 1978b; Snyder, Tanke, & Berscheid, 1977). Thus, if a supervisor believes that an employee has a "bad attitude" about his work, interaction is likely to result in confirmation of that hypothesis. The "naive advocate" model of information seeking (Hamilton, 1980) is a worthwhile addition to Kelley's (1971a) "naive scientist" model.

Holding hypotheses about the causes of another' behavior also affects how that person is treated in other ways. Swann and Snyder (1980) found that an instructor's theory about the nature of ability influenced the instructional strategy chosen. Those believing ability was acquired through experience produced higher performance in students randomly labeled high ability; those believing ability was innate produced higher performance in those labeled low ability. Further, regardless of actual performance, instructors always *rated* the "high-ability" students as the better performers and expressed more confidence in them than in the "low ability" students in spite of the fact that the high or low ability designations were randomly assigned to individuals.

Recategorization. Despite the conservative biases stressed above, people do change their beliefs about others. From time to time information is obtained which is so striking in its implications it can neither be discounted (Ross, 1977) nor interpreted consistently with previous categorizations, as when the respected businessman is revealed to be an embezzler. This is an extreme example, of course; even a series of consistent, less extreme departures from expected behavior may be enough to exceed the "threshold of discrepancy" postulated earlier (see, for example, Feldman, 1972; Feldman & Hilterman, 1975; Deaux, 1976). Linville and Jones (1980) can be interpreted as suggesting that this hypothetical threshold is lower for outgroup than ingroup members, due to the more complex schematic representation of the ingroup. Likewise, it may be that more cognitively complex individuals have lower thresholds overall than others and thus more "tolerance for ambiguity."

In such cases, a reorganization of memory seems to occur, such that memories consistent with the new categorization become selectively more available (Snyder & Uranowitz, 1978). this may be related to the increase in subjective probability of an event which occurs after the event has happened (Fischoff, 1975; Fischoff & Beyth, 1975); both seem to be functions of category salience (Wyer & Srull, 1979).

Integration. Two kinds of integration seem to be required for different sorts of tasks. *Cognitive* integration occurs when the task requires an estimation of probability or other behavioral prediction. Behaviorally anchored, checklist, or forced choice scales, as well as hiring or placement decisions, job assignments, and the like may require cognitive integration. "May require" is used advisedly, since the relevant prototype/schema may supply necessary information from memory without the need for integration. If not, the controlled processes come into play. Even though representable by the same sort of "cognitive algebra" as other decisions and integrations, these may not be the kind of judgments that are made when simple evaluations are required.

At least three theoretical orientations have addressed the issue of cognitive integration—attribution theory, decision theory, and social judgment theory. Unfortunately, in the brief amount of space allotted here we cannot provide a detailed reconciliation of attribution theory (used most in a performance appraisal context), psychological decision theory, and social judgment theory. The reader is directed to Fischoff (1976), Kahneman and Tversky (1979), and Hammond, McClelland, and Mumpower (Note 5) for treatment of these issues.

Evaluative integration likewise may or may not occur. If a stored impression exists and is sufficient to govern the overt response (as in a global rating or a ranking scale, or perhaps a hasty decision under pressure) no integration need take place. Where consideration of recalled material ostensibly forms the basis for evaluation, the recall processes noted previously will apply. Those aspects of the employee made salient by the context of evaluation, the rating task or decision (Hamilton, Fallot, & Hautaloma, 1978), recent events, and dispositions of the evaluator will be the basis for the overall evaluative response. These are most likely to be combined in a weighted-average fashion with whatever preexisting impression is available (Anderson, 1974, 1976). Salancik and Conway (1975) have shown that changing the salience of information in memory may alter an obtained evaluation. Fiske (1980) showed that the most "informative" or noticeable (negative/extreme) behaviors of the stimulus were given the greatest relative weight in impression formation.

An important point relevant to both cognitive and evaluative integration is raised by Tesser (1978). He supports the contention that increased *thought* about an object or person makes a perceiver's cognitions more consistent with whatever schema (or prototype) is being used to conceptualize that object or person. This, in turn, causes the evaluation of that object or person to become increasingly *polarized* or extreme. In other words, the more time a conscientious supervisor spends considering an employee's evaluation, the more biased in the direction of the governing prototype/schema (and therefore more extreme) the evaluation may become.

The use of evaluations based on group discussion of an employee is not likely to ameliorate this problem. Petty, Harkins and Williams (1980) have shown a similar polarization following group discussion. Such effects are not apparent in typical laboratory studies of performance appraisal, because judgments are made relatively quickly after the stimulus material is presented.

Sources of Validity in Evaluation. It seems that this discussion has focused on bias and invalidity almost exclusively, creating the impression that valid appraisals are rare. However, somehow, organizations do manage to function (sometimes remarkably well). We argue that the process by which valid appraisals are made is exactly the same as the one that generates biased ones, just as the forces determining an arrow's flight are the same whether or not the arrow is on target.

The categories that an appraiser uses are functions of education and experience. The cues that are salient to an appraiser are those that are significant; otherwise, their use would not have become habitual. To the extent that a job offers easily detectable cues of good or poor performance, and to the extent that training facilitates the detection of such cues, specialized category systems can readily develop. These job-relevant category systems, with their implications for treatment of employees (Swann & Snyder, 1980) are the source of valid variance in appraisals.

It is true that extraneous categorizations (based on age, dress, sex, race, etc.) may bias the use of job-relevant categorizations, but they are unlikely to remove all valid variance. Rather, they act so as to make *less* valid the appraisals of people in overly positive or negative categories (Zadny & Gerard, 1974; Taylor & Jaggi, 1974; Linville & Jones, 1980). The categorical nature of appraisals is thought to explain why those with more complex and differentiated category systems may use behaviorally-anchored rating scales better (Schneier, 1977); they are more able to separate job-relevant from irrelevant categorizations.

OUTLINE OF THE CATEGORIZATION AND APPRAISAL PROCESSES

The categorization and appraisal processes discussed earlier are admittedly complex, and we are far from certain that all of the issues that are (or will become) relevant have been covered. The reader should also be aware that many theoretical issues have been presented in a much simplified manner; the literature categorization, perception, problem solving, and decision making cannot be adequately summarized here.

The purpose of the present section is to provide a summary of what has gone before. The figures and text that follow should be considered a set of schematic diagrams or flow charts, and do not constitute "models" or "theories" except in the very crudest way. The labels and contents of the various boxes should be considered name-tags for the processes discussed earlier; there is no intention, for example, to postulate a recall mechanism as a separate entity. The intention is simply to show the place of recall in the sequence of cognitive activity.

Automatic Categorization.

Figure 1 outlines the automatic categorization process and the influences upon it.

As shown in the figure and accompanying legend, the distal stimulus (a complex of person and/or situational factors) impinges on the sensory organs, with two effects (1A and 1B): An automatic affective response is experienced, as discussed earlier, and the salience of certain person and situational features is increased. (These are also chronically affected by individual differences and ongoing situational factors acting both directly and through the habitual salience of given categories and their prototypes). In steps 2A, 2B, and 2C, which occur simultaneously, the affective response, category, and stimulus-salience parameters act on the "category selector," which may be seen as a subroutine directing the "recall" routine to retrieve particular types of category prototypes from long-and short-term memory. These salience parameters also influence the availability of categories in long-term memory. In step 3, the stimulus becomes "proximal," that is to say, perceived. It is explicitly assumed that perception does not occur without some form of categorization, however crude. Upon perception, step 4 occurs when the fit of the stimulus to the available prototypes is tested. The process itself is not experienced directly, but the outcome is. If the fit is satisfactory, the categorized stimulus goes to short-term memory, and from there to long-term storage (steps 5, 6). If not (step 5'), the individual experiences a state of subjective uncertainty as the controlled process is evoked (Fig. 2). Step 6' stores the rejection of the categorization in short-term mem-

Figure 1. Automatic Categorization Process

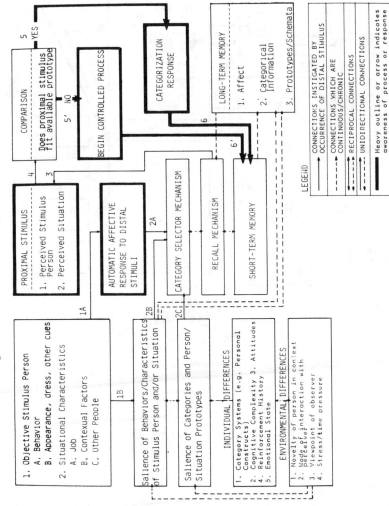

29

Figure 2.   Controlled Categorization Process

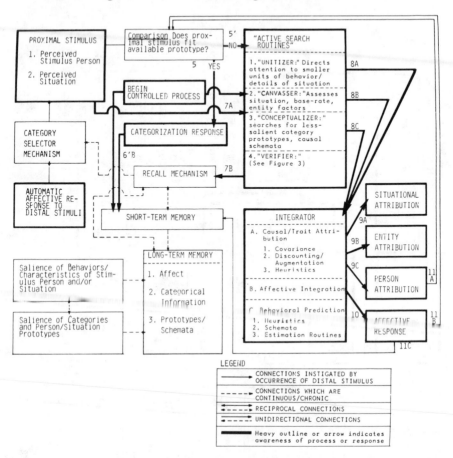

ory. (It is assumed that affect and categorization are stored separately, and that affect can be recalled without categorization, but categorization cannot be recalled without affect.)

The Controlled Process.

As shown in Figure 2, the controlled categorization process is complex and iterative in nature.

Step 5', resulting from an above-threshold discrepancy between proximal stimulus and category prototype, calls up to consciousness what we have termed an "Active Search Routine" (step 6'B). Three sub-parts are relevant here. the "unitizer" directs attention to smaller units of the proximal stimulus person's behavior; the "canvasser" directs attention to situation, base-rate, and entity aspects of behavior and its setting, and the "conceptualizer" directs a search of memory for less salient category prototypes and causal schemata. These steps involve both attention to the environment and memory search, and are influenced by category and stimulus salience as before. These are shown as steps 7A and 7B.

Following information-gathering, in steps 8A, B, C, informtion is transferred to the "integrator"; phenomenologically, the person is aware of "figuring things out," in a problem-solving sense. The attributional and affective integration subroutines are used in this process, and, should a person attribution result (step 9C), this decision together with an appropriate category prototype is sent for comparison (step 11A) as in step 3 earlier. Also communicated to short-term memory and the comparison routine (steps 11B and 11C) is the newly integrated affective response experience in step 10.

If an above-threshold discrepancy occurs, the process recycles (step 5'). If not, the categorization (step 5) is stored in short- and long-term memory. The information used in categorization is stored in short-term memory, but is eventually "cleared" and does not exist in long-term storage.

The Appraisal Process.

Figure 3 represents the events involved in the appraisal or decision process itself. The sequence begins at step 1, when a demand from the environment reaches awareness. This demand activates the "Active Search Routine," which begins scanning the proximal stimulus and seeking information from short- and long-term memory (steps 2A and 2B). Also brought from storage are causal schemata and, possibly, decision heuristics. Of course, retrieval of this information is influenced by the same salience-increasing or reducing factors discussed previously.

In step 3, the information is integrated by one or more of several processes into a trait or causal attribution, affective response, or prediction of behavior. These reach awareness, but are not yet at the level of overt responses. In step 4A, the internal response must be translated into an appropriate mode or level of response, as influenced by the type of rating form used and/or the kind of decision to be made. This is essentially a scaling problem for the respondent. Also simultaneously influencing the overt response are response biases (e.g., yeasaying) of which the person is unaware, the individual's standards of judgment, and explicit organizational demands (e.g., "We can't fire the boss' nephew"). Finally, in steps 5A and 5B, the integrated impression, attribution, or decision is returned to memory.

Figure 3.   Evaluation and Decision Process

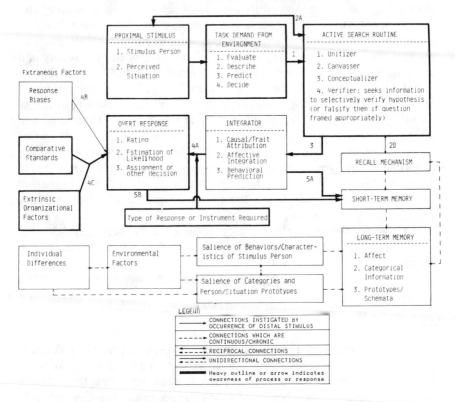

The role of the "verifier" is to support evaluations and decisions. In case justification must be presented, the verifier selectively searches memory and scans the proximal stimulus for consistent information. Of course, in case a falsification of an impression or decision is demanded, the verifying routine then searches selectively for inconsistent information.

Final Note.

As sketchy as the preceding representation has been, it may still generate testable hypotheses. For example, in Figure 3, the type of instrument used is presumed to influence only the final scaling of the integrated response, not the integration process itself. The individual's standards of comparison are likewise said to effect only the overt response. These propositions are eminently testable with known techniques. Likewise, we have proposed that individual differences influence the salience of stimulus characteristics and behaviors only through their influence on the habitual salience of particular person/situation categories and their prototypes. This assertion should also be tested. The reader can doubtless develop other hypotheses of interest.

APPRAISEES

For the most part, research on person perception has treated those who are being observed as passive objects in the perceiver's social environment—that is, as stimuli to be perceived and reacted to. In ongoing work groups, these individuals rarely are passive about the information they present to those evaluating their performance. On the contrary, the appraisee often actively attempts to manage performance-related information in order to present as favorable an impression as possible. Therefore, to understand the process of performance appraisal, we must consider how appraisees present themselves to appraisers independently of their "objective" performance. This process has been labeled *impression management* or *self-presentation*.

Our discussion will be based in large part on the arguments of Schlenker (1980), who has integrated much of the sociological and psychological literature on impression management (hereafter termed self-presentation). Inherent in Schlenker's view of interpersonal behavior is the idea of automatic and controlled processes governing self-presentation behavior, a view that distinguishes his approach from earlier ones, both sociological (e.g., Goffman, 1959) and psychological (e.g., Jones, 1964), which dealt with self-presentation as a controlled, conscious, decision making process. This two-process concept, unconscious and conscious (or automatic and controlled, respectively), has an appealing symmetry with the preceding discussion of appraisers, suggesting that many of the same concepts can be applied to self-presentation behavior in interpersonal settings as were applied to impression formation and evaluation.

Automatic Modes of Behavior

According to Schlenker, the automatic state is held to exist when people do not systematically monitor their own behavior and its consequences for interpersonal perception. The unselfconscious individual is thought to be responding to highly overlearned cues which elicit equally highly overlearned behavioral scripts appropriate to given settings (Shank & Abelson, 1977). Thus, for everyday social behavior, the individual does not have to monitor all of his activities, but can respond in terms of well-learned scripts. Presumably, only some interruption of the flow of normal interaction triggers conscious monitoring of behavior (e.g., Langer, 1978).

It is important to realize that such scripts can be highly specialized, like the performances discussed by Goffman (1959). An "executive," "iron-worker," or "fisherman" script is learned over a long period of time and is not experienced or perceived as a performance. Rather, it is seen as appropriate behavior for a person in a given role—behavior that is "given off" rather than "given" (Goffman, 1959). An important part of the training for particular positions, and thus an important component of evaluation, may be the presentation of appropriate dress and demeanor in a natural way. As Schlenker (1980) pointed out, these modes of behavior are often internalized, becoming part of a person's self-concept. Thus, the scripts associated with given roles provide the schematic basis for attention, organization, and recall of information about the self and others. The more these are internalized, the less the individual tends to be aware of his behavior with respect to them.

Controlled Modes of Behavior

The self-conscious state is held to occur during initial learning of role performance or scripts, and in situations where attention is drawn to the self as an object. It is characterized as a state in which the individual acts deliberately to foster a given impression, and attends to the responses of other people for feedback as to the success of his or her self-presentation efforts. It is akin to the controlled attribution process discussed earlier, but in this instance the actor is attempting to foster particular attributions by a particular observer. To do this, the individual must "take the role of the other," cognitively representing the other's probable interpretations of his or her behavior. In this, the individual is guided by what Schlenker terms the "association principle"; that is, people attempt to associate themselves with desirable images and dissociate themselves from undesirable ones. The association principle holds for both self-conceptions and other's conceptions of the person, basically reflecting the desire of individuals to see themselves (and have others see them) in the best possible light.

As a conscious process, self-presentation is said to be guided by a version of the commonly encountered expectancy model. Claims to particular images are made if the image has a positive expected value and if the individual believes he or she can successfully maintain a claim that indeed he or she is a person of that sort. Obviously, the extent to which this is possible depends upon the person possessing at least some of the requisite abilities and knowledge required of position occupants. The job interview is a case in point; the interviewee attempts to claim competence for a particular position and induce the interviewer to make appropriate attributions. The interviewer attempts to test the applicant by evaluating such factors as dress, mannerisms, social and professional skills. Often after hiring, the individual faces a similar on-the-job test that requires interaction with peers, supervisors, and subordinates in the context of a claimed identity (c.f. Dansereau, Graen, & Haga, 1975; Davidson, 1973, for discussions of the consequences of successfully or unsuccessfully substantiating a claimed identity).

Obviously, the more objective the criterion for a particular identity, the less likely it is that a person will attempt to claim it without proper credentials. A claim to be an artist may be somewhat difficult to refute, standards of artistic achievement being highly subjective, but a person claiming to be a computer programmer or a skilled machinist must, of necessity, be able to meet stringent performance criteria.

Likewise, a person may conceptualize himself or herself as fitting a particular identity, but these private claims can only be substantiated if the person receives proper feedback from others or arranges his life so that his claim is never seriously tested. Selective perception, distorted recall, and various self-serving attributional biases can also be seen as serving to protect an individual's private claim to an image (and, incidentally, interfering with the successful feedback of contradictory performance appraisals.)

Support for a Dual Process

Evidence for the two-process view is indirect. Duval and Wicklund (1972) and Wicklund (1975) describe states of objective and subjective self-awareness produced when situations focus attention on the self or on the external environment. Settings in which evaluation systems are quite salient and valued outcomes are linked to evaluations definitely should increase objective self-awareness. A state of objective self-awareness, according to Wicklund (1975), has motivational properties in that it leads the person to evaluate discrepancies between aspiration and achievement. Hull and Levy (1979) propose, however, that objective self-awareness is a cognitive rather than motivational process, causing increased salience of self-relevant schemata and stimuli and the consequent organization of information from a self-relevant perspective. Of course, it is entirely possible that both perspectives are valid—the motivational processes coming into play when the dimension of judgment has affective value for the person and the cognitive, informational processing factors operating when situations are new or less affectively relevant.

Research has shown behavioral differences between the two hypothetical states. For example, Feinigstein (1979) showed that self-aware people were more responsive to evaluation than non-self-aware subjects. Wicklund (1975) cites data showing that people are more self-critical and accepting of responsibility under conditions of objective self-awareness. At the same time, people tend to engage in more self-enhancing attributions when objectively self-aware (Arkin, Gabrenya, Appelman, & Cochran, 1979), although both results are moderated by situational factors (Hull & Levy, 1979). As Schlenker concludes, in agreement with Diener and Srull (1979), it seems as though objective self-awareness makes people "more conscious of the evaluative aspects of their actions. They . . . evidence a concern for their appearance before real or imagined audiences" (p. 110).

Evidence exists that a state of objective self-awareness is more chronic in some people than in others. Snyder (1979) defined "self-monitoring" as the degree to which a person is sensitive to the desires and expectations of others and subsequently uses other's behavior as a guide for controlling one's own presented identity. Snyder has validated a self-monitoring scale, and has shown that high self-monitors are both more skilled at presenting impressions and habitually take the social environment more into account in their behavior.[6] Snyder and Cantor (1980) have provided the link between self-monitoring and prototype- or schema-based categorization processes by demonstrating structural differences between high and low self-monitors' conceptual systems. Briefly, high self-monitors have more complex and differentiated category systems relevant to prototypical other people in various trait domains, while low self-monitors have a corresponding, highly articulated conceptual system about their own characteristics. This is consistent with the high self-monitor's ability to take a variety of roles, as the situation demands, and with the low self-monitor's greater cross-situational consistency in behavior (Schlenker, 1980).

Unfortunately, space does not permit a detailed discussion of the manifold ways in which self-presentation, deliberate or automatic, takes place. The many volumes advising people how to dress for success (Molloy, 1975), win friends and influence people (Carnegie, 1940), or achieve success and power (Korda, 1976, 1977) detail the strategies noted and systemized over the years by shrewd and practical observers. For example, "dressing for success" involves the presentation of a set of cues (an image) allowing an automatic fitting of the actor to a prototype representing a desirable category. This may, in turn, engage certain scripts of behaviors rather than others, resulting in better actual performance in some settings (e.g., sales). In other settings, it may offer the individual access to opportunities denied others (e.g., more challenging initial work assignments or a more favorable initial job interview). Advice to dress according to the standards of the firm in question to "dress for the job you want" indicates sensitivity to individual, organizational, and regional/cultural differences in desirable prototypes.

Professional actors, of course, are skilled in designing self-presentations which result in the desired automatic categorizations by their audience. It is interesting that some claim to need to "live" their roles while others can produce the desired image quite unemotionally. Of course, effects such as lighting, music, stage settings, and camera angles are all employed to enhance the performance, usually in ways unnoticed by the audience. It would not be surprising if similar techniques were used by employees to enhance their appraisals, for instance, by careful timing of the presentation of their work. This may be a fruitful field for the anthropologically oriented researcher, following Goffman's (1959) lead. Jones's work on ingratiation (Jones, 1964; Jones & Wortman, 1973) further details strategies of influence and self-enhancement in a more familiar experimental context. That these behaviors reported by Jones are not mere creations of the laboratory is evidenced by the following quotation, observed on the occasion of the firing of the Ford Motor Company's chief economic adviser: "Bill, in general, people who do well in this company wait until they hear their superiors express their view and then contribute something in support of that view" (Gainesville *Sun.* Aug. 7, 1980).

IMPLICATIONS FOR PERFORMANCE APPRAISAL

Our intention has been to describe the complexities of the performance appraisal process in organizations. As we see it, these complexities arise out of the human characteristics of the principals involved and out of the demands of the work setting itself. Having described each of the domains in considerable detail, we shall turn to what we feel are the implications of conditions described on performance appraisal.

Questioning Former Recommendations

Separation of Feedback and Rewards. As was mentioned earlier, performance appraisal information serves two functions. It provides feedback to the individual about the adequacy of past behavior, and it serves as a basis for personnel decisions linked to individual rewards. Most people follow the implications of the General Electric research (Kay, French, & Meyer, 1965; Meyer, Kay & French, 1965) and recommend that these two functions be separated. That is, performance appraisals intended to provide performance feedback, and counseling of employees should not occur at the same time that the reward implications of performance are discussed.

This advice seems faulty because recipients of feedback often cannot avoid considering reward implications even when they are not explicitly discussed. The appraiser is often in a position of authority, thereby controlling many of the individual's rewards. Although technically the feedback and reward discussions are separated, the feedback necessarily has reward implications. Attempting to separate the two promotes a benign fiction at best, hypocrisy at worst. Furthermore, without explicit information about the impact of the evaluation, more than likely employees will try to second-guess the meaning of the feedback. Since employees prefer less ambiguity in the evaluation-to-reward connection (Vitelas, 1953; Whyle, 1955), it would seem advisable to reduce such ambiguity by allowing appraisal feedback to serve both reward and coaching function.

Criteria for Effective Appraisal.   Although the ultimate goal of all performance appraisal systems is the development of procedures that provide *accurate* descriptions and evaluations of employee work behavior, the difficulty of obtaining measures meeting this criterion of accuracy led to the development of subcriteria for appraisal effectiveness. Most of these subcriteria focused on issues related to errors in the use of rating scales—in particular the problems of central tendency, leniency, and halo. Central tendency and leniency refer to general response styles of individuals using the scales. Halo errors occur when the rater fails to discriminate correctly among characteristics of the individual on aspects of job behavior. Thus, ostensibly different rating scales are correlated in use.

It is important to distinguish between correlation among ratings stemming from perceptual and memory bias, and correlation stemming from actual relationships among aspects of job behavior. It is only the former that constitutes error (Cooper, 1981).

Likewise, the presence of leniency/stringency biases or central tendency, depends upon the assumption of an "objective" performance criterion. Only if it can be demonstrated that the rank-order of performance within a group of employees or their position on some hypothetical interval or ratio scale of quality is dictated by a rating, can we claim that halo, leniency/stringency, or central tendency are "errors." Furthermore, it is entirely possible that a given set of ratings may be free from all three sources of "error" and still misrepresent the actual performance of a set of employees (Borman, 1974; 1978).

Either through scale design or through training, previous attempts to deal with the types of rating errors just described have focused on the way in which appraisers record information about appraisees. Yet, to attempt to correct these responses after behavior has been observed and stored in the observer's memory may be too late. This is particularly true of halo effects due to categorical distortions of recall.

Since, in our opinion, accurate ratings are the most basic goal of a performance appraisal system, and since the absence of central tendency, leniency, and halo neither logically implies accuracy—indeed their absence may not be possible given the cognitive limitations of appraisers— we concur with Borman's (1978) belief that accuracy rather than the presence or absence of the above-mentioned biases is a more reasonable criterion for judging the effectiveness of performance appraisal measures. However, we also realize that accuracy is not an easy objective. In most field settings, objective criteria against which to judge rating accuracy usually do not exist. Therefore, research has been, and needs to be, conducted in the laboratory (Hamner, Baird, Kim, 1975), in simulation conditions (Borman, 1978), and in limited settings where objective criteria do exist for a few dimensions of the job (Holman & Bass, 1972).

In addition to the setting limitations, statistical problems related to indices of accuracy also complicate attempts to use them to validate other criterion measures. Nevertheless, the overemphasis on central tendency, leniency, and halo should be corrected in the future, and continued research directed toward issues of accuracy should be encouraged.

Separation of Description and Evaluation. When the same individual is required to combine that information into an overall evaluative judgment, it often has been recommended that the descriptive, information gathering phase be separated from evaluation—preferably by having descriptions and evaluations done by different individuals or systems. For example, with respect to interviewing job candidates, relevant information about the candidates would be gathered from various sources—face-to-face interviews, letters of recommendation, and tests—and then combined by some empirical system to obtain an evaluation. The data clearly support the superiority of some empirical weighting system over the more clinical personal evaluation (Campbell, et al., 1970; Davis, 1979; Meehl, 1954).

With respect to performance appraisal, knowledge of the limited evaluative capabilities of raters has led to an emphasis on descriptive rather than evaluative judgments. For example, most texts recommend behaviorally based rating scales, because they force the observer to focus on more concrete behaviors rather than on evaluatively loaded traits.

The research in person perception suggests at least two reasons to question the extent to which a descriptive emphasis actually avoids problems of evaluation. First, unlike the interview setting, evaluators in performance appraisal settings normally work with the appraisee over an extended period of time. As a result of this continued exposure, the appraiser cannot avoid forming some rather firm evaluative judgments about the individual to be appraised. Once formed, this evaluation has several effects on future *descriptions* of that employee's behavior. At the unconscious (automatic) level, the evaluation will affect, (1) attention to and perception of the employee's behavior, (2) actual behaviors of the employee through the way in which the appraiser interacts with him or her and thus elicits behavior, and (3) the recall of behaviors at the time a formal evaluation is required. In all cases, the effect should lead to behavior descriptions that are biased in the direction of the evaluation. At a more conscious level, the individual may attempt to influence descriptions by (1) placing the employee in settings more likely to require the desired behaviors (assigning good salesmen to the best districts) or by (2) selecting those behaviors on the formal evaluation form that the appraiser believes reflect an evaluation at a given level. Finally, Zajonc (1980) contends that evaluations *precede* more descriptive judgments. To the extent that this is true in performance settings, there is little that can be done to separate descriptions from evaluations.

It is not our intention to suggest that descriptive scales should be avoided in performance appraisal—far from it. However, we caution against hoodwinking ourselves into believing that descriptive scales tend to isolate descriptions from evaluations. They do not and can not.

Coping with the Complex Process

Our analysis of the process of performance appraisal suggests three general areas of change. The first general approach is to develop rating instruments that take into account the nature of the performance appraisal process. The second is to design training programs that recognize and address the complexities of the task. The third is to construct rating procedures and performance appraisal settings in such a way that they enhance rather than detract from the appraiser's ability to judge others' performances validly. Each of these topics is addressed below.

Instrument Development. The strong emphasis on behaviorally oriented rating scales that has dominated thinking on performance appraisal scale construction since the early 1960s (Landy & Farr, 1980) is based, in part, on the assumption that behaviors provide a more concrete object to be rated. This more concrete stimulus should be less subject to perceptual and recall biases than other characteristics. Although nothing we have presented necessarily contradicts the behavioral focus, our perspective does question its objectivity. The person perception literature clearly shows that when asked to recall things that other people have said or done, recall is biased by the processes of information storage and retrieval (Cantor & Mischel, 1977; 1979). There is no reason to suspect that asking people to recall specific behaviors does not lead to these biasing effects. We would expect that appraisers, when given this task, report behaviors that they honestly believe they observed. These reported behaviors, however, may either (1) be somewhat altered from the actual behaviors in the direction of consistency with the appraisers' general impression of the employee and/or (2) be behaviors that were "constructed" by the appraiser and are consistent with his or her impression of the appraisee.

Let us first state three well-accepted assumptions, then consider the implications of these assumptions. First, assume that the behavior of employees is the most objective individual contributor to the individual's performance. Second, assume that appraisers are able to observe and evaluate the behaviors. Finally, assume that appraisers use some category system to store information about another's performance. Given these conditions, accurate appraisal is most likely if we understand (1) the relevant behavior set, (2) the relevant cognitive category set, and (3) we either develop rating scales that closely fit the match of these two, or we train people to use a new category system that incorporates (1) and (2).

It is not clear at this point what the resulting dimensions of such a match might be. However, it is likely that the interaction between behavior dimensions and information storage dimensions may alter our beliefs about what are the best dimensions for ratings. For example, recently behavior dimensions have been preferred for rating scales over trait dimensions for the reasons we have just described. Yet, there is evidence that information about people is stored in terms of traits (or trait categories). Thus, although we may quite validly consider traits very imprecise, it is not clear that behavior descriptions are more valid if, in fact, behaviors are encoded and stored in trait categories and then reconstructed upon demand. Furthermore, if the set for recall is expected behaviors rather than actual behaviors (as is often recommended; e.g., Smith & Kendall, 1963), these behaviors may be even more likely to be simple reflections of the stereotypic behaviors associated with the trait (see Bernardin and Smith, 1981). Clearly, if accurate ratings of others' performances are to be obtained from performance appraisal scales, we need to consider both the nature of the job behaviors that will be observed by an appraiser and the way in which the appraiser encodes, stores, and decodes information.[7]

The second implication for scale construction addresses the set created by the instructions for completing the scale. The person perception literature clearly demonstrates that the purpose to which the appraisal information is to be put affects the way individuals categorize information (Cohen & Ebbesen, 1979), the information they can recall (Hamilton, Katz, & Leirer, 1980; Lingle, Geva, Ostrom, Leippe & Baumgardner, 1979), and the attributions they use for performance (Harvey, Harkins, & Kagehiro, 1976). These data support the need for strict standardization of the instructions for the use of appraisal scales. Desire for standardization has always been stressed. However, recent data emphasize the need to make explicit how the data are to be used; past emphasis on standardization has ignored perceptions of use on the part of the appraiser. We cannot assume that the data collected will be valid for multiple uses if knowledge of the use affects the nature of the data obtained. Without specifying the use, unwanted between-person (appraiser) variance may be introduced as each appraiser forms his or her own perceptions of the uses to which the ratings will be put and then proceeds to complete the ratings. As a first step, common perceptions of use should be created by the instructions.

Training.   Training for performance appraisal has tended to focus upon the elimination of rating errors. Latham, Wexley, and Pursell (1975) were able to reduce the extent to which rating scale responses displayed patterns consistent with halo errors and leniency effects, although these training effects may not be especially long-lasting. Nevertheless, it seems clear that individuals can reduce such rating errors when they have been trained to do so.

A process-centered view of performance appraisal such as we are proposing suggests that the concern of training be greatly expanded from its previous almost exclusive concentration on rating errors. Training must concentrate upon the whole appraisal process if more accurate ratings are to result. In particular, training needs to expand its focus from that of the retrieval of information from memory (i.e., halo and leniency effects) to include that of encoding and storage (in-memory processes).

Considering first the encoding processes, at least two topics should be considered for training. The first of these deals with strategies and tactics of information gathering. We know, for example, that individuals are very poor at collecting information needed to reach decisions. They are much too likely to jump to a conclusion on the basis of far too little information. In addition, the information they do seek is usually what will confirm their previous expectations, in spite of the fact that seeking information that can disconfirm expectations is much more useful (Einhorn & Hogarth, 1978). Finally as perceivers of others, human beings tend to perceive novel events as co-occurring in the environment more frequently than is actually the case (Hamilton, 1979). For example, if very few telephone installers are women and also very few are lazy, the previous research data implies that telephone installers who are women will tend to be seen as lazy more frequently than the actual pairings of the two conditions would warrant.

The above information gathering and perception errors assume a relatively passive relationship between the encoder, in our case the appraiser, and the actor. Yet, we know appraisers are not passive. Their involvement leads to one additional problem that occurs at the initial stage of an evaluation. While interacting with appraisees under normal work conditions, appraisers may elicit from the appraisee behaviors that fit the appraiser's perception. This is known as self-fulfilling prophesy (Kipnis, 1974; Snyder & Swann, 1978b). Here the encoding may be accurate, but the observed behavior may have been created by the observer; the observer can hardly be considered an independent judge of behavior in such cases.

Appraisers can, and in our opinion should, be made aware of these issues that inhibit their ability to appraise others. Most research to date has been concerned only with describing the encoding difficulties. Yet, we know that people can be taught problem solving strategies. Certainly scientists learn this quite well as specific paradigms become firmly entrenched in various disciplines. Therefore, it is reasonable to expect that if people were made aware of common problems in collecting information about others and if strategies were developed for minimizing these errors, appraisers could be trained to gather more valid information. Empirical research is needed on such training to evaluate our assumptions.

With respect to memory, the major issue is that of the category system used to store information. Research shows quite clearly that differences exist across people in the specific categories they use to store information about others (e.g., Kelly, 1955; Markus, 1977). However, these differences may be minimized if people were aided, through training, in their development of job-relevant category systems. It has been shown that expertise tends to create more differentiated category systems (Rosch et al., 1976). Therefore, if people were subjected to similar experiences through training, we would expect that these people would be more likely to share a similar and highly differentiated category system. In a sense, the shared category set represents a common frame of reference for considering appraisees. The value of such a system has been stressed as one of the advantages of both assessment centers (Bray, Campbell,

& Grant, 1974; Finkle, 1976) and behaviorally based rating scales (Blood, 1973; Jacobs, Kafry & Zedeck, 1980). The use of both of these procedures communicates to the person what the expected or valued job behaviors are. Although not discussed in terms of category systems, shared expectations may also lead people to form a common hierarchical category system for relevant behaviors. This may be true particularly for assessment centers, where the dimensions used to judge others often contain a mixture of behavior and trait characteristics.

One final focus for training spans all three of the major subprocesses: encoding, storage, and retrieval. This has to do with attributions about the causes of performance. We have already shown that people do reach conclusions about the causes of performance at a given level, and that the ways these causal judgments are formed are subject to several common errors. In particular, appraisers underestimate the extent to which situational factors cause performance (and conversely, overestimate the performer's contribution), attend more to the most salient feature in the individual/task setting, emphasize those things that are likely to have the greatest impact on the appraisers' own outcomes, use their own behavior as a standard against which to judge others, and attribute positive characteristics to ingroups and negative to outgroups more than is objectively justifiable.

As was the case with the other information processing errors just discussed, researchers have been diligent in attempting to identify problems but have done little to explore how individuals may be helped to avoid them. Since most of these problems are quite straightforward and easily demonstratable, it should be possible to develop training programs designed to (1) make raters aware of these common attributional problems and (2) provide them with ways to avoid some of them. Work is just beginning in this area (Feldman, 1981b); more is needed.

Setting/Procedural Changes

A consistent theme running throughout this chapter is that systematic biases are present in all performance ratings. Although ideally one would like to eliminate all such biases, we recognize that it is impossible to do so. Therefore, we suggest that performance appraisal conditions should be established so as (1) to reduce, as much as possible, the conditions that lead to biased ratings in the first place and then (2) to assess the degree of bias remaining so that it can be controlled statistically. Each of these two procedures is discussed below.

Reduction of Bias. Systematic errors of rating are due to biasing factors inherent in both controlled and automatic modes of attention, categorization, and recall. They stem from the use of inappropriate cues/or rules of categorization, inappropriate integration strategies, and inappropriate category systems.

To minimize these errors, at the very least an opportunity for the appraiser to observe relevant behavior must be provided. This can be done by assuring that the appraisal occurs when adequate time has been allowed for relevant behaviors to have been exhibited by the appraiser. In addition, the assignment of appraisers to appraisees must insure that that appraiser is qualified to observe the person in question. Such qualifications include, at the minimum, the opportunity for frequent observation of the appraisee's behavior and sufficient knowledge of the appraisee's job to be able to evaluate the behavior. To obtain these conditions, it may be necessary to restructure the types of interactions that occur between appraisers and appraisees. It also may be necessary to be much more willing to consider appraisers other than or in addition to the appraisee's immediate superior. For example, peer ratings frequently have been demonstrated to be valid and often more valid than superior ratings, due, in part, to opportunities to observe behaviors without the biasing effects created by status differences between observers and actors. (See Kane & Lawler, 1978, for an excellent review of the peer rating literature.)

Statistical Control. Biases can also be controlled to a limited extent by statistical means. Kane and Lawler (1979) advocate the use of distributional measurement procedures to construct rating scales that are less skewed by halo or leniency biases. Their response to the distribution problems present in ratings biases is the development of Behavioral Distribution (BDS). While little empirical work exists at this time with the BDS, it does seem to deserve attention.

A second strategy for statistical control is to measure those conditions most likely to create rating biases then use those measures as controls in some partialing procedure or covariance analysis. Earlier we discussed such conditions as the amount of flexibility in attaching financial rewards to ratings, the number of times that the same appraiser rated the same appraisees in the past, the number of appraisees rated at one time by an appraiser, and the variance in performance among those being rated by the same appraiser as possible sources of systematic bias. Measuring these types of conditions and then treating these variables as statistical controls would be another method of addressing the problem of bias.

CONCLUSION

Future improvements in performance appraisal based upon attempts to eliminate rating errors through scale construction and administrative techniques are likely. However, advances probably will be very slow and of limited magnitude. Therefore, if performance appraisal is to advance, the total appraisal process must be better understood. To do this, we must focus upon the appraiser, the nature of the appraisal setting, and the motives and desires of those being appraised.

Fortunately for performance appraisal, the major sub-parts of the appraisal process have received considerable attention in the past, although often not in the context of performance appraisal. In particular, the study of human judgment processes is conceptually and empirically quite rich. We can learn much from the research in this area.

To improve our ability to develop effective performance appraisal systems in which the data represent a reasonably accurate assessment of the effectiveness of individuals in a work organization, we recommend that future work proceed on several fronts. First, it is necessary to continue to explore the way appraisers gather, process, and recall information about the performance of appraisees. Much has already been done by social psychologists in this area. However, more needs to be done in this area by creating experimental conditions that more closely resemble performance appraisal settings. The research to date has tended to ignore the parameters of performance appraisal because its primary purpose was not to focus on applied settings. The model presented in Figure 1-3 is a start at a more focused consideration of the appraiser's judgment process. More empirical research is needed.

Concurrently we should begin to develop methods for the diagnosis of biases due to conditions of appraisal settings. It has been argued that reward opportunities, the need to conduct several appraisals of the same people over an extended period of time, the performance mix among those being rated, and other contextual conditions may systematically bias responses from appraisers. At the very least, many of these contextual variables should be measured and their effects on appraisals assessed.

We believe that as the process becomes more completely understood interventions can take any or all of three forms. These are: (1) design of the appraisal instrument and the procedures for its use, (2) training of appraisers, and (3) engineering work settings to enhance the possibilities for accurate appraisals. We and others (e.g., Jacob, Kafry, & Zedeck, 1980; Landy & Farr, 1980; Latham & Wexley, 1980) have thoroughly discussed these alternatives. Training is an area that has been and should continue to be valuable. However, in order for training to be useful it is necessary that we expand our focus from the narrow consideration of rating errors to a broad concern for the functions of information gathering, storage, recall, and integration. Finally, one caution should be introduced. Although appraisal always has been and will continue to be an important process in organizations, it is not necessarily the most important process in the operation of an effective work unit. Therefore, the changes advocated must not only facilitate appraisal accuracy; they must do so in a manner that facilitates, or at least does not prevent, the timely accomplishment of other work group functions.

ACKNOWLEDGMENTS

This project was supported, in part, by Grant No. MDA 903-78-G-05 from the Army Research Institute for the Behavioral and Social Sciences as part of the technical-base research of the Organizational Effectiveness Unit. The ideas expressed herein are those of the authors and not necessarily endorsed by the supporting agency. We also want to thank Sandi Westfall for help in the preparation of the manuscript.

NOTES

1. Much of this section will summarize Feldman (1981a), though it has benefited from the inclusion of more recent literature.
2. A student of one of the authors was once offered a position with a large communications company. A finance/management MBA, her first position was to be a supervisor of a group of engineers, and she was expected to manage their work with no technical background whatsoever. This was common practice in the firm.
3. This is likewise a true incident.
4. What follows is a drastic oversimplification. In fact, the present treatment owes much to the work of Wyer & Srull, and readers are strongly advised to consult their work.
5. Lingle & Ostrom (1979) suggest that under some circumstances, people may seek disconfirming information. This seems to occur when they are asked to generalize from a judgment on one dimension to a judgment on a second, unrelated dimension. Snyder & White (1971) have also shown that people preferentially seek disconfirming information when instructed to falsify an hypothesis.
6. Self-monitoring should be distinguished from Machiavellianism (Christie & Geis, 1968, 1970). While high Machiavellians seem to consciously monitor their own behavior as do high self-monitors, the former are also characterized by cynical and manipulative interpersonal behavior (e.g. cheating; see Schlenker, 1980, p. 80–86).
7. Interestingly, this was apparently the original intent of the behaviorally anchored rating scale, an intent which seems to have been misinterpreted by many in the succeeding years (Bernardin & Smith, 1981).

REFERENCE NOTES

1. Bazerman, M. H., & Atkin, R. S. Performance appraisal: An information-processing and attributional perspective. Working paper, Graduate School of Industrial Administration, Carnegie-Mellon University, 1978.
2. Cantor, N. Perceptions of situations: Situation prototypes. Paper presented at the Stockholm Conference on *The situation in Psychological Research,* June 1979.
3. Cohen, C. E. Prototypes: Some properties of person categories. Paper presented at the symposium on Categorical Processing and Representation of Person Information,

Annual Convention of the American Psychological Association, New York, September 1979.
4.   Davidson, L. M. The process of employing the disadvantaged.
5.   Hammond, K. R., McClelland, G. H., & Mumpower, J. *The Colorado report on the integration of approaches to judgment and decision making.* (Report #213, Center for Research on Judgment and Policy). Boudler: Institute of Behavioral Sciences, University of Colorado, 1978.
6.   Smith, E. E., and Medin, D. Representation and processing of lexical concepts. Paper presented at the Sloan Conference, University of California at San Diego, March, 1979.

REFERENCES

Abelson, R. P. Script processing in attitude formation and decision making. In J. S. Carroll, & J. W. Payne (Eds.), *Cognition and social behavior.* Hillsdale, N.J.: Erlbaum, 1976.
Anderson, C. A., Lepper, M. R., & Ross, L. Perseverance of social theories: The role of explanation in the persistence of discredited information. *Journal of Personality and Social Psychology,* 1980, *39,* 1037–1049.
Anderson, N. H. Cognitive algebra: Integration theory applied to social attribution. In L. Berkowitz (Ed.), *Advances in experimental social psychology,* Vol. 7. New York: Academic Press, 1974.
Anderson, N. H. How functional measurement can yield validated interval scales of mental quantities. *Journal of Applied Psychology,* 1976, *61,* 677–692.
Arkin, R. M., Gabrenya, W. K. Jr., Appleman, A. S., & Cochran, S. T. Self-presentation, self-monitoring, and the self-serving bias in general attribution. *Personality and Social Psychology Bulletin,* 1979, *5,* 73–76.
Ashmore, R. D., & Del Boca, F. K. Sex stereotypes and implicit personality theory: Toward a cognitive social-psychological conception. *Sex Roles,* 1979, *5,* 219–248.
Bazerman, M. H., & Atkin, R. S. Performance appraisal: An information-processing and attributional perspective. Working paper. Graduate School of Industrial Administration, Carnegie-Mellon University, 1978.
Behling, V. W., Gifford, W. E., & Tolliver, J. M. Effects of grouping information on decision making under risk. *Decision Sciences,* 1980, *11,* 272–283.
Bem, D. J., & Funder, D. C. Predicting more of the people more of the time: Assessing the personality of situations. *Psychological Review,* 1978, *85,* 485–501.
Berman, J. S., & Kenney, D. Correlational bias in observer ratings. *Journal of Personality and Social Psychology,* 1976, *34,* 263–273.
Bernardin, H. J., Alvarez, K. M., & Cranny, C. J. A recomparison of BES to summated scales. *Journal of Applied Psychology,* 1976, *61,* 564–570.
Bernardin, H. J., & Pence, E. C. Effects of rater training: Creating new response sets and decreasing accuracy. *Journal of Applied Psychology,* 1980, *65,* 60–66.
Bernardin, H. J., & Smith, P. C. A clarification of some issues regarding the development and use of behaviorally anchored rating scales (BARS). *Journal of Applied Psychology,* 1981, *66,* 458–463.
Bernardin, H. J., & Walter, C. S. Effects of rater training and diary-keeping on psychometric error in ratings. *Journal of Applied Psychology,* 1977, *62,* 64–69.
Berscheid, E., & Walster, E. Physical attractiveness. In L. Berkowitz (Ed.), *Advances in experimental social psychology,* Vol. 7. New York: Academic Press, 1974.
Bigoness, W. J. Effect of applicant's sex, race, and performance on employer's performance ratings: Some additional findings. *Journal of Applied Psychology,* 1976, *61,* 80–84.
Blood, M. R. The validity of importance. *Journal of Applied Psychology,* 1971, *55,* 487–488.

Borman, W. C. Effects of instructions to avoid halo error on reliability and validity of performance evaluation ratings. *Journal of Applied Psychology*, 1975, *60*, 556–560.

Borman, W. C. Exploring the upper limits of reliability and validity in job performance ratings. *Journal of Applied Psychology*, 1978, *63*, 135–144.

Borman, W. C. The ratings of individuals in organizations: An alternate approach. *Organizational Behavior and Human Performance*, 1974, *12*, 105–124.

Borman, W. C., & Dunnette, M. D. Behavior-based vs. trait-oriented performance ratings: An empirical study. *Journal of Applied Psychology*, 1975, *60*, 561–565.

Bray, D. W., Campbell, R. J., & Grant, D. L. *The formative years in business: A long-term AT&T study of managerial lives*. New York: Wiley, 1974.

Brewer, M. B. In-group bias in the minimal intergroup situations: A cognitive-motivational analysis. *Psychological Bulletin*, 1979, *86*, 307–324.

Brown, E. M. Influence of training, method, and relationship on halo effect. *Journal of Applied Psychology*, 1968, *52*, 195–199.

Bruner, J. S. Social Psychology and perception. In E. E. Maccoby, T. M. Newcomb, & E. L. Hartley (Eds.), *Readings in social psychology*. New York: Holt, Rinehart, & Winston, 1958.

Burnsaka, R. F., & Hollmann, T. D. An empirical comparison of the relative effects of rater response biases on three rating scale formats. *Journal of Applied Psychology*, 1974, *59*, 307–312.

Campbell, J. P., Dunnette, M. D., Lawler, E. E. III, & Weick, K. *Managerial behavior, performance, and effectiveness*. New York: McGraw-Hill, 1970.

Cantor, J. H. Individual needs and salient constructs in interpersonal perception. *Journal of Personality and Social Psychology*, 1976, *34*, 519–525.

Cantor, N., & Mischel, W. Traits as prototypes: Effects on recognition memory. *Journal of Personality and Social Psychology*, 1977, *35*, 38–48.

Cantor, N., & Mischel, W. Prototypes in person perception. In L. Berkowitz (Ed.), *Advances in experimental social psychology*, Vol. 12. New York: Academic Press, 1979.

Carnegie, D. *How to win friends and influence people*. New York: Pocket Books, 1940.

Cash, T. F., Gillen, B., & Burns, D. S. Sexism and "beautyism" in personal consultant decison-making. *Journal of Applied Psychology*, 1977, *62*, 301–310.

Chapman, L. J. Illusory correlation in observational report. *Journal of Verbal Learning and Verbal Behavior*, 1967, *6*, 151–155.

Christie, R., & Geis, F. L. Some consequences of taking Machiavelli seriously. In E. F. Borgatta, & W. W. Lambert (Eds.), *Handbook of personality theory and research*. Chicago: Rand McNally, 1968.

Christie, R., & Geis, F. L. *Studies in Machiavellianism*. New York: Academic Press, 1970.

Cohen, C. E., & Ebbesen, E. B. Observational goals and schema activation: A theoretical framework of behavior perception. *Journal of Experimental Social Psychology*, 1979, *15*, 305–329.

Cooper, W. H. Ubiquitous halo. *Psychological Bulletin*, 1981, *90*, 218–244.

Dansereau, F., Graen, G., & Haga, W. J. A vertical dyad approach to leadership in formal organizations. *Organizational Behavior and Human Performance*, 1975, *13*, 46–78.

Davidson, L. M. The process of employing the disadvantaged. Unpublished doctoral dissertation. Massachusetts Institute of Technology, 1973.

Davis, R. M. The robust beauty of improper linear models in decision making. *American Psychologist*, 1979, *34*, 571–582.

Deaux, K. Sex: A perspective on the attribution process. In Harvey, J. H. et. al. (Eds.), *New Directions in Attribution Research*, Vol. 1. Hillsdale, N.J.: Erlbaum, 1976.

Dickinson, T. L., & Zellinger, P. M. A comparison of the behaviorally anchored rating and mixed standard scale formats. *Journal of Applied Psychology*, 1980, *65*, 147–154.

Diener, E., & Srull, T. K. Self-awareness, psychological perspective, and self-reinforcement in relation to personal and social standards. *Journal of Personality and Social Psychology*, 1979, *37*, 413–423.

Dowell, B. E., & Wexley, K. N. Development of a work-behavior taxonomy for first-line supervisors. *Journal of Applied Psychology*, 1978, *63*, 563–572.

Dreben, E. K., Fiske, S. T., & Hastie, R. The independence of evaluative and item information: Impression and recall order effects in behavior-based impression information. *Journal of Personality and Social Psychology*, 1979, *37*, 1758–1768.

Duncan, B. L. Differential social perception and attribution of inter-group violence: Testing the lower limits of stereotyping of blacks. *Journal of Personality and Social Psychology*, 1976, *34*, 590–598.

Duval, S., & Wicklund, R. A. A theory of objective self-awareness. New York: Academic Press, 1972.

Ebbeson, E. B., & Allen, R. B. Cognitive processes in implicit personality trait inferences. *Journal of Personality and Social Psychology*, 1979, *37*, 471–488.

Einhorn, H. J., & Hogarth, R. M. Confidence in judgment: Persistence of the illusion validity. *Psychological Review*, 1978, *85*, 395–416.

Eisen, S. V., & McArthur, L. Z. Evaluating and sentencing a defendant as a function of his salience and the perceiver's set. *Personality and Social Psychology Bulletin*, 1979, *5*, 48–52.

Enzle, M. E., & Schopflocher, D. Instigation of attribution processes by attributional questions. *Personality and Social Psychology Bulletin*, 1978, *4*, 595–599.

Fenigstein, A. Self-consciousness, self attention, and social interaction. *Journal of Personality and Social Psychology*, 1979, *37*, 75–86.

Feldman, J. Beyond attribution theory: Cognitive processes in performance appraisal. *Journal of Applied Psychology*, 1981a, *66*, 127–148.

Feldman, J. M. Perceptual variations in real-life interaction: Some selected examples. In H. C. Triandis (Ed.), *Variations in black and white perceptions of the social environment*. Urbana, Ill.: University of Illinois Press, 1976.

Feldman, J. M. Stimulus characteristics and subject to prejudice as determinants of stereotype attribution. *Journal of Personality and Social Psychology*, 1972, *21*, 333–340.

Feldman, J. M. Training and instrumentation for performance appraisal: A perceptual-cognitive viewpoint. *Proceedings of the American Institute for Decision Sciences Annual Meeting*. Boston, Mass., 1981b.

Feldman, J. M., & Hilterman, R. J. Sterotype attribution revisited: The role of stumulus characteristics, racial attitude, and cognitive differentiation. *Journal of Personality*, 1975, *31*, 1177–1188.

Feldman, J. M., & Hilterman, R. J. Sources of Bias in performance evaluation: Two experiments. *International Journal of Intercultural Relations*, 1977, *1*, 35–57.

Finkle, R. B. Mangerial assessment centers. In M. D. Dunnette (Ed.), *Handbook of Industrial and organizational psychology*. Chicago: Rand McNally, 1976.

Fischhoff, B. Attribution theory and judgment under uncertainty: In J. H. Harvey et al. (Eds.), *New Directions in attribution research*. Hillsdale, N.J.: Erlbaum, 1976.

Fischhoff, B. Hindsight = foresight: The effect of outcome knowledge on judgment under uncertainty. *Journal of Experimental Psychology: Human Perception and Performance*, 1975, *1*, 288–299.

Fischhoff, B., & Beyth, R. "I knew it would happen": remembered probabilities of once-future things. *Organizational Behavior and Human Performance*, 1975, *13*, 1–16.

Fishbein, M., & Ajzen, I. *Belief, attitude, intention, and behavior*. Reading, MA: Addison-Wesley, 1975.

Fisher, C. D. Transmission of positive and negative feedback to subordinates: A laboratory investigation. *Journal of Applied Psychology,* 1979, *64,* 533–540.

Fiske, S. T. Attention and weight in person perception: The impact of negative and extreme behavior. *Journal of Personality and Social Psychology,* 1980, *38,* 889–908.

Fleming, J., & Arrowood, A. J. Information processing and the perseverance of discredited self-perceptions. *Personality and Social Psychology Bulletin,* 1979, *5,* 201–205.

Furgeson, T. J., & Wells, G. L. Priming of mediators in causal attribution. *Journal of Personality and Social Psychology,* 1980, *38,* 461–470.

Gainesville *Sun,* "Always start at the end." (Anonymous Author), August 7, 1980.

Garland, H., & Price, K. H. Attitudes toward women in management and attributions for their success. and failure in a managerial position. *Journal of Applied Psychology,* 1977, *62,* 29–33.

Gibb, J. C. The meaning of ecologically oriented inquiry in contemporary psychology. *American Psychologist,* 1979, *34,* 127–140.

Goffman, E. *The presentation of self in everyday life.* Garden City, N.Y.: Doubleday/ Anchor, 1959.

Green, S. G., & Mitchell, T. R. Attributional processes of leaders in leader-member interactions. *Organizational Behavior and Human Performance,* 1979, *23,* 429–458.

Hamilton, D. L. A cognitive-attributional analysis of stereotyping. In L. Berkowitz (Ed.), *Advances in experimental social psychology,* Vol. 12. New York: Academic Press, 1979.

Hamilton, V. L. Intuitive psychologist or intuitive lawyer: Alternative models of the attribution process. *Journal of Personality and Social Psychology,* 1980, *37,* 767–772.

Hamilton, D. L., & Fallot, R. D., & Hautaloma, J. Information salience and order effects in impression formation. *Personality and Social Psychology Bulletin,* 1978, *4,* 44–47.

Hamilton, D. L., Katz, L. B., & Leirer, V. O. Cognitive representation of personality impressions: Organizational processes in first impression formation. *Journal of Personality and Social Psychology,* 1980, *39,* 1050–1063.

Hammond, K. R., McClelland, G. H., & Mumpower, J. *Human judgment and decision making: Theories, methods and procedures.* New York: Praeger, 1980.

Hamner, C. A., Kim, J. S., Baird, L., & Bigoness, W. J. Race and sex as determinants of ratings by potential employers in a simulated work-sampling task. *Journal of Applied Psychology,* 1974, *59,* 705–711.

Harvey, J. H., Harkins, S. G., & Kagehiro, D. K. Cognitive tuning and the attribution of causality. *Journal of Personality and Social Psychology,* 1976, *34,* 708–715.

Hastie, R. Memory for information that is congruent or incongruent with a conceptual schema. In E. T. Higgins (Eds.), *Social Cognition,* Hilldsale, N.J.: Erlbaum, 1978.

Hoffman, C., & Mischel, W. Objectives and strategies in the laypersons's categorization of behavior. Paper presented at the National Convention of the American Psychological Association, Montreal, Canada, September, 1980. Abstracted in *Personality and Social Psychology Bulletin,* 1980, *6,* 182–183.

Hull, J. G., & Levy, A. S. The organizational functions of the self: An alternative to the DuVal & Wicklund model of self-awareness. *Journal of Personality and Social Psychology,* 1979, *37,* 756–768.

Isen, A. M., Shalker, T. E., Clark, M., & Karp, L. Affect, accessibility of material in memory, and behavior: A cognitive loop? *Journal of Personality and Social Psychology,* 1978, *36,* 1–12.

Jacobs, R., Kafry, D., & Zedeck, S. Expectations of behaviorally anchored rating scales. *Personnel Psychology,* 1980, *33,* 595–650.

Jacques, E. *Equitable payment.* New York: Wiley, 1961.

Jacques, E. Equity in compensation. In H. L. Tosi, R. J. House, & M. D. Dunnette (Eds.), *Managerial motivation and compensation: A selection of readings.* East Lansing, MI.: MSU Business Studies, 1972.

Jones, E. E. *Ingratiation*. New York: Appleton-Century, 1964.

Jones, E. E. The rocky road from acts to dispositions. *American Psychologist*, 1979, *34*, 107–117.

Jones, E. E., & Baumeister, R. L. The self-monitor looks at the ingratiator. *Journal of Personality*, 1976, *44*, 654–674.

Jones, E. E., & Davis, K. E. From acts to dispositions. In L. Berkowitz (Ed.), *Advances in experimental social psychology*, Vol. 2. New York: Academic Press, 1965.

Jones, E. E., Davis, K. E., & Gergen, K. J. Role playing variations and their information value for person perception. *Journal of Abnormal and Social Psychology*, 1961, *63*, 302–310.

Jones, E. E., & McGillis, D. Correspondent inferences and the attribution cube: A reappraisal. In Harvey, J. H. et al. (Eds.), *New directions in attribution research*, Vol. 1. Hillsdale, N.J.: Erlbaum, 1976.

Jones, E. E., & Wortman, C. *Ingratiation: An attributional approach*. Morristown, N.J.: General Learning Press, 1973.

Kahneman, D., & Tversky, A. Propect theory: An analysis of decision under risk. *Econometrika*, 1979, *47*, 263–291.

Kane, J. S., & Lawler, E. E., III. Performance appraisal effectiveness. Its assessment and determinants. In B. M. Staw (Ed.), *Research in organizational behavior*, Vol. 1. Greenwich, CT: JAI Press, 1979.

Kay, E., French, J. R. P., Jr., & Meyer, H. H. *A study of the performance appraisal interview*. New York: General Electric, 1962.

Kelly, G. A. A theory of personality. *The psychology of personal constructs*. New York: Norton, 1955.

Kelly, H. H. Attribution in social interaction. In E. E. Jones, et al. (Eds.), *Attribution: Perceiving the causes of behavior*. Morristown, N.J.: General Learning Press, 1971a.

Kelley, H. H. Causal schemata and the attribution process. In E. E. Jones et al. (Eds.), *Attribution: Perceiving the causes of behavior*. Morristown, N.J.: General Learning Press, 1971 b.

Kimble, G. A., & Perlmuter, L. C. The problem of volition. *Psychological Review*, 1970, *77*, 361–384.

Kipnis, D. Does power corrupt? *Journal of Personality and Social Psychology*, 1972, *24*, 33–41.

Kipnis, D. The powerholder. In J. T. Tedeschi (Ed.), *Perspectives in social power*. Chicago: Aldine, 1974.

Korda, M. *Power!* New York: Ballantine, 1976.

Korda, M. *Success!* New York: Ballantine, 1977.

Kruglanski, A. W. Attributing trustworthiness in supervisor worker relations. *Journal of Experimental Social Psychology*, 1970, *6*, 214–232.

Landy, F. J., & Farr, J. L. Performance rating. *Psychological Bulletin*, 1980, *87*, 72–107.

Landy, F. J., Barnes, J., & Murphy, K. Correlates of perceived fairness and accuracy in performance appraisal. *Journal of Applied Psychology*, 1978, *63*, 751–754.

Langer, E. J. Rethinking the role of thought in social interaction. In J. H. Harvey et al. (Eds.), *New directions in attribution research*, Vol. 2. Hillsdale, N.J.: Erlbaum, 1978.

Langer, E. J., & Roth, J. Heads I win, tails it's chance: The illusion of control as a function of sequence of outcomes in a purely chance task. *Journal of Personality and Social Psychology*, 1975, *32*, 951–955.

Latham, G. P., & Wexley, K. N. Behavioral observation scales for performance appraisal purposes. *Personnel Psychology*, 1977, *30*, 255–268.

Latham, G. P., & Wexley, K. N. *Improving performance through effective performance appraisal*. Reading, MA: Addison-Wesley, 1980.

Latham, G. P., Wexley, K. N., & Pursell, E. D. Training managers to minimize rating errors in the observation of behavior. *Journal of Applied Psychology*, 1975, *60*, 550–555.

Lawler, E. E., III. Control systems in organizations. In M. D. Dunnette, (Ed.), *Handbook of industrial and organizational psychology*. Chicago: Rand McNally, 1976.

Lawler, E. E., III. *Pay and organization development*. Reading, MA: Addison-Wesley, 1981.

Lawler, E. E., III. *Pay and organizational effectiveness: A psychological view*. New York: McGraw-Hill, 1971.

Lingle, J. H., & Ostrom, T. M. Retrieval selectivity in memory—based impression judgments. *Journal of Personality and Social Psychology*, 1979, *37*, 180–194.

Lingle, J. H., Geva, N., Ostrom, T. M., Leippe, M. R., & Baumgardner, M. H. Thematic effects of person judgments on impression organization. *Journal of Personality and Social Psychology*, 1979, *37*, 674–687.

Lindville, P. W., & Jones, E. E. Polarized appraisal of out-group members. *Journal of Personality and Social Psychology*, 1980, *38*, 689–703.

Markus, H. Self-schemata and processing information about the self. *Journal of Personality and Social Psychology*, 1977, *35*, 63–78.

McCall, M. W., Jr., & DeVries, D. L. When nuts and bolts are not enough: An examination of the contextual factors surrounding performance appraisal. Paper presented at the American Psychological Association annual meetings, Washington, D.C., September, 1976.

McArthur, L. Z., & Solomon, L. K. Perceptions of an aggressive encounter as a function of the victim's salience and perceiver's arousal. *Journal of Personality and Social Psychology*, 1978, *36*, 1278–1290.

McCloskey, M. E., & Glucksberg, S. Natural categories: Well-defined or fuzzy sets? *Memory and Cognition*, 1978, *6*, 462–472.

McCloskey, M. E., & Glucksberg, S. Decision processes in verifying category membership statements: Implications for models of semantic memory. *Cognitive Psychology*, 1979, *11*, 1–37.

McCormick, E. J., & Ilgen, D. R. *Industrial psychology* (7th ed.), Englewood-Cliffs, N.J.: Prentice-Hall, 1980.

Medin, E. L., & Schaffer, M. M. Context theory of classification learning. *Psychological Review*, 1978, *85*, 207–238.

Meehl, P. E. *Clinical vs. statistical prediction: A theoretical analysis and review of the evidence*. Minneapolis: University of Minnesota Press, 1954.

Meehl, P. E. Theoretical risks and tabular asterisks: Sir Karl, Sir Ronald, and the slow progress of soft psychology. *Journal of Consulting and Clinical Psychology*, 1978, *46*, 806–834.

Meyer, H. H., Kay, E., & French, J. R. P., Jr. Split roles in performance appraisal. *Harvard Business Review*, 1965, *43*, 123–129.

Mintzberg, H. *The nature of managerial work*. Englewood Cliffs, N.J.: Prentice-Hall, 1973.

Mischel, W., Jeffrey, K. M., & Patterson, C. J. The layman's use of trait and behavioral information to predict behavior. *Journal of Research in Personality*, 1974, *8*, 231–242.

Mitchell, T. R., Green, S. G., & Wood, R. E. An attributional model of leadership and the poor-performing subordinate: Development and validation. In L. L. Cummings, & B. M. Staw (Eds.), *Research in Organizational Behavior*, Vol. 3. Greenwich, Conn: JAI Press, 1981.

Molloy, J. T. *Dress for success*, New York, N.Y., Wyndham Books, 1975.

Neisser, U. Toward a realistic cognitive psychology. Master Lecture on Cognitive Psychology, Annual Convention of the American Psychological Association, Montreal, Canada, September 1980.

Newtson, D. Foundations of attribution: The perception of ongoing behavior. In J. H. Harvey et al. (Eds.), *New Directions in Attribution Research*, Vol. 1. Hillsdale, N.J.: Erlbaum, 1976.

Newtson, D. Task and observer skill factors in accuracy of assessment of performance. *JSAS Catalog of Selected Documents in Psychology*, MS #1947, 1979, 9, (80).

Nisbett, R. E., & Wilson, T. D. Telling more than we can know: Verbal reports on mental processes. *Psychological Review*, 1977, *84*, 231–259.

Petty, R. E., Harkins, S. G., & Williams, K. D. The effects of group diffusion of cognitive effort on attitudes: An information-processing view. *Journal of Personality and Social Psychology*, 1980, *38*, 81–92.

Pryor, J. B., & Kriss, M. The cognitive dynamics of salience in the attribution process. *Journal of Personality and Social Psychology*, 1977, *35*, 49–55.

Pyszczynski, T. A., & Greenberg, J. The role of disconfirmed expectations in the instigation of attributional processing. *Journal of Personality and Social Psychology*, 1981, *40*, 31–38.

Quanty, M. B., Keats, J. A., & Harins, S. G. Prejudice and criteria for identification of ethnic photographs. *Journal of Personality and Social Psychology*, 1975, *32*, 449–454.

Regan, D. T., Strauss, E., & Fazio, R. Liking and the attribution process. *Journal of Experimental Social Psychology*, 1974, *10*, 385–397.

Rosch, E. Human categorization. In N. Warren (Ed.), *Studies in cross-cultural psychology*, Vol. 1. New York: Academic Press, 1977.

Rosch, E., Mervis, C. G., Gray, W. D., Johnson, D. M., & Boyes-Braem, P. Basic objects in natural categories. *Cognitive Psychology*, 1976, *8*, 382–439.

Rosenthal, R. *Experimenter effects in basic research*, New York: Appleton-Century-Crofts, 1967.

Ross, L. The intuitive psychologist and his shortcomings: Distortions in the attribution process. In L. Berkowitz (Ed.), *Advances in experimental social psychology*, Vol. 10. New York: Academic Press, 1977.

Ross, L., Greene, D., & House, P. The "false consensus effect": An egocentric bias in social perception and attribution processes. *Journal of Experimental Social Psychology*, 1977, *13*, 279–301.

Salancik, G. R., & Conway, M. Attitude inferences from salient and relevant cognitive content about behavior. *Journal of Personality and Social Psychology*, 1975, *32*, 829–840.

Schlenker, B. R. *Impression management*. Monterey, CA: Brooks/Cole, 1980.

Schmitt, N., & Lappin, M. Race and sex as determinants of mean and variance of performance ratings. *Journal of Applied Psychology*, 1980, *65*, 428–435.

Schneider, F. C. Operational utility and psychometric characteristics of behavioral expectations scales: A cognitive reinterpretation. *Journal of Applied Psychology*, 1977, *62*, 541–548.

Schneider, D. J., Hastorf, A. H., & Ellsworth, P. C. *Person perception* (2nd edition). Reading, MA: Addison-Wesley, 1979.

Schneider, W., & Shiffrin, R. M. Controlled and automatic human information processing: I. Detection, search, and attention. *Psychological Review*, 1977, *84*, 1–66.

Schneier, E. C. Operational utility and psychometric characteristics of behavioral expectations scales: A cognitive reinterpretation. *Journal of Applied Psychology*, 1977, *62*, 541–548.

Segall, H., Campbell, D. T., & Herskovitz, M. J. *The influence of culture on visual perception*. Indianapolis, IN: Bobbs-Merrill, 1966.

Sentis, K. P., & Burnstein, E. Remembering schema—consistent information: Effects of a balance schema on recognition memory. *Journal of Personality and Social Psychology*, 1979, *37*, 2200–2211.

Shank, R., & Abelson, R. P. *Scripts, plans, goals, and understanding.* Hillsdale, N.J.: Erlbaum, 1977.

Shaver, K. G. *An introduction to attribution processes.* Cambridge, MA.: Winthrop, 1975.

Shevrin, H., & Dickman, S. The psychological unconscious: A necessary assumption for all psychological theory? *American Psychologist,* 1980, *35,* 421–434.

Shiffrin, R. M., & Schneider, W. Controlled and automatic human information processing: II. Perceptual learning, automatic attending, and a general theory. *Psychological Review,* 1977, *84,* 127–190.

Smith, E. E., Adams, N., & Schorr, D. Fact retrieval and the paradox of interference. *Cognitive Psychology,* 1978, *10,* 438–464.

Smith, E. E., & Medin, D. Representation and processing of lexical concepts. Paper presented at the Sloan Conference, University of California, San Diego, March, 1979.

Smith, E. R., & Miller, E. D. Attributional information processing: A response-time model of causal subtraction. *Journal of Personality and Social Psychology,* 1979, *37,* 1723–1731.

Smith, P. C. Behavior, results, and the problem of criteria. In M. D. Dunnette (Ed.), *Handbook of industrial and organizational psychology.* Chicago: Rand McNally, 1976.

Smith, P. C., & Kendall, L. M. Retranslation of expectations: An approach to the construction of unambiguous anchors for rating scales. *Journal of Applied Psychology,* 1963, *47,* 149–155.

Snyder, M. Self-monitoring process. In L. Berkowitz (Ed.), *Advances in research in social psychology,* Vol. 12. New York: Academic Press, 1979.

Snyder, M., & Cantor, M. Thinking about ourselves and others: Self-monitoring and social knowledge. *Journal of Personality and Social Psychology,* 1980, *39,* 222–234.

Snyder, M., & Cantor, M. Testing hypotheses about other people: the use of historical knowledge. *Journal of Experimental Social Psychology,* in press.

Snyder, M., & Swann, W. B., Jr. Hypothesis-testing processes in social interaction. *Journal of Personality and Social Psychology,* 1978a, *36,* 1202–1212.

Snyder, M., & Swann, W. B., Jr. Behavioral confirmation in social interaction: From social perception to social reality. *Journal of Experimental Social Psychology,* 1978b, *14,* 148–162.

Snyder, M., Tanke, E. D., & Berscheid, E. Social perception and interpersonal behavior: On the self-fulfilling nature of social stereotypes. *Journal of Personality and Social Pshchology,* 1977, *35,* 656–666.

Snyder, M., & Uranowitz, S. W. Reconstructing the past: Some cognitive consequences of person perception. *Journal of Personality and Social Psychology,* 1978, *36,* 941–950.

Snyder, M., & White, P. Testing hypotheses about other people: Strategies of verification and falsification. *Personality and Social Psychology Bulletin,* 1981, *7,* 39–43.

Snyder, M. L., & Frankel, A. Observer bias: A stringent test of behavior engulfing the field. *Journal of Personality and Social Psychology,* 1976, *34,* 857–864.

Spiro, R. J. Remembering information from text: The "state of schema"approach. In R. C. Anderson, R. J. Spiro, & W. E. Montague (Eds.), *Schooling and the acquisition of knowledge,* Hillsdale, N.J.: Erlbaum, 1977.

Srull, T. K., & Wyer, R. S., Jr. The role of category accessibility in the interpretation of information about persons: Some determinants and implications. *Journal of Personality and Social Psychology,* 1979, *37,* 1660–1672.

Srull, T. K., & Wyer, R. S., Jr. Category accessibility and social perception: Some implications for the study of person memory and interpersonal judgment. *Journal of Personality and Social Psychology,* 1980, *38,* 841–856.

Stone, T. H., & Slusher, E. A. Attributional insights into performance appraisal. *JSAS Catalog of Selected Documents in Psychology,* MS#964, 1975, *5,* 253.

Strickland, L. S. Surveillance and trust. *Journal of Personality,* 1958, *26,* 200–215.

Swann, W. B., Jr., & Snyder, M. On translating beliefs into action: Theories of ability and their application in an instructional setting. *Journal of Personality and Social Psychology*, 1980, *38*, 879–888.

Tajfel, H. Social and cultural factors in perception. In G. Lindzey, & E. Aronson (Eds.), *Handbook of social psychology* (2nd ed.), 3. Reading MA: Addison-Wesley, 1969.

Taylor, D. M., & Jaggi, V. Ethnocentrism and causal attribution in a South Indian context. *Journal of Cross-Cultural Psychology*, 1974, *5*, 162–171.

Taylor, S. E., Fiske, S. T. Salience, attention, and attributions: Top of the head phenomena. In L. Berkowitz (Ed.), *Advances in experimental social psychology*, Vol. 11. New York: Academic Press, 1978.

Taylor, S. E., Fiske, S. T., Etcoff, N. L., & Rudderman, A. J. Categorical and contextual bases of person memory and stereotyping. *Journal of Personality and Social Psychology*, 1978, *36*, 778–793.

Teasdale, J. D., & Fogarty, S. J. Differential effects of induced mood on retrieval of pleasant and unpleasant events from episodic memory. *Journal of Abnormal Psychology*, 1979, *88*, 248–257.

Terborg, J. R., & Ilgen, D. R. A theoretical approach to sex discrimination in traditionally masculine occupations. *Organizational Behavior and Human Performance*, 1975, *13*, 352–376.

Tesser, A. Self-generated attitude change. In L. Berkowitz (Ed.), *Advances in experimental social psychology*, Vol. II. New York: Academic Press, 1978.

Thorngate, W. Must we always think before we act? *Personality and Social Psychology Bulletin*, 1976, *2*, 31–35.

Triandis, H. C. (Eds.), *Variations in black and white perceptions of the social environment* Urbana, IL: University of Illinois Press, 1976.

Tsujimoto, R. N. Memory bias toward normative and novel trait prototypes. *Journal of Personality and Social Psychology*, 1978, *36*, 1391–1401.

Tsujimoto, R. N., Wilde, J., & Robertson, D. R. Distorted memory for exemplars of a social structure: Evidence for schematic memory processes. *Journal of Personality and Social Psychology*, 1978, *36*, 1402–1414.

Tucker, D. H., & Rowe, P. M. Relationship between expectancy, causal attributions, and final hiring decisions in the employment interview. *Journal of Applied Psychology*, 1979, *64*, 27–34.

Tversky, A. Features of similarity. *Psychological Review*, 1977, *84*, 327–352.

Tversky, A., & Kahneman, D. Belief in the law of small numbers. *Psychological Bulletin*, 1971, *76*, 105–110.

Tversky, A., & Kahneman, D. Judgment under uncertainty: Heuristics and biases. *Science*, 1974, *185*, 1121–1124.

Viteles, M. S. *Motivation and morale in industry*. New York: W. W. Norton, 1953.

Warmke, D. L., & Billings, R. S. Comparison of training methods for improving the psychometric quality of experimental and administrative performance ratings. *Journal of Applied Psychology*, 1979, *64*, 124–131.

Weick, K. *The social psychology of organizing*. Reading, MA.: Addison-Wesley, 1979.

Whyte, W. F. (Ed.), *Money and motivation: An analysis of incentives in industry*. New York: Harper & Row, 1955.

Wicklund, R. A. Objective self-awareness. In L. Berkowitz (Ed.), *Advances in experimental social psychology*, Vol. 8, New York: Academic Press, 1975.

Wyer, R. S., & Srull, T. K. Category accessibility: Some theoretical and empirical issues concerning the processing of social stimulus information. In E. T. Higgins, C. P. Herman, and M. P. Zanna (Eds.), *Social cognition: The Ontario symposium on personality and social psychology*. Hillsdale, N.J.: Erlbaum, 1979.

Wyer, R. S., & Srull, T. K. The processing of social stimulus information: A conceptual integration. In R. Hatie, et al. (Eds.), *Person memory and encoding processes.* Hillsdale, N.J.: Erlbaum, 1980.

Zadny, J., & Gerard, H. B. Attributed attention and informational selectivity. *Journal of Experimental and Social Psychology,* 1974, *10,* 34–52.

Zajonc, R. B. The process of cognitive tuning in communication. *Journal of Abnormal and Social Psychology,* 1960, *61,* 159–167.

Zajonc, R. B. Feeling and thinking: Preferences need no inferences. *American Psychologist,* 1980, *35,* 151–175.

SELF-ASSESSMENTS IN ORGANIZATIONS:
A LITERATURE REVIEW
AND INTEGRATIVE MODEL

Susan J. Ashford

ABSTRACT

To regulate their behavior and, ultimately, to succeed in organizations, individuals must make a variety of self-assessments concerning their past performances, skills, and potential. While prior self-assessment research has attempted to document whether individuals are accurate self-assessors and provide some contextual factors governing accuracy, little theoretical attention has been given to explaining why individuals might deviate from accuracy. This chapter offers such as explanation. It is proposed that to assess their performance adequately, individuals must fulfill three tasks: They must establish the environment-specific standards on which they should judge their performance; they must learn which feedback cues among the many available they should attend to; and they must correctly interpret those cues. Individuals have three problems in successfully completing these tasks. First, they must complete them in an organizational environment that often provides only random and conflictual cues. These cues must be decoded accurately. Second, they must resolve the tension within them between wanting assessment information for its instrumental value while also wanting to protect their egos and self-esteem. Finally, they must reconcile their needs to maintain a self-presentation as a self-confident performer. The tension exists because such self-presentations often do not allow one to show an interest in how one is performing. The manner in which individuals resolve each of these problems can introduce distortions into the self-assessment process, resulting in less accurate self-appraisals. The outcomes of self-assessment, as well as some theoretical issues surrounding the measurement of accuracy, are also raised and discussed.

He told me I'd be pitching five minutes of batting practice today and that I'd be the last pitcher. . . . That might mean something. It's one of the tiny things you look for all during spring training. You watch who you follow in batting practice, try to find out how many minutes you've pitched compared with other pitchers, decide whether you're with the good squad or the bad squad, whether the morning workout is more important than the afternoon workout. . . . I can't really read anything into the way it is broken up [here]. And that makes me nervous.

Jim Bouton
Ball Four, p. 13

For it is my belief no man ever understands quite his own artful dodges to escape from the grim shadow of self-knowledge.

Joseph Conrad
Lord Jim, p. 102

Individuals at all levels in organizations make self-assessments. Whether they are new employees assessing their potential to survive in a company, more tenured employees wondering how they might fare in an upcoming organizational transition, or top-level executives interested in whether they made the right strategic decisions, managers and employees frequently wonder: Am I good enough? Was the action I took the right one? How am I doing? These questions and musing set managers and employees off on a process of self-assessment. The nature of that process is the topic of this chapter.

As the two quotations above indicate, the self-assessment process is not a simple one. It appears that assessing oneself and one's potential is not entirely the same process as, say, assessing the value of a new house or car. While both are complex, the self-assessment process is also often a conflictual one. Individuals, as evidenced by the Bouton quotation, at times go to great lengths to construct interpretive schemes that allow them to draw self-assessment conclusions from the events occurring around them. In other circumstances, individuals become masters at Conrad's "artful dodges" to avoid self-knowledge. That is, some people make complicated inferences about their abilities from what may have been a chance remark, while others are insensitive to "all but the most fulsome praise or devastating insult" (Jones & Gerard, 1967). Even those who are interested in drawing inferences about their behavior do not search indiscriminately for information. Rather, they pay particular attention to vivid cues and cues from those on whom they are dependent (Berscheid et al., 1976; Jones & Gerard, 1967). Turner (1970), for example, noted that despite the apparent clarity of any remarks or pronouncements that a CEO might make, they will be "ransacked for latent meanings" by those beneath him or her. Many aspects of the CEO's behavior will be treated as if they contained messages for others in the organization and examined accordingly. The complexity and conflictual nature of the self-assessment process make it an interesting area of inquiry.

There is also much to be gained from better understanding the self-assessment process. First, these processes highlight the self as a source of feedback. This focus may be valuable because several studies have shown the self to be the most available and trustworthy source of feedback (Greller & Herold, 1975; Hanser & Muchinsky, 1978). Indeed, Ivancevitch & McMahon (1982) found that self-generated feedback was superior to external feedback in increasing subsequent performance on five of seven performance dimensions assessed. Researchers also generally believe that further study of self-generated feedback is warranted (cf. Harold & Parsons, 1985) in that early self-assessment research suffered from methodological flaws (cf. Heneman 1980) and failed to address many theoretical issues.

Second, self-assessments pay a critical role in the self-regulation process. The aim of self-regulation is to enable an individual to achieve his or her goals in the organization—whether the goals are basic survival, good performance, collegial relationships, rapid advancement, or something else. Individuals are thought to set self-standards reflecting these goals and to evaluate their behavior with respect to those standards (cf. Manz, 1986). Thus, when making decisions about how intensely to work and how to allocate their efforts in making major career decisions, self-assessments of strengths, weaknesses, and the success of previous performances play an important role in individuals' abilities to regulate their behavior successfully. In short, self-regulation has become an increasingly important survival skill.

Further, organizations are becoming much more turbulent. Such fast-changing events as mergers, downsizings, and restructurings occur with increasing frequency (Kimberly & Quinn, 1985). Sorting out supervisory and peer preferences and evaluative criteria in such turbulent environments places added demands on the self-assessing individual. The pressing reality of having to survive in such settings makes the self-assessment process an even more important area of inquiry.

Finally, self-assessments are important in their effects. Self-assessments have been related to such outcomes as depression (Beck, 1967), emotional arousal (Dweck, 1975; Miller, 1976), efficacy expectations, aspiration level (Bandura, 1982), persistence (Janoff-Bulman & Brickman, 1981), effort, and subsequent performance (Brockner, 1979). Self-assessments give the individual the choice of when to obtain feedback, a choice associated with subsequent performance improvements (Ilgen & Moore, 1987). Self-assessments may also become more important at points when the individual experiences greater ambiguity about environmental demands. Thus, when individuals enter organizations, are transferred, or must cope with organizational change, the self-assessments they make will be important predictors of such variables as their willingness to stay in the organization or to perform duties beyond those strictly demanded by the job. The speed of their assimilation into the new role or setting is likely to be affected as well.

In the self-management literature, the subprocesses of setting standards for behavior and self-evaluation have been treated as fairly automatic (Bandura, 1982).

However, in organizational settings, we might expect that these processes are far from routine. In fact, it is not clear that individuals are very adept at the learning necessary to regulate their behavior effectively. Indeed, a variety of errors and misjudgments in self-assessments have been documented (see Mabe & West, 1982, Shrauger & Schoeneman, 1979, for reviews). The nature of these errors and why they might be particularly likely to occur in organizational settings are an additional focus of this chapter.

Given the ubiquity and importance of these processes and the potential for individual errors in carrying them out, this chapter undertakes the task of presenting a model of self-assessment tendencies that summarizes existing research on this topic and provides a systematic base for future research contributions. Before presenting this model, the chapter will (1) review prior literature on self-assessment, and (2) introduce the theoretical perspectives that motivate a more careful look at self-assessment processes in organizations.

SELF-ASSESSMENT LITERATURE

Many studies have attempted to establish whether individuals can accurately evaluate their own skills, abilities, and performances (see Mabe & West, 1982; Shrauger & Schoeneman, 1979; Thornton, 1980; for reviews). While these studies have produced inconsistent results, they differ in a variety of ways. These differences were examined as potential explanations for the conflicting findings. (Table 1).

First, the studies used different samples, varying from college students (Bailey & Bailey, 1971; Fisher, 1974; Reagan et al, 1975), to various work populations including nurses (Klimoski & London, 1974), assemblers (Shore & Thornton, 1986), clerical workers (Parker et al., 1959), and managers (Heneman, 1973; Meyer, 1980; Thornton, 1980).

Second, the studies differ in their motivation. In educational settings, researchers have examined self-assessments of basic skills and abilities because these assessments serve as an input to a variety of scholastic, vocational, and career decisions (cf. Lunnenborg, 1982; Mihal & Graumenz, 1984). In organizational settings, interest was sparked by the desire to substitute self-assessments for more costly supervisory appraisals (cf. Heneman, 1973; Klimoski & London, 1974, Lawler, 1968; Mihal & Graumenz, 1984). Self-assessments were attractive because of their lower cost (both financial and in supervisory time) and their potential to reduce defensiveness in performance appraisal interviews (Meyer, 1980) and improve performance (Bassett & Meyer, 1968; Meyer, Kay, & French, 1965).

Third, the studies differ methodologically in their sophistication, as well as in the specific methods employed. A variety of behavioral dimensions have been examined as the focus of self-assessment. Some studies have examined very general and subjective dimensions, such as one's self-image (Eledscoe & Wiggens,

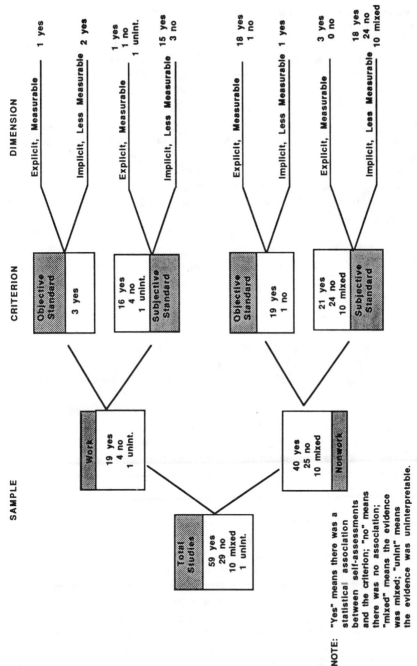

SAMPLE   **CRITERION**   **DIMENSION**

Explicit, Measurable   1 yes

Implicit, Less Measurable   2 yes

Objective Standard
3 yes

Work
19 yes
4 no
1 unint.

Explicit, Measurable   1 yes
1 no
1 unint.

Subjective Standard
16 yes
4 no
1 unint.

Implicit, Less Measurable   15 yes
3 no

Total Studies
59 yes
29 no
10 mixed
1 unint.

Objective Standard
19 yes
1 no

Explicit, Measurable   18 yes
1 no

Implicit, Less Measurable   1 yes

Nonwork
40 yes
25 no
10 mixed

Subjective Standard
21 yes
24 no
10 mixed

Explicit, Measurable   3 yes
0 no

Implicit, Less Measurable   18 yes
24 no
10 mixed

NOTE: "Yes" means there was a statistical association between self-assessments and the criterion; "no" means there was no association; "mixed" means the evidence was mixed; "unint" means the evidence was uninterpretable.

Table 1. Results of Previous Self-assessment Studies

63

1973), interpersonal skills (D'Augelli, 1973), or the level of various personality traits (Goslin, 1962; Hase & Goldberg, 1967; Miyamoto & Dornbusch, 1956). Others have focused on highly objective and presumably more measurable dimensions such as clerical and manual skills (Griffiths, 1975) and statistical ability (Kooker, 1974). Mihal & Graumenz (1984) concluded that individuals can more accurately assess their performance on more objective, easily measured dimensions than on a highly subjective dimension such as one's self-image or sensitivity. Both sets of dimensions, however, are important to understanding self-assessment in organizational contexts because most jobs involve both subjective and objective performance criteria.

Fourth, studies measured accuracy in a variety of ways. Some authors correlated self-ratings and relatively objective standards such as tests (e.g., DeNisi & Shaw, 1977; Fisher, 1974; Kooker, 1974), while others correlated self-ratings with ratings provided by peers, superiors, parents, and so fourth (e.g., Brams, 1961; Helper, 1958; Levine, Flory, & Ash, 1977). In all cases, accuracy was presumed when the correlation of self-ratings with the chosen criterion was either statistically significant or, for some, substantively important (of large size). Some authors also went beyond simply correlating self and other ratings to examine whether self-ratings overestimated or underestimated performance relative to the ratings of others.

Finally, the studies differ in that some asked individuals to estimate how well they might perform at some task (or test) that they would take in the future (cf. DeNisi & Shaw, 1977), while others asked how well they have performed at a task (or test) just completed (Mabe & West, 1982). It would seem that individuals should be more accurate at the latter assessment than the former because, in judging how well they might do in the future, individuals must reflect on past performances, estimate the contribution of ability, effort, and luck in achieving those performances, and extrapolate to the future (Mabe & West 1982). However, Mabe and West found no support for this proposition. Thus, while assessing future performance or potential may require more complex judgments than assessing past performance accomplishments, individuals are equally inaccurate in doing both.

As a whole, this research has produced few unequivocal conclusions regarding self-assessment accuracy. Even when studies are arrayed based on the six dimensions named (Table 1), no unequivocal conclusions emerge. That is, it is not clear that individuals are more accurate in their self-assessments of how well they performed in the past than they are regarding how they might do in the future. They are not more accurate on objective dimensions than they are on subjective ones. And the purpose for which the assessments were collected had little influence on accuracy. The only patterns that emerge from Table 1 are that self-ratings were associated with the criterion twice as often as they were not and that self-ratings were more often associated with the criterion in work samples than in nonwork samples. This difference is probably due to the fact that studies involving nonwork samples frequently examined rather ambiguous behavioral dimensions and often used subjective criteria to assess the accuracy of self-ratings. Finally, in studies that compared individuals' specific estimates of their performance to the estimates made by others, overestimation was far more common than underestimation.

The average correlation between self-ratings and the accuracy criteria (for the studies that reported these data) was small. In addition, Mabe & West (1982) concluded that while 88% of the correlations between self-ratings and the various criteria were greater than zero (average $r = .29$), general conclusions about the validity of self-evaluations cannot be made due to the large standard deviation of the correlations and the methodological weaknesses of the studies. Similarly, Thornton (1980) concluded that the findings regarding self and supervisory rating agreement have been inconsistent.

Shrauger and Schoeneman (1979), nevertheless, felt able to draw stronger conclusions. They reviewed 50 studies of the congruence between self and others' evaluations of various personality attributes and self-aspects (not abilities—only two studies were included in both the Shrauger & Schoeneman, 1979, and Mabe & West, 1982, reviews). They note that, overall, the studies showed a modest to strong correlation between individuals' perceptions of themselves and the way they assume others see them (link A in Figure 1). However, there was much less agreement between self-judgments and actual judgments made by others (link B): "Approximately one-half the studies showed no correlation, and the majority of the remainder showed either significant but low correlations or ambiguous results" (Shrauger & Schoeneman, 1979, p. 552). Finally, there was some correlation between individuals' views of how others see them and how others actually do see them (link C). Taking into account all the results, Shrauger & Schoeneman (1979 p. 558) concluded that individuals have "a tendency to assume greater similarity between one's own and others' attitudes than actually exists."

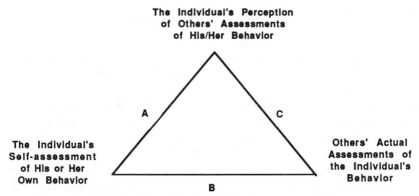

Figure 1   Relationships Examined by Shrauger and Schoeneman

Finally, considering the primary issue researched by organizational scholars—whether self-assessments are accurate—Heneman (1980) and others (Anderson, Warner, & Spencer, 1984; Cummings & Schwab, 1973; DeNisi & Shaw, 1977) cautioned against substituting self-appraisals for more costly supervisory appraisals. The modest correlations generally found between self-assessments and various accuracy criteria do not warrant their use in predicting job performance.

To a large extent, the organizational behavior scholars interested in self-assessment have been too narrow in their study of it by focusing solely on the adequacy of self-assessments as selection and performance appraisal mechanisms. In addition to self-assessments requested by the organization as part of selection and appraisal systems, individuals often spontaneously engage in a variety of self-assessments (DeNisi & Shaw, 1977; Heneman, 1980). Thus, irrespective of their status in personal evaluation, self-assessments are a natural and ongoing part of individuals' organizational experiences. As such, self-assessments are consequential in terms of decisions individuals make regarding their performance and the longevity in the organization. Given the importance of self-assessments, understanding how and why individuals deviate from accuracy remains an important issue that is unresolved and largely unaddressed by the self-assessment literature. The literature has focused on whether self-assessments are accurate at the expense of explaining why the accuracy or inaccuracy might occur (Heneman, 1980 p. 297). Recognizing this omission, Heneman (1980) and others (cf. Thornton, 1980) have called for a better theoretical explanation of individuals' self-assessments. By refocusing theoretical attention to explain self-assessment tendencies and inaccuracies, we will have a basis for some important new research on self-assessments.

My goal here is to provide such an explanation for the self-assessments that occur as part of an individuals' ongoing interaction with the organization. The theoretical underpinnings of this explanation are the subject of the next section.

Before turning to the theoretical grounding, one self-assessment literature issue remains. One question that has not been addressed in the self-assessment literature is, What criteria should be used to deem a self-assessment accurate or inaccurate?

Mabe and West (1982) note that 103 criteria have been used to judge self-assessment accuracy, with objective tests, class grades, and superior's ratings being represented most often. In their meta-analysis of those studies, however, they did not differentiate results by the type of criteria used. That is, we do not know whether individuals are more accurate predictors of test scores, class grades, or superior's ratings. They implicitly considered the criteria interchangeable. Further, each criterion, including superior ratings and, in more recent studies peer and subordinate ratings (Mount 1984), was treated as if it were error free. The only question posed was whether the individual's self-assessment matched it. This assumption, however, may not be warranted particularly for the "other's ratings" criteria.

Correlating self-assessments with assessments made by others begs the question of which set of ratings is most reflective of true performance. That is, it is clearly logically possible that the individual and other raters may agree that the individual is doing well, only to have the individual's objective performance (as indicated by an objective test or financial job outputs) fail. It may also be possible that the observer could be wrong about the individual's performance and the individual correct. Individuals often know more about their abilities, for example, than do observers because the abilities may not yet become manifest in actual behavior.

Although this argument is a valid criticism of an assumption tacitly made by the self-assessment literature, it can be overdrawn. In the political realities of organizational life, it is often the subjective assessments of others that must be understood and anticipated. In organizations, it frequently may not matter whose rating is more reflective of true performance. The ratings made by superiors, peers, and subordinates will have important consequences for the individual. These raters make decisions based on their rating of the individual such as whether to follow, to share resources, to promote, and so forth. These decisions are important for the individual being rated. Recognizing this, it seems reasonable to posit that individuals will attempt to assess accurately how these others see them.

For the purposes of this chapter I will continue, as has previous research, to consider other's ratings as one appropriate accuracy criterion. This assumption will be revisited in the final sections of the chapter.

THEORETICAL PERSPECTIVE

Two theories suggest the central role of self-assessments in understanding individual behavior. These theories, control theory and symbolic interactionism, motivate the current work and provide a framework for understanding self-assessment dysfunctions.

Control theory was articulated by Carver and Scheier (1981) and applied in organizational settings by Campion and Lord (1982) and Brief and Hollenbeck (1985). Control theory is based on the cybernetic notion of a negative feedback loop. It proposes that individuals survive by a continual process of matching their behavior to a goal or standard. When they detect discrepancies between the standard and their current behavior, this feedback causes them to take action to reduce the discrepancy (Carver & Scheier, 1981). Control theory integrates many notions used in organizational behavior for years, particularly with its emphasis on the importance of goals and feedback in the regulation of individual behavior.

Control theory adds to our understanding of self-regulation processes by positing the notion of goal hierarchies. Individuals are thought to have a variety of valued end states, which are nested in a hierarchy (or hierarchies) (Carver & Scheier, 1981; Miller, Galanter, & Pribran, 1960; Powers, 1973). Thus, obtaining a lower-order goal also represents progress toward a goal at a higher level in the hierarchy (Carver & Scheier, 1981; Powers, 1973). For example, successfully meeting their job performance goals also helps individuals attain the goal of career advancement. Attaining career advancement may help attain an even higher-level goal or guiding principle, such as "being a success in life." (See Carver & Scheier, 1981, for similar examples.)

According to control theory, individuals must accomplish three tasks to attain their goals. They must: (a) set standards for their behavior, (b) detect discrepancies between their behavior and those standards (feedback), and (c) enact behaviors to reduce these discrepancies. The second task is self-assessment. It suggests that individuals need to see where and how they are not meeting their goals. Recognizing these errors allows them to get their behavior back on track toward attaining their goals.

These three tasks are inadequate, however, for explaining self-regulation processes that occur within organizations. Because organizations have their own control systems, operative reward structures, and so forth (Manz, 1986; Mills, 1983), two additional self-assessment tasks not suggested by Carver and Scheier (1981) are relevant. First, individuals must be able to assess whether the standards they have chosen to guide their behavior actually enable survival and success within the environment. Second, they must develop proficiency in seeing and assessing their behavior in a manner consistent with how others perceive and evaluate it. This latter task is crucial in detecting discrepancies and determining how well they have been reduced. Thus, effective self-regulation in organizations requires attention to issues of veridicality and validity of one's self-assessment with respect to the assessments of others. Individuals do not self-regulate in a vacuum. The impressions and evaluations of others and the importance the organization places on a variety of goal options play a role in the individual's ability to attain valued goals.

An example might help. Control theory would study how individuals regulate their behavior to meet the standard of "achieving individual performance accomplishments." If they were engaged in this process in an organization where teamwork is valued, however, such a standard may actually be dysfunctional with respect to the individual's higher-order goal of surviving in the organization over the long term. Thus, to survive in an organization that can enforce the preferences of its leadership on its members, individuals must complete the two additional self-regulation tasks.

Considering how control theory's individual-level system might work within an organization's larger control system emphasizes the functional value of having an accurate self-view. Individuals cannot simply develop any self-assessment. At some level, they must be concerned with the accuracy of their self-view. Accurate self-appraisals have instrumental value (Ashford & Cummings, 1985); they allow employees to correct errors and better tailor their performances to the current situation and the demands of the larger control system. I will return to this argument when considering the various outcomes of self-assessments.

The importance of others's evaluations when considering control processes in organizations suggests the relevance of a second theoretical perspective,- symbolic interactionism. The core of this theory is the proposition that we develop self-concepts and make self-assessments based on our beliefs about how others perceive and evaluate us (Cooley, 1902; Edwards & Klockars, 1981; Mead, 1934). Over time, individuals learn to take on the role of others and see themselves from others' perspectives in order better to predict and control social interaction (Mead, 1934). Perspective taking occurs because individuals want a social world that is predictable and therefore more controllable (Mead, 1934). This assumption has been adopted by many behavioral scientists in recent years (Rosse & Hulin, 1985; Salancik 1977; Staw, 1977; Swann 1983; Touhey 1972). Symbolic interactionism argues that people gain predictability and control by considering how they will be viewed by the social environment surrounding them.

Symbolic interactionism has not been concerned with self-regulation per se but rather with the development of a self-concept. Nevertheless, this theory highlighted the importance of understanding the views of others in the environment. Epstein (1973), for example, proposed that the self-concept can be considered a self-theory that shares attributes of theories in general. Implicit in Epstein's argument was the assumption that if an individual's self-theory is to be valid, it must be congruent with reality (Bailey & Lazar 1976). Accurate self-assessments, ones that take into account how others view an individual's behavior, thus seem basic to the development of a useful self-theory (Bailey & Lazar, 1976).

Symbolic interactionism also gives a central role to the interpretations individuals make of the world around them (Blumer, 1969). Thus, individuals do not respond directly and instinctively to events but rather respond in terms of their interpretation of those events (Mead, 1934). This proposition is important to the current analysis because it is the interpretations (self-assessments) that we are trying to explain in terms of their congruence with external events. And it is through the process of interpretation that the individual's assessment can diverge from those made by others. The fact that individuals act on their interpretations, and not reality itself, means that understanding how they come to make particular interpretations and how their interpretations deviate from reality are important undertakings.

Symbolic interactionism and control theory provide the basis upon which to discuss how individuals regulate their behavior. Control theory articulates the structure of self-regulation and highlights the importance of standards (goals) and discrepancies. Symbolic interactionism leads us to highlight the importance of seeing ourselves as others see us, of developing accurate appraisals and of the

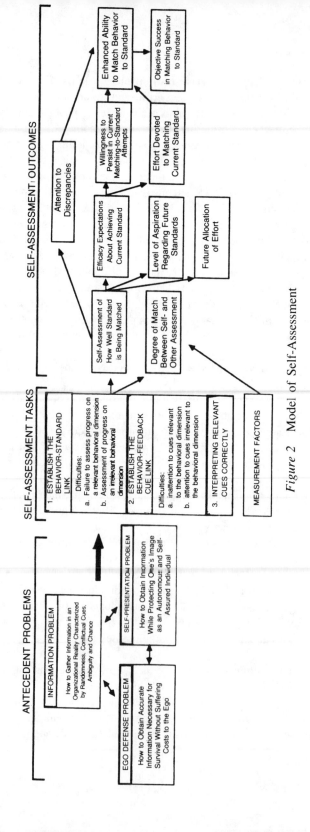

Figure 2 Model of Self-Assessment

role our interpretations play in the process. The remainder of this chapter will address the problems individuals experience in self-regulation, focusing on the self-assessment process.

MODEL OF SELF-ASSESSMENT

Figure 2 presents an integrative model of self-assessment. The model proposes that individuals face three general problems in making self-assessments in organizations. These general problems (an information problem, an ego defense problem, and a self-presentation problem) result in three specific self-assessment tasks. The self-assessment tasks in turn affect self-assessments (how well or poorly one feels one has performed, is performing, or might perform in the future) and the match between self- and other-assessments. Self-assessments are then related to various outcomes.

Self-Assessment Tasks

When assessing their behavior, individuals assess how well it matches a particular standard. For example, when assessing how well they are performing, individuals compare their current level of performance to some standard of adequate performance that they have adopted. In making such assessments, individual must complete several tasks.

First, they must establish the links between the standards they hope to achieve and the behavioral strategies required to meet them. There are often many ways to attain a given goal in a particular setting (i.e., the principle of equifinality). Therefore, individuals must determine which strategies will have the highest payoff. For example, an employee hoping for a high performance rating from his or her superior must determine the relative importance of working long hours, getting along with colleagues, and/or innovating on job to achieving this goal. Self-assessments ought to be less accurate when individuals either do not assess their progress on a dimension relevant to achieving the standard (e.g., employees do not consider their innovativeness in assessing progress when innovativeness is important in the eyes of relevant evaluators), or they assess their progress on a dimension that is irrelevant to achieving the standard (e.g., employees assess their progress based on the number of hours they spend on a job when this is irrelevant to evaluators). In both cases, employees will have a distorted view of the extent to which they have met the standard and the likelihood that they can meet it in the future.

This task may pose real difficulties for employees in organizations. Zammuto, London, and Rowland (1982) and Tsui (1984) documented that different groups (e.g., superiors, subordinates, peers, and the manager) hold quite different views about what it takes to perform well as a manager. Given this reality, employees attempting to evaluate their own behavior must determine if their notion of the relevant evaluative dimensions is faulty.

The second self-assessment task requires that individuals judge what cues should be interpreted as feedback messages. To understand this task, it is important to recognize that feedback is not simply the verbal messages directly provided by others. It also includes the observations individuals make of situations and others' actions (Ashford & Cummings, 1983). Once recognizing this, it is clear that any situation can provide feedback cues, as can the responses (or lack of responses) of any individual with whom the employee interacts (Ashford & Cummings, 1983; Jones & Gerard, 1967). The difficulty individuals face, then, is that they must judge which verbal messages, situations, behaviors, or lack of behaviors are relevant and should be considered feedback cues. This was the difficulty facing the ballplayer in the example that opened this chapter.

In the language of Sandelands, Brockner, and Glynn (1986), the individual's task is to determine the "self-diagnosticity" of each cue. Self-diagnosticity refers to the relevance of the cue to evaluating a particular performance. Inaccurate self-evaluations should occur when individuals do not attend to cues relevant to the behavioral dimension in question or attend to cues irrelevant to the particular dimension. Thus, in the example presented above, employees may correctly understand that "innovativeness" is important but may consider inappropriate cues as evidence of their success on this dimension (e.g., being asked to express an opinion in a staff meeting when newcomers are routinely queried in such meetings).

Qualitative studies of organizational culture suggest that difficulty with this task may be quite prevalent in the industrial sector. Turner (1971 p. 16), for example, noted:

> A person will not rely solely on the direct meaning of written and spoken messages for an understanding of his situation within the subculture, but will be attending to the whole range of signals, the whole range of experiences which are available to him, in order to ascribe meaning to these experiences. He will treat much of his physical and social environment as if it contained messages for him.

Organizational newcomers especially may fall prey to this difficulty. Newcomers are prone to misinterpret their situations by reading feedback in cues that were not intended as such. Louis (1980) believes that this practice results in overpersonalized attributions.

The third self-assessment task is to interpret the valid content of the cues themselves. In this task, too, individuals may experience difficulties. They may correctly sense that a cue represents a feedback message for them but then misconstrue the meaning of that message. Thus, praise for an idea in a staff meeting might be relevant feedback on one's innovativeness, but the importance of this cue as an indication of the praiser's true assessment must still be determined. It may be that the praiser is relatively indiscriminate and gives praise without thinking about it or remembering it. Because cues are subjectively interpreted, people can make of them what they wish. This fact often introduces error into the resulting self-appraisal. For example, a speaker may interpret an audience "nodding their heads" as a good sign that his speech is going well while the audience is intending their head nods to signal that the speaker should hurry and finish. Clearly feedback cues can be misinterpreted.

In fact, cues differ in their relative clarity and thus in their susceptibility to misperception and misinterpretation (Jacobs, et al., 1971; Neisser, 1976). Thus, we would expect difficulties handling this third self-assessment task will be more or less severe depending on the setting and the nature of the cues themselves.

The success individuals have with these three self-assessment tasks will contribute to accurate or inaccurate self-assessments. Our task is to explain why individuals experience difficulties carrying out these tasks, especially when it is often in their instrumental best interest to have an accurate sense of how well they are doing.

Antecedent Problems

Self-assessment difficulties arise from three broad problems individuals face: an information problem, an ego defense problem, and a self-presentational problem. Individuals' attempts to cope simultaneously with these problems can lead to self-assessment difficulties and inaccuracies. Each problem, along with its antecedents, will be discussed in turn. An additional determinant of self-assessments, "Measurement Factors," is included in Figure 2 in recognition of the measurement conditions identified by the self-assessment literature as conducive to more accurate self-appraisals (Mabe & West, 1982). These are not the focus of the current theoretical model; however, they will need to be taken into account in any empirical study of self-assessment.

The Information Problem. Organizations provide a rich and complex stimulus field within which individuals must discern cues relevant to their self-assessments of goal attainment. In addition to directly communicated information, any action or lack of action on the part of another individual, and indeed, virtually any event occurring in the situation, can be treated as if it contained messages for employees. The focus can be what they should be doing and/or how well they have done (Turner, 1971). This abundance of cues and information poses an interpretation problem for individuals. This problem stems not only from the environment itself but from individual interpretations as well.

Environmental antecedents. Hanser and Muchinsky (1978) label the stimulus field within which individuals work the "information environment." Within this environment, some information tells individuals what they should be doing, while other information (feedback) conveys how well they have accomplished what they set out to do (Harold & Parsons, 1985; Greller & Herold, 1975). Information environments affect self-assessments in two important ways: by the amount of information and feedback that they directly communicate to individuals and by the degree of uncertainty regarding appropriate behaviors and evaluations that exists in the environment.

In some environments a good deal of information is communicated directly. Information regarding appropriate standards and the relative merits of various strategies for attaining those standards is frequently part of the "sent-role" (Katz & Kahn, 1978) and is directly communicated to individuals by others in their role set. Indeed, role ambiguity is treated as an aberration from the optimal state of certainty about what one should be doing and how it should be done. Role ambiguity is seen as something both the individual and the organization try to reduce (Katz & Kahn, 1978). The organization does so by providing the needed standard information and specifying expected behaviors to meet those standards (Katz & Kahn, 1978).

While feedback on performance can also be communicated directly to individuals, the flow of such feedback often is very constricted. An American Management Association survey conducted in 1984 found that 75% of organizations provide formal feedback only once a year. The flow of informal feedback may vary according to the affective sign of the particular message. Felson (1980) and Blumberg (1972) noted that people withhold both positive and negative informal feedback from each other. Tesser and Rosen (1975) and Larson (1986) documented this tendency for negative feedback only. Finally, Ilgen and Knowlton (1980) and Fisher (1979) have shown that feedback providers tend to distort negative feedback in a positive direction. The picture that emerges from this research is that of an organizational environment in which individuals, particularly poor performers, hear something about what they should be doing but much less about how well they have done it.

When individuals do not receive direct positive and negative feedback messages, they must arrive at their own conclusions regarding their performance. To do so they must decide which of their colleagues' expressions and behaviors are intended to provide messages about their behavior (Felson, 1984). They may also use observational cues to determine appropriate standards of behavior by attending to various models (Weiss, 1978) or learning through vicarious reinforcement. In making such determinations, the important factor appears to be the relative mix of these two types of information—that given directly to individuals and that which they must discover through their own observations.

In environments that do not provide direct information, individuals can try to obtain it by seeking it out (cf. Ashford & Cummings, 1983; Weiss, Ilgen, & Sharbaugh, 1982). In organizations, this is not always an easy proposition. Such seeking goes against the norms in many companies. It may be fruitless in other companies, where evaluative standards are in flux. Indeed, Walsh, Ashford, and Hill (1985) argued that channels of inquiry in organizations are often obstructed, causing individuals to fall back on observed cues.

Environments will probably differ in the amount of feedback directly provided to individuals, the amount they must infer from their observations, and the amount they must seek from others. In environments where individuals must rely on observational cues and expressions given off by others, because little feedback is directly provided and/or feedback channels are relatively obstructed, self-assessment errors are more likely. They are more likely, first, because people tend to overestimate the amount of unity, order, and clarity present in the environment (Weick, 1979). However, they make this overestimation in a world where any action or lack of action on the part of others in the environment is available to be interpreted as feedback. Believing that the world is orderly, individuals are free to pick and choose among the abundance of available cues to construct any number of equally plausible self-assessments. Indeed, many different self-assessments can probably be supported by the available "data." In such environments, self-assessment errors are likely.

Self-assessments are also made more difficult by an environment where there is uncertainty or actual dissensus among potential evaluators. Evaluators can disagree and thus give off conflicting messages to those observing them. While disagreement between supervisors and coworkers regarding appropriate behavior is well documented (Rothlesberger & Dickson, 1939), disagreement among peers, subordinates, or between supervisors at different levels might also exist. Similarly, the organization itself may be in flux, causing a single individual (e.g., a superior) to communicate directly or give off quite different cues over time regarding appropriate behaviors. The superior might also reward different behaviors over time as the organization's needs change. Organizations experiencing major transitions, for example, may go through periods where it is difficult to specify what behaviors are appropriate or desired. Daft (1986, p. 2) labels such environments "equivocal": "Equivocality presumes a messy, unclear field. An information cue may have multiple interpretations. New information may be confusing and may even increase uncertainty."

When potential evaluators are uncertain or disagree about what is appropriate and how to evaluate behavior, the information environment takes on more of the character of equivocality. In such situations, evaluators are likely to communicate conflicting or confusing messages to individuals, either directly or through their actions. Individuals then pick up conflicting cues and/or cues that are unique to a specific evaluator or a specific moment. Self-assessment inaccuracies should be rife in such environments.

One implication of this discussion is that individuals who are active in seeking out information and feedback ought to fare better than those who are not. Individuals with histories of information-seeking may better understand the limitations of cues or messages from any particular evaluator. Further, barring completely obstructed information channels, active seekers may also be able to increase the proportion of direct messages obtained, thereby reducing their reliance on the more ambiguous messages given off by others. Even in equivocal environments, Daft (1986) speculates that multiple lines of inquiry may help reduce equivocality. Finally, Ammons (1956:292) summarized the existing empirical work and concluded that across studies, ''Where subjects are not being given supplementary knowledge of performance by the experimenter any longer, the ones who maintain their performance level probably have developed some substitute knowledge of performance.'' It seems, then, that individuals who develop a system that allows them to get the information they need to make sense out of an uncertain environment will be able to maintain their performance levels. These individuals also ought to have more accurate self-assessment.

In addition to the problem of random and uncertain cues, however, some environments contain cues that are systematically biased. For example, it is said that Henry Ford may have led his company into disaster by surrounding himself with ''yes-men'' and ignoring reality. It may be that when the self-assessor is a member of top management or the highest manager in a division or group, the assessment problem is not one of inscrutable cues but rather the fact that the cues are socially constructed by others to show that he or she is correct. Thus there may be unique problems associated with the attempt to get feedback from those below one in the organization's hierarchy. In these situations, the self-assessor must take additional steps if he or she is to obtain the information necessary to come to an accurate self appraisal.

Individual antecedents. The information problem does not stem just from the environment; it is also caused by the individuals who must perceive and interpret this environment. Consider the rather complex task that individuals must face in deciding if someone's behavior, or cues offered by a situation, ought to be construed as feedback. First, individuals must notice the behavior or cue. Given the amount of data they encounter each day, this is no small accomplishment (Markus, 1977). Second, they must rule out other causes for the behavior. These might include the personal disposition of the person they are observing, and situational demands (Ellis & Holmes, 1982; Pepitone & Wilpizeski, 1960). Third, they must make the connection between the observed behavior or the situational cue and their own behavior (Carver & Scheier, 1981). Given the inherent uncertainties in these judgments, individuals' perceptual processes and categorization tendencies will be important determinants of self-assessment proficiency.

The hypotheses that individuals hold about themselves, the setting, and the cues around them may distort the objective data and influence their self-assessment accuracy. For example, individuals have hypotheses about the kind of person they are and their capabilities for achieving a given goal. These hypotheses tend to direct attention toward certain cues and away from others and affect subsequent memory for information (Shrauger, 1975). At times, however, these hypotheses are incorrect, and the performer may attend to incorrect cues (Ammons, 1956). Individuals expecting to do quite well, for example, might ignore negative feedback cues, while those who are uncertain about their abilities or expect to do poorly might overattend to those same cues. As a result, each performer facing the same stimulus field would come to quite different conclusions about how well he or she had performed. This effect may perpetuate itself over time as feedback and information cues that confirm one's hypotheses are attended to, more accurately retained, and given more credence than those that are inconsistent (Shrauger, 1975). Hypothesis-consistent cues can influence beliefs and behavior quite strongly. When the initial hypothesis is incorrect, this influence can lead to distorted self-appraisals.

Because these hypotheses can be so easily sustained through time, the question of where they come from is important. We might expect that one's hypotheses about the self develop from past experience. Indeed, Lepper, Ross, and Lau (1986) found that initial success or failure with a new topic of subject had a strong perseverance effect on individuals' beliefs about their abilities. Individuals did not revise their original hypotheses about their capabilities, even when the experimenter told them to discount the initial feedback. Similarly, low self-esteem individuals tend to (1) distort ambiguous evaluations in a way that is consistent with their self-views (i.e., negatively), (2) underestimate positive evaluations from others (Jacobs, Berscheid, & Walster, 1971), and (3) underestimate the quality of their performances (Shrauger & Terbovic, 1976). High self-esteem individuals also appear to be more discriminating information users. For example, Bandura (1977) noted that low self-esteem individuals attend to models indiscriminatly to determine what they should be doing. In contrast, high self-esteem individuals attend to models only when they perceive the information they may gain is instrumental. Similarly, Shrauger and Lund (1975) and Baird (1977) found that high self-esteem individuals discriminated in their ratings of feedback sources between those who gave them positive feedback and those giving negative feedback. These individuals disparaged the negative feedback giver and thus accepted less negative feedback. In contrast, low self-esteem individuals accepted either source and thus accepted more negative feedback. While in certain task situations the broader and less discriminate search of low self-esteem people should give them a relative advantage (Weiss & Knight, 1980; Knight & Nadel, 1986), their tendency to distort ambiguous feedback and underestimate positive evaluations should bias their self-evaluations.

Given these findings, we would expect that self-esteem and early success or failure experiences anchor individuals with certain hypotheses about themselves and their potential. These hypotheses serve as a filter for subsequent information. The filtering process reduces self-assessment accuracy so individuals fail to see the cues for what they are but rather read into them what they expect. This information processing distortion can occur quite unconsciously until the individual is harshly confronted with disconfirming data.

Beyond hypotheses about themselves, individuals also develop hypotheses about the settings they encounter, generally based on their previously organized knowledge about an environment (Carver & Scheier, 1981). Accordingly, individuals entering an organization use their past experiences to hypothesize what they should be doing, what cues to attend to, and how to interpret these cues (Jones, 1983; Louis, 1980). To the extent that environments differ, the revision of hypotheses is required. Revision is also required if the environment changes dramatically (e.g., through merger, divestiture, or restructuring). However, we know that revision does not occur easily. Individuals tend to interpret discrepant information in a theory-consistent manner (Crocker, Fiske, & Taylor, 1984) and seek out data that confirm their hypotheses about themselves and the situation (Swann, 1983; Swann & Read, 1981). Thus, individuals may inappropriately carry over hypotheses useful in previous environments and fail to revise them adequately based on current information. This tendency should produce self-assessment inaccuracies as individuals overlook relevant cues, attend to incorrect standards, and weigh cues inappropriately.

In addition to being biased in testing their hypotheses, individuals also differ in the sheer amount of cues that they will consider as relevant feedback in the first place (Ammons, 1956). For example, individuals high in public self-consciousness are susceptible to feelings of being "observed" when in the company of others (Fenigstein et al., 1975) and tend to view many situational events and acts of others as feedback (Fenigstein, 1979). As a result, these individuals use social cues more as a basis for self-evaluation than do those low in public-consciousness. Their self-evaluations, then, should be less stable through time as these individuals, probably at times, interpret random behaviors of others as direct feedback messages. Individuals with low self-esteem also tend to view a greater range of situations and events as having evaluative implications (Brockner, 1983; Bandura 1977). Thus, these individuals not only see situations in evaluative terms but also have characteristic interpretations of cues. These twin tendencies should result in less accurate self-assessments.

A final aspect of the information problem lies not with the hypotheses individuals hold about themselves or their environment but with their ability to test their hypotheses over time. An adequate test requires a judgment of covariation between their actions and a set of reactions that can be considered feedback. Individuals, however, have difficulty making these judgments. They overrely on cues that are present (i.e., that actually occur) and virtually ignore the diagnostic implications of the absence of action or events (Crocker, 1981; Fazio, Sherman, & Herr, 1982; Nisbett & Ross, 1980; Ward & Jenkins, 1965). Consequently, individuals may overinflate their self-evaluations by considering all the positive feedback that they have received or "see" in the acts of others. They may not moderate their self-assessment, however, by considering the positive things that do not occur to them but may be occurring to others. Inflation in self-assessments will thus occur. The effect of this tendency will be compounded in organizations where feedback is delayed. In these situations, it is difficult to categorize a particular cue as an occurrence or nonoccurrence of a positive message. To be fair, a nonoccurrence often is not always directly interpretable. It may reflect the potential evaluator's inattention to the individual's behavior rather than a negative evaluation of that behavior. Nevertheless, these difficulties in judging covariation can result in more extreme self-assessments. These assessments may be more positive or more negative than is accurate, depending on whether the cues present are positive or negative. However, given research documenting the reluctance of evaluators to give negative feedback (Felson, 1980; Blumberg, 1972), the distortion will likely be a positive one.

Summary

It is not surprising that errors in self-assessments occur. Individuals work within an environment that is often complex and ambiguous and offers few direct feedback messages. In such an environment, individual hypotheses will play a large role in the ultimate assessment. They will direct attention to certain cues and away from others, affect what events are defined as feedback, and how these feedback events are interpreted. Thus, both the setting and the hypotheses themselves contribute to inaccurate self-assessments.

The Ego Defense Problem. The information problem is not the only one individuals must confront in assessing goal progress. Because feedback is information about the self, the processes of acquiring and using it are argued to be different from those used in more typical decision-making situations. Feedback always implicates the ego to some degree; thus, it raises affective as well as cognitive involvement in decision-making processes. Information about appropriate standards may also be seen as ego threatening. Discovering that one is pursuing the wrong strategy to obtain the standard in question, for example, may be taken as indirect feedback about one's understanding of the organization, as well as one's wisdom and perceptiveness. Individuals must balance their desire to assess their choice of behavioral strategy and their goal progress accurately, with the desire to maintain a positive self-image (Jones & Gerard, 1967). When the balance is tipped toward creating and maintaining a positive self-image, inaccurate self-assessments are more likely.

The ego affects the way people process information and respond to situations in a variety of ways (cf. Greenwald, 1980). In turn, the ego itself is protected by various means (Miller, 1976). For example, individuals might selectively attend to and seek out only certain types of information in the environment (Swann, 1983). They might see information that confirms, or comparisons that reflect, a positive view of them as particularly desirable (Friend & Gilbert, 1973; Swann & Read, 1981; Tesser, Campbell, & Smith 1984). Alternatively, individuals may avoid all information in order to avoid ego-threatening messages (Conolley, Gerard, & Kline, 1978; Sachs, 1982; Trope, 1980; Zuckerman 1979). As Janis and Mann (1977:218) note: "Restricting one's social contacts is sometimes tantamount to making a special type of auxiliary decision to avoid exposure to disquieting messages or to guarantee that one will only hear reassuring information." Individuals may also avoid direct personal feedback by choosing to work in groups as opposed to individually (Willerman, Lewitt, & Tellegen, 1960).

Individuals can cognitively defend the ego once they have obtained or inadvertently received ego-threatening feedback (Swann & Hill, 1982). They can do so by (1) defining dimensions on which they have performed well as more relevant to their self-definition than those on which they performed poorly (Tesser, 1983); (2) questioning the validity of ego-disparaging feedback (Harvey, Kelley, & Shapiro, 1957); (3) attributing disconfirming feedback to such external factors as luck (Feather & Simon, 1972; Simon & Feather, 1973); or (4) remembering only information consistent with a particular view (Mischel, Ebbeson, & Zeiss, 1976; Ross & Sicoly, 1979). If individuals do these things—defend their egos by searching selectively for information, avoiding all diagnostic information, or cognitively distorting the appraisals they receive—their self-appraisals will tend to be at odds with appraisals made by others. The tendency to take such defensive action, however, is not a random one. The research suggests that certain personality types will more readily fall prey to ego defensiveness.

Achievement motivation, for example, significantly and positively affects individuals' interest in and seeking of diagnostic information (Trope, 1982; Halish & Heckhausen, 1977). The interest that these high-need achievers have in attaining diagnostic information may overide their ego defensive needs. High self-esteem individuals also appear to defend their egos capably. Negative feedback seems to have less of an effect on them than it does on their low self-esteem counterparts. This differential effect may occur because low self-esteem individuals evaluate the source of negative feedback as more credible than that of positive feedback (Jones, 1973). Further, while desiring positive feedback and liking it better, low self-esteem individuals tended to believe negative feedback more (Shrauger, 1975).

It is interesting to note that Meyer and Starke (1982) found that the *belief* that one had high ability was unrelated to actual ability, suggesting that individuals' beliefs about their ability may be false. However, individuals act on their beliefs. Thus, if they believe they have low ability, they may avoid feedback and therefore never discover the true level of their abilities. They will also fail to obtain error-correcting information necessary for survival, making future negative appraisals more likely. In this sense, the belief that one's ability is low can be self-perpetuating. The individual breaks out of the loop only by risking hearing negative feedback. This observation suggests that self-esteem, a variable thought to index a chronic belief that one's ability is low, will be an important influence at all stages in the self-assessment process.

Across personality types, past successes or failures also contribute to ego defensiveness. People who have failed previously at a task tend to avoid diagnostic information (Modigliani, 1971; Zuckerman, 1979). This tendency clearly does not contribute to an accurate self-appraisal.

Even the most diagnostic individuals, however, will defend their egos in certain situations. For example, when people are new to a situation (i.e., new to a job or organization), less well-formulated self-views may be more open to disconfirming information. When they gain tenure, become certain of their self-conceptions, and invested in their continued existence, they will tend to avoid diagnostic information (Swann, 1983, p. 57).

Some contexts, however, preclude ego defensiveness. These settings are sufficiently demanding that the individual is almost forced to attend carefully to diagnostic information in order to cope. Thus, while many environments are not structured to show our limits (Slovic, Fischhoff, & Lichtenstein, 1977), it is easy to imagine organizational settings that are fairly strict and select individuals for survival based strictly on good performance (Lichtenstein, 1977). Stockbrokers and salespeople, for example, whose performance can be tied directly to numbers, may exist in organizations where bottom-line performance is strictly enforced. Pepsico is widely known as just an organization. Employees who fail to produce bottom-line results will not last long within this company (*Business Week*, 1980). Other things being equal, individuals desiring predictability in settings like Pepsi will value accurate information about their skills, abilities, and potential. The heightened importance and payoff of accuracy in these environments should override individuals' natural tendencies to avoid diagnostic information. Zuckerman et al. (1979) offer indirect support for this proposition. They found that when subjects are paid for accuracy, they are more willing to be diagnostic. Thus, in contexts offering rewards for accurate self-views and/or punishments for inaccuracy, individuals may seek more diagnostic information. They also should have more accurate self-assessments. Without such contextual demands, many individuals are likely to defend their egos at the expense of accurate self-assessments.

Summary

The self-assessment difficulties depicted in Figure 2 stem in part from the problem individuals face in the need to defend and maintain their egos. Information and feedback can cause anxiety and threats to self-esteem. By undertaking various strategies to avoid this information, however, individuals lose its utilitarian value. Thus, individuals are always balancing the utilitarian value of feedback with the potential pain it may cause. Individuals new to a situation or with a high need for achievement appear to tip the balance toward an emphasis on feedback's utilitarian value. More tenured and lower self-esteem individuals, on the other hand, forgo the utilitarian value to avoid the threat to their egos. These individuals may experience difficulty determining the relevant dimensions along which to measure goal progress, the cues relevant to their performance, and the appropriate evaluation of those cues. Inaccurate assessments of performance and potential may result. Interestingly, although many theories state that individuals' desires for predictability underlie their behavior, the logic of ego defense suggests that they will sacrifice some degree of predictability in order to maintain an enhanced self-view. It may be that what many individuals really prefer is not a perfectly predictable world (and the costs to self-esteem that this might involve) but rather the illusion of predictability and control that comes from maintaining a positive self-view, irrespective of the accuracy of that view.

Self-Presentation Problem. The self-presentation problem individuals face is how to obtain information while protecting their images as autonomous, self-assured people. It is not only information or feedback seekers who experience this problem; the self-presentation problem is generic to seeking any sort of help from others. Broll, Gross, and Piliavin (1974), for example, found that individuals responded more positively to help that was offered than to help that had to be requested. The primary cost of seeking help or information is that seeking exposes the seeker's uncertainty and need for help (Gergen, 1974). Such exposure may be at odds with the need to maintain a self-assured, confident self-presentation. To undertake social comparisons and seek external feedback publicly could be interpreted by others as a sign of insecurity (Schoeneman, 1981, p. 291). Recognizing this, individuals may rely more on self-observations as feedback in an attempt to appear self-sufficient and secure (Schoeneman, 1981). They do so even though they may have an actual need for information and feedback. Goffman (1956, p. 265) argues that people will:

> attempt to conceal evidence of their ineptness or deficiency because of the embarrassment they are likely to experience, because of the existence of norms which stress the importance of looking capable, and strong to others.

Such pressures to simultaneously conceal inadequacies and appear competent deter direct feedback and information seeking.

Self-presentation is very important to may employees in organizations. Tsui (1984), for example, has shown that effective managers develop a reputation and that it is their effectiveness as judged by others in their role set that determines their ultimate performance and progress. Mangers who recognize the evaluative role their constituencies play will clearly see the importance of their self-presentations in maintaining their managerial effectiveness.

Individuals worry about self-presentation because of their desire to please an audience (or audiences) and their desire to maintain public behaviors that match the concept of an ideal self (Baumeister, 1982). In organizations, managers and employees must please many audiences, including their superiors, subordinates, peers, and clients. Self-assessment difficulties occur when the need to maintain a particular self-presentation with an audience inhibits needed information and feedback search. Individuals who feel great pressure to maintain a self-confident, autonomous self-presentation will have trouble gauging the constituent's opinions of the appropriate standards they should be using to assess goal progress and detecting discrepancies between their behavior and the standard. They should be less accurate in their self-assessments than those who feel free to seek information and feedback. Individuals who feel the self-presentation pressures just described are forced, not by an ambiguous and uncertain environment but by their own perceptions of the costs involved, to forgo obtaining direct feedback and information. As a consequence, they are more dependent on observations made without the awareness of others. Relying on this more ambiguous data results in self-assessment inaccuracies.

Clearly not every employee suffers from such strict self-presentational demands. First, while certain audiences may have special value or meaning to the individual, others matter much less (Baumeister, 1982). Thus individuals may be able to ask their peers but not their superior for information. The more important the audience is, the more self-presentational needs will deter information search.

Important audiences, however, deter information search only in environments that define uncertainty as inappropriate. Organizations differ in the norms regarding information and help seeking (DeWhirst, 1971). In contexts where individuals sense rewards for managing their self-presentation, less direct seeking should occur.

Even in relatively competitive and closed contexts, expressing uncertainty may be more appropriate for some individuals than others. Both Ashford (1986) and Feldman and Brett (1983) found that new employees sought more information and feedback than did those longer tenured. These authors argue that they do so because they experience less of the self-presentational pressures that inhibit the information search of longer tenured employees.

Finally, the conditions prompting individuals to be more willing to bear the self-presentational costs of direct seeking must be noted. It seems logical to presume that on very important issues or for issues with a high cost to continuing on the wrong course of action, individuals should be willing to bear more self-presentational costs. They should seek more information and feedback on these issues even though they are less willing to seek less important issues.

Summary

In contexts where admitting uncertainly and doubt is not normatively sanctioned, individuals ought to seek less feedback and information. This will be the case unless individuals are new to the organization (and are essentially excused from following the norm for a period of time), face important issues on which appropriate behavior is critical, and are only concerned about maintaining a self-presentation with particular audiences, in these circumstances, that should feel free to seek from others.

The self-presentation problem is especially important as it reduces the possibility of resolving the information problem. One can resolve the informational problem of scarcity of feedback and information by direct search. Self-presentational constraints, however, make this option less viable because of the social costs inherent in such seeking.

Outcomes

Self-assessments, whether accurate or inaccurate, are judgments individuals make regarding something they have done, are doing, or will undertake in the future. These judgments are usually the outputs of an assessment process that uses some degree of feedback from others and the task, plus momentary feelings and responses within the self. They represent a conclusion, a judgment of the adequacy of past performances, and capabilities for handling future problems. As such, self-assessments should have a strong psychological impact, set a vari-

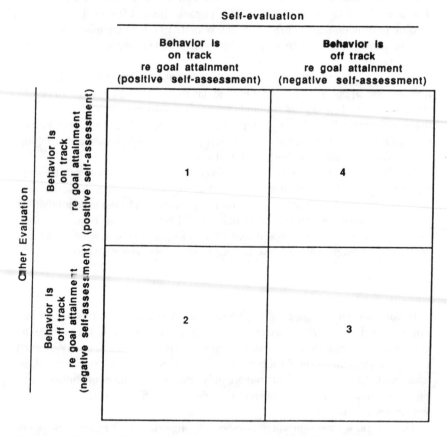

Figure 3   Possible Relationships between Other and Self-evaluations of Goal Progress

ety of processes in motion, and therefore be somewhat resistant to change.

Certain outcomes occur due to the assessment itself, regardless of its accuracy. Other outcomes stem from holding an inaccurate self-view. To clarify these outcomes, the heuristic presented in Figure 3 will be used. That is, once individuals make a self-assessment of their past or present performance, abilities, goal progress, and the like, they will fall into one of the four cells depicted in Figure 3. Individuals may come to one of two conclusions about their performance (abilities, goal progress, etc.): they may decide that their performance is on track with regard to attaining a particular standard or that it is off track. These assessments may or may not agree with existing objective or subjective evidence (i.e., others' opinions, tests, or objective performance). Thus, individuals may have accurate or inaccurate positive ("I'm on track") or negative ("I'm off track") views. Several outcomes are associated with each cell.

Many outcomes stem from the affective sign (positive, on track or negative, off track) of the assessment itself. Past research suggests that the sign of individuals' self-assessments, whether correct or incorrect, will likely affect their efficacy expectations concerning a given standard (Dweck, 1975; Shrauger & Rosenberg, 1970), the level of effort they devote to achieving the standard (Fisher, 1984; Felson, 1984), their persistence (Janoff-Bulman & Brickman, 1981), and their level of attention to the matching-to-standard process (Carver & Scheier, 1981). Self-assessments may also affect future aspiration levels (Heneman, 1980). In this way, self-assessments will affect both internal and external job mobility as an individual's willingness to try for various positions is affected by his or her self-assessments (Heneman, 1980). Thus, individuals who assess their behavior positively or on track ought to (1) develop favorable efficacy expectations regarding the standard in question (Bandura, 1982), (2) maintain their efforts toward standard attainment, (3) persist longer in their task efforts (Brown & Inouye, 1978; Janoff-Bulman & Brickman, 1981), and (4) have high levels of aspiration for their future performance. These individuals will probably not see the need to change either the strategies they are pursuing to attain a standard or the standard itself. A negative or off-track assessment with respect to the standard should result in (1) reduced efficacy expectations (Bandura, 1982), (2) less effort and persistence (Janoff-Bulman & Brickman, 1981), (3) lower levels of aspirations, and (4) some pressure to alter behavioral strategies to attain the standard in question. Individuals making a negative assessment may abandon the current standard altogether in favor of an easier one, and they may experience affective responses such as frustration and anxiety. These heightened emotions may debilitate subsequent performance (Bandura, 1982; Brockner, 1983).

Clearly an off-track assessment has some potential positive consequences as well. It gives individuals the abilities to make changes in their behavior, take corrective action, gather more information, and so forth. This utilitarian benefit is likely the primary reason why individuals would undergo the ego threat that comes with getting negative feedback. The critical question seems to be, then,

How do we provide individuals with feedback that is negative, indicating that they are off track in their goal-related efforts, in such a way as to avoid reducing their efficacy expectations and thereby their effort?

The final outcome associated with the affective sign of individuals' self-assessments is the extent to which the self-management, discrepancy-reducing process continues to capture the individual's attention. A positive, on track assessment requires only nominal future attention to the matching-to-standard process. In essence, with an on-track assessment, the individual needs only minimal attention to detect any future discrepancies. Thus, the individual's attention is drawn elsewhere. With an off-track assessment, the result is somewhat more complex. A discrepancy in this case is thought first to draw attention to the matching-to-standard process and to push individuals into remedial action. Depending on the outcomes of these actions, attention may subsequently increase or decrease. Carver and Scheier (1981) describe a likely scenario: individuals may examine alternatives, perhaps even try them out; if the alternatives fail or individuals feel they lack the necessary skills and abilities to take action, they will withdraw from matching-to-standard attempts.

The previous paragraphs described the outcomes associated with a positive or negative self-assessment, whether that assessment is accurate or inaccurate. We have argued, however, that the mismatch between self-assessments and some outside appraisal is also consequential. Such mismatches characterize individuals in cells 2 (who overestimate their performance) and 4 (who underestimate their performance.

Individuals in cell 2 believe their behavior is on track with respect to the standard in question. What they fail to realize is that relevant others in their environment or objective records or performance do not corroborate this view. While these individuals will likely enjoy feelings of accomplishment and efficacy, they probably do not believe they need to change either the strategies they are pursuing to attain the standard or the standard itself. Accordingly, they are likely to reduce the attention they devote to considering how well they are doing. The self-appraisals of cell 2 individuals should lead them to maintain their efforts due to high efficacy expectations away from any reallocation of their efforts through time.

In many contexts, there will be no costs for holding an inflated self-view. Imagine a stable environment where the organizational structure seldom changes, where employees are paid based on attendance and job tenure, and where employees are hired "for life." Having an overinflated self-assessment in this environment does not have many serious consequences. The environment is not set up to challenge any employee's self-view. Fast actions are seldom required, and a wrong step is not seriously sanctioned. Contrast this environment to one in which the organization is rapidly changing, with new structures, layoffs, and so forth occurring frequently, and where pay is based on performance. In this environment, individuals have to choose between courses of action with significant personal consequences. They must decide, for example, whether they will survive the next round of layoffs or whether they are doing enough to earn that next pay raise. In this environment, self-appraisals serve as important guides for action (Bandura, 1982), and inaccuracy can be costly. A wrong step will likely be sanctioned in some way. The cost of having an inaccurate inflated self-view is that no corrective action is taken when such action is in fact needed.. Other minor costs include damage to the ego when these individuals are confronted with other's actual appraisals of them and loss of face for any public planning they did based on their inaccurate self-view.

The real cost of holding an inaccurate self-view is that individuals lose the opportunity to alter their behavioral strategies aimed at goal attainment. I argued earlier that a positive self-assessment alters attention from the discrepancy-reducing process. Thus, accurate learning about the environment will likely come too late, and individuals will have little time to implement different behavioral options. In a sense, they end up persisting when there is less of a chance for payoff than they may think. They may also set unrealistic aspiration levels for the future and begin acting on those aspirations in the present (e.g., by allocating their current efforts to be more in line with the future higher level goal). These individuals will feel a sense of efficacy and accomplishment, at least until they are confronted with the view of others.

The situation faced by individuals in cell 3 is quite different. These individuals believe they are off track in their behavioral attempts, while others do not. Unless some intervention is made, one cost individuals in this cell may bear is the burden of a needless sense of inefficacy and desire to change. These individuals may mistakenly quit tasks in which they had a reasonable probability of success. They do so in response to their negative self-assessment and a felt need to alter their behavior. For individuals in this cell, however, no change is needed. Changes undertaken in fact may leave these individuals worse off than their current course of action with respect to task success. Thus, as they needlessly change their behaviors, their current negative self-assessment may cause them to undertake changes that actually impair performance, thereby making their current beliefs a future reality.

The costs of having an inaccurate self-view discussed so far have been personal ones. There may be organizational ones as well. For example there may be important consequences to the organization if individuals in cell 3 (who inaccurately underestimate their abilities): (1) act on their self-assessments and fail to persist even though the potential payoff is actually high (Janoff-Bulman & Brickman, 1981); or (2) act on a reduced level of aspirations and fail to apply for jobs or promotions that they could handle. The organization then loses the benefits of their efforts.

The organizational costs of having many employees in cell 2 (with inaccurate, overinflated self-views), however, are less clear. We might hypothesize, in fact, that organizational leaders will not care about self-assessment inaccuracies char-

acteristic of those in cell 2. These individuals overestimate their own performance, the correctness of the strategies they have chosen to achieve a goal, their
capabilities, and so forth relative to others' evaluations. This assessment may set
in motion several processes, including maintenance of task effort, the reallocation of effort from other tasks to this one, and decreased attention to self-management and discrepancy detection. Depending on the degree of overestimation
of abilities, performance strategies, and past performances, these processes are
not likely to be fruitful. They will be sustained only at increasing cost to the
individual in terms of self-esteem and opportunity cost of not pursuing other,
more likely goals. However, as Janoff-Bulman & Brickman (1981) point out, the
interests of society (or in this case, organizations) and the interests of the individual may not coincide. People who persist in struggling toward a worthy but
unlikely-to-be-achieved goal are valued because they contribute to others' well-
being, if not their own. People who quit are denigrated, not only because quitting
is seen as failing but because quitting is often a refusal to continue with a line of
action that other people may wish to see pursued (Janoff-Bulman & Brickman,
1981). Thus much like organizational leaders who have shown, under certain
conditions, to "throw good money after bad" (cf. Shaw & Ross, 1986), individuals in cell 2 may be prompted to continue devoting effort toward what may be
an ultimately losing proposition. It is interesting, then, that while the organizational literature decries the inflation of self-assessments that threaten their use as
selection and performance appraisal criteria, organizational leaders may have
vested interests in maintaining that inflation. Those same overinflated views spur
individuals to increase their efforts toward goals in which the organization has a
vested interest.

SUMMARY AND CONCLUSIONS

For both pragmatic and theoretical reasons, the debate about self-assessment accuracy has continued for a number of years. Interest continues because many
view self-assessments as central to self-concept development and change (Cooley, 1902; Mead, 1934). Others see them as important to adjustment to organizations (Ashford & Taylor, 1987); still others view them as potential tools to reduce the costs of selection and performance appraisal systems (DeNisi et al.,
1977; Heneman, 1980; Shore & Thornton, 1986).

This chapter suggests two new directions for the existing self-assessment literature. These are: (1) to focus more on explaining why inaccuracies occur rather
than continuing to document accuracies and inaccuracies, and (2) to increase the
attention given to naturally occurring, ongoing self-assessments relative to those
collected explicitly for formal organizational uses such as selection and performance appraisals.

To date little research attention has been paid to why individuals' assessments might or might not be accurate and how they might deviate from accuracy (Heneman 1980; Thornton, 1980). The little attention paid has focused primarily on issues surrounding the measurement of self-assessments. Thus, Mabe and West (1982) proposed that if individuals understand the dimension in question, accept the dimension, and perceive that the assessment will not be used against them, self-assessments will be more accurate. The focus solely on measurement factors, however, provides a relatively impoverished explanation of self-assessment accuracy.

To push self-assessment research toward a broader explanation, we offer a social-psychological model of self-assessment that takes into account both the psychological experiences of the individual and the nature of the organization as a social context for such assessments. We propose that self-assessment difficulties arise from problems individuals experience in (1) obtaining the information necessary to assess their performance accurately and interpreting this information in a veridical manner; (2) balancing the instrumental desire to understand what they should be doing and how well they have done with the costs to the ego that they suffer by hearing negative feedback; and (3) obtaining standard and feedback information within a social environment in which information seeking may have particular negative symbolic meaning as a sign of weakness or insecurity. Each of these problems and their interaction contribute to difficulties in completing three essential self-assessment tasks: (1) interpreting cues, (2) establishing the links between various behavioral strategies and one's goals, and (3) establishing the links between available feedback cues and one's own behavior. These difficulties result in self-assessment inaccuracies that produce a host of outcomes.

The model has several implications for managing people. The main performance appraisal system implication is an old one: that superiors should maximize the amount of feedback and standard information given directly to employees. This calls for both very honest formal performance appraisals and more frequent informal appraisals. Given the emphasis on accuracy, these appraisals should include both positive and negative feedback. Superiors need to recognize the ways that they introduce bias into situations. First, by not giving direct feedback, individuals are forced to rely on observational cues that are more subject to idiosyncratic interpretation. Second, by reducing interaction time with those they have negatively evaluated (Thornton, 1968), superiors cut these employees off from the most direct observational source of feedback: that of observing how the superior acts toward them. These employees then must use even more speculative cues to see where they stand.

In altering their feedback-giving behavior, supervisors face two obstacles: their own reluctance to give negative feedback (Fisher, 1979) and the subordinates's desire to avoid hearing negative news. It is not surprising, then, that in formal appraisal situations, these two factors combine, resulting in little sharing of information that may have the most instrumental value for the subordinate. To overcome these obstacles, work organizations must overcome our societal belief that equates giving negative feedback with giving offense or being rude. To the extent possible, organizations must create an ethos that affirms negative feedback as useful. To this end, superiors need to be trained to develop routines by which individuals can be given feedback without it's threatening their egos.

One way to avoid ego threat is to make individual feedback encounters seem less crucial by having them more of them. If a supervisor can establish a norm that feedback will be exchanged often and honestly, the tension surrounding both the giving and hearing of negative feedback will be reduced. Subordinates would understand that the negative feedback they hear today is not an indictment of their last six months' performance but rather a current impression that may likely be quickly followed by a more positive report. Another way to improve the tenor of feedback encounters is to let subordinates have some control over them. Perhaps subordinates will more readily receive information that they have sought actively. Active seeking gives the subordinate control over the timing of the feedback encounter, the setting in which it will occur, and so forth. If this is so, much can be done to reduce the self-presentational costs of seeking out feedback. Superiors can influence how this act is interpreted by work group members. Anything superiors can do to reduce the cost of search will result in feedback encounters that are timely and useful. In these encounters, subordinates, feeling more in control, may be more likely to "hear" negative feedback. Implicit in the discussion is the second suggestion for the self-assessment research: the need to move beyond its traditional focus on the use of self-assessments in selection and performance appraisal contexts to consider assessments that individuals make naturally in their ongoing organizational experiences.

This shift in focus is an important one for several reasons. First, employees do make self-assessments spontaneously as part of their ongoing decision making about what they should be doing, how they should allocate their efforts across tasks, and how they are faring in meeting their own goals. While these issues certainly arise in performance appraisal contexts, they also occur naturally at other times in an individual's worklife. Second, these naturally occurring assessments have important consequences. They serve as inputs to a variety of performance- and career-related issues that individuals face daily. Many of these decisions are important to the organization (i.e., an individual's decision to remain within an organization or leave it). From a human resource management standpoint, we would like to avoid having able individuals shy away from job opportunities they can handle. Third, employees see self-feedback as highly available and trustworthy (Greller & Herold, 1975). Thus self-assessments will likely be a primary source of employee feedback. Their effects on the employee's self-views are likely to be pervasive and only partially modified by formal and informal superior and peer assessments. Fourth, as organizations experience increasing amounts of change, their internal control systems may also be in flux and will arguably lose some rigor and potency. In such situations, organizational leaders may be increasingly dependent on the self-management practices of their employees. It is difficult to believe that individuals who have had four bosses and two new accounting or performance appraisal systems in a short time span are really under the rigorous control of the organization. In periods of great internal flux, organizations may only be able to establish parameters around the self-management processes of their employees. In such situations, we might expect that self-generated assessments will have more impact on an individual's behavior than will, say, feedback from a boss who is unfamiliar with the employee's work. Further, if we believe that individuals in these situations are operating primarily on their own assessments as they choose among task strategies, then any self-assessment problems will introduce inefficiencies as employees follow up incorrect strategies and overlook more efficient ones. In this way, self-assessment inaccuracies have important organizational consequences.

Fifth, periods or organizational change also bring career concerns to the fore. Consider a case of a merger between two companies. Between the announcement of a merger and the actual change, a high degree of career uncertainty exists as employees attempt to determine, "Will there be a place for me in the new structure? Do I have what it takes to survive here, or should I go elsewhere?" It is at just these times, however, that organizational leaders have few concrete answers. Thus, we would expect that self-assessments would be important determinants of action in these periods. Given the uncertainty and turmoil of the firm's internal environment in these periods, we would also expect that self-assessment errors will certainly occur. Thus transition periods pose a particular management challenge: that of helping employees make realistic self-assessments and career decisions in an ambiguous environment.

Finally, it is also important to remember that self-assessment capability is as much an organizational issue as it is an individual one. The self-assessment problems we have outlined apply as much to the firm's top managers plotting the strategic direction of firm as they do to the lowest-level employee determining how to survive in the firm. There are clear consequences to the firm and its members if the top management team is off track in its self-assessment of the firm's strengths, capabilities, and current strategy. When the CEO tries to determine whether he or she has chosen the best strategy for the firm, he or she faces an information problem consisting of random, or sometimes systematically, biased cues, an ego defense problem in that he or she chose the strategy and may not comfortably accept criticism, and a self-presentational problem in that seeking others' opinions may especially be inconsistent with our images of how a strong, capable leader acts. Understanding why individuals, including those that head up our organizations, may deviate from an accurate self-view gives us a basis to intervene in situations where inaccuracy has individual and/or organizational costs.

In taking these two new directions, the self-assessment literature must grapple with two thorny philosophical issues that have not been carefully addressed by the existing literature. These issues are: (a) Should accuracy be a goal for individuals? and, (b) What accuracy criteria really matter? These issues need to be addressed by subsequent empirical researchers as the issues relate to their specific research aims and context.

Scholars disagree about whether an accurate self-view is a goal worth striving for. Mechanic (1974, P. 37), for example, argues quite persuasively that

> there is perhaps no thought so stifling as to see ourselves in proper perspective. We all maintain our sense of self-respect and energy for action through perceptions that enhance our self-importance and self esteem, and we maintain our sample by suppressing the tremendous vulnerability we all experience in relation to the risks of the real world.

Ashford and Cummings (1985), however, have pointed out the instrumental value of having an accurate general sense of one's abilities, potential, and performance. Bailey and Lazar (1976) and Epstein (1973) also noted the functional value of having an accurate self-view. It may be that accuracy is more important in a contractually based organizational setting where there are some real benefits to be gained in terms of career and performance management from an accurate view of one's self. While individuals may be able to structure the rest of their lives so that they receive only self-enhancing feedback and lose little by doing so, in organizations much more may be at stake. In life, others may disagree with their assessment, but those others do not have power over them. In organizations, others have the power to hire, fire, promote, and reward.

In organizations, too, however, there may be certain situations where accuracy may be less desirable, For example, entrepreneurs may need to divorce themselves from receiving negative feedback through the early stages of an innovation. Many ideas that have ultimately paid off could have died had their inventors listened to early critics. Similarly organizational change agents who bring new members on board certainly do not want those members to base their self-assessments on either direct feedback from old-timers or on how they see the old-timers responding to them. In both of these cases, new employees may need specific guidance so that they do not attend to cues from others. These employees may not need an "accurate" view of how they are seen by these others.

Acknowledging the arguments on both sides, it is reasonable to say that there is a tension within individuals regarding how much accurate information they want about themselves. The important research concern, then, is to understand and account for the contextual pressures operating on the individual in each research setting. These pressures for or against accuracy need to be either explicitly examined as explanatory factors or controlled for in testing the effects of individual-level variables on accuracy.

The second issue is, What accuracy criteria matter? A subordinate question becomes, what criteria should we as researchers use to draw conclusions about self-assessment accuracy? The self-assessment literature has not differentiated between objective and subjective criteria in drawing cross-study conclusions. It does seem glib, however, to call a self-assessment accurate solely because it matches another's assessment when there is no evidence to suggest that the other's assessment is a valid measure of the individual's behavior or performance. For example, there has been much study of supervisors' biases in performance appraisal (Landy & Farr, 1980), so a correlation of self and supervisor assessment as an accuracy criterion should be somewhat suspect. There may also be circumstances in which we would expect an individual to know more about his or her performance than will an outside observer. In these situations, labeling the low correlation between the individual and others' assessment evidence of inaccuracy also seems suspect.

In thinking about what criteria probably matter most to individuals, however, it is clear that both objective and subjective indicators will matter under different circumstances. For example, if individuals are going to change organizations, they may want to know whether their skills will serve them well in the new environment. In this case, it may not be enough to know that all those in the current work setting feel their skills are adequate. They may want to have some objective evidence of their skills (e.g., test score or actual task performance) and will derive their self-assessment based solely on that objective evidence.

In many situations, however, such objective evidence does not exist (Festinger, 1954). Indeed, Jacques (1961) argued that the higher one is in the organization, the longer it takes to get any kind of objective evidence regarding the utility of one's actions. Therefore others' opinions, as biased and error filled as they might be, may be all that employees have to go on in guiding their immediate self-assessments. Thus, while others' opinions may be inadequate as the sole accuracy criteria in a study, they certainly can be realistically included as criteria of some importance to employees.

These opinions may also not be such a bad guide for employees. One's superior, peers, and subordinates use their opinions about an individual to make important decisions about whether to give or withhold their resources, their support, and their respect to him or her. Therefore, the ability to see oneself as these others do may be of crucial importance. Indeed employees from minority groups have complained that their careers reach dead ends because, while they do well at meeting objective performance indicators, they have trouble winning subjective favor with their superior, peers and subordinates (Davis & Watson 1982), For them, as I would argue for most other employees, those subjective, error-filled evaluations mattered; they were tied to important consequences.

Having recognized the importance of others' evaluations, an additional self-regulation task may emerge. That is, employees who discover that their self-views are at odds with how others see them may not alter their own view of their behavior but may attempt to influence the content of these opinions. This possibility suggests a more political model of self-regulation than has been considered to date. It may be that interpersonal influence and impression management are as important as accommodating others' opinions. Ashford and Tsui (1987) speak to this view in their model of managerial effectiveness.

The more general point, however, is that we as researchers would like to have objective performance data as a criterion in our quest to establish whether individuals are accurate self-assessors. However, in the socially constructed, political organizational worlds in which these individuals exist, the important reality may be others' opinions of them (no matter how biased). Thus, our continued use of these opinions as an accuracy criterion may be entirely appropriate. What we might do in empirical research is to use both objective performance indicators and subjective evaluations as criteria. If we assume that the objective indicator is error free (a major assumption in many cases), then we can estimate and control for the bias in others' evaluations.

My intent has been to broaden the scope of questions asked and the explanations considered in the self-assessment literature. The model presented in Figure 2 will provide a foundation for the new direction outlined. I have also focused on errors—ways that individuals go wrong in the assessment process. This focus is motivated by the sometimes unnecessary toll that these inaccurate assessments take on individuals. For example, Ernest Hemingway's suicide has been described as a reaction of someone who set high standards for himself and maintained a self-view that was inconsistent with how others saw his work and certainly how his work has been "objectively" appraised in recent years (Bandura, 1977, p. 142). Hemingway severely underestimated his considerable talent. While the organizational examples of human cost are probably far less dramatic than Hemingway's death, their very unnecessity motivates us to give them careful consideration.

ACKNOWLEDGMENTS

The author would like to thank Jane Dutton, Jay Hull, Lance Sandelands, Ralph Stablein, and Jim Walsh for their comments on an earlier draft of this manuscript. Stephanie Crewsell also deserves credit for her work in collecting and organizing the literature review materials.

REFERENCES

Ammons, R. E. (1956). Effects of knowledge of performance: A survey and tentative theoretical formulation. *The Journal of General Psychology, 54*, 279–299.

Anderson, C. D., Warren, J. L., & Spencer, C. C. (1984). Inflation bias in self-assessment examinations: Implications for valid employee selection. *Journal of Applied Psychology, 69*, 574–580.

Ashford, S. J. (1986). The role of feedback seeking in individual adaptation: A resource perspective. *Academy of Management Journal,* '*29*, 465–487.

Ashford, S. J., & Cummings, L. L. (1983). Feedback as an individual resource: Personal strategies of creating information. *Organizational Behavior and Human Performance, 32*, 370–398.

Ashford, S. J.. & Cummings, L. L. 1985. Proactive feedback seeking: The instrumental use of the information environment. *Journal of Occupational Psychology, 58*, 67–79.

Ashford, S. J., Taylor, M. S., K. M. Rowland and G. R. Ferris (Eds.), Toward a theory of individual adaptation. (Forthcoming). In Research in Personnel and Human Resource Management, 8.

Ashford, S. J., & Tsui, A. 1987. The self-regulating manager: A process model of reputational effectiveness and managerial success. Working paper, The Amos Tuck School of Business Administration, Hanover, NH: Dartmouth College.

Bailey, R. C., & Bailey, K. G. 1971. Perceived ability in relation to actual ability and academic achievement. *Journal of Clinical Psychology, 27,* 461–463.

Bailey, K. G., & Lazar, J. 1976. Accuracy of self-ratings of intelligence as a function of sex and level of ability in college students. *Journal of Genetic Psychology, 129,* 279–290.

Baird, L. S. 1977. Self and superior ratings of performance-related to self-esteem and satisfaction with supervision. *Academy of Management Journal, 20,* 291–300.

Bandura, A. 1977. *Social Learning Theory.* Englewood Cliffs, NJ: Prentice-Hall.

Bandura, A. 1982. The self and mechanisms of agency. In J. Suls (Ed.), *Psychological perspectives on the self,* (Vol. 1, pp. XX–XX), Hillsdale, N.J.: Erlbaum Associates.

Bandura, A., & Cervone, D. 1983. Self-evaluative and self-efficacy mechanisms governing the motivational effects of goal systems. *Journal of Personality and Social Psychology, 45,* 1017–1028.

Bassett, G. A., & Meyer, H. H. 1968. Performance appraisal based on self-review. *Personnel Psychology, 21,* 421–430.

Baumeister, R. 1982. A self-presentational view of social phenomena. *Psychological Bulletin, 91,* 3–26.

Beck, A. 1967. *Depression: Clinical, experimental and theoretical aspects.* New York: Harper & Row.

Berscheid, E., Graziano, W., Monson, T., & Dermer, M. (1976). Outcome dependency: Attention, attribution and attraction. *Journal of personality and Social Psychology, 34:* 378–389.

Bledscoe, J. C., & Wiggens, R. E. (1973). Congruence of adolescents' self-concepts and parents' perceptions of adolescents' self-concepts. *Journal of Psychology, 83,* 131–136.

Blumberg, H. H. (1972). Communication of interpersonal evaluations. *Journal of Personality and Social Psychology, 23,* 157–162.

Blumer, H. (1969). *Symbolic interactionism: Perspective and Method.* Englewood Cliffs, N.J.: Prentice-Hall.

Bogart, D. H. (1980). Feedback, feedforward, and feedwithin: Strategic information systems. *Behavioral Science, 25,* 237–249.

Bouton, J. (1970). *Ball Four* New York: Dell.

Brams, J. (1961). Counselor characteristics and effective communication in counseling. *Journal of Counseling Psychology 8,* 25–30.

Brief, A. P., & Hollenbeck, J. R. (1985). An exploratory study of self-regulating activities and their effects on job performance. *Journal of Occupational Behavior, 6,* 197–208.

Brockner, Joel (1979). The effects of self-esteem success-failure, and self-consciousness on task performance. *Journal of Personality and Social Psychology, 37,* 1732–1741.

Brockner, Joel (1983). Low self-esteem and behavioral plasticity: Some implications. In Wheeler & Shaver (Eds.), *Review of Personality and Social Psychology,* 4, 237–271. Beverly Hills, CA: Sage Publications.

Broll, L., Gross, A., & Piliavin, I. (1974). Effects of offered and requested help on help seeking and reactions to being helped. *Journal of Applied Social Psychology, 4,* 255–258.

Brown, Jr., I., & Inouye, D. K. (1978). Learned helplessness through modeling: The role of perceived similarity in competence. *Journal of Personality and Social Psychology, 36,* 900–908.

Business Week. (1980). Corporate Culture. The hard-to-change values that spell success or failure. October 26.

Campion, M. A., & Lord, R. G. (1982). A control system conceptualization of the goal-setting and changing process. *Organizational Behavior and Human Performance,* 30, 256–287.

Carver, C. S., & Scheier, M. F. (1981). *Attention and self-regulation: A control-theory approach to human behavior.* New York: Springer.

Conolley, E. S., Gerrard, H. B., & Kline, T. (1978). Competitive behavior: A manifestation of motivation for ability comparison. *Journal of Experimental Social Psychology, 14,* 123–131.

Conrad, J. (1949). *Lord Jim.* Harmondsworth, Middlesex, England: Penguin Books.

Cooley, C. H. (1902). *Human nature and the social order.* New York: Scribner.

Crocker, J. (1981). Judgment of covariation by social perceivers. *Psychological Bulletin, 90,* 272–292.

Crocker, J., Fiske, S. T., & Taylor, S. E. (1984). Schematic bases of belief change. In R. Eiser (ed.), *Attitudinal judgment.* New York: Springer-Verlag.

Cummings, L. L., & Schwab, D. P. (1973). *Performance in organizations.* Glenview, Ill.: Scott Foresman.

Daft, R. (1986). Organizational information requirements, media richness and structural design. *Management Science, 32,* 554–571.

D'Augelli, A. R. (1973). The assessment of interpersonal skills: A comparison of observer, peer and self-ratings. *Journal of Community Psychology, 1* (2), 177–179.

Davis, G., & Watson G. (1982). *Black life in corporate America: Swimming in the mainstream.* Garden City, N.Y.: Anchor Press, Doubleday.

Denisi, A. S., & Shaw, J. B. (1977). Investigation of the uses of self-reports of abilities. *Journal of Applied Psychology, 62,* 641–644.

DeWhirst, H. D. (1971). Influence of perceived information sharing norms on communication channel utilization. *Academy of Management Journal, 14,* 303–315.

Dweck, C. S. (1975). The role of expectations and attributions in the alleviation of learned helplessness. *Journal of Personality and Social Psychology, 31,* 674–685.

Edwards, A. L., & Klockars, A. J. (1981). Significant others and self-evaluation: Relationships between perceived and actual evaluations. *Personality and Social Psychology Bulletin, 7,* 244–251.

Ellis, R. J., & Holmes, J. G. (1982). Focus of attention and self-evaluation in social interaction. *Journal of Personality and Social Psychology, 43* (1), 67–77

Epstein, S. (1973). The self-concept revisited: Or a theory of a theory. *American Psychologist, 28,* 404–416.

Fazio, R. H., Sherman, S. J., & Herr, P. M. (1982). The feature-positive effect in the self perception process: Does not doing matter as much as doing? *Journal of Personality and Social Psychology, 42,* 404–411.

Feather, N. T., & Simon, J. G. (1972). Luck and an unexpected outcome: A field replication of laboratory findings. *Australian Journal of Psychology, 24,* 113–117.

Feldman, D. C., & Brett, J. M. (1983). Coping with new jobs: A comparative study of new hires and job changers. *Academy of Management Journal, 26,* 258–272.

Felson, R. B. (1980). Communications barriers and the reflected appraisal process. *Social Psychology Quarterly, 43,* 223–233.

Felson, R. B. (1984). The effect of self-appraisals of ability on academic performance. *Journal of Personality and Social Psychology, 47,* 944–952.

Fenigstein, A. (1979). Self-consciousness, self-attention and social interaction. *Journal of Personality and Social Psychology, 37,* 75–86.

Fenigstein, A., Scheier, M. F. & Buss, A. H. (1975). Public and private self-consciousness assessment and theory. *Journal of Consulting and Clinical Psychology, 43,* 522–527.

Festinger, L. (1954). A theory of social comparison processes. *Human Relations, 7,* 117–140.

Fisher, C. D. (1979). Transmission of positive and negative feedback to subordinates: A laboratory investigation. *Journal of Applied Psychology, 64,* 533–540.

Fisher, R. I. (1974). Cognitive appraisal: An examination. *Journal of Psychology, 88,* 147–152.

Friend, R. M., & Gilbert, J. (1973). Threat and fear of negative evaluation as determinants of locus of social comparison. *Journal of Personality, 41,* 328–340.

Gergen, K. (1974). Toward a psychology of receiving help. *Journal of Applied Social Psychology, 4,* 184–193.

Goffman, E. (1956). Embarrassment and social organization. *American Journal of Sociology, 62,* 264–71.

Goslin, P. A. (1962). Accuracy of self-perception and social acceptance. *Sociometry, 25,* 283–296.

Greenwald, A. G. (1980). The totalitarian ego: Fabrication and revision of personal history. *American Psychologist, 35* (7), 603–618.

Greller, M. M., & Harold, D. M. (1975). Sources of feedback: A preliminary investigation. *Organizational Behavior and Human Performance, 13,* 244–256.

Griffiths, R. D. P. (1975). The accuracy and correlates of psychiatric patients: Self-assessments of their work behavior. *British Journal of Social and Clinical Psychology, 14,* 181–189.

Halisch, F., & Heckhausen, H. (1977). Search for feedback information and effort regulation during task performance. *Journal of Personality and Social Psychology, 35,* 724–733.

Hanser, L. M., & Muchinsky, P. M. (1978). Work as an information environment. *Organizational Behavior and Human Performance, 21,* 47–60.

Harvey, O. J., Kelley, H. H. & Shapiro, M. M. (1957). Reactions to unfavorable evaluations of self made by other persons. *Journal of Personality, 25,* 393–411.

Hase, H. D., & Goldberg, L. R. (1967). Comparative validity of different strategies of constructing personality inventory scales. Psychological Bulletin, 67, 231–248.

Helper, M. M. (1958). Parental evaluations of children and children's self-evaluation. *Journal of Abnormal and Social Psychology, 56,* 190–194.

Heneman, H. (1973). Comparisons of self- and superior-ratings of managerial performance. *Journal of Applied Psychology, 57,* 49–54.

Heneman, H. G. (1980). Self-assessment: A critical analysis. *Personnel Psychology, 33,* 297–300.

Herold, D. M., & Parsons, C. K. (1985). Assessing the feedback environment in work organizations: Development of the job feedback survey. *Journal of Applied Psychology, 70,* 290–305.

Ilgen, D. R., Knowlton, W. A. (1980). Performance attributional effects on feedback from subordinates. *Organizational Behavior and Human Performance, 25,* 441–456.

Ilgen, D. R., & Moore, C. F. (1987). Types and choices of performance feedback. *Journal of Applied Psychology, 72,* 001–006.

Ivancevitch, J. M., & McMahon, J. T. (1982). The effect of goal setting, external feedback and self-generated feedback on outcome variables: A field experiment. *Academy of Management Journal, 25,* 359–372.

Jacobs, L., Berscheid, E., & Walster, E. (1971). Self-esteem and attraction. *Journal of Personality and Social Psychology, 17,* 84–91.

Jacques, E. (1961). *Equitable Payment.* New York: Wiley

Janis, I., & Mann, L. (1977). *Decision making.* New York: Free Press.

Janoff-Bulman, R., & Brickman, P. (1981). Expectations and learning from failure. In N. T. Feather (ed.), *Expectancy incentive and action.* Hillsdale, N.J.: Erlbaum Associates.

Johnson, T. W., & Graen, G. (1973). Organizational assimilation and role rejection. *Organizational Behavior and Human Performance, 10,* 72–87.

Jones, E. E., & Gerard, H. B. (1967). *Foundations of social psychology. New York: Wiley.*

Jones, G. (1983). Psychological orientation and the process or organizational socialization: An interactionist perspective. *Academy of Management Review, 8,* 464–474.

Jones, S. C. (1973). Self- and interpersonal evaluations: Esteem theories versus consistency theories. *Psychological Bulletin, 79,* 185–199.

Katz, D., & Kahn, R. L. (1978). *The social psychology of organizations.* 2 ed. New York: Wiley.

Kimberly I. R., & Quinn, R. E. (1984). *Managing organizational transitions.* Homewood, Ill. Richard D. Irwin.

Klimoski, R. J., & London, M. (1974). Role of the rater in performance appraisal. *Journal of Applied Psychology, 59,* 445–451.

Knight, R. A., & Nadel, J. I. (1986). Humility revisited: Self-esteem information search and policy consistency. *Organizational Behavior and Human Decision Processes, 38,* 196–206.

Kooker, E. W. (1974). Changes in ability of graduate students in education to assess own test performance as related to their Miller Analogies scores. *Psychological Reports, 35*, 97–98.

Landy, F. J., & Farr, J. L. (1980). Performance rating. *Psychological Bulletin, 87* (1), 72–107.

Larson, J. R. (1986). Supervisors' performance feedback to subordinates: The impact of subordinate performance valence and outcome dependency. Working paper. University of Illinois at Chicago.

Lawler, E. E., III. (1968). Equity theory as a predictor of productivity and work quality. *Psychological Bulletin, 70*, 596–610.

Lepper, M. R., Ross, L., & Lau, R. R. (1986). Persistence of inaccurate beliefs about the self: Perseverance effects in the classroom. *Journal of Personality and Social Psychology, 50*, 482–491.

Levine, E. L., Flory, A., & Ash, R. A. (1977). Self-assessment in personnel selection. *Journal of Applied Psychology, 62*, 428–435.

Louis, M. R. (1980). Surprise and sensemaking: What newcomers experience in entering unfamiliar organizational settings. *Administrative Science Quarterly, 25*, 226–251.

Lunnenborg, C. E. (1982). Systematic biases in brief self-ratings of vocational qualifications. *Journal of Vocational Behavior, 20*, 255–275.

Mabe, P. A., & West, S. G. (1982). Validity of self-evaluation of ability: A review and meta analysis. *Journal of Applied Psychology, 67*, 280–296.

Manz, C. C. (1986). Self-leadership: Toward an expanded theory of self-influence processes in organizations. *Academy of Management Review, 11*, 585–600.

Markus, H. (1977). Self schemata and processing information about the self. *Journal of Personality and Social Psychology, 35*, 63–78.

Mead, G. H. (1934). *Mind, self and society*. Chicago: University of Chicago Press.

Mechanic, D. (1974). Social structure and person adaptation: Some neglected dimensions. In G. V. Coelho, D. A. Hamburg, & J. E. Adams (Eds.), *Coping and adaptation*, 32–47. New York: Basic Books.

Meyer, H. H. 1980. Self-appraisal of job performance. *Personnel Psychology, 33*, 291–295.

Meyer, H., Kay, E., & French, J. R. P. (1965). Effects of threat in a performance appraisal interview. *Journal of Applied Psychology, 49*, 311–317.

Meyer, W. U., & Starke, E. (1982). Own ability in relation to self-concept of ability: A field study of information seeking. *Personality and Social Psychology, 8*, 501–507.

Mihal, W. L., & Graumenz, J. L. (1984). An assessment of the accuracy of self-assessment for career decision making. *Journal of Vocational Behavior, 25*, 245–253.

Miller, D. T. 1976. Ego involvement and attributions for success and failure. *Journal of Personality and Social Psychology, 34*, 901–906.

Miller, G. A., Galanter, E., & Pribram, K. H. (1960). *Plans and the structure of behavior*. New York: Holt, Rinehart & Winston.

Mills, P. K. (1983). Self-management: Its control and relationship to other organizational properties. *Academy of Management Review, 8*, 445–453.

Mischel, W., Ebbesen, E. B., & Zeiss, A. M (1976). Determinants of selective memory about the self. *Journal of Consulting and Clinical Psychology, 44*, 92–103.

Miyamoto, S. F., & Dornbusch, S. 1956. A test of the symbolic interactionist hypotheses of self-conception. *American Journal of Sociology, 61*, 399–403.

Modigliani, A. 1971. Embarrassment, facework, and eye contact: Testing a theory of embarrassment. *Journal of Personality and Social Psychology, 17*, 15–24.

Mount, M. K. 1984. Supervisor, self- and subordinate ratings of performance and satisfaction with supervision. *Journal of Management 10*, 305–320.

Neisser, V. (1976). *Cognition and reality: Principles and implications of cognitive psychology*. San Francisco: Freeman

Nisbett, R., & Ross, L. (1980). *Human inference: Strategies and shortcomings of social judgment*. Englewood Cliffs, N.J.: Prentice-Hall.

Parker, J. W., Taylor, E. K., Earrett, R. S., & Martens, L. (1959). Ratings scale content III: Relationship between supervisory and self-ratings. *Personnel Psychology, 12*, 49–63.

Pepitone, A., & Wilpizeski, C. (1960). Some consequences of experimental rejection. *Journal of Abnormal and Social Psychology, 60*, 359–364.

Powers, W. T. (1973). *Behavior: The control of perception.* Chicago: Aldine Publishing Company.

Reagan, J. W. Gosselink, H., Hubsch, J., & Ulsh, E. 1975. Do people have inflated views of their abilities? *Journal of Personality and Social Psychology, 31*, 295–301.

Roethlisberger, F. J., & Dickson, W. J. (1939). *Management and the worker.* Cambridge, Mass.: Harvard University Press.

Ross, M., & Sicoly, F. (1979). Egocentric biases in availability and attribution. *Journal of Personality and Social Psychology, 37*, 322–336.

Rosse, J. G., & Hulin, C. L. (1985). Adaptation to work: An analysis of employee, health, withdrawal and change. *Organizational behavior and Human Decision Processes, 36*, 324–347.

Sachs, P. R. (1982). Avoidance of diagnostic information in self-evaluation of ability. *Personality and Social Psychology Bulletin, 8*, 242–246,

Salancik, G. R. (1977). Commitment and the control of organization behavior and belief. In B. M. Staw and G. Salancik (Eds.), *New directions in organization behavior.* Chicago: St. Clair Press.

Sandelands, L. S., Brockner, J., & Glynn, M. A. (1988). If at first you don't succeed, try, try again: Situational and dispositional determinants of persistence. *Journal of Applied Psychology, 73*, 208–216.

Shoeneman, T. J. 1981. Reports of sources of self-knowledge. *Journal of Personality, 49*, 289–293.

Shore, M. L., & Thornton, G. C. (1986). Effects of gender on self and supervisory ratings. *Academy of Management Journal, 29*, 115–129.

Shrauger, J. S. (1975). Responses to evaluations as a function of initial self-perceptions. *Psychological Bulletin, 82*, 581–596.

Shrauger, S., & Lund, A. K. 1975. Self-evaluation and reactions to evaluations from others. *Journal of Personality, 43*, 94–108.

Shrauger, J. S., & Rosenberg, S. E. 1970. Self-esteem and effects of success and failure feedback on performance. *Journal of Personality, 38*, 404–417.

Shrauger, J. S., & Shoeneman, J. 1979. Symbolic interactionist view of self-concept: Through the looking glass darkly. *Psychological Bulletin, 86*, 549–573.

Shrauger, J. S., & Terbovic, M. L. 1976. Self-evaluation and assessments of performance by self and others. *Journal of Consulting and Clinical Psychology, 44*, 564–572.

Simon, J. G., & Feather, N. T. 1973. Casual attributions for success and failure at university examinations. *Journal of Educational Psychology, 64*, 46–56.

Slovic, P., Fischhoff, B., & Lichtenstein, S. 1977. Behavioral decision theory. *Annual Review of Psychology, 28* 1–9.

Staw, B. M. 1977. Motivation in organizations: Toward synthesis and redirection. In B. M. Staw and G. Salancik (Eds.), *New directions in organization behavior.* Chicago: St. Clair Press.

Swann, W. B. 1983. Self-verification: Bringing social reality into harmony with the self. In J. Suls and A. G. Greenwald (Eds.), *Psychological Perspectives on the Self,* (Vol. 2, pp. 33–66). Hillsdale, N.J.: Lawrence Erlbaum Associates.

Swann, W. B., & Hill, C. A. (1982). When our identities are mistaken: Reaffirming self-conceptions through social interaction. *Journal of Personality and Social Psychology, 43*, 59–66.

Swann, W. B., & Read, S. I, 1981. Acquiring self-knowledge: The search for feedback that fits. *Journal of Personality and Social Psychology, 41*, 1119–1128.

Tesser, A. (1983). The definition of self: Private and public self-evaluation management strategies. *Journal of Personality and Social Psychology, 44*, 672–682.

Tesser, A., Campbell, J., & Smith, M. (1984). Friendship choice and performance: Self-evaluation maintenance in children. *Journal of Personality and Social Psychology, 46*, 561–574.

Tesser, A., & Rosen, S. (1975). The reluctance to transmit bad news. In L. Berkowitz (Ed.), *Advances in Experimental Social Psychology,* (Vol. 8, pp xx-xx) New York: Academic Press.

Thornton III, G. C. (1968). The relationship between supervisory and self-appraisals of executive performance. *Personnel Psychology, 21*, 441–455.

Thornton, III, G. C. (1980). Psychometric properties of self-appraisals of job performance. *Personnel Psychology, 33*, 263–271.

Touhey, J. C. (1972). Studies in symbolic interaction: II. An experimental analysis of self-referent behavior. *Psychological Record, 22*: 325–331.

Trope, Y. (1980). Self-assessment, self-enhancement, and task preference. *Journal of Experimental Social Psychology, 16*, 116–129.

Trope, Y. (1982). Self-assessment and task performance. *Journal of Experimental Social Psychology, 18*, 201–215.

Tsui, A. S. (1984). A role set analysis of managerial reputation. *Organizational Behavior and Human Performance, 34*, 64–96.

Turner, Barry A. (1971). *Exploring the industrial subculture.* London: Macmillan.

Walsh, J. P., Ashford, S. J., & Hill, T. E. (1985). Feedback obstruction: The influence of information environment on employee turnover intentions. *Human Relations, 38*, 23–46.

Ward, W. D., & Jenkins, H. M. (1965). The display of information and the judgment of contingency. *Canadian Journal of Psychology, 19*, 231–241.

Weick, Karl. 1979. *The social psychology of organizing.* 2d ed. Reading, MA: Addison-Wesley.

Weiss, H. M. 1978. The social learning of work values in organizations. *Journal of Applied Psychology, 63*, 711–718.

Weiss, H. M., Ilgen, D. R., & Sharbaugh, M. E. 1982. Effects of life and job stress on information/search behaviors of organization members. *Journal of Applied Psychology, 67*, 60–66.

Weiss, H. M., & Kinght, P. A. (1980). The utility of humility: Self-esteem, information search and problem solving efficiency. *Organizational Behavior and Human Performance, 25*, 216–223.

Willerman, B., Lewitt, D. & Tellegen, A. (1960). Seeking and avoiding self-evaluation by working individually or in groups. In D. Wilner (Ed.), *Decision, values and groups.* New York: Pergamon Press.

Zammuto, R. F., London, M. A., & Rowland, K. M. (1982). Organizational and rater differences in performance appraisals. *Personnel Psychology, 35*, 643–658.

Zuckerman, M. (1979). Attribution of success and failure revised or: The motivational bias is alive and well in attribution theory. *Journal of Personality, 47*, 245–287.

Zuckerman, M., Brown, R. H., Fox, G. A., Lathin, D. R., & Minasian, A. J. 1979. Determinants of information seeking behavior. *Journal of Research in Personality 13*, 161–174.

A PROCESS ANALYSIS OF THE ASSESSMENT CENTER METHOD

Sheldon Zedeck

ABSTRACT

The processes underlying the assessment center method are explored from three perspectives: (1) information processing, (2) categorization and social cognition, and (3) group dynamics. These perspectives are used to explain the dynamics that operate when observing behavior of managerial candidates in simulated exercises and when processing information for the purpose of evaluating candidates. In addition, concepts such as categories and management behavior schema are used to explain how assessors recall information and make predictions and judgments. Finally, these perspectives shed light on the conclusions of several recent studies that suggest that evaluation on general assessment dimensions provides a limited contribution to the process.

An *assessment center* is a method for describing, evaluating, or predicting effectiveness as a manager. It has been in use in the United States since World War II (MacKinnon, 1977), and its increasing popularity is evidenced by the fact that literally thousands of people a year are now processed through these centers (Thornton & Byham, 1982). Within the research literature, it too can be considered a popular topic—one recent examination of computer searches found approximately 500 studies related to assessment centers (Bentz, 1984). The overall general conclusion from such research has been positive. That is, assessments derived from the method have been found to be correlated with (and predictive of) subsequent performance in managerial roles. In brief, the results of most of the research have been of one form—"another positive finding."

A missing link in the study of assessment centers is a full understanding of the particular cognitive and behavioral processes involved in assessment center dynamics. Though the components of the process have been studied, we need a better understanding of the dynamics involved in the process. Even if the bottom line for assessment centers is positive, in terms of both validity and utility, a useful scientific endeavor would be to study the person x situation interaction dynamics that intercede between the components and the end product of any method (see Figure 1). That is, whereas most of the research literature has focused on what the components of the method ought to be, and how these components affect outcomes, there is little, if any, research on how the components–results link is impacted by a particular group of persons—the assessors—and the dynamics of the situation in which they are functioning.

It is the contention of this paper that any interpretation of the relationship between a component variable (e.g., the number of dimensions to be assessed) and the adequacy of the prediction needs to be viewed in light of how the assessor processes information, or deals with the information, in a group discussion setting. Thus the person x situation interaction depicted in Figure 1 is not concerned with the characteristics of the candidate

Figure 1. The person × situation link between assessment center components and results.

and how he/she does in the center, but is concerned with how the candidate's results are impacted by characteristics of the assessor and by the group nature of decision making.

This paper will (a) describe the assessment center process; (b) present the issues regarding the components of the process; and (c) introduce three particular perspectives on aspects of the process and dynamics of the method that need examination, clarification, and research. These perspectives have the potential to illuminate and explain what goes on during assessment, but also to explain some of the recent findings that have been viewed as critical of the procedure. These three perspectives are (1) information processing; (2) categorization and social cognition; and (3) group dynamics.

ASSESSMENT CENTER PROCESS

Overview

Excellent sources for the history of assessment centers can be found in MacKinnon (1977) or Thornton and Byham (1982). Several landmark studies and projects have influenced the way in which assessment centers have been conducted. The first project in the United States was conducted by the Office of Strategic Services for the purpose of selecting intelligence agents to serve during World War II. This program used subjective and objective methods for assessment; it assessed cognitive abilities and personality as well as situational behavior. The first industrial application was by AT&T (Bray, Campbell, & Grant, 1977). This project was a longitudinal study of approximately 400 managers who were assessed soon after employment. They were assessed on 25 dimensions, including managerial functions, interpersonal relations, general abilities, and values and attitudes. Among the assessment techniques were intelligence and personality tests, interviews, leaderless group discussions, business games, and personal history questionnaires. Examination of the salary progress and management level attained by the subjects about 8 years later showed that the predictions of the assessment staff were largely successful, and this finding provided evidence that the assessment process yields valid prediction of the future success of young managers.

Since the AT&T study was reported, literally hundreds of organizations have implemented assessment centers. Many have modified their centers to accommodate their unique situations. The research that has been reported has generally focused on the impact of components of the method (see Thornton & Byham, 1982, for a description of the research projects in various organizations). Given the multitude of companies using the method, there is no single description of *the* assessment center. Perhaps the best example of an "ideal" center is found in a document, "Standards for Ethical Considerations for Assessment Center Operation," endorsed in May 1975 by the Third International Congress on the Assessment Center Method (this document can be found in the appendix of Moses & Byham, 1977). The center that will be used for illustrative purposes throughout this chapter, is the one described in this section, one that approximates the ideal of the "Standards." Specific methods, procedures, and rules for specific organizations have evolved over time and are shaped, in part, by one's experience and one's preference for particular types of assessment.

The following description of assessment centers is by necessity brief. The description is of a rather comprehensive though generic center. A key point to be made at the outset is that an assessment center is not a place, but rather a method, technique, or procedure. Specifically, an assessment center is a comprehensive, structured procedure essentially designed to reduce rater bias or error and in which multiple assessment techniques are used to evaluate candidates' performances for one of various purposes. Multiple assessors use subjective and objective data-gathering procedures to assess the candidate's performance. The assessment is a behaviorally oriented procedure in which judgmental methods are used to combine and integrate information relevant to the candidate's performance. The procedure is one that needs to be adapted to the organization in which it will be used, for the specific jobs that are of interest, and for the purpose for which the results will be applied.

Most often the procedure has been used for individuals being considered for selection, promotion, or special training and development in management. It can be used for entry-level or advanced levels of management. During the course of an assessment center, candidates partake in a number of exercises as well as respond to paper-and-pencil instruments. The exercises are performed in either a one-to-one interaction between the candidate and a role player (an assessor), or a group situation. The key to the exercises is that they are simulations or mini samples of the type and kind of work that is performed in the position for which one is being assessed. Assessment centers have been conducted in a one-day session, in which a candidate may be exposed to 3 or 4 exercises, or in two- or three-day sessions, in which perhaps 8 to 10 exercises are used.

When a particular assessment center is completed the group of assessors first, independently, prepares written reports on the behaviors observed, and then meets as a group for the purpose of disseminating that observational information, integrating the data in some fashion, and deriving a consensus recommendation for the candidate.

The purpose of the preceding brief overview is to highlight five important aspects of the process that are crucial to the consideration of the issues that this paper suggests need exploration:

1. job behaviors
2. multiple exercises
3. multiple assessors
4. assessment process
5. consensus discussion

Also, as previously indicated, the overview is a representation of an assessment center design that can be considered to be somewhat more comprehensive and elaborate than the typical center. The center described in the overview represents the ingredients of most assessment centers, but in practice the emphasis may vary from center to center. This variability is due, in part, to personal preference of the organization as well as to historical trends and influences.

Job Behaviors

Most of the exercises that are used in an assessment center are based on the types and kinds of behaviors that represent or sample the job for which candidates are being evaluated. For the present purpose, we will adopt the example of an assessment center that is to be used to select candidates for a middle manager position in sales. (Although the behaviors and exercises may differ for different purposes, such as developmental purposes, the issues are the same.)

To develop the exercises, one most often conducts a job analysis of the position of interest. Regardless of the particular job analytic technique used, the emphasis for most of them is on *specific* tasks performed or *specific* abilities needed to perform those tasks (see McCormick, 1979, for a review of job analysis procedures). In essence, the analysis can be considered to be a *micro* analysis of the job. For example, some task statements that one may find in a job analysis of a managerial position are the following:

1. Makes presentations to senior management regarding projected sales goals.
2. Sets priorities and allocates resources to staff.
3. Prepares a product package to meet needs of high-potential clients.

Such specific statements have two purposes. First, the task statements are used to prepare exercises. For example, one exercise based on the preceding statements could require the candidate to make an oral presentation to a group. Another exercise could involve a situation in which a candidate meets with a potential client, determines that client's needs, and then returns to make a formal presentation regarding a product that the candidate believes meets the needs of the client.

The second purpose of the generation of the task statements is to develop criteria that will be used for evaluation of a candidate's performance in the center. Whereas performance appraisals for the purpose of evaluating incumbent performance can involve the use of specific checklists, assessment centers ordinarily require the evaluation of candidate performance on *dimensions*. These dimensions are *macro* assimilations of the specific task statements. The word *dimensions* is italicized because, as will be shortly developed, it is at the root of most of the controversy about, as well as the focus of, many of the process concerns discussed in this paper.

What follows is a very short list of dimensions and typical definitions, based on the foregoing task statements, that may be used for evaluating performance in the exercises:

1. Oral Communication: The ability to express oneself, to effectively convey one's ideas, thoughts, and concepts
2. Organizing and Planning: The ability to set priorities for oneself or others; to schedule and allocate resources.
3. Decision-making: The ability to analyze information and develop courses of action that are based on logical and rational assumptions that reflect factual information.

The important point to keep in mind is that the tasks themselves are at the root of the development of the exercises. Whether a center sinks or swims is based on the adequacy of task sampling. There is an obvious *inferential* leap on the part of the developer of the assessment center exercises as he/she goes from the delineation of specific tasks to abilities and skills on which candidates will be evaluated. One may make the leap in several ways. One way is for the developer to obtain the opinion of experts in the subject matter as to the abilities needed to perform the tasks. A second way is to conduct factor analyses (intuitive or statistical) of task or ability data to derive dimensions. Yet a third way to develop dimensions is based on group discussion as to which characteristics managers need to be successful. The point that will be emphasized is that the use of dimensions is a means by which specific micro information is integrated into macro categorizations for the purpose of condensing data and facilitating information processing as well as communication among assessors. Dimensions are a convenient way of summarizing information.

Multiple Exercises

As indicated earlier, the exercises represent samples or simulations of the position for which one is being evaluated. Typical kinds of exercises used are as follows:

1. In-basket. This is a simulation of administrative tasks of a manager's job. It includes letters, reports, memos, documents, phone messages, and "junk mail" that can accumulate over time and appear on a manager's desk. The items vary in urgency, complexity, and impact on the organization. Furthermore, to enhance complexity, several items are often interrelated. The candidate is told that he/she has 2 hours to work on the in-basket, alone, and without being able to ask questions of anyone else. The only information that can be gathered to deal with the items would be contained in documents that explain history, policy and practices of the organization (a fictitious one).

Candidates are required to respond as if they were actually in the position. Responses are in the form of written letters and memos that represent real products of the candidate's decision; they represent what the candidate actually did as opposed to what he/she might do.

After the in-basket exercise, the candidate is interviewed by an assessor for the purpose of reviewing the actions, determining the reasons for the actions and alternatives considered, and for inferring the orientation/style of the candidate regarding completion of the in-basket.

2. Role plays. These often are simulations of the types of one-on-one encounters in which a manager might be engaged. For example, the exercise could involve a confrontation with a problem subordinate, an encounter with a client, or a negotiation setting with a peer or a supervisor. An assessor would role play a fairly standardized scenario with the candidate that would permit the candidate to emit behaviors needed in such environments; the candidate would play the role of the manager and the assessor would play the role of the subordinate, client, or peer.

Here, again, the candidate needs to respond directly to the situation and be able to do so as the situation/context evolves. The candidate should be able to bring the situation to closure.

3. Group exercises. These are group situations, with or without a designated leader, in which several candidates work together, either cooperatively or competitively. For example, the exercise could be one in which six candidates, each playing the role of a different manager within the organization, are required to come up with a joint recommendation to the president of the organization regarding an issue of importance to the company (e.g., future direction of the company into a new market). The decision reached by the group may differentially impact each of the managers.

Regardless of which of the preceding exercises is used, the essential aspect is the opportunity they provide for the candidate to directly respond to a situation with behavior; behavioral intentions or statements of what one "might" do in an abstract situation are practically nonexistent.

Multiple Assessors

Typically, there is a 2:1 ratio of candidates to assessors. The role of the assessor is threefold. First, as noted earlier, he/she plays the role of a particular person—a boss, peer, or client—depending on the exercise. For example, in a "problem with a subordinate" role play, the assessor plays the role of the subordinate. Thus, the assessor is the stimulus to which the candidate responds. In essence, the assessor can be viewed as a standardized test; to attain a degree of standardization across candidates, the assessors need to be thoroughly trained (see Moses, 1980, for a discussion of assessor training). During training, assessors are exposed to the exercises, practice both their roles and the candidates' roles, and have an opportunity to discuss *expected* behaviors on the part of the candidate. This latter opportunity is crucial to one of the positions to be developed in this paper. That is, although the assessors usually have direct experience in management, it may be that, during training for assessment, many of their notions about the types and kinds of management behaviors that one desires become crystallized and explicit. In addition, discussion among assessors has the potential to lead to a group norm for managerial behaviors and to the development of uniformity among assessors. But perhaps of greater import is the fact that *most* of the discussion centers on the candidate's performance and behavior in the exercises. Thus, here again, the emphasis is on the exercises, the simulation of the job.

The second purpose of the assessor's role is to be a recorder of behavior. That is, the assessor is required to prepare a report that *describes* the behavior of the candidate during the exercise. Though the purpose of the center is assessment, the emphasis during the center is on behavior description. The report typically takes one of two formats. Behavior can be described either in a narrative manner in which the assessor reports the actions and behaviors of the candidate as they occurred in sequence and in response to particular cues, or a form is filled out in which behaviors are provided for specific dimensions. Whereas the latter format is directly driven by dimensions, the former format *implicitly* requires that behaviors be cited and reported that reflect the dimensions that are to be assessed subsequently.

Given the usual candidate-to-assessor ratio, and depending on the number of exercises, each candidate will be seen, interact with, and subsequently be described by each of the assessors, with some assessors perhaps being involved in more than one exercise with the same candidate. Thus, you have the situation where reports of the candidate's behavior will be generated by different assessors on different exercises, but on the same dimensions. The latter is an important characteristic of the process; different assessors observe the same candidate in different exercises, but each of their evaluations will be relevant to the same dimensions. For example, one observer will report on decision-making results based on the in-basket while another assessor will report on decision making in a role play involving a problem subordinate. Should the evaluation results be comparable? The answer depends, in part, on the expectations each assessor has for the type and kind of performance to be emitted by the candidate in the particular *exercise*. Yet, as will be indicated in a later section, the evaluations are based on inferences to dimensions and not on specific exercise performance.

The third role of the assessor is to make predictions. This usually occurs in the final stage of the process, but in fact, there has been no study to determine whether prediction occurs in the exercise review, dimension discussion, or integration stage.

Assessment Process

Assuming a 2-day center, reports will be prepared by the assessor in the evenings of those two days (or at any other free time) and carried over to a third day if necessary. Then, on the fourth day, discussion takes place. The time at which reports are generated and when discussion begins are mentioned because they may be relevant to long-term memory and recall issues that will be discussed later in the paper.

Typically, evaluations are conducted in groups of four assessors. In this case, the group is composed of three assessors (managers who were role players and who were actually involved in the assessment process and exercises) and a fourth person, designated as director or coordinator (one who has not been involved in the particular assessment setting but is experienced in assessments).

That which takes place during the evaluation discussion can be described in four stages: (1) behavior description; (2) dimension evaluation; (3) dimension consensus discussion; and (4) overall assessment rating.

1. *Behavior description.* One candidate is discussed at a time. Each assessor presents a report, in behavioral terms, on the exercise in which he/she was involved. The report describes, in objective terms, the specific actions taken or things said by the candidate. The report generally does not contain any interpretation or evaluation of the performance. The other assessors listen and take notes. Questions of clarification by other assessors

can be asked regarding that which was reported, but generally there is no discussion of the relevance or significance of the cited behavior. After all reports on the candidate are presented, evaluation of dimensions begins.

2. *Dimension evaluation.* Each assessor independently evaluates the candidate on each of the dimensions that were identified in the job analysis as relevant to the position. The evaluations by a particular assessor for a particular dimension should be based on *all* of the behaviors cited that pertain to the particular dimension, and not based solely on the behaviors reported or observed by the assessor.

The example presented earlier contained 3 dimensions. The number of dimensions actually evaluated varies from about 10 to 25. The following is a short list of dimensions (see Thornton & Byham, 1982, for a comprehensive list of dimensions and their definitions):

1.	Delegation	6.	Control
2.	Analysis	7.	Judgment
3.	Risk Taking	8.	Tolerance for Stress
4.	Behavior Flexibility	9.	Adaptability
5.	Interpersonal Skills	10.	Autonomy

The above dimensions are presented for two purposes, both of which are crucial to later arguments. First, they show the diversity of skills needed for most managerial jobs. It should also be realized that the dimensions are not mutually exclusive and that they are overlapping with regard to the type of behavior that reflects them. Recall from our earlier argument that the dimension labels are macro assimilations of many diverse tasks. Thus, the same behaviors can be used to reflect performance on several dimensions. For example, a candidate's well-developed argument as to why a subordinate should consider enrolling in a drug detoxification unit can be used to represent oral communications, decision-making, and interpersonal skills.

Second, not only does the assessor need to consider a number of behaviors per dimension, he/she also needs to consider a number of dimensions. The question to be pursued later in this paper deals with the issue of information-processing capacity.

The actual evaluation of a candidate for each dimension is typically made on a 5-point scale where 1 indicates "low" and 5 indicates "high." After all four group members have independently made their evaluations, the coordinator reviews the dimension evaluations to begin the process of consensus discussion.

3. *Dimension consensus discussion.* Not all dimension evaluations are discussed by the assessor group. A rule of thumb used by many organi-

zations is that a discussion takes place for a dimension if there is a discrepancy of more than one point among the four evaluations of the four assessors. If, for example, two assessors indicate a value of 3, the third assessor indicates a value of 4, and the fourth assessor indicates a 5, then this set of ratings is open for discussion. This set of ratings will be referred to as the "preliminary set" in order to distinguish it from a subsequent set that will be discussed shortly.

The basic goal of the discussion is to understand why trained observers see things differently, to discuss these differences, and to reach consensus. Practically, however, consensus is achieved when the 5 moves to a 4 or the two 3s move to a 4, or in some way all four evaluations come to within a point of each other. One means for beginning the discussion of such a set of ratings is to have the assessor who gave the 5 rating explain his/her basis for that rating. During this discussion, each of the assessors can participate and may introduce *new* behavioral information. If, on the other hand, three assessors indicate a 2 and one indicates a 3, the recorded value is the modal value, 2. If two assessors indicate a 1 and two indicate a 2, because there is no discrepancy greater than 1, the value provided by the coordinator usually becomes the value assigned to the dimension.

The discussion can have several impacts, each of which is important to our subsequent process discussion. First, new information or clarification of information leads to explicit change in some assessors' ratings. For our purposes, assume that the assessor who initially presented a 5 now moves to a 4. This would result in moving on to consider a different dimension, because now there would be two 3s and two 4s. This set of data will be referred to as the "secondary set," the set that is a result of discussion.

Second, new information may result in reconsideration by an assessor(s) of his/her rating on a dimension already considered and discussed. Suppose the dimension discussion has moved on the the eighth dimension on the list. The introduction of information for this eighth dimension may cause an assessor to reconsider how he/she evaluated the candidate on the fifth dimension. The fifth dimension which has already been discussed, is not reopened for discussion, but the assessor may now have his/her own "secondary set" of ratings for that dimension that may influence his/her subsequent overall rating. This implicit secondary set is an unknown in any statistical analysis of assessment center data.

Third, new information/clarification may cause one of the 3s to move to a 4, but if the 5 has already indicated he/she is willing to move to a 4, then the 3 does not need to reveal a change. The point of this, again, is that the dynamics of the situation need to be considered if one is to better understand a process and subsequently modify it. The modification should not be made solely on statistical analyses, but should involve process analyses. Reliance on a particular set of data, whether they be "prelim-inary" or "secondary" sets, can be misleading.

4. *Overall assessment rating (OAR).* Once all of the dimensions have been discussed and agreed upon with respect to how much of the behavior was shown in the exercise, each assessor provides an evaluative OAR in terms of the candidate's probability of success if placed into the man-agement position. Often, a 4-point scale is used where 1 represents "low potential" and 4 represents "excellent potential." Each assessor forms his/her OAR based on his/her own method or rules for combining and integrating information. It should take into account all of the behaviors on all of the tasks—behaviors that are described in the reports and those generated by the discussion. No rules or formula are provided for forming the final judgment. After each assessor's OAR is revealed, a consensus discussion on the OAR would take place if there were a discrepancy of greater than 1, just as there was for the individual dimension ratings.

Summary

This section provided a brief overview of one kind of assessment center process. It is important to recognize that this assessment center process involves *multiple* exercises, behaviors, assessors, and dimensions Whereas the development of the assessment center is based on micro tasks, by necessity, judgment of performance in the assessment center is more macro and varied. That is, several kinds of judgments take place (Moses, 1983): judgments are made of normed (expected), typical, and predicted behaviors.

Reviews of criterion-related validity studies have shown that assessment center results can predict management performance and progress (Thorn-ton & Byham, 1982). Likewise, there are data to indicate that assessment centers have utility in terms of monetary payoffs for the organization (Cascio & Ramos, 1984). The question now seems to be, If it works, do you fix it? The answer will be, Don't fix it until you understand it.

RECENT ASSESSMENT CENTER ISSUES

As indicated, most of the research on assessment centers has focused primarily on their validities. Within the last few years, however, Sackett and his associates have begun to investigate several aspects of the as-sessment center process (Sackett, 1982; Sackett & Dreher, 1982, 1984; Sackett & Harris, 1983; Sackett & Wilson, 1982). The issues raised deal with (a) the content or construct validity of assessment centers; (b) the results that show higher correlations between dimensions within exercises than do the correlations between the same dimensions across exercises; and (c) the value of mechanical combination of individual assessor ratings. The results and interpretations made by Sackett and his associates may lead one to suggest that the same assessment center results could be achieved without going through the consensus process (Sackett & Wilson, 1982) and that there is little support for the view that dimensional scores can be interpreted as representative of complex constructs (Sackett & Dreher, 1982). The essence of the findings and arguments is to reconsider both the emphasis on dimensions and their contribution to the assessment center process, and the value of the consensus discussion.

One of the practical implications of the above findings is that exercises should be the focus of development and validation of assessment centers, and that dimensions be used as guides in documenting and categorizing behaviors (Sackett and Harris, 1983; Zedeck & Cascio, 1984). An implication that should *not* be made is that dimension assessment and consensus discussion be eliminated from the process—at least at this point in time. As suggested earlier, there has not been any empirical or systematic assessment of the dynamic process that takes place during discussion and its impact on assessment center outcomes. Sackett and Wilson (1982) reported that consensus discussion occurred in approximately 22% of the specific cases they looked at. This is sufficient to suggest that we *study* the consensus process to determine the dynamics of the process and how it is impacted by particular factors, as well its impact on the OAR.

An analysis of the assessment center literature reveals that most of the research, and implications drawn from it, can be characterized as "static" and as raw empiricism. Little, if any, of the research has modeled the assessment center process; i.e., the assessment center is a dynamic process that results in rich information on candidates, yet little research has been undertaken to study how that information is gathered, processed, and used in a dynamic context.

Even though the bottom line for assessment centers has been positive (i.e., satisfactory levels of validity and utility), it would be premature at this point to modify or depart from the current practice and assume that the results would be maintained. There simply is insufficient research on the assessment center process to provide an understanding of the dynamics involved.

The purpose of the remainder of this paper is to explore three particular perspectives that are relevant to an assessment center process and may impinge on the results, but more importantly, may serve as a framework for future study and clarification of the process. The areas for review are (1) information processing, (2) categorization and social cognition, and (3) group dynamics. These three perspectives relate to the aspects of assessment centers that involve observation, judgment and evaluation, and consensus discussion. There may be other relevant and salient foci, but these three capture the richness of the process as well as serve as a framework for developing a research agenda.

INFORMATION PROCESSING

The end product of an assessment center is a *decision*—a decision to promote, select, or develop a candidate. Analysis of how this decision is derived can be undertaken from two perspectives: (1) an *individual* assessor's recommendation, and (2) the assessor *group's* final recommendation. In order to improve decision making, we need to understand how decisions are made. In this section, we will discuss individual decision making; a subsequent section will explore the group dynamics that relate to group decision making.

This paper will consider two issues, not mutually exclusive, that underly decision making: (1) the *sequence* in which information is gathered and used; and (2) *how* and *what* information is combined, integrated, and used. Much of what follows is drawn from the cognitive psychology and information processing literatures, though little, if any, of the theories and results have been applied to the assessment center method. It is known that information processing in decision making is highly contingent on the demands of the task (Einhorn & Hogart, 1981; Payne, 1982). The difficulty in generalizing from typical cognitive research is due to the dynamic nature of the assessment center process. This process, as detailed at the outset of the paper, involves judgment and evaluation by an assessor who is playing an active role in a process that provides information via observation and reporting, all of which takes place in a concentrated, fast-paced environment where decisions actually impact people's lives.

Sequence

To understand decision making in the assessment center process, it is necessary to capture how information goes from an observation to a recommendation; however, there are several steps between these endpoints that need clarification. Whereas others such as Cooper (1981) and Lord (1985) have outlined the sequence of information-processing events as they are related to other issues in organizational behavior, it is the contention of this paper that the assessment center process is somewhat different and thus requires an extension of some of the steps.

Cooper (1981) presented 11 stages in a performance appraisal process: (1) observation of actions, (2) encoding, aggregation, and storage in short-term memory, (3) short-term memory decay, (4) transfer to long-term storage and aggregation, (5) long-term memory decay, (6) presentation of categories to be rated, (7) observation/retrieval from long-term storage, (8) relating observations to rating categories, (9) comparison of observation to rater's standards, (10) incorporation of extraneous considerations, and (11) rating. Lord (1985), on the other hand, has identified 5 basic stages in studying information processing for social perceptions and leadership perceptions and behavior: (1) selective attention/comprehension of information in environment, (2) encoding and simplifying of information, (3) storage and retention, (4) retrieval, and (5) judgment.

The components from each of the preceding sets of stages are generally appropriate for understanding the assessment center process. However, there is additional complexity in the assessment center, complexity that derives in part from the different roles that an assessor assumes as well as different requirements of input at different points in time. Figure 2 illustrates this complexity. With regard to the roles assumed by the assessor, in some exercises, the assessor is only an observer and/or recorder of behavior. This is true for any of the group exercises and, in part, for the in-basket interview. The latter exercise, however, permits the assessor to ask questions and thus provides an opportunity for clarification and elaboration of information. A different role for the assessor is that of active participant in the exercise such that during the course of a role play the assessor must be a stimulus, or a respondent, as well as an observer. Both of these roles within the same exercise require strict attention by the assessor with regard to the information that he/she is processing. To distinguish between these two roles in an exercise, *active processing* will be used to describe the assessor who observes and role plays, whereas *passive processing* describes an assessor who only observes.

With regard to input required from the assessor during discussion, the assessment process calls for the assessor to provide a report of his/her observations and exchanges with the candidate for those exercises in which he/she was directly involved—this is referred to as *active participation.* However, for those exercises in which the assessor does not partake in the exercise with the participant, the source of information is from another assessor. Thus, our assessor of interest is a *passive processor* and *passive participant.* To now go through the stages of processing, the assessor relies on recall of the behaviors reported.

With the preceding dynamics in mind, let us review Figure 2 to try and understand the sequence of steps that lead from an observation to a judgment, and at the same time, identify issues that need to be explored in future research. Start with the assessor who is an observer and passive processor on a particular exercise. The following steps (indicated by an X in Figure 2) take place:

1. *Observation* of behavior and actions taken by the participant. The assessor selectively attends to behaviors, actions, and responses that he/she was trained to attend to. The information that is attained through

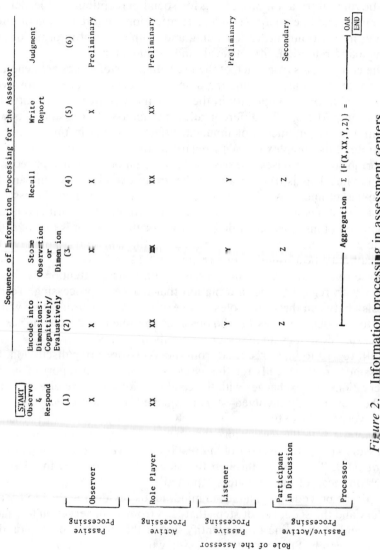

Figure 2. Information processing in assessment centers.

116

observation is a function of salient characteristics of the behaviors and is guided, in part, by automatic and unconscious processing.

2. *Encoding* the behaviors/actions into dimensions. The observations are assimilated and encoded into categories or dimensions. (This topic will be explored in greater depth in the next section.)

3. *Storing* the observations/dimensions for later use. An obvious question at this point is what is stored and whether the information is stored cognitively (a behavioral representation) or evaluatively (in terms of whether one behavior was appropriate/inappropriate, effective/ineffective, etc.). That is, does the assessor store the behavior/dimension in terms of characteristics of the event or in terms of its relationship to an affective attribution? Also, how much information does not get stored because of the rapid nature of events? Storage into memory is a strained and labored process, since time and effort are required to insert new material into memory (Lindsay & Norman, 1977).

4. *Recall* of the behaviors and dimensions is necessary in order for the assessor to prepare a report. (Recall is not an issue if the exercises are taped and the assessor uses the tape to prepare his/her report.) Here there is concern for selective recall. Is that which is recalled consistent with a first or general impression of the candidate? Is that which is recalled consistent with the assessor's expectations of a manager's performance? Sackett and Dreher (1982) found a general factor among the dimensions. This could occur if recall is based on a global macro assimilation and evaluation of observations.

5. *Writing* the report in behavioral terms without being evaluative.

6. The preceding five steps contribute to the formation of two preliminary *judgments:* (1) preliminary judgment of the dimension scores, and (2) preliminary judgment of a final recommendation. They are preliminary in the sense that group discussion could change one's judgments.

If, on the other hand, the assessor was involved in a role play and therefore was an active processor, then the steps are the same as above, but the dynamics differ (indicated by XX in Figure 2). Specifically, the first step of observation is influenced and impacted by the need for the assessor to be a stimulus (provide cues to the candidate) as well as be responsive to the behavior and actions of the candidate. Posner (1982) has concluded that people manage several tasks and simultaneously monitor several informational channels with almost no interference. Yet, the active role playing can interfere with the ability to observe as well as impact the *selectivity* of that which is observed. Nevertheless, during the course of the exercise, the assessor still needs to encode (Step 2) and store (Step 3) the information, and later that evening to recall (Step 4) and write a report (Step 5) and subsequently to form a judgment (Step 6). Particularly in regard to recall, the obvious question is whether recall is influenced by reaction of the assessor to the exchange. For example, in a problem subordinate exercise, if an assessor is treated in a rude or hostile manner, the recall may be more vivid than if the exchange was more amicable.

The preceding two roles are parallel in terms of the sequence that goes from observation (Step 1) to preliminary judgment (Step 6). Another condition exists, however, when the assessor is a "listener" to other reports during the "behavior description" phase of the actual assessment process (indicated by Y in Figure 2). In this situation, forming of preliminary judgments (Step 6) for an exercise is *not* based on direct observation, but is a function of how another assessor encoded behaviors (Step 2), stored the observations (Step 3), recalled the information (Step 4), and reported it (Step 5). A key point in this sequence is that the reporter of behavior may encode behavior in one way, but the listener encodes the behavior in a different way. Also complicating the process is the fact that while listening to others' reports, the assessor is "aggregating" the information. That is, assessors are comparing the information that was presented by an observer to represent a dimension with the information that he/she has accumulated and processed based on his/her own direct observations.

After hearing all of the reports, the assessor aggregates information and produces his/her preliminary dimension evaluations. Consensus discussion then takes place for those dimensions for which there was disagreement. This situation (indicated by Z in Figure 2) allows for the introduction of new information by any of the assessors. If it is by the assessor whose information processing we are studying, then the recall phase is particularly activated. During the discussion, the assessor may change his/her encoding (i.e., place a behavior into a different dimension) and/or may change how he/she evaluates the behaviors and/or dimensions. In addition, the aggregation of information may result in other changes. The result of these dynamics is a "secondary set" of evaluations that are group derived, but which may not be consistent with one's own "secondary set." That is, suppose the group begins with three 3s and one 5, and that the assessor whom we are studying initially indicated a 3. The result of the discussion is that the 5 moves to a 4 and thus the recorded value for the candidate can then be recorded as a 3 on the particular dimension. In final processing by this particular assessor whom we are studying, he/she may have been influenced by the discussion and viewed the behavior as a 4, although he/she did not indicate such a movement, because the 5s movement to a 4 ended the need for further discussion.

Finally, the assessor becomes a processor of information (last row of Figure 2) for the purpose of making an overall recommendation (OAR). Here the assessor relies on aggregated dimension and behavior information that was encoded and stored during the active and passive processing stages and also includes that which was encoded and stored immediately preceding the request for an overall recommendation. (Because the data show that only 1% of the OARs require discussion as a result of disagreement [Sackett & Wilson, 1982], the processing issues in such decisions will not be pursued.) At this point, the overall recommendation is a function of some combination of the information processed (X, XX, Y, and Z). As will be indicated subsequently, little is known about how X, XX, Y, and Z impact the final recommendation.

Information Integration: How and What

To understand an assessor's recommendation, we need to understand *what* information (behaviors and dimensions) is used and *how* that information is combined or integrated in forming the judgment. The results of such analyses may not be independent of the stage at which decisions are made by the assessor.

As implied by Figure 2, there are several points at which the assessor needs to integrate information; i.e., to combine two or more bits of information into a preliminary or secondary judgment. These points are: (1) at the time the assessor recalls specific behavioral information in order to form a preliminary evaluation for a dimension that is subsequently reported to the group; and (2) at the time the OAR is made based on integration of dimension data. Thus, these two types of judgments can be distinguished by whether specific behavioral information is integrated or whether dimension data are integrated.

An alternative view of the first integration is to assume that the integration can be decomposed into bits of information for each exercise rather than for each dimension. An unknown in the process is whether assessors are oriented to exercises or to dimensions. Though dimensions are emphasized in evaluation, the exercises are emphasized in training and report writing.

Assuming that a linear prediction model is adequate for representing information integration (Slovic & Lichtenstein, 1971), the various integration strategies cited above can be represented as follows:

1a. Integrating behavioral information within an exercise to form a dimension score:

$$b_1B_1 + \ldots\ldots + b_nB_n = D_x$$

where B_1 to B_n represent different behaviors that can be quantified; b_1 to b_n represent the statistical weights associated with the behaviors, and D_x represents the score on the xth dimension provided by an assessor.

1b. Integrating behavioral information across exercises to form a dimension score:

$$\underbrace{b_{1j} B_{1j} + \ldots.. + b_{nj} B_{nj}}_{\text{Exercise } j} + \underbrace{b_{1k} B_{1k} + \ldots.. + b_{nk} B_{nk}}_{\text{Exercise } k} = D_x$$

where the j and k subscripts represent two exercises, j and k.

2. Integrating dimension scores to form an OAR:

$$b_X D_X + \ldots\ldots + b_Y D_Y = OAR$$

where D_X and D_Y represent different dimensions. Attempts to determine the strategies for information integration in assessment centers are almost nonexistent. There is no study that looks at 1a or 1b. A limited amount of research, however, has addressed an issue related to 2, i.e., the issue of whether clinical or statistical combination is more predictive. The results, however, are equivocal (Thornton & Byham, 1982).

One study that has addressed the issue of the number of dimensions needed to predict the OAR is by Sackett and Hakel (1979). In an assessment center context in which evaluations were made on 17 dimensions, results indicated that 5 to 7 dimensions could capture variance in an individual assessor's OAR. Also, there were some individual differences that contributed to assessor's ratings. Implications that can be drawn from such results are that not all dimensions are needed and/or that the final OAR can be predicted by use of an equation, the weights of which are generated by the organization.

It is generally accepted that people use simplifying heuristics to deal with complex judgments (Pitz & Sachs, 1984). Many factors other than those to which a person is asked to respond can be shown to affect the judgment. This is true for performance appraisal (Landy & Farr, 1980), and there is no reason to suspect it is different for assessment centers. Payne (1982) has concluded that understanding judgment processes is likely to be advanced if we adopt a "time-dependent" view or process analysis of decision behavior. Process-tracing studies would be most useful for describing strategies.

Regression analysis of decision making, often referred to as policy capturing, is limited in determining what and how information is integrated. The results reveal the optimal strategy for *statistically* combining information when forming a judgment; they indicate the degree to which the decision can be predicted or modeled. Yet, they are not necessarily precise in the actual representation of the processing. The model that results from such analyses usually is one that finds the smallest set of dimensions needed to predict judgment; redundancy among dimensions is avoided. There are, however, arguments that redundancy is beneficial, particularly in the information search phase of the judgment process. Some benefits include reduced dimensionality of the information space and thus less likelihood of information overload; interchangeability of cues; increased reliability; and higher selective attention (Einhorn, Kleinmuntz, & Kleinmuntz, 1979).

Given the preceding limitations of policy capturing as a means for *understanding* what information assessors combine and how they combine it, another strategy is to combine a regression model with a process-tracing model (Einhorn et al., 1979) to study assessors. Specifically, process-tracing methods involve the construction of a detailed model of the cognitive rules used by a person to form a decision rule. The bases for extracting the rules are verbal protocols or "thinking out loud" sessions of the assessor. The rules are then formulated into a computer algorithm. Such a procedure could maintain the sequential nature of most decision rules as well as result in a configural representation. It would be especially useful for studying information search, whereas the linear regression model would complement it with a focus on information integration. In essence, the two approaches treat the underlying processes at different levels.

CATEGORIZATION AND SOCIAL COGNITION

The preceding information-processing section dissected judgments into their components. This section has two purposes: (1) to further dissect a bit of information into a specific category or dimension and, in addition, (2) to be more global and to look at the gestalt of a behavioral evaluation. As described previously, a key component of the assessment center process has been the use of dimensions. In a formal sense, dimensions have provided the basis for quantification of performance in the assessment center. This is true regardless of whether the required reports specifically request dimension information or are completed in narrative form. As also described earlier, recent statistical analyses suggest that dimension evaluations within an exercise are more highly correlated than are the evaluations on the same dimensions across exercises. One implication of the results of these analyses is to minimize the importance of dimensions, particularly as an evaluation aid. The position of this paper, however, is that it is premature to take such action. As described in the preceding section, information processing underlies the whole assessment process. Before information can be processed, however, it needs to be attended to and recognized as information that is useful for the assessment purpose. Implicit or explicit use of dimensions reduces the amount of information that must be stored and processed as well as facilitates its recall and interpretation. Dimensions may reduce the complexity of the information received by the assessor, because they facilitate the grouping of objects, people, and events according to similarities in their essential features. Labeling the dimensions also facilitates communications about the similarities and differences. Dimensions allow the assessor to go beyond the information given and to infer some of its nonperceptible attributes. Each unique event per se is not perceived, remembered, and discussed; rather, the focus is on the behavior as an instance or example of a class or concept about which something is known. In the assessment center process, behaviors are provided as examples of dimensions; it is the dimension evaluations that are then used, at least explicitly, to form evaluations.

Given this viewpoint, considerable research needs to be done on the development, activation, and use of dimensions within an assessment center context. Assessors view behavior, interact with participants, write reports, and discuss behavior and candidates. Each of these roles involves recall, inference, and prediction. This section will explore how categories and schemas help us understand these processes. In doing so, that which has been found and studied by cognitive and social cognitive psychologists will be selectively cited.

Dimension Development

It is given that the developer of an assessment center determines the relevant dimensions on which candidates will be evaluated. However, a key concern is how a particular assessor forms his/her view of the dimensions. To explore this issue, reference will be made to the literature that relates to category and concept formation.

At the outset, assume that dimensions, as used and defined in the assessment center literature, are equivalent to concepts as used in the cognitive psychology literature. Concepts have been defined by Medin and Smith (1984) as "mental representations of a simple class (i.e., a class denoted by a single word);" a category is a set of objects considered to be equivalent (Rosch, Mervis, Gray, Johnson, & Boyes-Braem, 1976). Concepts are taxonomies or pattern-recognition devices that are used to classify novel entities and to draw inferences about such entities. To have a particular category called X is to know something about the properties of entities that belong to the class of X, and such properties can be used to categorize novel events, objects, etc. (Smith & Medin, 1981). The use of single cognitive categories about, for example, people, generally reduces and simplifies what one needs to know and look for in particular people (Cantor & Mischel, 1979).

In the assessment center literature the word *dimension* is used to denote a set of tasks and behaviors that are similar in features, or the performance of which requires the same or equivalent ability. Everything that was stated for concepts or categories can be stated for dimensions. Assessors are trained in the definitions of dimensions and are provided examples of tasks or behaviors that are illustrative of the dimensions. However, when used in assessment centers, the assessor needs to place observed behavior into a dimension based on the similarity of that behavior to the examples provided in training or to the similarity of features as perceived by the assessor.

Categorization is a function that involves determining that a specific action, event, object, etc., is a member of a concept or category (Smith

& Medin, 1981). The question of interest is this: What rules guide one's categorization of objects, events, or people? A categorization process, such as delineating observed behaviors into dimensions, allows the assessor to structure and provide coherence to his/her information.

The cognitive literature generally has explored three views of concepts and categorizations: (1) classical; (2) probabilistic; and (3) exemplar (Smith & Medin, 1981). The classical view holds that all instances of a concept share common properties, and that these common properties are *necessary* and *sufficient* to define the concept. The probabilistic view, also known as the prototype view, assumes that not all instances of a concept are equal, but *vary* in the degree to which they represent the concept. The third and most extreme view is the exemplar view, that holds that there is no single representation of an entire class or concept; the representation of a concept consists of *specific* and separate descriptions of some of the instances of the concepts as opposed to any abstractions. Whereas cognitive psychology generally is interested in how people use natural concepts with one-word names (e.g., the word *square*) to classify things (e.g., pictures of objects), the focus of this paper is on how assessors classify complex or simple behaviors into dimensions.

To apply the preceding classification system to assessment center dimensions, it is necessary to view a dimension such as "oral presentation" as a concept under whose rubric can be placed behaviors, events, or people if they share features that define the dimension. For example, a candidate who is observed to give a fixed, 10-minute address to a group of potential clients can be described as one who has exhibited behavior on the "oral presentation" dimension, because the behavior is part of an "oral presentation" definition that emphasizes *formal* presentations to *others* in an *oral* mode. The italicized words are the properties that behaviors need to exhibit to be categorized under "oral presentation." A classic view of concepts would argue that any behavior that is a formal presentation orally conveyed to others is an "oral presentation"—the behavior needs to possess all of these features to be classified as such. However, some behaviors that could be labeled as "oral presentation" would not involve the formal feature—for example, a 3-minute spontaneous and extemporaneous recitation to an audience of the benefits of a product. The probabilistic view states that the latter behavior is an example of "oral presentation" because it contains *most* of the *critical* features. The exemplar view requires that there be different models or representations of what "oral presentation" is, and that particular behaviors be compared to these models or exemplars. The distinction between these views may be fine and fuzzy, but their impact as a whole is important for understanding the assessment center process and its results.

The view of this paper is that the probabilistic or prototype view is most appropriate. That is, behaviors observed in assessment center activities are categorized under particular dimensions because the behaviors contain or reflect most of the *expected* features to be found in that category. Behaviors are categorized by virtue of the degree to which they are "prototypical" of the dimension in question. The categorization decision will, therefore, be probabilistic in nature, with different behaviors varying in degree of representativeness (prototypicality) and with many ambiguous behaviors resulting in overlapping and fuzzy boundaries between dimensions. This view may, in part, explain the results for generally high correlations across dimensions within an exercise. Since the behaviors are exercise specific, these behaviors can contain features of several dimensions. For example, the previously noted oral presentation can reflect the dimensions of "decision making," "organizing and planning," "oral communications," "persuasiveness," and the like. Thus, when evaluating behavior that can be a prototype of several dimensions, it is not surprising that there is correlation among dimensions. Nevertheless, there is value in adopting some dimension under which to store and record the behavior, since it will facilitate recall and communication. The reason for adopting the prototype view is that research in cognitive psychology has shown that it is easier to learn to classify, to name, and to image prototypical members than nonprototypical exemplars (Rosch, 1978). An issue that needs to be explored in the assessment center process, however, is the finding that traits (dimensions) are recalled more readily than behaviors (Jeffrey & Mischel, 1979).

In sum, categorization of a behavior into a particular dimension is based on prototypes. That is, knowledge about a dimension is provided by its definition and the training the assessor receives; the latter provides typical or ideal instances of that behavior on the dimension. When observing actual behavior in an assessment center, the observer decides whether the observed behavior is a member of that dimension by assessing its similarity to the prototype. The more similar it is, the more certain the assessor is that the behavior represents the dimensions. The similarity is based on features and resemblances. There is no *single set* of features that must be present in a behavior that would then define the dimension; rather, any of several features contribute to the judgment that a behavior resembles the dimension prototype. The more features a behavior shares with other dimension behaviors, the more consistently, consensually, and quickly it is identified and posited as a reflection of the dimension (Rosch, 1978). However, because dimensions, like categories, are not fixed, an expectation should not be made for rigid, well-defined, formal dimensions. A particular behavior observed/reported by an assessor and categorized into one dimension may be viewed as a prototype of another dimension by another assessor. Consequently, within an exercise, we should expect dimension intercorrelation.

It is the contention of this author that assessors observe behavior and attempt to store it in "dimension bins" which are categories or dimension labels. The encoding process serves to organize information by comparing its features with that of the dimension. Observations of behavior are automatically encoded into general dimensions. What happens to this information when it is stored is not totally clear, but retrieval depends on the dimensions into which it was encoded. If we apply the results from sentence memory research, we can conclude that information is recalled better when it has an integrated structure than when it does not; i.e., when there is consistency and a coherent whole. Narratives with a consistent point of view are remembered better and rated as more comprehensible than those with a change in point of view. Recall, also, is better if new information is consistent with prior information. Finally, "chunks" are better recalled (Horton & Mills, 1984). All of this argues for the view that information that is stored in dimension bins will be recalled more efficiently and perhaps with less distortion. Furthermore, it suggests that, in fast-paced discussions, memory will be searched for consistent information, that is, selective searching will take place. If consistency is the goal, there should be high dimension intercorrelations within an exercise.

Dimension Activation

An observed behavior often may be interpreted in different ways (Wyer & Srull, 1981). The interpretation that happens to be made of the behavior may determine the category in which the behavior is placed. Prediction of the nature of the impression or evaluation one is likely to form on the basis of observed behavior requires an understanding of how individuals code information, for categories, and for related categories.

Wyer and Srull (1981) have empirical support for several assumptions that relate to social information processing, each of which can also be applied to assessment center processes. Their first assumption is that social information often is interpreted and encoded into memory as a complex configuration of concepts, the features of which overlap but are not necessarily identical to those actually contained in the stimulus information. To elaborate upon this, Wyer and Srull draw upon the concept of schema.

Whereas categories and concepts help us understand the observation and storage of information, in order to understand the recall process, we will refer to the literature in social cognition that deals with schema. As we have indicated, the processing of information involves observing behaviors, selecting instances to attend to, taking in information about those instances, and storing it so that it can be retrieved when it is time to prepare the report, to discuss the candidate, and to evaluate the candidate. In social cognition, the term *schema* is defined as a cognitive structure that consists in part of the representation of some defined stimulus domain (Taylor & Crocker, 1981). The schema contains general knowledge about that domain, including a specification of the relationships among its attributes as well as specific instances of the stimulus domain.

The distinction that this paper draws between schema and category is one of level. That is, a category or dimension is a particular representative of similar and specific behaviors. We can describe a particular behavior as possessing features that imply that it is representative of a category. On the other hand, schemata are broader representations of a series of events; e.g., the total behavior in an exercise. A schema can be thought of as a pyramidal, hierarchical structure (Taylor & Crocker, 1981) that is organized with more abstract or general information at the top, but with *categories* of specific information nested within the general categories.

Fiske and Taylor (1984) indicate that there are four types of schemata in social cognition:

1. *Person schemata.* Includes prototypic conceptions, impressions, and representations of specific people; composed of traits and goals; helps one to categorize others and to remember schema-relevant behavior.
2. *Self-schemata.* General information about one's own psychological make up.
3. *Role schemata.* Schemata for particular occupations, social roles, or social groups; involves social norms and expectations.
4. *Event schemata.* Knowledge of the typical sequence of events on standard social occasions that helps one to understand ambiguous information.

The schema concept maintains that information is stored in an abstract form, as a general case. There are schemata for people, roles, and events. The schema organizes incoming information theoretically.

This paper argues that in the assessment center literature, there is a fifth type of schema, that in part subsumes several of the previously cited schema. That is, given that assessors are usually trained and experienced managers, they have a "management behavior schema" that enables them to attend to, store, and retrieve information relevant to a candidate's behaviors. This schema develops by abstracting from similar events and experiences the manager has accumulated. The more variety one has experienced, the more complex will one manager's schema be, and, in addition, the more schemata he/she will possess. Thus, the schemata of some managers will differ from the schemata of others; the former's schemata may be more complex and may also be better organized than the latter's. During discussion of a candidate, the focus may be on dimensions, but it is the "management behavior schema" for a particular exercise that allows one to organize the interrelated sequences of events in that exercise.

With regard to observation of assessment center behavior, observed events are compared to cognitive schemata or scripts, i.e., configural representations of objects and events that provide the basis for interpreting information. As an assessor observes behavior, he/she may be forming a new cognitive structure that contains one's *beliefs* about the behavior, which influences the interpretation of new information, and which serves as the basis for anticipating future behavior. An observed behavior is interpreted with reference to previously formed representations of persons or events that have been stored in memory. Thus, at the outset, an assessor draws upon his/her experience as a manager in the process of comparing and consequently storing observed events. However, the representation of the observation as it is reported during discussion contains both aspects of the behavior as it actually occurred and features of the assessor's script or schema, as a basis for intepreting and organizing it.

When behavior in an exercise is encountered by the assessor, it is matched against one's specific "management behavior schema" for that simulation—the exercise. The ordering and relations among the specific behaviors of the schema are imposed on the elements of the encounter. Having a schema allows one to relate various behaviors to each other. The different "management behavior schemata" could represent such activities as a manager performing administrative tasks (in-basket), dealing with subordinate problems (role play), and working on an organization task force (group discussion). Each of these activities forms a different schema within the "overall management behavior schema." Each schema may involve the same dimensions (e.g., organizing and planning), but within each dimension there may be different expectations regarding the behaviors for the different situations. Thus, it is not surprising to find lower correlations between exercises (schemata) than are found within exercises.

Specific schemas are connected to other schemas through a web of associations. One specific behavior in an exercise may be represented in each of several categories. But as one puts together a schema for a person across exercises, the web of associations influences the interpretation and recall of specific behaviors.

Figure 3 shows the hierarchical relations between behaviors, categories, and schemata as adapted to assessment centers. At the basic level, there is an exercise in which the candidate emits behaviors b_i. These behaviors are encoded and stored in dimension bins (D_i). Some of the same behaviors can be stored in different dimensions. The specific exercise is a representation of a particular "management behavior schema." The multiple

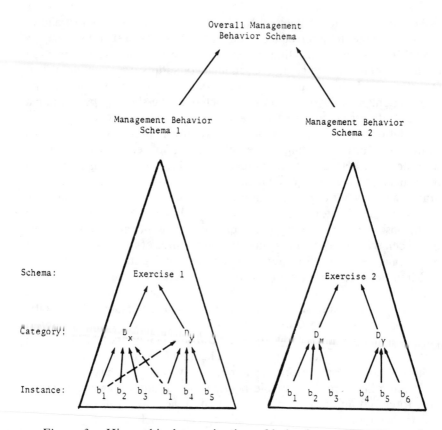

Figure 3. Hierarchical organization of behaviors, categories, and schema.

exercises in the center represent the "overall management behavior sche-ma." Within each of the schemata, given that behaviors can be in more than one dimension, there is greater overlap of dimension evaluations. However, the expectations for each schema can vary and thus there is less likelihood of correlation between exercises.

The structuring function of schemata influences subsequent recall and provides the basis for inferences and predictions. These latter aspects—recall, inferences, and predictions—are the end products of the assessment center process. By using schemata, assessors facilitate their ability to participate in and contribute to the consensus discussions; this also facilitates their ability to evaluate the candidates. There is evidence that information that represents a schema or is matched to it does increase recall (Cantor & Mischel, 1979); material that has an integrated structure is recalled better than material that is not integrated (Horton & Mills, 1984).

Wyer and Srull (1981), also, assume that when people are called upon to judge a person, or to report on a person, they do not perform an exhaustive search of memory for all required information that is relevant to the judgment or description. Rather, they sample only a subset of this information that is most easily accessible and, given that this subset is sufficiently consistent in its implications, may base their judgment on the implications alone. Thus, in an assessment center environment, we have an assessor who needs to encode information when he/she is observing it, recall it when preparing a report or participating in a discussion, encode new information when listening to others describe the candidate, and recall all the information when evaluating the candidate on dimensions and the final OAR. If not all of memory is searched, which of the information is used as the basis for one's evaluation—the information one has observed and presented, or the information provided by another?

Another value of schemata is that there is evidence that people who are told to form an "impression" of an individual have better recall of information than do people who are simply told to memorize information. Though assessors are told to observe and record behavior, by doing so and then relating it to schemata, they increase their recall of macro events. Assessors essentially impose a meaningful organization for the observed behaviors. By focusing on dimensions, assessors are clustering information according to categories or person schemata, a situation that occurs to a greater extent in impression formation than in memory (Hamilton, 1981).

In discussions, assessors need to rely on the reports presented by the other assessors. One of the issues in assessment centers is whether reports should be written in the narrative form or according to dimensions. Examination of recent studies concerned with memory for sentences and stories suggests that the narrative form is better. Reviews have concluded that when the following three conditions exists, recall is better: (1) information is integrated in a coherent whole; (2) the information in one part is causally related to another part, and (3) narratives have a consistent point of view. In sum, memory is coded by organization of relational processing of meaning (Horton & Mills, 1984), an effect achieved by reliance on schemata.

Schemata also influence inferences, which, in turn, can be regarded as the filling in of gaps in the representation of a problem (Pitz & Sachs, 1984). During report writing or discussion, once a schema is initiated and activated, the assessor may *assume* other things to be relevant to the candidate who is being evaluated. That is, schemata enable the observer to fill in data missing from the report. A schema can direct a search for missing information from one's own report or direct the assessor to question another assessor's report/description. Or, the schema may fill in missing values with best guesses regarding what the value should be (Taylor & Crocker, 1981). Such assessor behavior is another contribution to increased correlation among dimensions within an exercise, a phenomenon often referred to as the *halo effect*.

Activation of a schema also may be the basis for inference about a person's behavior in relation to content contained in another schema (another exercise). If the information is consistent for the two exercises, then one can expect that there would be correlation between the two exercises. Whereas there is some evidence that little correlation occurs between dimensions across exercises (Sackett & Dreher, 1982), there is less evidence on the correlation between exercise evaluation results. However, if the information is inconsistent within or between exercises, how does the assessor deal with inconsistency when he/she provides a dimension value, participates in discussion, or concludes with an OAR? Attribution theory (Kelly, 1972) can be adapted to assess such a predicament. When inconsistency exists, people seek out information to validate a tentative impression of what is occurring or to develop an explanation of what is occurring. Thus, one embarks on a causal analysis.

To date, it is not known how assessors resolve inconsistency in what they observe or hear. The inconsistency can be between dimensions, within exercises, or across dimensions and exercises, and it can be within one's own view or between two assessors. The bottom line, however, is that the end result of assessment usually reveals remarkably consistent OARs.

Several important attribution theory principles are relevant to the present discussion. First, there is the principle of covariation, which states that a perceived cause of an event is a function of the observed co-occurrence of two events. Behaviors in an assessment center can vary because of the specific *task* (information that the participant works on), the *context* (alone, in a role play, or in a group), or the other *people* involved (nature of the role player and other group members). The assessor needs to decide if the inconsistent behavior is due to this participant, or to the task, situation, or other people. To answer the question, the assessor needs to consider three factors: (1) Could the inconsistent behavior for that person have occurred with others or in the absence of the participant? (2) Does similar behavior occur each time a particular person is involved? (3) Does similar behavior occur in relation to others? To answer all of these questions, the assessor draws on his/her schemata and their corresponding expectations, and infers whether the cause of the inconsistent behavior is due to the person or to the situation. However, as will be indicated shortly, the role of the assessor himself/herself influences the attribution.

Another principle in Kelly's model is that of *augmentation*. Does the behavioral outcome result from facilitative or inhibitory factors? Did the candidate perform well in the light of obstacles (e.g., insufficient information or negative reaction from others in the group)? Yet another principle is that of *discounting,* which states that a single behavior will be discounted if there are other potential causes.

In addition to the preceding factors, Ross (1977) has identified a number of others that influence inferences. He has noted a tendency to underestimate the importance of situational factors and overestimate dispositional or person factors as causes of behavior. Furthermore, actors and observers differ in their attributions such that actors emphasize situational factors and observers emphasize personal dispositions. Finally, there is a *hedonic relevance* factor, whereby if the behavior has positive or negative consequences for the observer, the attribution is more in terms of personal dispositions.

The relevance of the preceding discussion is that we know almost nothing about the processes of inference as they occur in assessment centers. This is unfortunate because some of the dilemma in the results (i.e., correlations higher between dimensions within an exercise than across exercises) may be due to the fact that the assessor has two roles during the exercises: (1) observer, and (2) actor. As an actor, the assessor is influenced by how he/she was treated by the candidate and by the particular actions taken by the candidate; as an observer, the assessor may be influenced by how other candidates treat the particular candidate. Also, during discussion, the assessor is a reporter of his/her experience as well as a recipient of others' information. Does the dual role impact one's evaluations?

The final step in the assessment center process is to derive the OAR. Here, too, schemata may be relevant. Given that a schema represents a *normative* structure (Taylor & Crocker, 1981), it functions as a *standard* for explicit evaluations of a stimulus configuration. In assessment centers, managers have an "overall management behavior" schema of what a future manager ought to be like; i.e., they have a representation of a stimulus configuration. Overall evaluations will be based on each of the categories, whether the categories are or are not a central part of the schema and whether the categories are negatively or positively evaluated. Each manager has his/her own schema and needs to find participants who match or fit that schema.

Summary.

This section emphasized the role of categories (dimensions) and schemata in the assessment center steps of observation and evaluation. However, a point that still needs to be addressed pertains to individual differences. As previously mentioned, the assessors usually are managers who are one or two levels above the position for which one is assessing candidates. Though the assessors may each be at the same organizational level, there is still some variability in their experiences as managers. This variability in experience could be associated with variability in the degree to which their schemata are developed. This is important, because Taylor and Winkler (1980) have found that experience promotes conservative processing strategies. Experienced assessors perhaps have a greater wealth of knowledge about the position, and also a greater complexity, but their well-developed schema implies that it is compact and well organized. Consequently, they can attend to more behavior, use schema-relevant information more, and perhaps deal with inconsistency better than the less experienced assessor. However, another side of the issue relates to findings by Tesser (1978) showing that those with well-developed schemata make more extreme evaluations for schema-relevant material than do people whose schemata are less well developed.

Yet another relevant assumption is found in Wyer and Srull's (1981) social inference model which posits that once information has been organized and encoded, this encoding rather than the information itself, serves as the primary basis for subsequent judgments of the candidate. Thus, given that individual differences exist in the way the same information can be encoded, there may be variablity in evaluation at the dimension discussion and at the OAR stage.

GROUP DYNAMICS

Group dynamics is an area that seems to be totally ignored within the assessment center literature. Although there is some process literature, it focuses on the individual as the unit of analysis. This omission in research is somewhat surprising given that the emphasis in assessment centers is on consensus discussions. The purpose of this section is to highlight some of the issues that pertain to group dynamics research and which are relevant to the assessment center process. In particular, we will explore three interdependent aspects: (1) characteristics of groups; (2) characteristics of group members and their interaction with the group entity; and (3) dynamics of group processing.

The Assessment Group

The assessor group in both consensus and OAR discussion typically is composed of three assessors and a coordinator. The decisions made by individuals must reach consensus. There is little research on why these two constraints—size and consensus—are part of the process, or how the process is improved because of these characteristics.

With regard to size, it could be argued that an odd number should be used in order to break ties in situations where no discussion is needed (e.g., two 3s and two 4s). But more importantly, the impact of group size on the process and on the final OAR must be assessed.

The larger the group, the broader the range of knowledges, skills, and abilities among its members, and, also, the broader the range of schemata. Is this an advantage or disadvantage? If the group grows too large, the opportunity for conflict increases, there may be less time for each assessor to comment on the candidate, and the group may have greater difficulty in achieving consensus. With regard to the latter, however, there may be more pressure to reach consensus in larger groups. Though the literature is not clear about the exact relationship between group size and conformity, the trend is that conformity increases with increasing group size (Shaw, 1976). Research is needed to determine the optimal size of the group— optimal in terms of quality of decision (OAR), time to reach decision, and quality of information generated (that may be used as feedback to the candidate).

Another issue pertains to the practice whereby the tie-breaking vote is given to the coordinator. The reason for this practice is not obvious, given that the coordinator often has *not* interacted with the candidate and is not a manager. Coordinators usually are representatives from the training or human resource department (or psychologists). Thus, they are likely to have the least managerial experience and, consequently, the least developed "management behavior schema."

Group Composition

The characteristics of assessor group members determine to some extent what their own behavior in the group will be and how others will react to them. Thus, it is imporant to study the interaction of group-member characteristics and its relationship to the quality of the discussions and the OAR.

Obvious characteristics of group members that can be considered are background factors (age, sex, race), general abilities and skills (e.g., cognitive skills, leadership skills), and personality characteristics (e.g., social sensitivity, authoritarianism, risk taking). There is an abundant literature on the relationship between such factors and degree of participation in discussion, amount of influence, and quality of decisions (see Shaw, 1976). A factor for which there is little research, in any literature, is the degree to which an observer actually has an observational skill. It is the contention of this author that differences exist among individuals' skills to observe, to recognize an important behavioral action, and to record and report such observations. When information is presented on the candidate's performance in the exercises, the crux of the discussions is the description of behaviors in nonevaluative and nonjudgmental terms. Lack of this skill

on the part of the assessor decreases the influence of the assessor in a
group discussion and diminishes the validity of the process.

Types of Group Dynamics Interactions

The dynamics of the assessor group are such that interactions take place
between the group as an entity, the characteristics of the group members,
and the mechanics of the group process. The dynamics have an obvious
impact on the OAR, but the nature and type of impact has not been studied.
An alternative to consensus discussion would be to average individual
ratings on dimensions and the OAR and use those results to make decisions. An argument against this suggestion is that it ignores the essence
of the assessment center process, which is to generate a rich source of
information (on the candidate's performance on multiple tasks in multiple
situations). Discussion contributes to this multiplicity in that it allows for
additional information to surface. Furthermore, the group dynamics literature shows, in general, that group judgments are superior to individual
judgments, and that groups usually produce more and better solutions to
problems. These results are particularly important when the assessment
decisions involve either selection of employees or developmental needs.
However, there is also some evidence that decisions made after group
discussion are usually more risky than decisions made by the average
individual prior to group discussion (Shaw, 1976). Selection decisions, in
particular, involve risk, and there must be willingness to take it, whether
it is due to diffusion of responsibility or to accountability.

To return to the interaction, there is little research on what the mix
ought to be for the group. A particular combination of individual characteristics should produce a significant effect upon group processes. The
purpose of discussion is to persuade another assessor to "move" his/her
rating. Thus, there must be concern for assessors' persuasiveness skills,
receptivity to change, behavioral flexibility, and the impact of polarization.
An emerging literature on group polarization implies that there is group-
produced enhancement of a prevailing individual tendency (see Lamm &
Myers, 1978). Studies have indicated that group discussion can polarize
judgments of fact, particularly when discussing tasks that require subjective evaluation. Furthermore, discussion tends to strengthen initial
impressions. If the latter is true for assessment centers, why does anyone
in the assessor group ever "move" his/her rating? Is it simply to move
the process along?

A possible explanation for the high OAR agreement, even after dimension discussion, is that a "*group management behavior schema*" emerges
over time. Given that assessors usually receive extensive training and that

they serve in the assessor role for a reasonably long period of time, the group members begin to follow some rules for combining their individual views into a group decision. Schemata develop and change over time. As one gains more experience in assessment, a schema emerges that is similar to other schemata. This happens without any a priori, explicit statement of the organization's expectations. Theories are needed to explain this development.

CONCLUSION

This paper briefly presented a description of a typical assessment center procedure that has been used for selection and development of managers. Much of the research on assessment centers has focused on statistical analyses of data collected during assessment; e.g., dimension ratings and an overall assessment rating. These data have been examined for relationships among themselves and for their relationship to an external criterion. Recently, some analyses have pointed to some potential faults in the process, or at least to some faults in the implicit assumptions; these analyses also have questioned the need for some parts of the method— dimension ratings and consensus discussion. This paper, however, pointed to the almost total lack of research on process issues in assessment center methods, and, consequently, posited three perspectives that could contribute to an understanding of the process as well as highlight the need for research in order to gain a better understanding of the process. These perspectives are (1) information processing, the concern of which is to understand the sequence in which information is gathered and used as well as how and what information is combined, integrated, and used; (2) categorization and social cognition, which focuses on learning how dimensions are developed and activated as well as how dimensions and schemata are used to facilitate encoding, recall, inference, and prediction; and (3) group dynamics, wherein the interest is in how characteristics of groups and their members interact to influence the dynamics of processing of information. The final conclusion is that something that works should not be fixed until we understand what we are fixing.

ACKNOWLEDGMENTS

The author would like to thank Drs. Larry Cummings, Joel Moses, Robert Ramos, Barry Staw, and Philip Tetlock for their review of an early draft of this manuscript and for their constructive comments.

REFERENCES

Bentz, V. J. (1984, April). *Assessment center technology in perspective: Hard won gains and missed opportunities.* Paper presented at the meeting of the 12th International Congress on the Assessment Center Method, Lincolnshire, IL.

Bray, D. W., Campbell, R. J., & Grant, D. L. (1977). *Formative years in business: A longterm AT&T study of managerial lives.* New York: Wiley.

Cantor, N., & Mishcel, W. (1979). Prototypes in person perception. In L. Berkowitz (Ed.), *Advances in experimental social psychology: Vol. 12* (pp. 3–52). New York: Academic Press.

Cascio, W. F., & Ramos, R. (1984). *Development and application of a new method for assessing job performance in behavioral and economic terms.* Manuscript submitted for publication.

Cooper, W. H. (1981). Ubiquitous halo. *Psychological Bulletin, 90,* 218–244.

Einhorn, H. J., & Hogarth, R. M. (1981). Behavioraaal decision theory: Processes of judgment and choice. *Annual Review of Psychology, 32,* 52–88.

Einhorn, H. J., & Hogarth, R. M. (1981). Behavioral decision theory: Processes of judgment and choice. *Annual Review of Psychology, 32,* 53–88.

Fiske, S. T., & Taylor, S. E. (1984). *Social cognition.* Reading, MA: Addison-Wesley.

Hamilton, D. L. (1981). Cognitive representations of persons. In E. T. Higgins, C. P. Herman, & M. P. Zanna (Eds.), *Social cognition: The Ontario symposium, Vol 1* (pp. 135–159). Hillsdale, NJ: Erlbaum Associates.

Horton, D. L., & Mills, C. B. (1984). Human learning and memory. *Annual Review of Psychology, 35,* 361–394.

Jeffrey, K. M., & Mischel, W. (1979). Effects of purpose on the organization and recall of information in person perception. *Journal of Personality, 47,* 397–419.

Kelly, H. H. (1972). Attribution in social interaction. In E. E. Jones, D. E. Kanouse, H. H. Kelly, R. E. Nisbett, S. Valins, & B. Weiner (Eds.), *Attribution: Perceiving the causes of behavior.* Morristown, NJ: General Learning Press.

Lamm, H., & Myers, D. G. (1978). Group-induced polarization of attitudes and behavior. In L. Berkowitz (Ed.), *Advances in experimental social psychology: Vol. 11* (pp. 145–195). New York: Academic Press.

Landy, F. J., & Farr, J. L. (1980). Performance rating. *Psychological Bulletin, 87,* 72–107.

Lindsay, P. H., & Norman, D. A. (1977). *Human information processing: An introduction to psychology.* New York: Academic Press.

Lord, R. G. (1985). An information processing approach to social perceptions, leadership perceptions and behavioral measurement in organizational settings. In B. M. Staw & L. L. Cummings (Eds.), *Research in organizational behavior: Vol 7.* Greenwich, CT: JAI Press.

McCormick, E. J. (1979). *Job analysis: Methods and applications.* New York: AMA-CON.

MacKinnon, D. W. (1977). From selecting spies to selecting managers in the OSS Assessment program. In J. L. Moses & W. C. Byham (Eds.), *Applying the assessment center method.* New York: Pergamon.

Medin, D. L., & Smith, E. E. (1984) Concepts and concept formation. *Annual Review of Psychology, 35,* 113–138.

Moses, J. L. (1980). Assessing the assessor. *Journal of the Assessment Center Technology, 3,* 1–5.

Moses, J. L. (1983). *Using clinical methods in a high-level management assessment center*. Paper presented at the Sixth Annual Symposium on Applied Behavioral Science, Blacksburg, VA.

Moses, J. L., & Byham, W. C. (Eds.). (1977). *Applying the assessment center method*. New York: Pergamon.

Neidig, R. D., & Neidig, P. J. (1984). Multiple assessment center exercises and job relatedness. *Journal of Applied Psychology, 69,* 182–186.

Payne, J. W. (1982). Contingent decision behavior. *Psychological Bulletin, 92,* 382–402.

Pitz, G. F., & Sachs, N. J. (1984). Judgment and decision theory and application. *Annual Review of Psychology, 35,* 139–163.

Posner, M. I. (1982). Cumulative development of attentional theory. *American Psychologist, 37,* 168–179.

Rosch, E. (1978). Principles of categorization. In E. Rosch & B. B. Lloyd (Eds.), *Cognition and categorization*. Hillsdale, NJ: Erlbaum Associates.

Rosch, E., Mervis, C. G., Gray, W. D., Johnson, D. M., & Boyes-Braem, P. (1976). Basic objects in natural categories. *Cognitive Psychology, 8,* 382–439.

Ross, L. (1977). The intuitive psychologist and his shortcomings: Distortions in the attribution process. In L. Berkowitz (Ed.), *Advances in experimental social psychology: Vol. 10* (pp. 173–220). New York: Academic Press.

Sackett, P. R. (1982). A critical look at some common beliefs about assessment centers. *Public Personnel Management Journal, 11,* 140–147.

Sackett, P. R. & Dreher, G. F. (1982). Constructs and assessment center dimensions: Some troubling empirical findings. *Journal of Applied Psychology, 67,* 401–410.

Sackett, P. R. & Dreher, G. F. (1984). Situation specificity of behaviors and assessment center validation strategies: A rejoinder to Neidig and Neidig. *Journal of Applied Psychology, 69,* 187–190.

Sackett, P. R., & Harris, M. M. (1983, August). *A further examination of the constructs underlying assessment center ratings*. Paper presented at the meeting of the American Psychological Association, Anaheim, CA.

Sackett, P. R., & Hakel, M. D. (1979). Temporal stability and individual differences in using assessment information to form overall ratings. *Organizational Behavior and Human Performance, 23,* 120–137.

Sackett, P. R., & Wilson, M. A. (1982). Factors affecting the consensus judgment process in managerial assessment centers. *Journal of Applied Psychology, 67,* 10–17.

Shaw, M. E. (1976). *Group dynamics: The psychology of small group behavior* (2nd ed.). New York: McGraw-Hill.

Slovic, P., & Lichtenstein, S. (1971). Comparison of Bayesian and regression approaches to the study of information processing in judgment. *Organizational Behavior and Human Performance, 6,* 649–744.

Smith, E. E., & Medin, D. L. (1981). *Categories and concepts*. Cambridge, MA: Harvard University Press.

Taylor, S. E., & Crocker, J. (1981). Schemata bases of social information processing. In E. T. Higgins, C. P. Herman, & M. P. Zanna (Eds.), *Social cognition: The Ontario symposium: Vol 1* (pp. 89–134). Hillsdale, NJ: Erlbaum Associates.

Taylor, S. E., & Winkler, J. D. (1980, September) *Development of schemas*. Paper presented at the meeting of the American Psychological Association, Montreal.

Tesser, A. (1978) Self-generated attitude change. In L. Berkowitz (Ed.), *Advances in experimental social psychology: Vol. 11* (pp. 289–338). New York: Academic Press.

Thornton, G. C., III, & Byham, W. C. (1982). *Assessment centers and managerial performance*. New York: Academic Press.

Wyer, R. S., Jr., & Srull, T. K. (1981). Category assessibility: Some theoretical and empirical issues concerning the processing of social stimulus information. In E. T. Higgins, C. P. Herman, & M. P. Zanna (Eds.), *Social cognition: The Ontario symposium: Vol 1* (pp. 161–197). Hillsdale, NJ: Erlbaum Associates.

Zedeck, S., & Cascio, W. F. (1984). Psychological issues in personnel decisions. *Annual Review of Psychology, 35,* 461–518.

SEX BIAS IN WORK SETTINGS:

THE LACK OF FIT MODEL

Madeline E. Heilman

ABSTRACT

Asserting that occupational sex bias is not inevitable nor invariable but
can be situationally influenced, a Lack of Fit model is presented to describe
the dynamics of sex bias and the conditions which prompt and support its
occurrence in organizational settings. The model uses a single principle
to explain how both self-directed sex bias (self-limiting behavior) and other-
directed sex bias (discrimination) operate before and after a woman's entry
into an organization. A review of the relevant literature demonstrates the
integrative capacity of the Lack of Fit model, and a consideration of the
model's implications illustrates its practical utility in furthering organizational change efforts to reduce sex bias in the workplace.

Research in Organizational Behavior, Vol. 5, pages 269–298
Copyright © 1983 by JAI Press Inc.
All rights of reproduction in any form reserved.
ISBN: 0-89232-271-3

Women are not yet fully integrated into the mainstream of American organizational life. Despite the fact that they now comprise nearly half of all wage earners, they continue to be grossly underrepresented in organizational roles associated with power or status. As recently as 1979, for example, only 6.4% of the employed women as compared to 14.0% of the employed men in the United States were managers and administrators. Moreover, this 6.4% figure represents an increase of only 1.3% over that of twenty years before (U.S. Bureau of Labor Statistics, 1980). Thus, the considerable increase in the number of women in the labor force in recent years has not been accompanied by a corresponding expansion in the range of their work activities and roles.

Few would dispute the contention that sex bias prevails in organizations. What to do about it has increasingly become cause for concern. It generally is agreed that cultural stereotypes depicting women as deficient in achievement-oriented traits are the root cause: they produce both self-limiting behavior on the part of women themselves and the discriminatory treatment they receive. Consequently, many organizations have developed educational and consciousness raising programs aimed at altering these stereotypic beliefs. Such programs are costly to run and time-consuming to plan and execute; however, these would be small costs to pay if success were assured. But changing stereotypes is no easy task. They very often are deeply rooted in value systems and maintained by diverse motivations. Not surprisingly, programmatic efforts in this area often are unsuccessful and optimal strategies have not emerged. An alternative approach to the sex bias problem clearly is needed.

Current ideas about how to combat sex bias are built upon the assumption that if we are to eliminate the consequences of sex stereotypes, we must do away with the stereotypes themselves. Thus, change activities are directed at individuals in an effort to challenge their beliefs. But, we know from research on related issues that regardless of the strength of a belief an individual might hold, the degree to which that belief will influence behavior is dependent upon situational factors (see, for example, Ajzen & Fishbein, 1973). It therefore is conceivable that sex bias can be inhibited by changing aspects of the work environment, even if the stereotypic beliefs giving rise to it remain intact. This idea, which stands in sharp contrast to the ones which currently dominate organizational efforts in this area, provides a new and potentially fruitful perspective from which to view the problem of occupational sex bias.

But to capitalize on this new perspective it is essential to understand the process by which sex stereotypes give rise to sex bias. Only then can we identify aspects of the work environment which are the critical moderators of sex bias and, accordingly, establish guidelines for bias-minimizing changes in organizational procedures and practices. Unfortunately, few attempts have been made to examine the dynamics of sex bias; far more energy has gone into documenting its existence. This chapter is written in the hope of remedying that lack.

In the following pages we introduce a model, here termed the "Lack of Fit" model, describing the dynamics of sex bias and the conditions which prompt and support its occurrence in organizational settings. The model uses a single principle to explain how both self-directed sex bias (self-limiting behavior) and other-directed sex bias (discrimination) operate before and after entry into the organization's ranks. A review of the relevant literature demonstrates the integrative capacity of the Lack of Fit model, and a consideration of research designed to test the model and its implications illustrates its potential utility in furthering organizational efforts to reduce sex bias in the workplace. Before proceeding with a description of the model, however, it is critical to review the two elements which, together, lie at its core: sex stereotypes and the sex-typing of jobs.

SEX STEREOTYPES

What, exactly, is a stereotype? It is a set of attributes ascribed to a group and imputed to its individual members simply because they belong to that group (Taylor, Fiske, Etcoff, & Ruderman, 1978)[1]. Thus, individuals who attach stereotypes to blacks will believe certain attitudes to be possessed by a significant proportion of blacks (e.g. laziness and musicality) and certain others to be lacking in a significant proportion of blacks (e.g. intelligence and dominance). The more traits included in the stereotype, and the larger the proportion of the group assumed to be characterized by the stereotyped attributes, the more stereotyping exists.

Stereotyping can be a work-saving, efficient cognitive enterprise, serving to simplify and organize the complex world we encounter. And, indeed, in many instances it is. Knowing that rocks are hard, for instance, and that they do not melt when submerged in water enables us to act upon our environment far more effectively than if we had to test for these qualities every time we chanced upon a rock. The problem is that stereotypes about groups of people often are *overgeneralizations* and are *either inaccurate or do not apply to the individual group member in question*. In these cases, stereotypes become the basis for faulty reasoning leading to biased feelings and actions, disadvantaging (or advantaging) others not because of who they are or what they have done but because of what group they belong to.

There are stereotypes associated with the sexes. If asked to describe a "typical man" or a "typical woman" most people are able to do so. The descriptions of the two tend to differ dramatically and in predictable ways, and are assumed to apply to nearly all men and women as members of their respective groups. In fact, inquiries about the nature and scope of sex stereotyping have discovered that men and women are often portrayed as polar opposites (Sheriffs & McKee, 1957; Broverman, Vogel, Clarkson, & Rosenkrantz, 1972). With regard to achievement-oriented traits, men are thought to be competent and strong and women are thought to be incompetent and weak. Thus, whereas men are described as independent, active, competitive, self-confident, and ambitious, women are described as dependent, passive, uncompetitive, unconfident, and unambitious. Men and women also are described differently with respect to qualities of warmth and expressiveness, with women being rated more positively: they are described as tender, understanding, concerned with others, and comfortable with their feelings, whereas men are described in opposite terms.

The traits associated with women and men are not only different, but they are also seen as differentially desirable. Although each are credited with a number of positive traits, individuals of both sexes concur that those associated with men are more valued than those associated with women (Rosenkrantz, Vogel, Dee, Broverman & Broverman, 1968). There is much additional evidence supporting this point (Fernberger, 1948; McKee & Sheriffs, 1957; 1959). Simply put, achievement-related attributes seem to be more highly valued in our society than those concerning nurturance or affiliation. One would thus expect the differential desirability of masculine and feminine traits to be even further exaggerated in work settings. A number of research investigations have indeed documented this fact (Darley, 1976; Zellman, 1976).

Sex stereotypes are widely shared within our culture. Whatever the age, religion, social class, marital status, or educational background of research participants, researchers have consistently found remarkable agreement about the traits that are characteristic of men and women (Broverman et al., 1972). Even sex makes no difference. Whether male or female, people seem to concur about the different attributes of men and women, and that those associated with men are more desirable. This lack of difference between the sexes has held despite the date in which the investigation has occurred or the type of methodology it has employed.

The fact that sex stereotypes are subscribed to by members of both sexes raises an interesting and important question about the extent to which they are reflected in the self-concepts of women and men. Researchers who have examined the self-descriptions of women and men have found them to be very much in accordance with sex stereotypes (Rosenkrantz et al., 1968). It is important to note that women seem to accept the societal view of themselves and do not reject the less favorably valued characterizations associated with their sex. In fact, there is some evidence which suggests that women tend to adhere to sex stereotypes in their self-descriptions even more forcefully than do men (Sheriffs & McKee, 1957). The implication of this for women's behavior and the self-inflicted inhibition of their career progress will be discussed later in this chapter.

To what extent are sex stereotypic conceptions accurate reflections of reality? Are males and females actually as different as commonly is assumed?

Answering this question is more complex than at first it may appear. Until recently it generally was accepted that the biological differences between women and men were paralleled by distinct psychological differences. In fact, several reviews of the research literature focused on the nature of these sex differences (Garai & Scheinfeld, 1968; Maccoby, 1966; Tyler, 1965). In 1974, however, Maccoby and Jacklin published their comprehensive book, *The Psychology of Sex Differences*, which prompted a reassessment of the actual existence of sex differences. This reassessment grew from the recognition of measurement problems inherent in many of the research efforts in which sex differences had been identified and from issues surrounding the reporting of data relevant to sex differences.

The type of measure used to capture differences between the sexes is critical in evaluating the data that results. For the data may in fact yield more information about sex stereotypes than about actual sex differences. This is particularly true when verbal measures are used, for respondents in this case are providing subjective impressions of others or of themselves rather than rating or engaging in real behavior. Beliefs and expectations about how males and females do behave or should behave are very likely to influence such ratings. It therefore is not surprising to find discrepancies in the magnitude of sex differences found when verbal measures, as opposed to direct observation, are used as the primary data collection procedure (Maccoby & Jacklin, 1974).

Another measurement issue which has recently emerged in the sex difference literature concerns the sex of the researcher. It has been found in a meta-analysis of social influence studies, for instance, that sex differences were much more prevalent when the investigator had been a male than a female; in fact, no sex differences were evident at all when the investigator had been a female (Eagly & Carli, 1981). This suggests that even in studies where people engage in behavior, the nature of this behavior may be biased by factors having little to do with sex differences and far more to do with the sex stereotypes which are made salient by the context in which the research is occurring.

Finally, Maccoby and Jacklin (1974) made the important point that the many studies in which sex differences might have occurred but did not have not been widely disseminated. They argued that because scientific journals publish almost exclusively those studies in which statistically significant differences have been obtained, the evidence contradictory to a sex difference hypothesis never gets heard, and the literature over-represents the differences between the sexes. In fact, after reviewing the array of studies in which sex differences *could* have occurred, they conclude that many of the presumed differences between males and females are based in myth, not in reality.

These problems aside, however, it is useful to briefly review the literature pertaining to sex differences relevant to work behavior. Such a review follows.

Aggression

The studies of aggression have yielded one of the most consistently found sex differences: males behave more aggressively than females. This finding has held regardless of type of measure, age of actor, or culture in which the research takes place. There is some indication, however, that females may not, in fact, differ from males in aggressive motivation, and when aggression takes a nonphysical form, such as verbal aggression (Oetzel, 1966) or aggression through rejection and exclusion (Feshbach and Jones, 1971), females have been found to be more aggressive than males.

Dependency

Females are believed to be more passive and dependent, and more easily influenced than males. But support for this is very mixed. In observational studies, no systematic sex differences in dependency-related behaviors have emerged (Oetzel, 1966; Maccoby and Jacklin, 1974). However, in many verbal report studies, more females are rated as dependent than males. This suggests that bias rather than fact may be operating.

Social Orientation

Findings from early research suggest that females are more socially oriented and nurturant than males. However, many recent research efforts have found no differences in these behaviors. Of particular relevance here, studies measuring social orientation in task situations typically find no sex differences (e.g. Ruble, 1975), and when differences are found, sometimes they demonstrate females to be more socially oriented than males and sometimes they demonstrate males to be more socially oriented than females, showing no particular trend in one direction or the other.

Verbal Skills

By age 10 or 11, girls clearly surpass boys in verbal performance and, continuing through the high school and college years, females are superior to males in a variety of verbal skills (Maccoby & Jacklin, 1974). However, there is no evidence that verbal reasoning ability (Oetzel, 1966) or communication skills (Higgins, 1976) differ among males and females at any age.

Mathematical Skills

Males are clearly superior to females in mathematical reasoning and problem solving (Oetzel, 1966; Maccoby & Jacklin, 1974). Recent studies have suggested, however, that this finding is due to the content of the problems used in such research, not to the type of logic required to solve them (e.g. Leder, 1974).

What can we conclude from this brief review? First, there is little support for the ideas that sex stereotypes do, in fact, accurately reflect powerful and consistent differences between the sexes. However, it is apparent that when sex differences occur, they tend to be in the direction of the stereotype. What is not clear is whether such differences actually are a function of the methodology employed in studying them. The sex of the researcher, the sex-related content of the problem or issue presented, and/or the type of measure used may all be sources of bias that are inadvertently introduced in the research situation. Often when these types of factors are controlled, sex differences disappear.

Of course, even if one were to take the point of view that stereotypes *are* based on true differences between the sexes, it must be remembered that there is a great deal of overlap in the distribution of males and females on any one stereotyped attribute. In other words, while the average level of the attribute may differ across the sexes, all males and all females will not be different from one another and, at times, a female may be more like the average male and a male like the average female with respect to that attribute. Thus, even stereotypes based on an accurate overall assessment of a sex group may be totally inappropriate to apply to an individual member of that group. Whether the stereotype is correct or incorrect on the average, using it to characterize a given male or female can become the basis of faulty reasoning due to overgeneralization.

The current controversy about whether or not sex differences exist raises some important questions about the veracity of the stereotypes used to characterize males and females. An additional body of literature examining women's feelings toward and behavior at work raises similar questions. Results from many of these studies also contradict the notion that women are fundamentally different from men. For example, women when compared to men have been reported to have much the same leadership abilities (Day & Stogdill, 1972), problem-solving abilities (Matthews, 1972), leadership styles (Chapman, 1975), and motivation to manage (Miner, 1977). Thus it seems that in many areas critical to work behavior men and women might be more alike than different. Nonetheless, sex stereotypes obstinately persist.

Most investigators have found little evidence that sex stereotypes have changed within the culture in recent years. Even today's college students seem no different than their predecessors in their attitudes and beliefs about women. This lack of change is particularly evident when researchers take precautions to limit the pressures on subjects to give socially appropriate responses (see Spence, Helmreich, & Stapp, 1975). There is, however, some evidence suggesting that current societal changes may ultimately give rise to altered views of women. If a person's mother has worked, for instance, that individual has been shown to have a less stereotyped view of women than one whose mother has not (Vogel, Broverman, Broverman, Clarkson & Rosenkrantz, 1970). Thus, exposure to a woman in a nontraditional role (a working mother) is a factor that can influence one's general view of women. Extrapolating from this finding, one might expect that changes in the way women are portrayed by the media, in the way they are depicted by our educational institutions, and in their visibility and importance in the work force will slowly contribute to an evolved view of women in the coming generations. There is, therefore, some room for optimism about the future. But, for the present, sex stereotypes are very much with us.

SEX-TYPING OF JOBS

Not only is there concurrence about the attributes of men and women but also about the gender classification of jobs. Sex-typing of jobs has its origins in the traditional view that paid work—especially if it is important, demanding, and lucrative—is a man's domain. Women's lack of mobility, their failure to maintain career continuity, and their seemingly lesser ambition with regard to livelihood all have served to reinforce that image throughout the years. Now, when these factors no longer weigh so heavily in women's life plans, the view of work as primarily a man's activity remains.

There have, of course, always been some positions and occupations that are considered female in sex-type: librarian, nurse, secretary, and elementary school teacher, to name a few. By and large such jobs are believed to require the skills and talents that society attributes to women—nurture, social sensitivity, and service. Occupations of higher status, however, apparently are the province of men. They not only have fewer women in their ranks but also are thought to require an achievement-oriented aggressiveness that rarely is associated with women.

Evidence exists in many forms documenting the fact that being successful at work in high status jobs is generally thought to be reserved for men and not women. Research conducted by Feldman-Summers and Kiesler (1974) is a case in point. In the course of designing a research procedure, these researchers administered a pretest survey to approximately 85 male and female undergraduates at the University of Kansas. Each was shown descriptions of several different professionals and was asked to indicate how successful he or she believed them to be. For each subject, half were presented as male and the other half as female. The results were dramatic. In no instance was a woman expected to be more successful than a man! The authors also report that in later work they were unable to find even a single professionally-oriented occupation in which women rather than men were expected to be more successful. This is indeed a very compelling indication that success at high status work has been generally associated with men more than women.

To bring this point a bit closer to organizational life it is useful to consider the work of Schein (1973; 1975). She asked both male and female management personnel in insurance companies to describe either women, men, or successful middle managers. She found that "men" and "successful middle managers" were described in very similar terms whereas "women" were described quite differently. Apparently, those attributes thought to characterize a successful manager (the high status role in organizations) are not at all those typically ascribed to women. Thus, not only are most managers men, but good management is also thought to be a manly business.

The work of Kiesler (1975) suggests an alternative to the point of view that sex-typing of jobs is based on the perceived content of the job and the sex-related attributes linked with it. She proposes that a job becomes sex-typed as male or female according to the sex of the usual job-holder. Thus, the disproportionate representation of one sex in a job results in the belief that the job is appropriate for those of that sex and inappropriate for those of the other sex. Judgments of sex-typing are therefore essentially actuarial in nature.

Research pitting this point of view against others has, unfortunately, been difficult to interpret due to methodological problems. In the two studies by Krefting et al. (1978) which seek to demonstrate the strength of this argument, subjects were asked to assign jobs which objectively differed in both sex-related job content and proportional representation of male and female job holders to male or female categories. However, the criteria for categorization confounded assessment of the capability of those of the two sexes with the assessment of their likely satisfaction with such a job, creating problems in interpreting just what the resulting sex-type categories mean. Also problematic is the way in which the masculine and feminine content of jobs was determined, leaving much room for debate about the authors' conclusion that the sex-related attributes of jobs had no effect on perception of job sex-types. Thus the relative importance of these two explanations for the sex-typing of jobs has not yet been established.

Although it is quite plausible that the perceived representation of the sexes within a job category affects how that job is viewed with respect to gender, it is not reasonable to discard the notion that the perceived sex-related attributes of jobs are a critical aspect of the sex-typing process. Everyday notions differentiating "women's work" from "men's work" on the basis of job content, as well as the empirical work of Schein (1973; 1975) and others, attest to its importance. But whether such perceptions are a contribution to, or an outcome of, the sex-typing process remains to be determined in future research. The answer is important, for the implications of these two explanations are quite different with respect to the likely ease of changing the sex-typing of jobs. It is clear, however, that many jobs are seen as predominantly masculine or predominantly feminine (Shinar, 1975); they are believed to require the skills and talents associated with one or the other sex. And, with few exceptions, the jobs that carry with them power, prestige, and authority in our culture are cast as male rather than female in sex-type.

THE LACK OF FIT MODEL

How do stereotyped conceptions of women and the sex-typing of jobs detrimentally affect women's acceptance, participation, and advancement in the work world? It is instructive to consider the role that "perceived incongruity" or "lack of fit" play in this process.

Expectations about how successful or unsuccessful an individual will be when working at a particular job are determined by the fit between the perception of an individual's attributes and the perception of the job's requirements in terms of skills and abilities:

$$\left.\frac{\text{Perceived Attributes}}{\text{Perceived Job Requirements}}\right\}\text{Fit Assessment} \longrightarrow \text{Performance Expectations}$$

If, for example, an individual is believed to be high on verbal but low on quantitative ability, one would not expect him or her to be successful at a job thought to require sophisticated mathematical skills. There seemingly is a poor fit between the individual's attributes and the requirements of the job. But, the same individual may be viewed as a likely success when a job is thought to require skills in writing and communication. Here, the perceived fit between the individual's attributes and the job requirements is a good one. Thus, perception of a good fit gives rise to expectations of success and perceptions of a poor fit give rise to expectations of failure:

$$\left.\frac{\text{Perceived Attributes}}{\text{Perceived Job Requirements}}\right\}\begin{array}{l}\text{poor fit} \longrightarrow \text{expectations of failure}\\ \text{good fit} \longrightarrow \text{expectations of success}\end{array}$$

These performance expectations have critical consequences. There is a cognitive tendency to perpetuate and confirm them. Viewed in the context of these expectations, the identical data about an individual is subjected to differential interpretation (Feldman, 1981). As in the classic social psychological research in which the same statement was shown to be interpreted quite differently depending upon whether the source was said to be John Adams or to be Karl Marx (Asch 1948), performance expectations create a predisposition, or a cognitive set, toward negativity or positivity that colors judgments of self and others. And such judgments have behavioral consequences. They influence whether people choose and are chosen for employment, they influence how work outcomes are evaluated and rewarded, and they influence whether and how individuals seek to advance their careers:

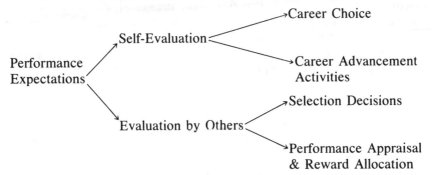

Applying this reasoning to women in the work world it is clear that skills and abilities perceived to be required to effectively handle masculinely sex-typed organizational jobs, such as managerial ones, do not correspond to the attributes believed to characterize women as a group. Taking a leadership role, making hard-nosed decisions and competing for resources simply are not activities that are consistent with a view of women as the gentle and/or helpless sex. One thus would expect that if a stereotyped view of women were taken when considering an individual woman in a managerial role, expectations of failure would ensue creating a clear bias toward negativity. She would not be believed or believe herself capable of handling such a job adequately or, if she did, her success would tend to be discredited by both herself and critical others in her work setting. This sequence of events is depicted in Figure 1. Thus it is proposed that *the presumed lack of fit that arises from a perceived attributes-job requirements incongruity underlies each of the many varieties of sex bias encountered in the work world.* It is further proposed that *the larger this perceived incongruity, the worse the presumed lack of fit and therefore the greater the likelihood and/or magnitude of sex-biased judgments or behaviors.*

It should be noted that this is a cognitive model. It asserts that rational information processing, not some irrational imperative, underlies occupational sex bias. Whether self-directed or other-directed, sex bias is conceived of as a logical result of the combined impact of stereotyped characterizations of an individual woman and sex typed conceptions of the nature of a job. Following this reasoning, *variations in the presumed lack of fit, either due to the extent stereotypes are applied to an individual woman or due to the extent a given job is masculinely sex-typed, should correspondingly influence the degree and the frequency of sex bias that results.*

As will become evident in the subsequent sections, this model and the lack of fit principle provide a parsimonious explanation for much of the existing research conducted in this area. Presumed lack of fit can be viewed as the source of occupational sex discrimination. It functions as a barrier against women competing equally with men in the initial acquisition of employment and, if hired, in the distribution of performance rewards. Additionally, presumed lack of fit can be regarded as the source of women's self-limiting behavior both in job choice and in career advancement activities.

DISCRIMINATION

Pre-Entry Discrimination

Sex discrimination has been repeatedly demonstrated in employee selection processes. While some researchers have found no differences in the willingness to hire men and women for traditionally male positions, most have indeed discovered such a tendency (e.g., Rosen and Jerdee,

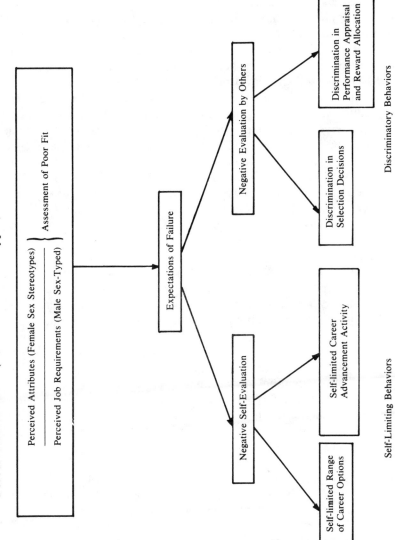

Figure 1. The Lack of Fit Model Regarding Occupational Sex Bias
Perceived Attributes (Female Sex Stereotypes)

1974; Zickmund, Hitt, and Pickens, 1978). This has been found to be the case regardless of whether those making the selection decisions are students or professional interviewers (Dipboye, Fromkin, & Wiback, 1975), or are male or female (Dipboye, Arvey, and Terpstra). Moreover, sex bias has been shown to prevail regardless of the discipline base of the job applicant (Shaw, 1972). Not only are males judged preferable to females and evaluated more favorably in selection deliberations, but several investigations have indicated that they are likely to be offered higher starting salaries (Terborg & Ilgen, 1975; Dipboye, Arvey, & Terpstra, 1977) and higher level positions (Fidell, 1970).

These research findings and the real-life organizational events they reproduce can be readily understood in terms of the lack of fit principle. The perceived incongruity between a woman's characteristics and the requirements of a masculinely sex-typed job results in the expectation that the woman will not be effective. Such expectations no doubt have impact on selection decisions. Individuals believed to be unqualified for a job are unlikely to be hired and, if they are, are likely to be compensated less generously than others whose prognosis for performance success seems more favorable. Here the conversion of expectations into action is direct and uncomplicated.

But how about the studies in which no differences have been found in the evaluations of male and female job applicants? Here, too, the Lack of Fit model is useful; it provides an explanation for these apparently contradictory results. According to our formulation, perceived lack of fit due to an attribute-job requirements incongruity is key to the occurrence of sex bias. But this does not imply that whenever job applicants are women such a lack of fit will automatically ensue. In some instances the job in question may not be perceived as male sex-typed. This is a reasonable assumption in, for instance, the Renwick and Tosi (1978) study in which the job was said to involve training and development activities, functions consistent with the ostensibly womanly talents of teaching, counselling, and being sensitive to the problems of others. Or, alternatively, in some instances the information provided about a woman may have far more influence on the impressions formed of her than do sex stereotypes. This may be due to either the job relevance of the information (which also is a possible factor accounting for the Renwick and Tosi results, for example) and/or the impact it makes because of the way it is conveyed (e.g. videotaped job interviews in Dipboye and Wiley, 1977). In any of these cases, the comparing of an applicant's perceived attributes with the perceived job requirements would not give rise to an assessment of "poor fit" for women more than men and, accordingly, sex bias would not be expected.

Finally, results of several investigations in which no *general* tendency to devalue female job applicants has been found lend direct support to the lack of fit principle as an explanation for sex bias in selection processes. Both Cohen and Bunker (1975) and Cash, Gillen and Burns (1977) systematically varied the sex of job applicants and the gender orientation of job types, thereby confronting research subjects with varying degrees of sex-job incongruence. These manipulations should, according to our ideas, directly affect the degree of lack of fit perceived. Consistent with our notion that the extent of the presumed lack of fit influences the degree of negativity that a female job candidate will receive, both studies indicated that females were found to be less acceptable than male job candidates only when the job was a masculinely sex-typed one. It thus appears that there was nothing about females *per se*, but about the meshing of their assumed attributes with the job type, that determined whether discrimination in selection processes occurred. Results from an additional study lend support to this point of view: whereas male managerial applicants were favored over female ones when subordinates were said to be male, female managerial applicants were favored over male ones when subordinates were said to be female (Rose & Andiappan, 1978). Again, the perceived nature of the job and its likely sex-typing (it is likely that more masculine attributes would be perceived necessary to supervise males than females) was shown to be a critical factor in determining whether sex discrimination occurred.

The degree of presumed lack of fit should be affected not only by the conception of the job and its responsibilities but also by the conception of the woman and the degree to which she is characterized by feminine attributes. Thus, according to our formulation, women considered more feminine or womanly should be judged less suitable than others for masculine positions. Consistent with this idea, Heilman and Saruwatari (1979) found that exceedingly attractive females, who were considered more feminine than their less good-looking counterparts, were evaluated less favorably for a managerial position. Results from other investigations support their findings. Cash et al. (1977) found that attractive applicants were favored over unattractive ones when the gender classification of the job was congruent with the sex of the applicant, but were found less favorable when the gender classification of the job was incongruent with the sex of the applicant. Finally, data patterns produced in another investigation (Dipboye, Arvey and Terpstra, 1977) also are consistent with these findings, although the authors did not directly focus on them. These data lend added support to the lack of fit principle as an underlying dynamic influencing and biasing personnel decision processes.

Post-Entry Discrimination

In recent years there have been many claims that sex bias permeates decisions about pay raises, promotions, employee utilization, and training opportunities. Indeed there is a growing realization that women, simply because they are women, are treated shabbily by the organizations for which they work. How women are treated within organizations derives from judgments made about their performance. Below two critical aspects of this process are described: sex bias in the performance evaluation process itself and sex bias in causal explanations of success.

Sex Bias in Performance Evaluation. Although she achieves the identical outcome as a man, a woman's work is often not regarded equivalently. Inquiries in the past several years have been designed to examine the scope and parameters of this sexually based bias.

A study by Goldberg (1968) indicated that college students rated professional articles more highly when they were attributed to male authors than to female authors. Using the same experimental procedure, however, Pheterson (reported in Pheterson et al., 1971) found sex bias to be absent in a group of uneducated middle-aged women. A subsequent study (Pheterson, Kiesler, & Goldberg, 1971) attempted to reconcile the divergent results from these two investigations. The authors speculated that, as contrasted to the college students in Goldberg's study, the uneducated women in Pheterson's study were likely to view the very fact that an article is published to be an indication of proven success. It thus was postulated that only when a work product has uncertain status is it valued more highly when ascribed to a man than a woman. The data supported this idea: when paintings were said to be art contest entries, male work was judged superior, but when paintings were said to be prize winners this did not occur.

The lack of fit principle not only can account for but also can expand the implications of these results. Sex stereotypes function to make the world less complex and therefore more manageable. By treating an individual woman as a member of a category and ascribing attributes to her that presumably characterize her sex, a great deal of information about that woman and what she is like can be inferred. Thus, there is an impetus to use stereotypes in forming impressions of women. When specific information about a given woman is provided, however, and that information is apparently more informative than sex stereotypes, stereotypic attributions are precluded. If stereotyped attributes do not predominate, presumed lack of fit does not ensue even though the evaluatee is a woman.

This formulation reconciles many divergent results obtained by researchers in this area. In the Pheterson et al. study the information value of sex stereotypes was superceded by the unequivocal fact that the woman being judged was capable and talented—she was a prize winner. However, the information value of sex stereotypes can be superceded by other means as well. Heilman (1975), for instance, found that evidence of a woman's success in a field ordinarily populated only by men was sufficient to totally eliminate biased evaluations of her. Similar explanations can be made of the results of Hamner, Kim, Baird, and Bigoness (1974) and Bigoness (1976) in which women were rated as superior to men when they were shown to perform equivalently doing the heavy physical chores of a grocery store stock clerk. Indeed, these latter studies suggest that when stereotypes are not operative, women may be judged to be even more effective than similarly performing men, perhaps because of all of the forces assumed to have worked against them.

These findings demonstrate that it is not under all conditions that women and their work are subjected to prejudiced judgments. Moreover, they suggest that when the information value of sex stereotypes is undermined, bias is not evident. Since in each of these studies reducing the utility of sex stereotypes in forming impressions of a given woman reduced the perceived incongruity between her attributes and those requisite for the job or task, the results lend support to the Lack of Fit model.

Sex Bias in Causal Explanations of Success. Even when a successful performance outcome is acknowledged, interpretations of that success differ when the one who has achieved it is a woman rather than a man. A subtle prejudicial dynamic comes into play. When equally successful, a woman is viewed as less skilled than a man. This tendency to discredit the success of women as not being skill-related is of critical importance in organizational settings. Its origins also can be understood in terms of lack of fit.

According to attribution theory, it is only when an individual performs in accordance with expectations that the outcome is attributed to skill. When he/she performs inconsistently with expectations, the outcome is attributed to factors that enable interpretation of this event as an exception, unlikely to occur repeatedly. Such factors include aspects of the situation that are totally irrelevant to the individual, such as luck or the easiness of the task, or which are temporally limited such as effort. Through such attributions the original expectations about the individual can be maintained and the observer spared the cognitive strain of revising them.

Applying these ideas to the case of women at work, it can readily be seen that women's success at masculinely sex-typed jobs constitutes an inconsistency with expectations. Thus, female success might well be expected to be explained by factors other than skill more often than male success (see Deaux, 1976 for more on this). There is, in fact, research evidence attesting to this point. A woman's success on a masculine task has been found to be attributed to luck rather than ability, while the reverse was true for men (Deaux and Emswiller, 1974) and greater effort has been found to be attributed to females than males for identically successful performances (Feldman-Sumners & Kiesler, 1974). However, when the task is female rather than male in sex-type (Deaux & Emswiller, 1974) or when those making the attributions do not have a stereotyped view of women (Garland & Price, 1977), such discrepant attributions are less likely to occur. These latter findings support the notion that it is the perceived attributes-job requirement incongruity, not a woman's gender per se, that gives rise to these nonskill attributions.

The fact that women are prone to suffer from an underestimation of the extent to which their successes are skill-derived is, in and of itself, of little consequence. It is only if such underestimation results in differential allocations of organizational rewards that it is of importance in understanding occupational sex discrimination. Accordingly, a study was undertaken exploring the relationship between causal explanations of success and organizational reward allocation (Heilman & Guzzo, 1978). Results unequivocally demonstrated that the types of causal attributions typically made when women are successful (1) detrimentally affect the degree to which organizational rewards are viewed as appropriate personnel actions and, (2) if a reward is indeed seen as suitable, detrimentally affect the scope and magnitude of the reward viewed as preferable. Furthermore, it was found that males and females were treated identically if the causal basis of their behavior was thought to be the same. This investigation verifies the link between biased causal attributions and inequitable treatment of female employees and, as such, is indicative of one more way in which presumed lack of fit can contribute to sex discrimination in organizations.

SELF-LIMITING BEHAVIOR

Pre-Entry Self-Limitation

As recently as 1979 only 12.4% of all lawyers and judges, 2.9% of all engineers and 11.9% of all physicians and dentists were women (U.S. Bureau of Labor Statistics, 1980). One common explanation of these facts and figures is the discriminatory admissions policies of the institutions responsible for professional training. There is, no doubt, merit in that argument. However, if one were to follow the career paths of those women who do in fact gain entry to professional schools and advanced degree programs and compare them with the career paths of their male counterparts, a discrepancy still is apparent. Gross (1967) reported that women who do enter professions are disproportionately represented in those specialties considered to be lowest in status. In law, women are more frequently in practices involving juvenile, divorce, or welfare cases than in practices involving tax and corporate litigation. The same tendency has been found to predominate in medicine with women typically having practices as pediatricians, dermatologists, or psychiatrists and not as surgeons, internists, or neurologists. This pattern is noteworthy. It suggests that women may *choose* to pursue lower status careers even when the opportunity to do otherwise is available to them.

Returning for a moment to our Lack of Fit model, it is clear that women's perceptions of the conditions under which they would be likely to be successful may be a contributing factor. Careers in which work with children, families, or giving of nurturant support is the central activity is consistent with the societal views of women and what their strengths are and therefore lead to expectations of success. However theSe careers also tend to be those that are lowest in status—whatever the professional category. But performance expectations for more masculinely defined (and often higher status) jobs are apt to be low because of the presumed lack of fit between perceived qualities of oneself and the perceived requirements of these jobs. Thus, if they accept societal stereotypes, women are caught in a perpetual bind.

Results of a recently conducted experiment (Heilman, 1979) lends some support to this formulation. In it, the sex-linked perceptions of occupations, one component of the fit ratio, was systematically varied. College-bound high school students were exposed to information about one of two occupations that currently are dominated by males. Projections of the proportions of women expected to populate the occupation in the future were systematically manipulated. The results indicated that the projected sexual composition of an occupation had a great deal of influence on the degree to which women considered it a viable career choice. Their estimates of likely success were higher for each of the two occupations when the ratio of women to men was to rise above token level in the future. And the degree of occupational interest they expressed in each stimulus occupation closely paralleled these success estimates.

These findings make sense in terms of the Lack of Fit model. Shifts in women's perceptions of the maleness of an occupation can be viewed as creating a better fit between it and a woman's perceived attributes. The increased goodness of fit would be accompanied by higher expectations of success which in turn would mediate attitudes such as occupational interest. Thus, these results are supportive of the idea that perceptions of fit can be of critical importance in determining the types of careers women do and do not choose to pursue.

Post-Entry Self-Limitation

Research on women has produced a well-documented disturbing finding. Women consistently devalue themselves and their contributions to the work setting. Given the actual equivalence of women and men in many achievement-related characteristics, one would expect that the tendency to minimize their capabilities would dissipate once women had the opportunity to work alongside men and make comparisons. However, this is not the case.

Women continue to maintain their negative self-views despite their experiences. This is in part a consequence of attributional processes: on many work tasks they see themselves as responsible only for negative, not for positive, performance outcomes. Success is explained away as a lucky break or a result of an easy task, whereas failure is regarded as a reflection of self. Indeed, as compared to males whose performance is of comparable quality, females have been shown to accept less personal responsibility for success and more personal responsibility for failure (Deaux & Farris, 1977; Nicholls, 1975). Attributing responsibility in this fashion, because it dismisses favorable information, perpetuates a self-fulfilling cycle of negative self-regard. There no doubt are costly consequences. Women's willingness to take risks, their desire to be visible, and their general presentation of themselves are all likely to be affected in a manner that hinders career progress.

It has been suggested that the asymmetry in men's and women's attributional patterns originates from the different expectations men and women bring with them to work settings. According to Deaux (1976), when a performance outcome is inconsistent with one's expectations of oneself, personal responsibility is rejected or denied. Therefore, one might argue, women (who by-and-large have negative expectations relevant to achievement in traditionally masculine areas) are loath to take credit for success and are willing to take blame for failure, whereas men (who by-and-large have positive expectations relevant to achievement in these areas) do just the reverse. Because of cognitive set, the identical outcome is interpreted differently. In fact, it has been found that when they do start out with comparable performance expectations, no differences are observable in how men and women react to success or failure on several different tasks (McMahon, 1973; Feather & Simon, 1975).

It thus appears that the acceptance of responsibility for positive and negative performance outcomes is determined by the match between the outcome and an individual's performance expectations. Since according to our model, expectations are a result of an assessment of the degree of fit between one's perceived attributes and one's perceptions of the task requirements, one would expect that variations in this fit ratio would in turn affect self-expectations.

There is in fact some evidence to this effect. Heilman and Kram (1978) conducted a study in which subjects worked in pairs and received feedback about the pair's joint outcome. They then were asked to indicate how much responsibility they took for the joint outcome. It was found that women's tendencies to reject responsibility for success (take less than 50%) and accept it for failure (take more than 50%) were only evident when their coworkers were men. Moreover, when paired with a female as compared to a male, they were shown to be more optimistic and confident about upcoming work sessions in which they were to work alone. If one accepts the notion that the sex of one's coworker can influence one's perception of the job at hand and/or one's sense of self, these data can be interpreted as supportive of the idea that variations in perceived fit can influence women's expectations and evaluations of themselves and therefore their career-oriented behavior.

Thus, diverse findings relevant to women at work reported by different investigators working in different settings with different subject populations all can be viewed as deriving from the same root cause: the incongruity between the attributes assumed to characterize women and the skills and abilities believed necessary for work success, and the negative performance expectations this lack of fit produces. We now turn to address the question of how these various forms of sex bias might be reduced.

INFLUENCING THE INCIDENCE OF SEX BIAS

If the magnitude of the incongruity between a woman's inferred stereotypic attributes and the perceived requirements of masculinely sex-typed jobs is the pivotal point upon which bias rests, one would expect that variations in either of these components of the fit ratio would affect the resulting degree of sex bias. The literature just reviewed indeed suggests that this is the case. Moreover, the literature, taken as a whole, is suggestive about situational variables that can influence one or the other of these perceptions. A summary of these situational variables follows.

Sex-Typing of the Job

It is when the nature of a job and/or those who work at it is viewed as overridingly masculine that it is sex-typed as "masculine." Thus there are a number of ways in which such sex-typing can conceivably be avoided or altered:

a. *Emphasizing Feminine Aspects.*   A job that is sex-typed as masculine tends to be perceived as requiring skills assumed to characterize men, not women. But many so-called masculine jobs in fact require skills typically considered feminine. Managerial responsibilities, for instance, include tasks such as handling interpersonal conflicts and dealing with problems of subordinates, both necessitating interpersonal skills and sensitivity. These, however, are not the tasks most salient when the role of manager is brought to mind. If such aspects of the job were to be highlighted, then the gender classification of that job might become more ambiguous.

A recent study in which overall reactions to the same job were found to differ depending upon the sex-related skills and abilities used to describe the job demands lends support to this idea (Vance, Note 1). However, whether the actual sex-typing of a job can be influenced by these differential descriptions remains to be demonstrated.

b. *Changing the Perceived Exclusivity.*   Masculinely sex-typed jobs are those traditionally held by men. Continued perception of this exclusivity perpetuates sex-typing. The Heilman (1979) investigation discussed earlier, in which it was shown that the belief that more women were to populate an occupation spurred greater occupational interest, makes this point quite dramatically. Thus, one would expect that increasing the number of women working in traditionally male-dominated jobs would go a long way toward altering the sex-type of a job.

However, one would also expect that organizational actions which clearly indicate that the job is not an excusively male one would have a similar impact. Some such actions might be the acknowledgement of women who are successfully functioning in traditionally male jobs, the explicit recruiting of women as well as men for such jobs, and the availability of opportunities to train for such jobs for women as well as men. In short, perceived exclusivity is not only contingent upon numerical facts but upon the spirit in which efforts are made to sexually integrate a job category or, for that matter, an occupation.

Inferring Stereotyped Attributes

Assumptions about women as a group provide the basis for stereotyped inferences about an individual woman's attributes. But if sex as a characteristic were to appear as less informative than other information, stereotypic assumptions would not result. There are several ways in which the information value of stereotypes can be reduced:

(a) *Rendering Sex a Non-salient Characteristic.*   Only when it is salient does an individual's sex influence impression formation. Like other characteristics, sex is salient when highlighted perceptually. According to Gestalt principles, such highlighting should be unlikely to occur when it is non-unique (McArthur & Post, 1977; Taylor, et al., 1978). Thus situational factors that act to downplay the distinctiveness of the sex dimension should limit its salience and therefore its information value. One such factor is the sex composition of a work group.

In her book, *Men and Women of the Corporation*, Kanter (1977) claims that the proportional representation of women in work settings not only influences their feelings and attitudes, but also influences the way in which they are treated by others. When there is a great disproportion in the size of the minority and majority groups she believes there is cause for concern. Tokens (the members of that piddling minority) are isolated from the informal social networks, they are viewed as alien and different, and their characteristics are distorted to fit stereotyped conceptions. According to Kanter tokenism is deadly, fostering reliance on stereotypes no matter what the personal characteristics of the individuals involved.

The implications of this point of view are simple enough. Batch hiring, not one-by-one hiring of women for male-dominated positions should be far more satisfactory. Additionally, when a number of women are to be brought into positions where there are few other women, clustering, not dispersing should be preferable; women should be clustered in numbers large enough so that they are not tokens even if it means that some units have no women at all. Simply by avoiding numerical scarcity, and providing evidence of the variety and differences among women, reacting to them all as if they were the same should become cognitively unjustifiable.

Although there is not much documentation about the consequences of these procedures, there are some data which demonstrate the power of the sex composition variable in selection decisions. MBA students evaluated a women applicant for a managerial position when the proportion of women in the applicant pool was varied (Heilman, 1980). The focal woman applicant was found to be in a far worse position in terms of employment opportunity when the representation of women was at or below the 25% level than when it was above it. In these token or near-token conditions, she was judged to be less qualified, was regarded as lower in potential, and was less likely to be recommended for the position. Also, as expected, she was viewed in far more stereotypic terms. Thus, proportional representation of women and men has been shown empirically to be a potent force in determining reactions to individual women.

(b) Making Other Information More Attention-worthy. It already has been pointed out that stereotypes about women in general are most likely to be employed when ambiguity exists. Terborg (1977) also has made

this point. Specific information about a woman is often more compelling than beliefs about stereotypic attitudes. There is reason to believe, for instance, that sex is unlikely to be viewed as the ultimate source of information about an individual when more job-relevant information is available (Renwick & Tosi, 1978), when that information is clear-cut and not subject to reinterpretation (Pheterson et al., 1971), when performance is directly observable in a job interview (Dipboye and Wiley, 1977), when performance is directly observable in a job sample (Bigoness, 1976; Hammer, Kim, Baird, & Bigoness, 1974), or when the causal basis of performance is known (Heilman & Guzzo, 1978).

However, not all types of information are sufficient to counteract the considerable power of sex stereotypes in determining inferences about the attributes of an individual woman. This point was demonstrated in an investigation in which subjects, who were MBA students, were asked to do some initial screening of job applicants for employment interviews (Heilman, Note 2). Only job-relevant information was found to produce less stereotyped views of women than did no information; when the information provided was not job-relevant, i.e., not diagnostic of occupational success, more stereotyping of women applicants occurred than when no information whatsoever was supplied. Thus, information, in and of itself, does not mitigate against stereotypes under all conditions. The type of information, its dramatic impact, and its specificity all are likely to be of importance. Drawing from Kelley (1967), it would also seem that information about which there is consensus (multiple sources) and which is consistent over time would be a forceful antidote to stereotypic processes.

Practical Implications

We have identified four general classes of sex bias: pre- and post-entry discrimination as well as pre- and post-entry self-limiting behavior. In terms of organizational action these can be facilitated or hindered by critical organizational processes such as recruitment, selection, performance appraisal, and feedback mechanisms. Each of these organizational processes are amenable to changes that preclude stereotypic beliefs from coloring inferences about a specific woman and/or short-circuit the gender-related assumptions held about many organizational roles. In this way organizations can structure such processes so as to *control* sex bias without necessarily eliminating the prejudiced beliefs and attitudes that give rise to it.

One might question why any measures at all should be taken to remedy sex bias in organizational life. After all, the sharp increase in the number of women enrolling in business schools, the cumulative effects of affirmative action programs, and the slow but steady increment in women managers should result in this problem working itself out over time. Indeed, social science research about racial integration suggests that discriminatory attitudes toward those in minority groups declines with increased exposure and disconfirmation of prior fears and expectations (e.g. Hamilton & Bishop, 1976). Nonetheless, there is reason to facilitate this process.

For one, societal stereotypes about women are extremely tenacious. We already have discussed the fact that sex stereotypes have changed only minimally over the years. It is clear that changing the attitudes and beliefs of an individual, male or female, who has accepted a traditional view of women is problematic. As Rosen and Jerdee (1975) have pointed out, there are many potential motivations for holding on to such sex stereotypes, some of which are quite complex. They suggest, for example, that men may view women as a potential threat or may react to them on the basis of earlier experiences with women. It also is conceivable that members of both sexes have a commitment to traditional values generally, and therefore are resistant to embracing a new image of what women are like. Any of these motives, and many more as well, are potential reasons for a rigid adherence to stereotypic thinking.

Secondly, there are organizational factors which can obstruct the evolution of a new view of women as competent, effective, and capable. An important one is the implementation of affirmative action programs. Recent data make painfully evident that if women placed in important positions are assumed to have obtained those positions only because they are women, not because they are deserving of them, the consequence is to reaffirm, not to disconfirm, stereotyped attitudes (Heilman, Note 3). Thus the very practice which should progress the cause of women at work can, unless cautiously implemented, work against them.

It therefore seems important to supplement the naturally occurring destereotyping process with planned efforts at reducing sex bias. For there are no guarantees that it will happen by itself. This chapter has carefully documented the cognitive calisthenics that we engage in which keep sex stereotypes intact and unchanged. It may well be that the wait for a shift in the conception of "woman" will be long and unrewarded. The capacity to *control* sex bias ultimately may be the best means we have to combat it.

CONCLUDING COMMENTS

We began this chapter by proposing that the impact of sex stereotypes on the career opportunities of women is neither inevitable nor invariable but can be situationally determined. The Lack of Fit model, by describing the dynamic giving rise to sex bias, is suggestive of how organizational procedures and practices can facilitate or hinder the adverse consequences of these stereotypes. According to the model, by restructuring critical processes in the work environment so as to minimize presumed lack of fit, the effects of stereotypes can be contained, and sex bias, whether other-directed or self-directed, can be reduced.

Although our discussion has been limited to examining sex bias as it pertains to women, it would be erroneous to leave readers with the impression that women alone suffer as a result of sex stereotypes. This is not so. There is evidence, for instance, that men are at a disadvantage when they apply for "feminine" jobs (Cohen & Bunker, 1975; Cash et al., 1977). Presumed lack of fit between person and job can have negative consequences for both sexes and sex bias can be directed at men as well as women. Typically, however, because few organizational positions are believed to require predominantly feminine skills for success, and these positions are rarely upper level ones, women bear the brunt of sex bias in efforts to advance up the organizational ladder.

Lastly, it should be noted that while this chapter has focused on bias in the work world that arise from *sex* stereotypes, the model and the research findings presented have relevance for any negatively stereotyped group. Assumptions of incompetence or of unsuitability for responsible positions are not unique to women. Others, also regarded as representatives of negatively viewed groups rather than as individuals in their own right, are equally susceptible to the discriminatory and self-limiting consequences of stereotypes, be they ethnic, racial, religious, or age-related in origin.

NOTES

1. This working definition confines the scope of sex stereotyping to the ascribing of sex-related traits. Readers should be aware that Terborg (1977) has made an important distinction between this aspect of sex stereotypes and a normative aspect which, rather than being descriptive of what males and females are like, dictates how they should behave.

REFERENCE NOTES

1. Vance, S. M. Male and female reactions to job descriptions as a function of job content and base-rates. Unpublished manuscript, New York University, 1981.

2. Heilman, M. E. Information as a deterrent against sex discrimination: The effects of applicant sex and information type on preliminary employment decisions. Submitted for editorial review.

3. Heilman, M. E., & Herlihy, J. M. Affirmative action, negative reaction? Manuscript in preparation.

REFERENCES

Ajzen, K. & Fishbein, H. Attitudinal and normative variables as predicators of specific behaviors. *Journal of Personality and Social Psychology*, 1973, *27*, 41–57.

Asch, S. E. The doctrine of suggestion, prestige and imitation in social psychology. *Psychological Review*, 1948, *55*, 250–276.

Bigoness, W. J. Effect of applicant's sex, race, and performance on employers' performance ratings: Some additional findings. *Journal of Applied Psychology*, 1976, *61*, 80–84.

Broverman, I. K., Vogel, R. S., Broverman, D. M., Clarkson, T. E., & Rosenkrantz, P. S. Sex-role stereotypes: A current appraisal. *Journal of Social Issues*, 1972, *28*, 59–78.

Cash T. F., Gillen, B., & Burns, D. S. Sexism and "beautyism" in personnel consultant decision making. *Journal of Applied Psychology*, 1977, *62*, 301–311.

Chapman, J. B. Comparison of male and female leadership styles. *Academy of Management Journal*, 1975, *18*, 645–650.

Cohen, S. L. & Bunker, K. A. Subtle effects of sex role stereotypes on recruiters' hiring decisions. *Journal of Applied Psychology*, 1975, *60*, 566–572.

Darley, S. Big-time careers for the little woman: A dual-role dilemma. *Journal of Social Issues*, 1976, *32*, 85–98.

Day, D. R., & Stogdill, R. M. Leader behavior of male and female supervisors: A comparative study. *Personnel Psychology*, 1972, *25*, 353–360.

Deaux, K. Sex: A perspective on the attribution process. In J. Harvey, W. J. Ickes & R. F. Kidd (Eds.), *New directions in attribution research*, Vol. 1. New Jersey: Lawrence Erlbaum Associates, 1976.

Deaux, K., & Emswiller, T. Explanation of successful performance on sexlinked tasks: What is skill for the male is luck for the female. *Journal of Personality and Social Psychology*, 1974, *29*, 80–85.

Deaux, K., & Farris, E. Attributing causes for one's own performance: The effects of sex, norms, and outcome. *Journal of Research in Personality*, 1977, *11*, 59–72.

Dipboye, R. L., Arvey, R. D., & Terpstra, D. E. Sex and physical attractiveness of raters and applicants as determinants of resume evaluations. *Journal of Applied Psychology*, 1977, *62*, 288–294.

Dipboye, R. L., Fromkin, H. L., & Wiback, K. Relative importance of applicant sex, attractiveness, and scholastic standing in evaluation of job applicant resumes. *Journal of Applied Psychology*, 1975, *60*, 39–43.

Dipboye, R. L., & Wiley, J. W. Reactions of college recruiters to interviewer sex and self-presentation style. *Journal of Vocational Behavior*, 1978, *10*, 1–12.

Eagly, A. H., & Carli, L. L. Sex of researchers and sex-typed communications as determinants of sex differences in influenceability: A meta-analysis of social influence studies. *Psychological Bulletin*, 1981, *90*, 1–20.

Feather, N. T., & Simon, J. G. Reactions to male and female success and failure in sex-linked occupations: Impressions of personality, causal attributions, and perceived likelihood of different consequences *Journal of Personality and Social Psychology*, 1975, *31*, 20–31.

Feldman, J. M. Beyond attribution theory: Cognitive processes in performance appraisal. *Journal of Applied Psychology*, 1981, *66*, 127–148.

Feldman-Summers, S., & Kiesler, S. B. Those who are number two try harder: The effect of sex on attributions of causality. *Journal of Personality and Social Psychology*, 1974, *30*, 846–855.

Fernberger, S. W. Persistence of sterotypes concerning sex differences. *Journal of Abnormal and Social Psychology*, 1948, *43*, 97–101.

Feshbach, N., & Sowes, G. Sex differences in adolescent reactions toward newcomers. *Developmental Psychology*, 1971, *4*, 381–386.

Fidell, L. A. Empirical verification of sex discrimination in hiring practices in psychology. *American Psychologist*, 1970, *25*, 1094–1098.

Garai, J. E., & Scheinfeld, A. Sex differences in mental and behavioral traits. *Genetic Psychology Monographs*, 1968, *77*, 169–299.

Garland, H., & Price, K. H. Attitudes toward women in management and attributions for their success and failure in a managerial position. *Journal of Applied Psychology*, 1977, *62*, 29–33.

Goldberg, P. A. Are women prejudiced against women? *Transaction*, April, 1968, 28–30.

Gross, E. The sexual structure of occupations over time. Paper presented at the meeting of the American Sociological Association, August, 1967.

Hamilton, D. L. & Bishop, G. D. Attitudinal and behavioral effects of initial integration of white suburban neighborhoods. *Journal of Social Issues*, 1976, *32*, 47–67.

Hammer, W. C., Kim, J. S., Baird, L., & Bigoness, W. J. Race and sex as determinants of ratings by potential employers in a simulated worksampling task. *Journal of Applied Psychology*, 1974, *59*, 705–711.

Heilman, M. E. Miss, Mrs. Ms., or none of the above? Effects of an instructor's title on course desirability. *American Psychologist*, 1975, *30*, 516–518.

Heilman, M. E. High school students' occupational interest as a function of projected sex ratios in male-dominated occupations. *Journal of Applied Psychology*, 1979, *64*, (3), 275–279.

Heilman, M. E. The impact of situational factors on personnel decisions concerning women: Varing the sex composition of the applicant pool. *Organizational Behavior and Human Performance*, 1980, *26*, 386–395.

Heilman, M. E., & Guzzo, R. A. The perceived cause of work success as a mediator of sex discrimination in organizations. *Organizational Behavior and Human Performance*, 1978, *21*, 346–357.

Heilman, M. E., & Kram, K. Self-derogating behavior in women—fixed or flexible: The effects of co-worker's sex. *Organizational Behavior and Human Performance*, 1978, *22*, 497–507.

Heilman, M. E., & Saruwatari, L. When beauty is beastly: The effects of appearance and sex on evaluations of job applicants for managerial and nonmanagerial jobs. *Organizational Behavior and Human Performance*, 1979, *23*, 360–372.

Higgins, E. T. Social class differences in verbal communicative accuracy: A question of "which question?" *Psychological Bulletin*, 1976, *83*, 695–714.

Kanter, R. M. *Men and women of the corporation.* New York: Basic Books, 1977b.

Kelley, H. H. Attribution theory in social psychology. In D. Levine (Ed.), *Nebraska Symposium on Motivation*, Vol. 15 Lincoln: University of Nebraska Press, 1967.

Kiesler, S. Acturial prejudice toward women and its implications. *Journal of Applied Social Psychology*, 1975, *5*, 201–216.

Krefting, L. A., Berger, P. K., & Wallace, M. J., Jr. The contribution of sex distribution, job content, and occupational classification to job sex typing: Two studies. *Journal of Vocational Behavior*, 1978, *13*, 181–191.

Leder, G. C. Sex differences in mathematics problem appeal as a function of problem context. *Journal of Educational Research*, 1974, *67*, 351–353.

Maccoby, E. E. *The development of sex differences.* Stanford, Calif.: Stanford University Press, 1966.

Maccoby, E. E., & Jacklin, C. N. *The psychology of sex differences.* Stanford, Calif.: Stanford University Press, 1974.

Matthews, E. Employment implications of psychological characteristics of men and women. In M. E. Katzell, & W. C. Byham (Eds.), *Women in the work force*. New York: Behavioral Publications, 1972.

McArthur, L., & Post, D. Figural emphasis and person perception. *Journal of Experimental Social Psychology*, 1977.

McKee, J. P., & Sherriffs, A. C. The differential evaluation of males and females. *Journal of Personality*, 1957, *25*, 356–371.

McKee, J. P., & Sherriffs, A. C. Men's and women's beliefs, ideals, and self concepts. *American Journal of Sociology*, 1959, *65*, 356–363.

McMahon, I. D. Relationships between causal attributions and expectancy of success. *Journal of Personality and Social Psychology*, 1973, *28*, 108–114.

Miner, John B. Motivational potential for upgrading among minority and female managers. *Journal of Applied Psychology*, 1977, *62*, 691–697.

Nicholls, J. G. Causal attributions and other achievement-related cognitions: Effects of task outcome, attainment value and sex. Journal of *Personality and Social Psychology*, 1975, *31*, 379–389.

Oetzel, R. M. Annotated bibliography. In E. E. Maccoby (Ed.), *The Development of Sex Differences*. Stanford: Stanford University Press, 1966.

Pheterson, G. I., Kiesler, S. B., & Goldberg, P. A. Evaluation of the performance of women as a function of their sex, achievement, and personal history. *Journal of Personality and Social Psychology*, 1971, *19*, 114–118.

Renwick, P. A., & Tosi, H. The effects of sex, marital status, and educational background on selection decisions. *Academy of Management Journal*, 1978, *21*, 93–103.

Rose, G. L., & Andiappan, P. Sex effects on managerial hiring decisions. *Academy of Management Journal*, 1978, *21*, 104–112.

Rosen, B., & Jerdee, T. H. Effects of applicants' sex and difficulty on evaluations of candidates for managerial positions. *Journal of Applied Psychology*, 1974, *59*, 511–512.

Rosen, B., & Jerdee, T. H. The psychological basis for sex-role stereotypes: A note on Terborg and Ilgen's conclusions. *Organizational Behavior and Human Performance*, 1975, *14*, 151–153.

Rosenkrantz, P. S., Vogel, S. R., Bee, H., Broverman, I. K., & Broverman, D. M. Sex-role stereotypes and self-concepts in college students. *Journal of Consulting and Clinical Psychology*, 1968, *32*, 287–295.

Ruble, D. N. Visual orientation and self-perceptions of children in an external-cue-relevant task situation. *Child Development*, 1975, *46*, 669–676.

Schein, V. E. The relationship between sex-role stereotypes and requisite management characteristics. *Journal of Applied Psychology*, 1973, *57*, 95–100.

Schein, V. E. Relationships between sex-role stereotypes and requisite management characteristics among female managers. *Journal of Applied Psychology*, 1975, *60*, 340–344.

Shaw, E. A. Differential impact of negative stereotyping in employee selection. *Personnel Psychology*, 1972, *25*, 333–338.

Sherriffs, A. C., & McKee, J. P. Qualitative aspects of beliefs about men and women. *Journal of Personality*, 1957, *25*, 451–464.

Shinar, E. H. Sexual stereotypes of occupations. *Journal of Vocational Behavior*, 1975, *7*, 99–111.

Spence, J. T., Helmreich, R., & Stapp, J. Likability, sex-role congruence of interest, and competence: It all depends on how you ask. *Journal of Applied Social Psychology*, 1975, *5*, 93–109.

Taylor, S. E. Fiske, S. T., Etcoff, N. L., & Ruderman, A. J. Categorial and contextual bases of person memory and stereotyping. *Journal of Personality and Social Psychology*, 1978, *36*, 778–793.

Terborg, J. R. Women in management: A research review. *Journal of Applied Psychology*, 1977, *62*, 647–664.

Terborg, J. R., & Ilgen, D. R. A theoretical approach to sex discrimination in traditionally masculine occupations. *Organizational Behavior and Human Performance*, 1975, *13*, 352–376.

Tyler, L. E. *The Psychology of human differences*. New York: Appleton-Century Crafts, 1965.

U. S. Bureau of Labor Statistics. *Employment and Earnings*, January, 1980.

Vogel, S. K., Broverman, I. K., Broverman, D. M., Clarkson, F. E., & Rosenkrantz, P. S. Maternal employment and perception of sex-roles among college students. *Developmental Psychology*, 1970, *3*, 384–391

Zellman, G. The role of structural factors in limiting women's institutional participation. *Journal of Social Issues*, 1976, *32*, 33–46.

Zickmund, W. G., Hitt, M. A., & Pickens, B. A. Influence of sex and scholastic performance on reactions to job applicant resumes. *Journal of Applied Psychology*, 1978, *63*, 252–255.

UNDERSTANDING COMPARABLE WORTH:
A SOCIETAL AND POLITICAL PERSPECTIVE

Thomas A. Mahoney

ABSTRACT

The topic of comparable worth elicits various extreme reactions from individuals, interest groups, labor unions, and employers. The topic appears in civil rights litigation, National Academy of Sciences research, presidential campaigns, and legislative proposals at both state and federal levels. What is analyzed here as the comparable worth *doctrine* is reasonably straight-forward—equal pay for jobs of comparable (equal) worth. As such, the doctrine probably enjoys relatively wide acceptance in society.

What we analyze as the comparable worth *phenomenon* can be characterized as a social–political movement with associated extreme advocacy and extreme criticism and rejection. The comparable worth doctrine is a general philosophical approach to compensating work in different occupations. And the comparable worth phenomenon is characterized as seeking a restructuring of occupational wages to increase the relative economic power and influence of women in our society.

The comparable worth phenomenon is best understood as seeking redistribution of economic power in our society through restructuring occupational earnings. It appears as a challenge to existing social norms of occupational worth. As such it is more of a social–political movement than a challenge to the process of job evaluation. The process of job evaluation can accommodate any criterion of job worth, but is dependent on some prior consensus of relative job or occupational worth. Achieving consensus on a norm of occupational worth is primarily a political task.

"The looniest idea since Looney Tunes came on the screen" is the topic of this essay. While this characterization may have been appropriate for other concepts of interest to organization behaviorists in the past, it was publicly assigned to the concept of comparable worth in 1984 by Clarence M. Pendleton, Jr., chairman of the U.S. Civil Rights Commission (*Wall Street Journal*, December 10, 1984). Despite Mr. Pendleton's assessment, the concept of comparable worth has advanced from a slogan of various women's interest groups to a major social phenomenon evidenced in enactments by state legislatures, proposals for national legislation, and espousal by one candidate for the presidency in the 1984 elections. Looney or not, the emergence of social and political activity associated with the concept of comparable worth provides abundant research opportunities for organizational behavior scientists and provides challenges to behavioral scientists to explain the extreme attention achieved by and controversy generated around an allegedly "looney idea."

Issues related to the concept of comparable worth have stimulated considerable research (largely by economists and sociologists), attracted ardent advocate groups as well as equally ardent groups of critics, stimulated a major research effort sponsored by the Equal Employment Opportunities Commission and conducted by the National Academy of Sciences, engendered position papers and books advocating and criticizing the concept, and was the subject of public hearings by the U.S. Civil Rights Commission (Treiman & Hartman, 1981; Livernash, 1980; Grune, no date; U.S. Commission on Civil Rights, 1984). Positions taken range from the "looniest idea" characterization to "*the* civil rights issue of the 1980s" and "a moral idea that deserves to be taken seriously" (Gardner, 1985). It is impossible in the available space to provide the definitive statement on comparable worth. Nor is it likely that the statement presented here will win unquestioned acceptance by the combatant scholars, attorneys, and spokespersons for the various political interest groups aligned with comparable worth issues. Of necessity, this statement is a personal statement from an interested, reasonably objective observer of the comparable worth phenomenon. It is intended to provide a general context for understanding the broad phenomenon and to serve as a stimulant for scholarly analysis and research.

What is termed here the *phenomenon* of comparable worth refers to the emergence and development of a social movement translated into political action interest groups working through judicial and legislative processes to secure change in the way wages and earnings are determined for occupations staffed predominantly by women. The stated objective or doctrine appears relatively simple. It is to obtain "equal pay for jobs of comparable (e.g., equal) worth" or, in more recent terminology, to secure "pay equity." Stated at this level of doctrinal abstraction, there is little basis for disagreement with the objective of the advocates of comparable worth. In fact, the objective of "equal pay for jobs of equal worth" might well have been enunciated by management, labor, and public spokesmen for at least the last half-century, long before the origin of what is termed the *comparable worth movement*.

Controversy arises only when we examine proposed policies and programs to achieve pay equity through equal pay for jobs of comparable worth, and the theories of equity and worth that support these proposed policies. *At present there is no single, accepted construct of comparable worth*. Different constructs are advanced by different interest groups, usually to rationalize or justify different policies and programs for wage determination. The confusion over the construct of comparable worth can be understood only within the context of competing policies for wage determination, policies with different effects on the structuring of income distribution in society. This essay advances the argument that the comparable worth phenomenon can be understood only through consideration of social values and issues as well as traditional economic models of wage determination.

Much of what is known as "organizational behavior" (OB) addresses issues of employee behavior and motivation, issues such as commitment, turnover, productivity, decision making, and the like. The phenomenon of comparable worth may be less familiar to readers than more traditional OB topics, in part because it often is cast as an issue of economics or of political and social analysis. *What makes comparable worth such a fascinating topic is that it truly lies at the intersection of so many related disciplines*. No single discipline can provide an adequate analysis of the comparable worth phenomenon although many contribute relevant concepts and theories. Analysis of the phenomenon provides an opportunity for re-integration of organizational behavior with other related disciplines in focusing on an important phenomenon concerning work, motivation, poverty, social justice, political activity, and conflict.

Our analysis begins with an examination of the background and problem or issue motivating the comparable worth movement. Next we review the theories of wage determination and relevant research based on those theories. Finally, we examine constructs of comparable worth advanced as policy proposals and the likely effects of their implementation in policy. Throughout we suggest topics for further study and analysis.

BACKGROUND

The term *comparable worth phenomenon* has been employed advisedly in the introduction. It is meant to connote that the subject of this inquiry is the full spectrum of political, social, and legal concerns relative to the concept of comparable worth. It is argued, for example, that analysis of the concept in merely legal or economic terms is inadequate for understanding the range of social and political efforts associated with comparable worth. Understanding of the phenomenon requires analysis of the historical evolution and development of labor markets, processes of wage determination, gender composition of the workforce, and values held in our society.

Although the doctrine of equal pay for jobs of comparable (equal) worth is gender neutral, the phenomenon of comparable worth has developed as a gender-related movement. Given long-term acceptance of the doctrine of comparable worth, why has the phenomenon of comparable worth developed only recently and why is it a gender (female) concern? The comparable worth phenomenon emerged with and reflects the profound changes in labor force participation and employment patterns of women over the past 40 years. Another related influence has been the associated change in social values and political influence of women beginning in the 1960s and evidenced in part by the civil rights movements of that time. Examination of the comparable worth phenomenon requires an understanding of the context, particularly (1) the changed role of women in the workforce, (2) women's earnings, and (3) civil rights legislation. All bear upon the issue.

Women in the Workforce

Female participation in the labor force, working outside the home for wages, has changed dramatically during this century, particularly during the period 1950–1980. In 1890, only 15% of women in the age group 25–44 were wage earners; by 1980, the participation rate had increased to 60%. The most dramatic increases occurred during the period 1950–1980, when the participation rate increased from 29% to 60%. Analyses of the increased employment of women indicate that the largest increases were due to increased employment of women with children. About 80% of single women without children were wage earners in both 1950 and 1980. However, the employment rate increased from 12% to 45% for women with children under 6-years-old, and increased from 26% to over 60% for women with children aged 6–17 (Fuchs, 1983). Clearly there has been a dramatic change in the employment of women, particularly married women and women with children, over the past 30 years. In consequence, the proportion of the labor force which is female increased from 18% in 1900 to 28% in 1950 and 47% in 1980.

The increased employment of married women has been attributed to a variety of influences and is cited as influencing various changes in family consumption patterns, the education and upbringing of children, and family and social values. Although causal inferences are limited, there are a number of social changes that at least paralleled the increased employment of married women. For example, the increase in female wage earners occurred as the service industries expanded and grew relative to goods-producing sectors. It was only natural that the service industries provided most of the employment opportunities for women entering the workforce. Over three fourths of the expanded employment of women occurred in the finance, trade, and service industries. The market for services doubtless also expanded as women became employed and were less able to perform traditional household services.

Divorce rates in the United States also rose during the last 30 years as well as the number of single-parent families; the annual divorce rate doubled from 10 to 20 per thousand between 1965–1975, for example, and the proportion of children living with a single parent rose from 10% in 1950 to 25% in 1980 (Fuchs, 1983).

Cultural values concerning the role of women in society and particularly the role of women in the workplace have been changing. The historical presence of a Women's Bureau in the Department of Labor evidences a predominantly male orientation, as did the designation "manpower" and the commonly employed gender references in the *Dictionary of Occupational Titles,* which were changed only recently. Norms of male dominance were clearly associated with the role of males as family breadwinners prior to the 1950s; movies of the 1940s and 1950s as well as the television series "The Honeymooners" clearly display these values. Women, if employed outside the home, typically were found in the needle trades or in office and secretarial jobs, and were considered to be working only until marriage when they would withdraw from the labor force. Only 26% of the population aged 65 and older in 1985 reported mothers who had worked at least one year after marriage; by contrast, 80% of the population aged 18–24 reported mothers working at least a year after marriage (*Public Opinion,* 1985). Family and home were considered the domain of women and work was the domain of men. As recently as 1974, 63% of women reported that they would prefer to stay home rather than work; this proportion declined to 48% by 1983 (*Public Opinion,* 1984).

The large-scale introduction of women into employment and work roles brought about a clash between traditional male values, norms, and behaviors and those of working women. This clash is evidenced in part by the many seminars and self-help manuals that counsel working women about traditional male work norms and how to cope with them. It is evidenced also by potential conflict between the work and job demands of working spouses; 47% of adults even today report that a husband's job demands should take priority as compared with 1% giving priority to a wife's job demands (*Public Opinion*, 1984). Finally, the changing work and household roles of men and women provide the focus for at least two popular daily comic strips (Adam; Sally Forth), comic strips that would have had no audience 20 years ago.

Earnings of Employed Women

Work norms and values are expressed in many ways—job titles, dress, and particularly pay systems. Pay is often analyzed as an economic exchange, which it is. But pay and pay systems also symbolize many values regarding work, and these values may be more important at times than the economic-exchange aspect of pay. Pay differentials, for example, signify hierarchy, power, and status aspects of work relationships. It is important, for example, that a supervisor be paid more than those supervised if the authority of the supervisor is to be accepted (Mahoney, 1979b). Status relationships also exist among nonsupervisory workers, and pay relationships inconsistent with those status relationships are not accepted by the workforce. Whyte (1955) has reported on the dysfunctional consequences of wage incentives that permit workers to earn more than nonincentive workers with higher-status jobs; and Goodman (1979) reported similar consequences for a Quality of Work Life (QWL) experiment that altered traditional pay relationships. We know relatively little about the origins or determinants of job status other than the association with hierarchy and pay. Certainly pay relationships symbolize status, particularly in an organizational context, and evidence value conflict if confronted with a competing and contradictory status hierarchy.

A world of work dominated by males could be expected to express status and value systems supportive of male values. Women workers traditionally were viewed as less committed to a work career and less valuable to an employer. Caricatured as less responsible for family financial support and working only for "pin money," employment of women at lower rates of pay than males was rationalized as consistent with dominant work values. Today the reasons for and motivation to work are more similar for men and women. A 1983 opinion survey reported that 63% of employed women and 66% of employed men gave economic necessity as their primary motivation for work (*Public Opinion*, 1984). This comparability of employment motivations of men and women provides challenge to the value system underlying traditional pay systems and pay relationships.

In summary, our society changed dramatically during the period 1950–1980, particularly with respect to the roles enacted by women. Women today are more likely to seek advanced education in professional and technical fields, to seek career employment outside the home, and, in consequence, to be influenced by values competing with those associated with motherhood and homemaking. These changes have been manifested in women's clothing styles, the use of time-saving household appliances, the growth of eating out and of ready-to-serve packaged foods, and the demand for childcare facilities to serve working mothers.

There is one characteristic of working women that has demonstrated little change over the period, however. The earnings of working women average about 60% of the earnings of employed men, only slightly higher than the proportion observed 50 years ago. Despite the success of women in securing legal equal access to jobs, credit, and education, the earnings of women as a class have not improved significantly relative to men's earnings. Job and career have become important sources of self-identity and worth to employed women and these are threatened by social comparison of earnings of men and women.

Economic equity and justice concepts are based in social comparison. Relative deprivation is experienced when one perceives that he or she receives less than a comparison other. Women, as a class, have sought and, in many ways, achieved treatment equal to that of men as a class. And yet women's earnings average less than men's earnings, occasioning perceptions of relative deprivation. Despite rights to equal access and treatment, the consequence or impact does not appear equal as regards earnings.

This sense of relative deprivation is intensified by the fact of higher divorce rates over the past 20 years, with the consequence of a larger incidence of female single-parent households and the related financial obligations. Twenty-five percent of children were living in single-parent households in 1980 (usually female), and 51% of those lived in poverty conditions as compared with only 8% of children in husband–wife households (Fuchs, 1983). Perceptions of relative deprivation doubtless relate to living standards as well as to earnings for employment.

Stimuli for the comparable worth phenomenon doubtless include perceptions of personal relative deprivation and inequity and perceptions of class relative deprivation with regard to both rewards for employment and incomes and associated living standards. *The comparable worth phenomenon is a mixture of employment issues (earnings) and social issues (status, income and power).* Concern for equity in earnings is motivated in part by concern for gender equality in income, status, and economic power in society at large. These concerns blend as motivation for the comparable worth movement, although the comparable worth doctrine speaks strictly to employment and earnings issues and only indirectly to social and income issues.

Civil Rights Legislation

Development of the comparable worth phenomenon also has been influenced by legislation during the 1960s, particularly the Civil Rights Act of 1964, Title VII of which relates to employment discrimination. There had been concern about wage differentiation between men and women prior to the 1960s, but it was only in 1963 that it was addressed in public policy despite numerous prior attempts to enact similar legislation. The Equal Pay Act of 1963 specifically forbids wage discrimination "between employees on the basis of sex when employees perform equal work on jobs in the same establishment requiring equal skill, effort, and responsibility and performed under similar working conditions," unless based on a seniority system, merit system, quality or quantity of performance, or any other factor other than sex. It became public policy that men and women performing substantially identical jobs should be paid equally, unless different payment is justified on the basis of specified criteria "other than sex." The work performed and not the gender of the worker should be the basis for pay.

The civil rights movement of the 1960s accomplished significant change in the social order and structure of the United States. In a very real sense, that movement was directed toward change in the power structure of society by opening access to power to various protected classes. Title VII of the Civil Rights Act of 1964 focused on discrimination in employment and sought change in employment practices that had discriminated among classes in the distribution of economic opportunities, rewards, and power associated with employment. Although women were specified as a protected class almost at the last minute in the legislative process, they are as a class protected against discrimination in employment practices including compensation. What constitutes discrimination under the provisions of Title VII has been the subject of guidelines and rulings of the EEOC and litigation in the courts. One significant aspect of the comparable worth phenomenon has been a series of efforts to incorporate particular comparable worth constructs into accepted definitions of discrimination.

Two broad definitions of discrimination under Title VII have evolved, one relating to access and treatment and the other relating to outcome and impact (Ledvinka, 1982). Briefly, the first definition *(disparate treatment)* identifies as discrimination any intentional, prejudicial treatment in employment practices for individuals or classes of individuals protected under the act. For example, systematic exclusion of members of a protected class from employment, as in a "men only" requirement or subjecting members of a protected class to more-stringent hiring criteria, would be judged as discriminatory unless demonstrated as necessary for job performance. Similarly, a practice of systematically paying women less than men in the same job would be discriminatory treatment (also prohibited by the Equal Pay Act of 1963). Members of protected classes are to be provided access and treatment equal to that of nonprotected classes. The second definition *(disparate impact)* identifies as discrimination any employment practice with unequal or disparate outcomes or impacts upon protected classes, despite equal treatment. Discriminatory impact would apply to any non–job related practice which, although applied equally to all applicants, excludes a larger proportion of protected class applicants. An example might be physical requirements for employment, not truly required for successful performance, which exclude a larger proportion of women than men applicants. Similarly, it might be argued that a pay system that rewards tall people (more often males) more than short people (more often females) discriminatorily impacts on women unless it can be shown that height truly is indicative of greater productivity and, thus, worth to the employer. In practice, discriminatory treatment has been identified for individuals and classes of individuals, while discriminatory impact has been identified for classes, and is usually demonstrated with statistical analysis; large numbers permit statistical analysis that may be irrelevant for a single individual (Bohlander, 1980).

The argument for comparable worth usually addresses differential payment for occupations dominated by men and occupations dominated by women.[1] Whatever the rationale and intent of differential payment, it is argued that women's occupations are underpaid relative to men's occupations of comparable (equal) worth. It is argued that lower wages for women's occupations of worth equal to higher-paid men's occupations is discriminatory. Advocates of a comparable worth concept argue that female-dominated occupations are undervalued by employers and in market surveys. This undervaluation may reflect normative values of a previously male workforce and/or perpetuation of historical occupational wage differentials from the labor market, whatever the original cause of those differentials. It is not clear what standard is proposed for the valuation of jobs in the determination of comparable worth discrimination, but some standard other than existing historical wage differentials is sought. Proof of nondiscrimination requires advancement of a measure of occupational or job worth to challenge differential payment, and much of the argument about comparable worth revolves around definition of a measure of worth.

At present, comparable worth discrimination is not an accepted legal doctrine and there has been no clear test of a comparable worth interpretation of Title VII (See Bureau of National Affairs, 1984b, for an overview of legislation and litigation). Judicial decisions to date, for example, have accepted market survey evidence in justification of occupational wages despite plaintiffs' arguments to reject market comparisons as a measure of worth. Similarly, job evaluations of worth have not been rejected if applied equally to the affected jobs. The U.S. Civil Rights Commission announced an opinion in April 1985, that the concept of comparable worth should not be developed as a test of wage discrimination under Title VII and should not be the basis for new wage-discrimination legislation (*Wall Street Journal,* April 12, 1985). The commission is only advisory, however, and federal legislation concerning wage discrimination is pending. Further, the courts have not rejected the concept of comparable worth as invalid. At time of writing, the ultimate legal status of comparable worth definitions of wage discrimination is still uncertain.

Responding to advocates and critics of the comparable worth criterion, the EEOC commissioned a study into the topic by the National Academy of Sciences. A report of that study has been published, but the EEOC has not chosen to provide any clarifying interpretations based on that report (Treiman & Hartmann, 1981). Most recently, the EEOC announced in a policy decision that it will only pursue cases of wage discrimination where employer intent to pay different wages to men and women in comparable jobs can be demonstrated (*Wall Street Journal,* June 18, 1985). At the time of writing, it does not appear that the EEOC will pursue the differential impact test of wage discrimination; differential payment of comparable jobs will be judged as discriminatory only where a consequence of intent to discriminate is found.

Despite the inconclusive status of the comparable worth criterion in federal legislation, state legislation has proceeded more rapidly to address the issue, particularly with respect to public employees (Bureau of National Affairs, 1984b). In general, state legislation is directed toward achieving what is termed "equitable compensation" relationships between female-dominated and male-dominated classes of employees. The Minnesota law, for example, defines *equitable relationships* as existing "when the primary consideration [in setting compensation] . . . is comparability of the value of the work" and goes on to define *comparability* as "the value of the work measured by the composite of skill, effort, responsibility, and working conditions." It is interesting that some comparable worth criterion of equity has been endorsed by states as employers in advance of judicial clarification of the concept within the framework of Title VII and in advance of clarifying legislation by the federal government. It is also interesting that state legislation has addressed wage equity issues directly in legislation without incorporating the issue with civil rights and discrimination concerns; wage equity is prescribed as an employment practice. Reasons for the concentration of comparable worth and pay equity efforts in the public sector are suggested later (pp. 237–238). The redirection of efforts toward individual employer pay practices rather than toward incorporation of the comparable worth doctrine in interpretations of civil rights protection probably reflects the relative lack of success to date in the latter effort as well as increasing awareness of the responsiveness of individual employers to direct action.

What we have termed the comparable worth phenomenon is an amalgam of attitudes, values, and behavior, particularly concerning women in our society. Women have entered the workforce on a large scale with expectations for careers and incomes comparable to those of men, yet their earnings approximate only 60% of male earnings. Not unexpectedly, many experience frustration as they seek to realize the prestige, power, and independence typically associated with male employment. Civil rights legislation appeared to promise equality, and the lack of realized equality in earnings tends to be attributed to discrimination. The comparable worth doctrine of equal pay for work of comparable worth suggests to many a means of reducing the earnings gap and thus attracts considerable attention. Evaluation of the likely effects of application of this doctrine, however, requires examination of reasons for the earnings gap and of links between those reasons and practical application of the comparable worth doctrine. Whether comparable worth is a "looney idea" or not depends critically on the standard advanced for measuring job and occupational worth and the theory supporting that standard. What we call the comparable worth doctrine may well be supported on moral and philosophical grounds, while a proposed application of the doctrine in a standard for assessing worth for purposes of judging wage discrimination is rejected as a looney idea. We turn next to explanations of the earnings gap and theories of job worth as they bear upon the concept of comparable worth.

Wage Theory and the Earnings Gap

Broadly speaking, the comparable worth phenomenon focuses attention on the gap in earnings between employed men and women, and advocates of comparable worth seek to reduce that gap. Advocates of comparable worth charge that much of the earnings gap is due to pay discrimination of one sort or another and seek to overcome the effects of alleged discrimination through alteration of the pay structure in society. The existence of a male–female earnings gap in the U.S. has been widely documented and is not disputed. What is disputed are the reasons for that earnings gap and, thus, policy implications for change in the earnings gap. Note that the earnings gap refers to employed men and women as classes in society and not necessarily to employed men and women in a single organization. Title VII addresses discrimination at the level of the employing organization; yet, most research into potential explanations of the earnings gap is macro in orientation and any inference of findings to individual employers is limited.

Measures of the gender earnings gap cited in the literature vary depending on the measure of the earnings that is employed. Annual earnings, for example, vary with both the rate of payment and the amount of time worked. In 1979, for example, it is estimated that only 35% of white females worked full-time all year as compared with 75% of white males, with consequent lower annual earnings for the women (Berger, 1984). Similarly, employed women work on average fewer hours per week than do employed men. Reasons for this difference in employment experience doubtless are varied and would include personal choices about time allocation. Estimated weekly earnings of full-time employed women in 1982 are reported to average 65% of the weekly earnings of full-time employed men, for example, a ratio somewhat larger than the often cited 59–60% ratio for annual earnings. Nevertheless, there remains an earnings gap regardless of the measures chosen for comparison.

Examination of wage rates and earnings in our society reveals an array of different rates of payment. Rates of payment vary from less than the federal minimum wage of $3.35 an hour to more than one million dollars a year. Many factors other than gender are associated with this array of wage rates and, to the extent that these factors also vary with gender, must be considered in the explanation of a gender earnings gap before discrimination can be accepted as a major cause of the earnings gap. The explanation of differentials in wages and earnings is an issue addressed in economic theory. Traditionally, economics has been relatively more concerned with the explanation of observed wage differentials, and other social sciences such as psychology and sociology have been relatively more concerned with the consequences of wage and earnings differentials. The various economic theories of wage determination are of more relevance to an understanding of reasons for the earnings gap and thus the likely consequences of policy proposals addressing comparable worth as they affect the earnings gap. The theories and concepts reviewed are classified into traditional market and institutional models of wage determination, reflecting the degree of dependence upon market concepts.

Market models. Most of the traditional economic analyses of wage structure are cast in terms of market models in which wages are viewed as the price of labor and are the consequence of various influences of labor demand and supply. The market model, while useful as a guiding concept, is difficult to apply in the empirical analysis of wage structures. In simple form, the market model implies a single wage rate at which demand and supply are equated. There is, however, no single market for labor and we observe a wide array of wage rates. A troublesome issue in any attempt to define parameters of the labor market is the definition of the item being traded. Analyses of labor supply tend to be cast in terms of the characteristics of workers who offer services for hire; analyses of labor demand, however, tend to be cast in terms of the job to be staffed and performed as represented by occupation and industry. In abstract terms we can conceptualize a match between worker characteristics and job requirements, but this match is difficult to identify in operational terms, as decades of selection research in industrial and personnel psychology testify. Analyses of wage structures relevant to explanation of the gender earnings gap have addressed both worker and job characteristics as explanations for differences in earnings; the first addresses human capital characteristics of men and women and the second addresses occupational and industrial employment of men and women.

1. *Human capital.* The general concept of human capital that has received attention from economists in recent years is based on assumptions that productive capabilities of workers are valued by employers and can be acquired and developed by workers (Becker, 1964). Employers seek more-skilled workers because they are more productive, and hence employers are willing to pay a wage differential for skill. Workers are willing to invest in acquisition of a skill to the extent that loss of current earnings will be compensated for by a higher future earnings stream. Human capital theory predicts wage differentials associated with labor-supply characteristics such as education, skill, and experience, which presumably are more productive of output in a job and thus more valuable to an employer.

Human capital theory provides one potential explanation of the gender earnings gap. To the extent that men possess greater education, skill, and experience than women, they would be expected to earn more than women. Because, in general, males historically have constituted a larger proportion of university graduates and apprenticeship program trainees, and have acquired more experience through continuous labor force participation, we might expect males to possess greater human capital than females and to receive relatively higher earnings.

Various analyses of human capital explanations of the gender earnings gap have been conducted with mixed results, partly as a function of sample differences and partly as a function of consideration of different explanatory variables (see Treiman & Hartmann, 1981, for a summary). Most of these analyses examine some measure of earnings (hourly or annual) at a given point in time. Observed earnings ratios vary from 46% (annual) to 82% (hourly). Typical human capital measures analyzed include education, age, labor market experience, and tenure; other control variables occasionally included are race, mental ability, training, marital status, health, hours of work, size of city, region, and absenteeism. The adjusted earnings ratios obtained from these analyses range from 56% (Sawhill, 1973) to 85% (Corcoran & Duncan, 1979); up to 41%–44% of the observed earnings gap is attributed to differences in human capital measures (Corcoran & Duncan, 1979; Mincer & Polachek, 1974).

A recent study by Smith and Ward (1984) is illustrative of human capital analyses of the earnings gap. Smith and Ward examine the earnings of men and women as a function of years of education and years of labor force experience, which they term *skill-related variables*. The lower earnings of working women are attributed to lower levels of education and of work experience. Until recently, the average education of working women was lower than that of all women because of lower labor force participation rates for educated women; the average education of women also lagged behind that of men. Similarly, because of lower labor force participation of women, the years of work experience for working women was considerably less than that for working men. Increased education and work experience of women are projected, and Smith and Ward estimate that the wages of working women will increase at least 15% faster than the wages of working men over the next 20 years. Thus the earnings gap is attributed to differences in productive potential of working men and women and it will narrow and disappear as differences in productive potential narrow and disappear.

A basic issue of concern in these analyses is the specification of personal characteristics to be analyzed as human capital indicators. Human capital concepts are rationalized as contributing to greater productivity, yet this productivity typically is assumed and not demonstrated. Thus, although variance in earnings may be associated with the measures, variance in productivity is only assumed. Polachek (1975) goes farther than others to argue that human capital accumulation throughout life also influences earnings, and he advances continuity of labor force experience as a human capital indicator. Intermittent experience, he argues, is associated with depreciation of prior skills acquired as well as loss of continued skill development. Women typically interrupt their employment more than men, and factoring continuity of labor force experience into the analyses permits attribution of nearly 100% of the earnings gap to male–female differences in human capital characteristics of labor supply.

Empirical analyses of the earnings gap employing concepts from human capital theory suffer from imperfect linkages between human capital concepts and indicator variables used to measure human capital. In theory, employers should be willing to pay a premium for more-productive employees. Lacking direct measures of individual productivity potential, we can only infer this potential productivity on the basis of logical argument. The history of employee-selection research and the typical constraint of validity coefficients to $r = .40$ suggests the difficulty of identifying valid indicators of employee performance even within relatively controlled contexts. Thus, although most of the earnings gap might be statistically attributed to personal characteristics termed *human capital*, it is unlikely that these characteristics are valid indicators of productivity potential and that the earnings gap is solely a function of productivity potential.

Human capital concepts from economics employed in the explanation of earnings differentials parallel concepts often advanced from social comparison models to explain perceptions of equity and inequity (Homans, 1961; Adams, 1965). Briefly, so-called equity theory proposes that individuals judge the equity of their outcome relative to that of someone else. It is hypothesized that these judgments focus on ratios of outcome to input, and that a disadvantageous comparison with another evokes judgments of inequitable treatment. This social comparison model would argue that equity of treatment consists of equivalent outcomes for equivalent inputs, and proportionally different outcomes for different inputs. Applied to the context of employment and earnings, human capital models and social comparison models both arrive at the same conclusion—that equivalent units of labor input ought to be paid the same—although for different reasons. Human capital theory bases that conclusion on assumptions of efficient market exchanges, whereas social comparison theory bases the conclusion on social norms of equity. In the first instance, the conclusion is a predicted outcome, and in the second instance it is a prescribed outcome. Although the same comparison variables (e.g., education) often are employed in both models, human capital theory rationalizes the variables in terms of imputed productivity and social comparison theory rationalizes the variables in terms of prior investment.

Human capital concepts are applied in a social comparison framework to focus attention on the inequity of the gender earnings gap when it is observed that lifetime earnings of male high school drop-outs exceed those of female college graduates (*Wall Street Journal*, 1983). They also are presented in allegations of discrimination when, for example, it is noted that female nurses with more education are paid less than male tree trimmers. Human capital measures are more closely associated with individuals than with occupations, however, and thus are of more direct relevance for analysis of a gender earnings gap in society than for analysis of occupational wage differentials. Given considerable variability of human capital and related concepts of labor supply inputs within any occupation (e.g., high school drop-outs and college graduates driving cabs), there is no unique set of human capital measures associated with a single occupation. Thus, human capital concepts are only of peripheral relevance in comparing the earnings of different occupations.

Links between human capital theory and equity models of social exchange have not been exploited in conceptual analysis or empirical investigation. Human capital concepts are rationalized in terms of presumed productivity, whereas social comparison models tend to focus more on investment regardless of productivity. Social comparison theory might predict the adverse productivity effects of a more highly educated person being paid less than a less-qualified person, whereas human capital theory would predict greater productivity (and pay) for the more educated person.

Integration of human capital and social comparison models in at least conceptual analyses of expected productivity effects of raising nurses' pay relative to the pay of tree trimmers would be interesting. Social comparison theory would suggest that nurses, perceiving underpayment with respect to education, would reduce other inputs such as effort and loyalty. To the extent that tree trimmers perceive overpayment relative to education, they would increase other inputs. A change in relative pay might be expected to reverse the contributions of other inputs. Merging human capital theory and social comparison theory might suggest that the productive potential of human capital can be realized only if relative pay is truly related to relative investments in human capital. Also, because social comparison models permit selective choice of comparison others, it would be valuable to investigate the consistency of choices and equity comparisons with those predicted from the human capital model. Finally, the presumed human capital–productivity linkage assumed in the human capital model cries for empirical assessment.

2. *Occupational factors.* Human capital concepts focus directly on measures of worker input in explaining earnings differentials, it being assumed that an efficient market rewards inputs in proportion to their productivity. Another set of concepts and analyses address the work performed or demand aspects rather than supply aspects. Measures of occupation and industry are presumed to reflect more directly aspects of labor demand and wage differentials.

Occupational differences in wages, status, and prestige are common in all societies (Phelps Brown, 1977). Based on 1980 U.S. Census data, for example, physicians were paid on average 6.5 times what nursing aides and orderlies were paid. Rationalizations of occupational wage differentials typically are based on conceptualizations of worth to an employer as well as on supply constraints such as worker ability and qualifications. Physicians are paid more than hospital orderlies, for example, because of the greater value placed on their services by the consuming society as well as because of the relatively more limited supply of physicians.

To the extent that employed men and women work in different occupations, they might as classes earn differing amounts, and different occupational distributions of the sexes have been advanced as one explanation of the gender earnings gap. Men and women do in fact tend to work in different occupations, and predominantly female occupations typically are paid relatively less. Occupational earnings vary such that each additional percentage of females in an occupation in 1970 was associated with about $42 less income per year (Treiman & Hartmann, 1981). Results of analyses of the earnings gap that can be associated with occupational distributions vary depending on degree of specificity in occupational classification. Treiman and Hartmann (1981) report, for example, that 35%–40% of the earnings gap can be attributed to occupation, and Sanborn (1964) accounts for 70% of the earnings gap with detailed occupational classifications. As with human capital analyses, doubtless 100% of the gap could be attributed to occupation if the classification were refined to the point of individual jobs. Also, occupation and human capital concepts doubtless are confounded, both being alternative ways of measuring labor supply and demand.

Occupational segregation of men and women is characteristic of the American labor force. In an analysis of 553 occupations as of 1970, for example, 310 occupations were staffed with 80% or more males and 50 occupations were staffed with 80% or more females. Conversely, 70% of males were in predominantly male occupations and 54% of females were in predominantly female occupations (Treiman & Hartmann, 1981). A commonly employed index of occupational segregation measures the percentage of women (or men) who would have to change occupations to balance the gender proportions across occupations; this index was about 62% in 1980, down slightly from 1970.

Why, however, are wages lower in occupations dominated by women? Explanations of the relationship between wages and gender composition of the occupation are varied. One set of explanations employs a concept of "crowding" (Bergmann, 1974). The concentration of women employees in relatively few occupations, it is argued, results in relatively abundant labor supplies in those occupations and minimal competitive pressure to pay higher wages; relatively less-abundant labor supplies in male-dominated occupations result in increased pressure to pay higher wages. The crowding hypothesis remains just that—a hypothesis, without adequate testing to date. It has been observed, however, that the occupations experiencing the greatest increases in demand and job opportunities during the past 20 years were precisely those dominated by women, casting some doubt on the validity of the crowding hypothesis.

Assuming the validity of the crowding hypothesis, activists in the comparable worth movement argue that the resulting wage differences are imperfect measures of relative occupational worth and are attributable to "discrimination by the labor market" (Berger, 1984). Because of employment discrimination, women were not permitted access to higher-paying occupations. Although employment discrimination is prohibited under Title VII, it is argued that basing wage rates on market rates achieved under conditions of employment discrimination now constitutes wage discrimination. To the extent that crowding and gender segregation of occupations was a result of employment discrimination, we might expect less segregation to have occurred during the last 20 years. However, as noted previously, occupational segregation has declined only slightly in recent years and projections of segregation rates into the future suggest that segregation will be eliminated only in 25 to 100 years (Beller, 1984). Occupational crowding as a consequence of choice, interest, or ability could not, of course, be argued as evidence of discrimination.

The effect of relative occupational wages on occupational choices is relatively unexplored. The expectancy model of motivation suggests that both wages (outcomes) and employment opportunities (expectancy) affect occupational choice (Vroom, 1967). Which is more functional in altering occupational supplies is not well known. The relative rigidity of the occupational wage structure despite change in occupational openings and supplies suggests that demand expressed in employment opportunities rather than in wage is more operational (Thurow, 1975). Shifts in college enrollments away from education majors 10 years ago and, more recently, back toward education majors would appear to be more reflective of varying job opportunities than variation in relative earnings of teachers. The reported adjustment by employers of occupational hiring standards (rather than wages) to adjust to changing occupational supplies also suggests that there are expected relative occupational wage rates below which labor supplies are extremely elastic—almost no applicants are available at lower-than-anticipated relative wage rates (Reder, 1955). The psychology of occupational choice, particularly with respect to wages, expected wages, and employment opportunities is still relatively unexplored.

3. *Industry factors.* Another characteristic of labor demand also has been related to wage differences, although it has not figured prominently in analyses of the gender earnings gap. There are persistent wage differentials among industries, some industries consistently paying more than others. A classic analysis by Dunlop (1957) identifies sizeable wage differences within a single occupation (truck driver) in a single geographic labor market (Boston). The differentials were associated with industry or product market of the employer. These differences in wage behavior, which Dunlop calls "wage contours," can be related to the elasticity of labor demand, labor cost as a proportion of total cost, and the elasticity of product demand. Certain industries appear better able to pay than do others, and exploit this ability by offering higher wages. In a very real sense, a given occupation is worth more in one industry than in another.

Although occupation and industry of employment may independently influence relative earnings, occupation and industry are often correlated. Thus, for example, skilled crafts occupations tend to be concentrated in construction and manufacturing whereas office and clerical occupations are concentrated in finance, insurance, and service industries. Those industries that experienced the greatest growth in employment following 1950 were the industries with relatively large proportions of jobs in traditionally female-dominated occupations (see Table 1). About 41.5 million new jobs were created during the period 1950–1980, and almost 63% of those new jobs were staffed by women, as the participation of women in the workforce increased. Of these new jobs, 75.6% were in the finance, trade, and service industries; almost 64% of the employment expansion in these industries was staffed by women and accounted for 77% of the expansion in the female labor force. By 1980 more than 50% of the workforce in these industries was female. The finance, trade, and service industries have typically paid relatively less than industries such as manufacturing and construction. It is likely that industry of employment accounts for a portion of the gender earnings gap independent of occupation, but it is difficult to isolate the effects of each. Certainly the expansion of employment during the period 1950–1980, when women entered the workforce in large numbers, occurred in the lower-wage industries and occupations, and female employment today is relatively concentrated in these lower-wage industries and occupations.

A recent analysis of earnings data provides some support for the hypothesized influence of industry of employment upon the gender earnings gap. Johnson and Solon (1984) analyzed individual earnings as a function of selected human capital variables, occupation, and industry. Occupation was operationalized as percent female in the occupation, and an inverse relationship with earnings was observed. This inverse relationship of

Table 1. Labor Force Comparisons, 1950 and 1980

	1950			1980		
	Labor force (%)	Female labor force (%)	Percent female	Labor force (%)	Female labor force (%)	Percent female
Agriculture, fishing mining, construction	20.2	4.5	6.3	9.9	2.7	11.7
Durable manufacturing	13.8	7.9	16.0	13.8	8.4	26.0
Nondurable manufacturing	11.9	15.1	35.3	8.6	8.4	41.4
Transportation, utilities, communications	10.3	7.4	20.2	7.3	4.2	24.7
Wholesale & retail trade	18.8	22.6	33.7	20.4	21.9	45.8
Finance, insurance	3.4	5.0	40.7	4.3	8.2	58.0
Services	18.0	34.2	53.0	28.7	41.1	61.1
Public administration	4.4	4.1	26.2	5.3	5.1	40.8
Total	100.0	100.0	28.0	100.0	100.0	46.6

Prepared from U.S. Census data.

earnings and percent female in the occupation was reduced substantially when industry of employment was taken into account. The results suggest interaction between occupation (measured as percent female) and industry, and that industry can be attributed with a substantial proportion of the earnings gap.

The preliminary analysis of likely industry effects on wage differentials sketched here requires elaboration and further investigation. Most investigations have defined *work* in terms of tasks and duties. Consideration of industry of employment extends that definition to encompass product and consumer market. Definition of comparable worth in terms of product valuation would be consistent with the tradition of economics, although perhaps not consistent with norms of social comparison. Examination of industry effects on both actual wage payments and perceptions of fair pay would be revealing. We hypothesize that industry differences of consumer demand elasticity, labor costs as a proportion of total costs, product market concentration, and capital investment per worker are significant independent influences on actual wages as well as influences interacting with occupation. The effect of industry upon norms of fair pay is by no means as easy to hypothesize.

Institutional influences. Two institutional or nonmarket models of wage determination also are offered in the explanation of wage differentials. The first model views wage determination as a function of collective bargaining between employer and union. Although there are broad market constraints on wage determination, it is argued that there is considerable latitude for wage negotiation through collective bargaining. It has been difficult in empirical investigation to isolate the effects of unionization and collective bargaining from the influence of industry, occupation, and productivity. Nevertheless, the evidence suggests that the effect of collective bargaining raises the wage rate above that which would have prevailed in the absence of collective bargaining (Freeman & Medoff, 1978).

To the extent that women are underrepresented in labor unions, the collective bargaining model would predict a gender earnings gap. And women have traditionally been underrepresented in labor union membership; women constituted only 31% of unionized workers in 1980, although 47% of the workforce (Marshall, Briggs, & King, 1984). Female employment tends to be more concentrated in those occupations and industries where collective bargaining is not the modal form of wage determination, and relatively more male employment is concentrated in industries and occupations with collective bargaining. Whether the difference in union representation is due to different values and behavior associated with gender, occupation, or industry of employment, the bargaining model would attribute at least part of the gender earnings gap to differences in union organization and collective bargaining.

The effects on organized labor of the comparable worth phenomenon have not been studied to any extent, although organized labor provides a unique setting for research. In a very real sense, a union is a miniature society and can be viewed as a laboratory for the study of social effects of the comparable worth phenomenon. Traditionally, women have not had a major role in the labor movement. The occupations and industries traditionally most highly organized have been those dominated by male employment. This is changing, however, due in part to shifts of employment and in part to growing organization in nontraditional sectors. Certain occupations (e.g., teaching) have been relatively highly organized for some time, but their concern over wage differentials focuses on other occupations in other industries; teachers may seek higher wages relative to other occupations but this typically does not challenge wage relationships within the membership of the union. Unions representing employees in the public sector (e.g., American Federation of State, County, and Municipal Employees) are more likely to confront issues of realignment of wage relationships within the membership. Organization in the public sector has grown to about 34% of the workforce compared to 20% of the overall workforce, and women represent about 41% of the public-sector workforce. Not surprisingly, unions in the public sector appear to have been more responsive to calls for realignment of wages for women's occupations. The effects on male members of the union have not been investigated in detail, but there are reports of unions representing predominantly male occupations (e.g., police and fire protection) resisting realignment of wages for women's occupations in the public sector. Longitudinal analysis of the comparable worth phenomenon within the context of organized labor would provide a fascinating study of the effects of gender competition for power within a more limited society.

A second model of institutional wage determination focuses on employer determination of wage differentials within the employing establishment, often through a process known as job evaluation. Job evaluation is a process for determining relative wages to be paid to different jobs in an establishment, and has been advanced in past years as an alternative to strict market pricing of jobs (Livernash, 1957). Compensation texts typically present job evaluation as a method of assuring "internal equity" of relative wages in an establishment, and discuss market surveys in the determination of "external equity." Although available as a process for quite some time, job evaluation as a formal process has developed largely since World War II, when the War Labor Board required job evaluation in the justification of realignment of wage rates (Northrup, 1980). Although there are several different approaches to job evaluation, all require the specification and application of some method for scaling and assessing the relative worth of different jobs in an organization. There is no limit to the number of different scales employed in job evaluation and, in fact, it is not uncommon for different scales to be used in a single organization for clusters of different types of jobs (e.g., production, office, professional, managerial).

Job evaluation is an administrative process for determining relative wage rates for different jobs in an organization that are judged to be equitable and acceptable to those affected, a process that is simpler and more orderly than attempting to identify relevant market rates or to bargain individual rates for each of the different jobs in an organization (Schwab, 1980). A process for scaling the relative worth of different jobs is developed and validated with a sample of jobs, key jobs that are highly visible, easily compared with similar jobs in other organizations, and for which there are accepted social norms in the workforce concerning the relative worth of the jobs. Job factor scales are specified that attempt to capture content variations among the jobs, and points are assigned for different degrees of the factors. After description and rating of the jobs, points presumed to be reflective of relative worth of the jobs are then assigned. The structure of points assigned to different jobs must be reflective of workforce norms of relative job worth of the key jobs.

The rationalization and practice of job evaluation are not always consistent and often occasion confusion to observers. Job evaluation is rationalized as a process for determining intrinsic worth of different jobs in an organization. The process is presented as a rational and pseudo-scientific assessment of worth. Dimensions of a conceptual criterion of worth are defined, weighted, and scaled for application to job descriptions. Measures of jobs are then obtained, usually expressed in points or numbers, which indicate the relative worth of jobs one to another. This conceptualization of job evaluation assumes some intrinsic criterion of job value or worth that can be scaled and that meets some test of construct validity.

In practice, the typical development of job evaluation proceeds quite differently. It proceeds from the assumption that there exists some relative consensus within the workforce concerning a ranking or hierarchy among jobs with respect to appropriate relative pay, whatever the origin or content of that ranking. A system of scaling jobs to replicate that consensual ranking is sought in development of a job evaluation system. Predictive validity is sought rather than construct validity (Livernash, 1957; Schwab, 1980).

A typical installation of job evaluation begins with analysis and description of all jobs in the organization. Descriptions of work performed and qualifications required for all positions are combined into generic descriptions of a more limited set of jobs. Some jobs will have a single incumbent but more commonly a single job will have multiple incumbents. A sample of jobs (key jobs) is selected for development purposes and the system of job evaluation developed and validated using that sample is later generalized in application to all jobs.

There are clusters of jobs in every organization that are related by skill, work process, or work location and that are compared with each other by job incumbents when assessing the equity of pay relationships. These jobs exemplify the "comparison other" specified in equity or social comparison theory. Employees working in a job cluster evolve a set of work and value norms about the relative status, prestige, and worth of jobs in the cluster. Similarly, there will be one or more jobs in every cluster that typify the entire cluster of jobs and provide a basis for comparison among job clusters. These so-called key jobs usually are relatively visible to all, have large numbers of incumbents, and have a relatively stable job content. Again, there is an accepted hierarchy of status, prestige, and relative pay for the key jobs; in fact, one criterion for the selection of key jobs is the existence of an accepted norm of appropriate pay relationships among the key jobs.

Relatively little is known about the origins of normative pay hierarchies within work groups except for anecdotal accounts of these hierarchies (Livernash, 1957). They appear to be a function of social influences and tradition and may vary from one work setting to another. Probable influences are skill levels, number of job incumbents, centrality in the work process, usual patterns of job progression, and market demand. That these influences do vary from one company and industry to another is evidenced by the tradition of a multi-graded hierarchy in the automobile industry and the tradition of a single-grade hierarchy in the brewing industry. Whatever the origin and influences of job-status hierarchy, job evaluation as practiced assumes the existence of a hierarchy of key jobs and rarely challenges that hierarchy.

Dimensions or factors for the evaluation of job worth are specified and weights may be judgmentally proposed or empirically derived. Traditionally, judgmental weights have been used and then altered as necessary to produce job evaluations consistent with the key job hierarchy; increasingly, empirical weighting through some form of policy-capturing analysis is employed. A test of predictive validity is applied in either case using the key-job hierarchy before the system is accepted for extension to non-key jobs. The criterion of a key-job hierarchy may be operationalized as existing wage rates, observed market wage rates, or a negotiated set of key job wage rates.

Because social norms of job worth and value vary from one setting to another, the factor weights and often factor definitions employed in job evaluation also differ. Not uncommonly, they also vary for different groups of jobs in a single organization because consensual hierarchies are more apparent in relatively more homogeneous job groups, and because the variance in job-factor measures often differs among job groups. For example, the dimensions of physical requirements, which vary among production jobs, often do not vary among office jobs where they tend to be defined differently. It is common then to employ different job evaluation systems for plant, office, professional, and managers' jobs, just as different employee-selection criteria are developed for different sets of jobs (Bellak, 1984). Each such system is developed, validated, and applied within a different specified population of jobs.

To the extent that job evaluation introduces bias and discrimination into the evaluation of traditionally female occupations, it may contribute to the gender earnings gap. Obvious potential sources of bias are the description of jobs for evaluation and the application of evaluation scales in the rating of jobs. It might be argued that job analysts (often male) and job raters (often male) unconsciously bias their descriptions and ratings of jobs on the basis of gender of job incumbents. Investigations of these potential sources of bias in recent years have manipulated sex of rater, sex of job incumbent, amount of job information presented, and amount of interest expressed in the job (Grams & Schwab, 1985; Arvey, Passino, & Lounsbury, 1977). In general, none of these has been identified as a major source of bias. However, manipulations of the job stereotype (male or female) and of traditional wage levels associated with the job do affect judgments of relative worth of jobs (Mahoney & Blake, in press; Grams & Schwab, in press). Traditional occupational pay relationships appear to reflect or to be projected into global judgments of job worth

A valid system of job evaluation at best captures the norms of the workforce concerning relative job worth. Lack of validity is demonstrated in pay grievances, turnover, unwillingness to accept promotion or transfer, and inability to recruit employees for certain jobs. Lacking evidence of nonvalidity of the job evaluations, employers accept them as measures of relative worth in the organization. Social norms of relative job worth may be such that traditionally female jobs are judged less worthy than traditionally male jobs, however, and job evaluation may in that sense explain some of the gender earnings gap. It is incorrect, however, to label this a consequence of bias in job evaluation; rather, it might better be labeled as bias present in social norms of the workforce.

The process of job evaluation has elicited more research interest in recent years than has the validity criterion for job evaluation. Relatively little is known about the content and origin of norms of equitable pay relationships in organizations. Although job evaluation may replicate judgments of equitable pay relationships, it does not explain their origins. Given current research interest in organization cultures and organizational symbolism, it is surprising that so little attention has been directed toward pay relationships as symbols and as expressions of organization culture. It is likely that equitable pay relationships are a function of other critical aspects of organization culture, such as style of management, promotion and career ladders, and degree of specialization in job design. For example, it is likely that the number of levels and range of compensation varies inversely with norms of egalitarianism in an organization and thus inversely with degree of participation and power sharing. Similarly, one might expect greater pay differentiation with norms of vertical (as opposed to horizontal) mobility, and with job specialization as opposed to job enlargement and enrichment. These relationships remain unstudied and, while relevant to analysis of comparable worth issues, are also relevant for a more complete understanding of organizational behavior.

Constructs of Comparable Worth

We advanced earlier a framework for the analysis of the comparable worth phenomenon. The problem addressed relates to an observed gender gap in earnings, women earning less than men. Examination of various models of wage determination indicated that it appears that women earn less than males in large part because they work in different occupations and industries with different worker qualifications and different pay practices. Female dominated occupations and industries pay less than male dominated occupations and industries. Reasons for the differential payment probably are several and the theories examined attempt to explain these differences.

The doctrine of equal pay for jobs of equal worth is advanced as a philosophical principle but has no obvious relationship to the perceived problem of a gender earnings gap. Any relationship with the earnings gap depends on the definition of some measure of worth to be applied with the doctrine. Various constructs of worth are advanced, among which some appear to address the earnings gap and others do not.

Several competing concepts of comparable worth are implicit in the previous discussion. All relate to concepts of job worth and each relies on a slightly different theoretical base. In a sense, the differences relate to differences in concepts of worth called out over 200 years ago by Adam Smith (1937). Struggling with the concept of economic worth, Smith identified two different bases for determination of worth, market value and use value. The market value concept states that something is only worth what another is willing to offer in exchange for it. The use value concept states that something is worth whatever value the owner obtains through use of the item. Incorporated in a broad theory of market exchanges, use value and market value should be equivalent for the marginal exchange because a purchaser would offer at most the use value of the item. However, for individuals the two concepts of value need not be equal, as in the case of an old automobile that has far greater use value to the owner than could be obtained in any market exchange. In any economic exchange, market value tends to exceed use value to the seller, and use value tends to exceed market value for the buyer. However, the distinction between market value and use value underlies much of the debate over comparable worth, because they imply different methods of assessing worth or value (Mahoney, 1979a).

Market-based constructs. It is argued that market rate for a job or occupation is the only true measure of worth. Worth or value is subjectively determined by individuals and differs among individuals and over time. Some individuals would willingly employ another at $10 an hour to rake the leaves on their lawns, and others, who enjoy raking leaves, would not willingly employ another to rake leaves. Similarly, the first person might refuse employment at $25 an hour to rake another's leaves, whereas the second person might rake another's leaves for a token amount. The value of a job in society can only be estimated through the market rate, that rate at which marginal trades of labor and compensation are made. Given the usual assumptions of efficient markets and general equilibrium, market rates of wages for different occupations are indicative of the value or worth of work in those occupations to marginal workers and employers. Any wage differential between occupations reflects both employer valuations of work in those occupations (demand) and worker valuations of the disutility of qualifying for and working in the occupations (supply).

The market-rate construct of job worth has been incorporated in various employer compensation policies relating compensation to surveys of what other employers pay (market rate) and has been accepted in litigation as a rationale for compensating occupations at different rates. Acceptance of market rate as the criterion for comparable worth is not satisfactory, however, to those seeking to reduce the earnings gap between men and women. The policy implications of that criterion are to seek efficient labor markets with freedom of access to alternative occupations and removal of barriers to mobility. Wage differentials between male- and female-dominated occupations will diminish only to the extent that women shift to higher paying occupations, increasing those supplies of labor and reducing supplies to lower-paid occupations. Further, reliance on a market criterion of worth is unacceptable to those with a social/political objective of elimination of the gender earnings gap. They prefer to define equitable pay in terms of impact or outcome rather than in terms merely of nondiscriminatory treatment.

Acceptance of a market-based criterion of job worth effectively denies wage discrimination as an overall cause of the gender earnings gap. Individual employers might attempt to discriminate by paying lower-than-market wages for female-dominated occupations, but a market wage differential between male- and female-dominated occupations would not evidence wage discrimination. The rationale for a market wage criterion assumes that any market wage differential between occupations is a consequence of market demand and individual supply choices. The gender earnings gap will diminish to the extent that women obtain employment in higher-paying occupations and industries, and the occupational wage structure will change only as a consequence of changing occupational demands and supplies of labor. Limited evidence that this might be occurring is provided in comparison of male–female earnings by age; the 60% ratio of female/male hourly earnings increases to 80% for workers aged 25–34 and to 89% for workers aged 19–24 (Bureau of National Affairs, 1984a). Lacking more definitive analyses, it cannot be determined whether the reduced earnings gap is due to redistribution of male and female employment among occupations and industries, or merely similarity of labor force exposure at young ages, which disappears as the cohort ages, as might be inferred from Polachek's research (1975). For example, men and women may begin their work careers with comparable labor force exposure and that comparability may diminish over time as women exit from and reenter the workforce; alternatively, entry jobs for men and women may pay comparably while men work in occupations with more advancement opportunities that result in noncomparable earnings at later career stages. Only time will tell whether or not the earnings gap remains at the same level for each age cohort over time.

Employer use value. Adam Smith's concept of use value underlies many of the criteria of worth advanced as alternatives to market value determination. Markets are not perfectly efficient and change occurs slowly in the occupational wage structure. Thurow (1975) has observed the remarkable stability of the occupational wage structure over time despite change in occupational demands and supplies. He and others suggest that the occupational wage structure is more a function of social values than of market influences. Advocates of comparable worth advance nonmarket criteria of worth rationalized as reflective of employer use value. These alternative criteria of job worth are advanced within the context of job evaluation as a measure of job worth.

To many it appears that job evaluation was advanced by employers for years as a means of determining relative worth of jobs independent of the market. The specification of job evaluation scales has been arbitrary and, although there may have been no disparate treatment in the application of job evaluation, the relative underpayment of female-dominated occupations is presented as evidence of disparate impact of traditional job evaluation. Alternative factors or criteria of worth are propoed for job evaluation, criteria which, it is presumed, would eliminate the disparate impact effects of job evaluation.

Human capital concepts provide the basis for a widely discussed measure of use value to be employed in achieving comparable worth: the education and training requirements for occupations. It can be argued, for example, that use value of an occupation varies directly with occupational requirements for education and training, particularly if presumed, as in human capital theory, that education and training increase worker productivity. Level of required education and training would provide a measure analogous to skill, effort, and responsibility that is independent of task content and would permit comparison of the use value of nurses and tree trimmers.

It is unclear what the effect would be on the gender earnings gap of using education as a measure of job worth. Certainly some female-dominated occupations with high educational requirements (nursing) are paid relatively less than some male-dominated occupations with lower education requirements (tree trimmers), but the same can be observed between male occupations as well (university professors of history earn less than professional football coaches). The strict application of education as a measure of relative occupational worth would totally restructure relative occupational wages that have enjoyed traditional acceptance and it is likely that it would be overwhelmingly rejected by much of the workforce. Some observers have attacked the suggestion as an elitist approach to social structuring and destined to intensify class antagonism in society (Berger, 1984). Finally, although women working in occupations requiring advanced educations might benefit, the majority of poverty-level families headed by working women probably would be unaffected.

To what extent is it possible to employ job evaluation as a measure of use value and, presumably, of comparable worth? Despite past employer rhetoric about measuring use value through job evaluation, the typical test of the validity of job evaluation has been acceptance of the results by the affected workforce (Livernash, 1957). Job evaluations that are not accepted occasion grievances, strikes, turnover, and other forms of withholding of labor services. The outcome of job evaluation is more important to the affected workforce than is the particular method employed in evaluation. Except for certain widely publicized cases in litigation, it is not apparent that there is any widespread challenge of existing wage structures by the affected workers. Despite charges that female-dominated occupations are underpaid relative to male-dominated occupations, the validity of job evaluation in individual employing organizations is not challenged widely except in the public sector.

Consensus within an employer's workforce regarding the appropriate or equitable structure of relative job worth is a precondition for successful job evaluation. Consensus concerning social norms is more easily achieved in relatively small, interacting societies and thus it is not surprising that successful applications of job evaluation typically are constrained to a single employer and often to related clusters of jobs (e.g., office or plant) within an organization. The social norms of one work group do not often generalize to other work groups.

The relative underpayment of female-dominated occupations in society, which some argue evidences disparate impact discrimination, does not appear to be evidenced as much within employer organizations when examined singularly, perhaps because of the occupational and industrial segregation of males and females noted previously; men and women tend to be segregated by industry (and thus employer) as well as by occupation. Occupational wage structures accepted as equitable with the steel industry and within retail trade are criticized at the societal level when they result in relatively higher wages for furnace tenders than for sales clerks. Cross-employer and cross-industry wage comparisons are not commonly accepted as evidence of wage discrimination nor are they commonly addressed in job evaluation.

It is revealing to observe that some of the most widely publicized comparable worth challenges to job evaluation have occurred in the public sector, particularly in state and local government. Speculation concerning the reasons suggests research opportunities. One likely reason is that public sector employment is not dominated either by men or by women; about 41% of employment in public administration was female in 1980. Further, there appear to be both male- and female-dominated occupations in the public sector (e.g., police, nursing), and the range of occupations in the public sector probably is more similar to the range in society than is the case in other industries such as steel, auto, insurance, and hospital care. Equity norms of occupational payment in public employment may be more reflective of those in society at large as a consequence. Further, it is likely that the degree of union organization of female employees in the public sector is greater than in other industries. Female employees in a public sector jurisdiction thus experience within the enterprise wage differentials others might encounter primarily in comparison with employees in other enterprises, constitute a relatively large segment of the total enterprise workforce, and are able to employ collective bargaining in their efforts to change the occupational wage structure. In contrast, employees in female-dominated occupations of secretary and file clerk in a manufacturing enterprise constitute a relatively small proportion of the total workforce and are less likely to be represented in collective bargaining. A final difference lies in the likely greater responsiveness of public sector employers (elected officials) to criticism by any major bloc of the voting public.

Challenge of the occupational wage structure in the public sector is analogous to challenges that have occurred in the private sector, with the exception of the likely responsiveness to public pressure. The Title VII prohibition of discrimination in wages provides an element of legitimacy for comparable worth arguments not otherwise available, and legislative initiatives for public employees provide an alternative to collective bargaining. For these reasons, the effectuation of change in the occupational wage structure to favor female-dominated occupations is more likely in the public sector than in the private sector.

The likely spillover effects of realignment of occupational wage structures in the public sector are unpredictable. Job evaluation does not normally generalize from one employer to another, particularly across industries, thus limiting spillover effects. Further, public sector employment is not so large that occupational wage realignment there is likely to impact significantly upon labor supplies to other industries, again limiting spillover. Spillover effects to other industries likely will depend on an emergent norm consensus concerning relative occupational worth throughout society, a norm consensus that appears unlikely for some time. Revalidation of job evaluations in the public sector will likely impact only on the individual organizations involved and any broader effects will depend on emergence of a broader norm consensus. This broader social consensus on norms of occupational worth will more likely emerge through political action and public discussion than through challenge of the occupational wage structure of individual employers. Challenges to pay equity in the public sector probably do raise social awareness of challenge to traditional norms of pay and thus promote emergence of some new norm consensus in society.

CONTRADICTIONS

The comparable worth phenomenon arises out of broad social issues of poverty among single-parent (usually female) families, the earnings gap between employed men and women, gender-dominated occupations, and increased participation of women in employment and in political action. Over the course of the last 35 years women have achieved essentially equal access to the previously male-dominated world of work, yet the outcome of that increased access has not achieved equality of power, status, and incomes. The prevailing value system implicit in occupational rankings of status and earnings still appears to be weighted toward traditionally male occupations. In the broadest sense, the comparable worth phenomenon provides a challenge to the traditional value system. It calls for reorientation of values to elevate the status and earnings of certain female-dominated occupations, particularly those occupied by women with higher education.

In the broader social context, most attention has been directed to disparities in earnings associated with education and skill, female school teachers with college degrees earning less than male mechanics without higher education. If education were established as the criterion of job worth, as often implied, this would substitute an elitist structuring of society for a more competitive economic structuring. If successful, such a program might significantly reduce the earnings gap, but it is not clear that it would benefit the poverty-level families headed by females, many of whom probably lack higher educations.

Advocates of the comparable worth doctrine appear to be seeking a restructuring of occupational wages across society, yet must direct their actions toward wage restructuring in individual employing establishments as a practical necessity. Prescription of occupational wage rates required throughout the economy would be infeasible and is caricatured by opponents of comparable worth as the outcome sought by advocates. Although social norms and values might be made supportive of occupational wage restructuring, any change in wage rates must be sought at the level of the employer or, perhaps, industry. Where restructuring is sought through collective bargaining, the constraint is individual bargaining units. Where restructuring is sought through EEO litigation and/or guidelines, the implementation effects are again constrained to individual employer establishments. The effect in both instances is analogous to revalidation of job evaluation in those establishments, perhaps restructuring pay relationships in the organization to reflect then-existing norms of pay equity in the organization. As noted previously, validated job evaluations cannot be easily generalized across employment settings. Men and women employees are unequally distributed among industries as well as among occupations. Job evaluation, validated at the enterprise level, will achieve internal equity of pay relationships in the employing establishment but it is not likely to have any effect on inter-industry differences in wage rates. Nursing and teaching may appear to be low paid relative to craft occupations such as plumbing and bricklaying, but the health care and education industries are low paid relative to construction. Internal equity within hospitals, schools, and building contractors has no bearing upon inter-industry wage differentials.

At base the comparable worth phenomenon is best interpreted as a clash of values, the values assigned to different types of work and particularly those types of work associated with different genders. Differential values are associated with different occupations and these change only slowly. Also, these values tend to parallel traditional differential rates of occupational earnings, which also change slowly (Thurow, 1975). Although market forces doubtless have some effect on relative occupational earnings, the occupational wage structure in the United States has been relatively constant over time. There is some evidence to the effect that adjustments to occupational demand–supply imbalances take the form of relaxing and tightening occupational entry requirements rather than adjusting relative wage rates (Reder, 1955). Thus, for example, a relative shortage of workers to an occupation (e.g., nursing) occasions expanded employment of less-qualified substitutes (e.g., nursing aides) more than it does a relative increase in wages for the occupation. Extreme imbalance of occupational supply and demand may occasion relative wage adjustments, but only if expected to persist indefinitely. Individual employers, for example, may establish what are termed "red circled" rates of pay, rates of pay greater than what is accepted as correct and authorized only as long as required to secure qualified employees.

Social values and attitudes are most likely to change during times of crisis (e.g., war) or social upheaval. Any significant restructuring of occupational earnings probably will follow or accompany major change in social attitudes, and the major effects of the comparable worth phenomenon are most likely to be evidenced in this manner, challenging and seeking change in social norms. Certainly the rapid feminization of the workforce and the emergence of women's interests as major political issues evidence significant change in social attitudes and behavior. The controversy about comparable worth is merely one aspect of the larger changes occurring in our society.

The comparable worth phenomenon is basically a political issue with a focus on the redistribution of power in society. It is addressed as a discrimination issue under Title VII of the Civil Rights Act merely because that act provides the opportunity to address the issue in the judicial system and provides a forum for national consideration of the issue. Advocates have had very limited success in obtaining acceptance of the comparable worth concept in the definition of discrimination under Title VII, however, and it is interesting that the social focus has changed. The broad comparable worth phenomenon seeking to reduce the earnings gap through restructuring of occupational wages has achieved more success in the attainment of "pay equity," particularly in the public service, than in implementing a comparable worth definition of discrimination. Comparable worth was proposed for implementation under existing legislation, and pay equity is advanced through new legislation. Viewed in a political context, elected officials appear to have been more responsive to constituents' desires than have been regulatory agencies and the court system.

Comparable worth and pay equity represent a variety of convergent issues in society. The philosophical basis for these concepts lies in economics and the determination of occupational wage structures. However, the concepts are advanced in the service of restructuring the relative power and status of men and women. Challenges to relative occupational earnings occur inevitably in any workforce. However, because of occupational segregation of the sexes, comparable worth has been advanced as a gender issue in addressing the distribution of economic power and social status of men and women.

This essay began with characterizations of comparable worth as a "looney idea," a "moral idea," and the "issue of the 1980s". Comparable worth is all of these despite probable general acceptance of the principle of "equal pay for work of equal value." Determination of the comparable worth of jobs and occupations is not a new challenge; it is addressed directly in the establishment of a wage structure for any employing organization. The comparable worth phenomenon of the 1980's differs significantly in several respects, however, from more traditional concerns about the equity of wage differentials.

First, the overriding concern of the comparable worth advocates of the 1980s is the wage differential existing between predominantly male and predominantly female occupations evidenced especially in the earnings gap. The comparable worth phenomenon of the 1980s is a gender issue first and a pay equity issue second. More traditional concerns about pay equity have addressed job and occupational wage differentials independent of gender of the concerned employees. Traditionally, the concerned employees were predominantly male (e.g., firemen vs policemen). The comparable worth phenomenon of the 1980s is thus an outgrowth of the large-scale entry of women into the workforce since 1950 and the efforts of women to participate equally with men in the exercise of economic and political power.

The comparable worth concern of the 1980's addresses occupational wage differentials throughout the economy and not merely wage differentials within an employing establishment as in the past. Change in the structure of relative occupational wages throughout the economy is sought.

The approaches being employed to achieve comparable worth today also differ somewhat, for several reasons, from those employed in the past. The traditional approach of seeking realignment of wage differentials in the employing establishment through collective bargaining and/or through grievances is being followed in some organizations, particularly those in the public sector with a wide range of occupations. The primary nontraditional approach being used is legal charges of discrimination under Title VII. This approach was not available before 1964 and, more relevantly, does not bear upon occupational wage differentials among occupations staffed predominantly by members of one sex. Only gender-associated issues of comparable worth can be considered as a discrimination issue.

Finally, achieving comparable worth defined as a gender issue requires a political movement throughout society and cannot be achieved through action at the level of individual employers. Gender-associated occupational wage differentials are also industry wage differentials and the achievement of pay equity at the employer level need not occasion any change in the occupational wage structure of the economy. The frame of reference for gender-defined comparable worth must be broader than the individual employer establishment and requires political activity on a broader scale.

The comparable worth phenomenon of the 1980s is basically a struggle over the distribution of power in our society. It seeks realignment of social values and norms that will increase the earnings, status, and prestige of traditionally women's occupations. The phenomenon offers a variety of research challenges to scholars from a range of disciplines; it invites analysis and interpretation from the standpoints of political science, philosophy, social psychology, economics, law, and organizational behavior. Relevant issues relate to the evolution of social norms and values, the politics of social movements, reaction to perceptions of equity and inequity, the role of the judiciary in achieving social change, and the conflict between market and nonmarket systems of wage determination.

It is impossible at this stage of the comparable worth debate to predict exactly what the outcome will be. Certainly comparable worth is not an accepted legal doctrine at the moment. However, the issue of gender-associated occupational wage differentials has been raised to a national consciousness and possible realignment of social norms and values is being addressed in the political arena. The movement is not likely to fade away as long as gender-associated occupational wage differentials continue. Those differentials may disappear over time with redistribution of male and female employment among occupations and industries as traditionalists would prescribe, or through some alteration of the occupational wage structure. Strictly speaking, the comparable worth doctrine of equal pay for work of equal value is likely to continue as an accepted philosophical principle addressed in wage and employment issues. As such, it is far from being a "looney idea." As an objective criterion of worth to be applied in realignment of occupational wage structures, it is a "looney idea" and has progressed little beyond a doctrine with widely varying applications among employers. Finally, as a means of challenging traditional social norms and values, the comparable worth phenomenon has been influential and will likely continue as such. Whatever the outcome, the phenomenon will provide abundant exciting research opportunities for scholars in organizational behavior.

ACKNOWLEDGMENT

Support for the preparation of this report was provided by the Dean's Research Fund of the Owen Graduate School of Management. Helpful comments on earlier versions were provided by John Deckop and Donald Schwab.

NOTE

1. Comparable worth has been advanced as a gender issue and not as a racial issue, although blacks as a group are paid less on average than are whites. However, blacks constitute a smaller proportion of the workforce than do women, there is growing convergence of black–white earnings and not a convergence of male–female earnings, and occupational segregation of blacks is less than occupational segregation of women (Smith & Welch, 1978; Treiman & Hartmann, 1981). The only black-dominated occupation that comes to mind is that of professional basketball player, not a low-paid occupation.

REFERENCES

Adams, J.S. (1965). Inequity in social exchange. In L. Berkowitz (Ed.), *Advances in Experimental Social Psychology: Vol. 2.* (pp. 272–283). New York: Academic Press.

Arvey, R., Passino, E., & Lounsbury, J. (1977). Job analysis results as influenced by sex of incumbent and sex of analyst. *Journal of Applied Psychology, 62,* 411–416.

Becker, G.S. (1964). *Human capital,* New York: National Bureau of Economic Research.

Bellak, A. (1984). Statement to U.S. Commission on Civil Rights. In U.S. Commission on Civil Rights, *Comparable Worth: Issue for the 80's:* (Vol. 2: Proceedings) 47–50, Washington, DC: Author.

Beller, A.H. (1984). *Occupational segregation and the earnings gap.* Paper presented to the U.S. Commission on Civil Rights.

Berger, B. (1984). Statement to U.S. Commission on Civil Rights. In U.S. Commission on Civil Rights, *Comparable Worth: Issue for the 80's:* (Vol. 2: Proceedings) 26–28, Washington, DC: Author.

Bergmann, B.R. (1974, April–July). Occupational segregation, wages and profits when employees discriminate by race or sex. *Eastern Economic Journal, 1,* 103–110.

Bohlander, G.W. (1980, Fourth Quarter). A statistical approach to assessing minority/white pay equity. *Compensation Review, 12,* 15–24.

Bureau of National Affairs. (1984a, August 9). *Bulletin to Management,* Washington, DC: Author.

Bureau of National Affairs. (1984b). *Pay Equity and Comparable Worth,* Washington, DC: Author.

Civil rights chief provokes anger, *The Wall Street Journal* (1984, December 10) p. 48.

Corcoran, M., & Duncan, G.J. (1979). Work history, labor force attachment, and earnings differences between the races and the sexes. *Journal of Human Resources, 14,* 3–20.

Dunlop, J.T. (1957). The task of contemporary wage theory. In G.W. Taylor & F.C. Pierson (Eds.), *New Concepts in Wage Determination* (pp. 117–139). New York: McGraw-Hill.

EEOC rejects worth concept as proof of bias, *The Wall Street Journal* (1985, June 18) p. 12.

Freeman, R.B., & Medoff, J.L. (1978). *The Percent Organized Wage (POW) relationship for union and nonunion workers* (Working Paper, No. 305). Washington, DC: National Bureau of Economic Research.

Fuchs, V.R. (1983). *How we live.* Cambridge, MA: Harvard University Press.

Gardner, M. (1985, January 14). Comparable worth: Is fairness practical? *Christian Science Monitor,* pp. 29–30.

Goodman, P.S. (1979). *Assessing organizational change: The Rushton quality of work experiment,* New York: Wiley.

Grams, R., & Schwab, D. (1985). An investigation of systematic gender-related error in job evaluation, *Academy of Management Journal, 28,* 279–290.

Grune, J.A. (Ed.). (no date). *Manual on pay equity,* Washington, DC: Conference on Alternative State and Local Policies.

Homans, G.C. (1961). *Social behavior: Its elementary forms.* New York: Harcourt.

Johnson, G., & Solon, G. (1984). *Pay differences between women's and men's jobs: The empirical foundations of comparable worth legislation* (Working Paper No. 1472). Cambridge, MA: National Bureau of Economic Research.

Labor letter, *The Wall Street Journal* (1983, March 14) p. 1.

Ledvinka, J. (1982). *Federal regulation of personnel and human resource management.* Boston: Kent.

Livernash, E.R. (1937). The internal wage structure. In G.W. Taylor & F.C. Pierson (Eds.), *New concepts in wage determination* (pp. 140–172). New York: McGraw-Hill.

Livernash, E.R. (Ed.). (1980). *Comparable worth: Issues and alternatives,* Washington, DC: Equal Employment Advisory Council.

Mahoney, T.A. (1979a). *Compensation and reward perspectives.* Homewood, IL: Richard D. Irwin.

Mahoney, T.A. (1979b). Organizational hierarchy and position worth. *Academy of Management Journal, 22,* 726–737.

Mahoney, T.A., & Blake, R.H. (in press). Judgments of appropriate occupational pay as influenced by occupational characteristics and sex characterization. *International Review of Applied Psychology.*

Marshall, F.R., Briggs, J.M., and King, A.G. (1984). *Labor economics,* Homewood, Il: Richard D. Irwin

Mincer, J., & Polachek, S.W. (1974, March–April). Family investments in human capital. Earnings of women. *Journal of Political Economy, 82* (Part II), S76–S108.

Northrup, H.R. (1980). Wage setting and collective bargaining. In E.R. Livernash (Ed.), *Comparable worth: Issues and alternatives.* Washington, DC: Equal Employment Advisory Council.

Phelps Brown, H. (1977). *The inequality of pay.* Berkeley: University of California Press.

Polachek, S.W. (1975, June). Differences in expected post-school investments as a determinant of market wage differences. *International Economic Review, 16*(2), 451–490.

Public Opinion (1984, August–September), pp. 35–36.

Public Opinion (1985, February–March), p. 32.

Reder, M.W. (1955). The theory of occupational wage differentials. *American Economic Review, 45*(5), 833–852.

Sanborn, H. (1964). Pay differences between men and women. *Industrial and Labor Relations Review, 17,* 534–550.

Sawhill, I.V. (1973). The economics of discrimination against women: Some new findings. *Journal of Human Resources, 8,* 383–396.

Schwab, D.P. (1980). Job evaluation and pay setting: Concepts and practices. In E.R. Livernash (Ed.), *Comparable worth: Issues and alternatives* (pp. 49–78). Washington, DC: Equal Employment Advisory Council.

Smith, A. (1937). *The wealth of nations: Inquiry into the nature of causes of the wealth of nations* (Canaan edition). New York: Random House.

Smith, J.P., & Ward, M.P. (1984). *Women's wages and work in the twentieth century.* Santa Monica, CA: The Rand Corporation.

Smith, J.P., & Welch, F. (1978). *Race differences in earnings: A survey and new evidence,* Santa Monica, CA: The Rand Corporation.

Thurow, L.C. (1975). *Generating inequality,* New York: Basic Books.

Treiman, D.J., & Hartmann, H.I. (Eds.) (1981). *Women, work, and wages: Equal pay for jobs of equal Value.* Washington, DC: National Academy Press.

Vroom, V.H. (1967). *Work and motivation.* New York: Wiley.
Use of comparable-worth idea to fight job sex bias opposed by rights panel, *The Wall Street Journal* (1985, April 12) p. 60.
U.S. Commission on Civil Rights. (1984). *Comparable Worth: Issue for the 80's.* Washington, DC: Author.
Whyte, W.F. (1955). *Money and motivation,* New York: Harper & Row.

THE MEANINGS OF ABSENCE:

NEW STRATEGIES FOR THEORY AND RESEARCH[1]

Gary Johns and Nigel Nicholson

ABSTRACT

The central thesis of this chapter is that the gap between experiential accounts of absence from work and the inferred accounts derived from conventional research should be reduced. First, six "propositions in use" that have tacitly guided conventional absence research are presented. These include the assumptions that empirically similar absence events have equivalent meanings; most absence is volitional; absence is best conceived as a function of individual differences; absence is a static phenomenon; absence is strictly an "organizational" behavior; absence occurs only among blue-collar and clerical workers. Second, six "counterpropositions" are introduced, which, if adopted, should lead to the use of new research methods and the development of fresh theory to study absence. Finally, seven research issues, which derive from the joint application of the counterpropositions, are presented to illustrate their value. These include a reevaluation of proneness; attribution processes and absence; the relationship between absence and other behaviors; absence and time allocation; absence as coin of exchange; normative control of absence; absence climates and cultures.

I am sometimes prevented from attending work through no fault of my own.
You lack motivation to attend work regularly.
They are lazy malingerers, willfully milking the system.

Thus might a cynical grammarian conjugate the verb "to be absent
from work." Cynicism aside, there is a grain of truth here: Accounts
of absence often refer to a "generalized other," and one need not be
a committed attribution theorist to see that the terms in which we explain
our own behavior and that of people we know well differ from those we
offer for strangers. It is the main theme of this chapter that the gap
between behavioral scientists' accounts of absence as a "social problem"
and its experiential reality to the worker should be closed by the adoption
of new frames of reference for research and theory building.

Evidence of the need to close this gap is abundant if indirect. Concern
about the social and organizational costs of absence has generated a vast
amount of research and some theorizing. However, reviews of this work
(Chadwick-Jones, Brown, & Nicholson, 1973a; Muchinsky, 1977; Porter
& Steers, 1973; Steers & Rhodes, 1978) reveal a rather depressing state
of affairs. Relationships of other variables with absence are often inconsistent. Even when well established and of practical magnitude, such
relationships may be poorly understood (e.g., the tendency for women
to exhibit more absence than men; Steers and Rhodes, 1978). In short,
a heavy investment of research effort has failed to generate significant
dividends, whether one's criterion is the prediction, explanation, or control of absence.

It is our contention that the implicit boundaries within which absence
research has been conducted, drawn by metatheoretical assumptions and
unstated premises, are overly restrictive and inappropriate. In turn, these
boundaries have led to theoretical and empirical vacuity. In this chapter
we shall first delineate these boundaries by presenting the hidden axioms
of absence research in the form of six propositions in use (PIUs). We
borrow here from Argyris and Schon's (1974) notion of "theories in use"
to distinguish the premises that underpin action from those that may be
"espoused" by actors. Following this, we shall outline six counterpropositions (CPs), which, if adopted, would radically reorient absence research toward theoretical innovation, fresh methodologies, and neglected
content areas. Finally, we shall illustrate this consequence by discussing
seven potentially fruitful approaches to the study of absence, each of
which derives from our CPs rather than from the paradigms of the PIUs,
which have long dominated the field.

The PIUs and CPs are developed first in outline form. This is done in anticipation of our intention to draw out their implications in the extended discussion of the seven research issues.

PROPOSITIONS IN USE IN ABSENCE RESEARCH

The PIUs that are discussed in the following paragraphs stem from our review of the methods behavioral scientists have used to study absence. In several cases these PIUs also correspond to managerial treatments of the "absence problem." This correspondence between research strategies and management interests is, of course, not uncommon (Nord, 1977).

PIU 1: *Empirically similar absence events have functionally and psychologically equivalent meaning for all workers.*

It is nearly universal for organizations to classify and label absences in accordance with this assumption. For example, the worker who misses a day and fails to offer an acceptable explanation or produce a medical certificate is likely to have his or her absence labeled "voluntary," "illegitimate," "unexcused," or "casual." Such labels impute motives, and it is apparent that supervisors and personnel managers often exercise extreme discretion in assigning absence to these or other categories. Moreover, there are indications that such judgments and assignments are frequently unreliable (Ilgen, 1977; Latham & Pursell, 1975) and culture-bound (Smulders, 1980). Despite this, it is common for absence researchers to adopt organizational measures of absence without comment or criticism (see Rhodes and Steers[2] for documentation of the prevalence of this practice).

Even when researchers adopt more objective criteria for absence classification, such as frequency and time lost, the naming of the resultant absence classes sometimes "smuggles in" causal attributions (e.g., Huse and Taylor, 1962, "Attitudinal Index" denoting short-spell frequency; see also Chadwick-Jones, Brown, Nicholson, and Sheppard, 1971). In other cases, researchers have made use of less value-laden distinctions, such as "medically certificated" versus "uncertificated," or "paid" versus "unpaid." However, often these are then adopted as operationalizations of *causal* categories, notably the "voluntary" versus "involuntary" distinction. The operationalizations upon which these distinctions are made are likely to tell us more about organizational and external controls than about the causal dynamics of the behavior.

PIU 1 is also evident in the great favor with which the notion of "withdrawal" is embraced to encompass not only different types of absence but also to link it with other behaviors such as turnover and lateness (Beehr & Gupta, 1978; Bernardin, 1977; Waters & Roach, 1971; Gupta & Jenkins, 1980[3]). This label imputes similar motivational states to superficially similar behaviors.

PIU 2: *Individual volitional processes underlie most psychologically interesting and potentially controllable forms of absence.*

While it is a profound misreading of motivational theory to assume that *motivated* behavior is *willed* behavior, it is commonly assumed by otherwise sophisticated scientists that most absence is provoked by desires to avoid work and to "consume" alternative satisfaction (Argyle, 1972). Indeed, this assumption is enshrined in the use of the term "voluntary" to describe unsanctioned absence (Behrend, 1959) and in managerial treatments of control strategies (CBI, 1970). Despite this, the hedonistic, rationalistic, and normative character of "push–pull" or "pain avoidance" treatments of motivated behavior has not gone unchallenged (Nicholson, 1977). It is now widely recognized that feelings of satisfaction and dissatisfaction may be peripheral to the core motivational process, as in expectancy theory, where they are cast in the role of potentially transient outputs (cf. Campbell & Pritchard, 1976). Similarly, rational calculations of subjective utilities and the probabilities of outcomes may be less important than behavioral and attitudinal commitments to habitual acts or constructions of the situation. Such relatively unconsidered factors are important and relevant motivational dynamics, yet ones that may only be obliquely glimpsed when the focus is fixed on conscious volitional states.

There is a curious exception to this emphasis on the volitional aspects of absence: the problem of bypassing significant motivational processes for those absences that have the appearance of being "involuntary." Even where the locus of control for absence can be attributed to factors external to the person, they are nonetheless mediated by the person's construction of reality, and their impact may be significantly moderated by the person's motivational state (as in the case of much nonchronic illness).

PIU 3: *Absence is essentially an individual-level phenomenon, best predicted and explained via individual differences.*

The reviews of the literature show that two strategies have dominated absence research. On one hand, absence has been correlated with personal characteristics such as age, sex, and family size. On the other, it has been associated with individually generated measures of work attitudes and perceptions, such as job satisfaction and job characteristics. The individualistic paradigm has proved so pervasive as to even lead researchers to apply explanations appropriate to individual variations to data in which groups are the operational units of analysis (e.g., Dittrich & Carrell, 1979; Kerr, Koppelmeier, & Sullivan, 1951).[4] As Hulin and Rousseau[5] point out, individual responses and rates of behavior do not tap the same pool of variance, and certainly in the absence literature there has been a relative neglect of factors potentially underlying sources of variation in group-level absence, such as norms, cohesiveness, and climate.

In their review of studies of absence and job satisfaction, Nicholson, Brown, and Chadwick-Jones (1976) found that 13 of 29 studies based their conclusions about the potency (or otherwise) of dissatisfaction as a cause of absence upon analytical techniques that took no account of individual variance on either variable. That is, all were group level investigations that resorted to individualistic explanatory frameworks. A related logic may be observed in many research treatments of job characteristics. Instead of viewing absence in light of workplace structural influences that distinguish *work roles*, job characteristics are abstracted as psychological dimensions that attach to *jobholders* (e.g., Turner & Lawrence, 1965). Although some positive findings have been reported by such studies, their efficacy is directly limited to those features that are suitable for psychometric analysis (i.e., displaying reliably quantifiable individual variation). They typically tell us little about other dimensions of jobs that may be of crucial relevance to understanding absence (e.g., payment systems and supervisory regimes), and that may underlie relationships between perceived job characteristics and absence behavior. These considerations suggest that subjective perceptions of job dimensions and work attitudes should be restored to their logical research roles as individual-level *intervening* variables, lying between the structure of work environments and worker behavior, rather than treated as intrapsychic *independent* variables without reference to their situational antecedents.

PIU 4: *Absence is a static phenomenon.*

Although fairly wide variations may be observed in rates, absence is almost always sufficiently infrequent among employee populations to be considered a low base rate phenomenon. A recent Canadian report judged the average industrial time lost rate to be around 4 percent of scheduled working days, with a range of approximately 1 to 10 percent ("Absenteeism," 1980), and one writer has recently assessed the United States average time lost to be 3.5 percent (Hedges, 1977). As Rousseau[6] and Hulin and Rousseau[5] have pointed out, a consequence of this has been the common practice of aggregating absence data over time (usually 6 to 12 months) to yield sufficient reliable variance for conventional analyses. The conceptual corollary of this, to which many researchers are prey, is to discuss absence as if it were timeless and absolute (i.e., an attribute or property of an individual or an organization): this person "has" high absence; that organization "has" low absence. Changes in absence levels are usually treated as problems of reliability (Chadwick-Jones et al., 1971; Huse & Taylor, 1962; Latham & Pursell, 1975). However, as Hulin and Rosseau[5] argue, the unreliability of behaviors such as absence may be a function of "lawful changes," meaning that the occurrence or nonoccurrence of the behavior may increase or decrease its probability in the future.

PIU 5: *Absence is best viewed as strictly an "organizational" behavior.*

In urging managers and researchers to measure work *attendance* rather than absence, Latham and Pursell (1975) state that "absenteeism is a *nonevent* in that no behavior can be observed or recorded *on the job*" (p. 369, italics added). This statement is a truism, and it indicates the profound lack of interest exhibited by researchers in the extraorganizational factors that may influence absence. For example, in their review of the absence literature, Porter and Steers (1973) partition the investigated correlates into four categories, three of which are solely concerned with the organization (organization-wide, immediate work environment, and job-related). Similarly, a later summary compiled by Rhodes and Steers[2] divides the factors associated with absence into seven categories, five of which are exclusively organizational.[7] When one examines individual studies more closely, this extreme "organization-centric" perspective is confirmed. Let us consider briefly how this arises.

In most regular employment, workers enter into a quasi-contractual exchange of a fixed quota of time to fulfill organizational goals for a schedule of rewards. Within this framework, unscheduled absence becomes deviant behavior in relation to organizational expectations, because it imposes direct costs upon organizational efficiency and profitability. This often leads to absence being viewed as an index of organizational effectiveness and individual performance, and as a criterion for the success of change programs (many basic organizational behavior texts stress this point of view). The assumption underlying this kind of treatment is that absence is "management's problem" (see Fox and Scott, 1943, for an early influential stimulus for this view), and that it falls within the organization's sphere of legitimate and intended control (Gaudet, 1963). In other words, there is a logical drift from awareness of the significance of absence for organizational functioning to a belief that causes and corrections lie within the workplace. A stimulus for this logical drift is the very ease with which absence is quantifiable as a performance measure, and the legalistic, contractual terms in which it is interpreted. Unfortunately for would-be agents of organizational control, however, absence events that are responses to aspects of work experience are identical in appearance to those that are prompted by extraorganizational factors.

PIU 6: *Absence occurs only among blue-collar and clerical workers.* In treating absence as "management's problem," commentators usually mean that it is a problem for the regulation of managers' *subordinates.* The mechanisms organizations institute to record and discipline absence are applied primarily to those areas of the enterprise where it is visibly related to output and requires adjustment to the programming of work systems (e.g., rescheduling tasks, reallocating manpower). For these reasons, reliable records of employee absence are usually only maintained at the lower levels of organizations. This is reflected in the great volume of research data pertaining to blue-collar and some lower level white-collar populations, and the dearth of information about higher level employees (consult the reviews cited earlier). The relative "invisibility" of absence among managers, professionals, and entrepreneurs has meant that these groups are generally exempted from generalizations about the causes of absence, and it seems to be assumed that no comparable "problem" exists among them. Among blue-collar workers the problem is often cast as one of "malingering" (Dennett, 1978), whereas among executives "stress" is the fashionable explanation for aberrant behavior, even though close scrutiny of the evidence shows that stress symptoms are in fact most prevalent among lower level occupations (Fletcher, Gowler, & Payne, 1979). As we shall be arguing in due course, one may certainly expect absence to have different meanings for people in contrasting occupational circumstances, but this in no way buttresses the fiction that absence is a problem or a behavior peculiarly characteristic of lower organizational levels.

It should be recognized that the six PIUs presented do not constitute a coherent "theory in use." Strictly interpreted, there are logical inconsistencies among them. For example, the normative view of absence causation seen in PIUs 1 and 6 is contradicted by methodologies that individualize its causation in accordance with PIU 3. Similarly, seeing absence as a means of fulfilling various conscious purposes (PIU 2) is potentially at odds with the assumptions underlying its aggregation in measurement (PIU 4) and its treatment as a species of organizational performance (PIU 5). Why should this be so? First, all these PIUs are supportive of the traditional positivist ethos of investigative methods. Each derives from the assumption that absence is a "problem" that can be "solved" by the application of normal science treatments, characterized by a value-free orientation, an acultural and ahistorical perspective, an emphasis on quantitative rather than qualitative explorations of data, and the application of the logic of hypotheticodeductive verification. For positivist methods to succeed, it is necessary that they be applied within carefully bounded limits that are specified by subtopic areas and internally consistent partial models of the phenomena in question. The result is a fragmentation of different approaches to absence, each invoking a different set of supportive PIUs. Some aspects of absence may be illuminated by such approaches, though it is our contention that alternatives are necessary to advance understanding in areas where research has reached an impasse or where there has been neglect by researchers.

Absence research, like much other research in organizational behavior, is method-driven. The ease with which absence data may be collected at different levels of analysis suggests facile possibilities for data analysis at these various levels. Consequently, the multiplexity of absence causes is simplified, and questions about its social and personal meanings are shelved in the interests of easy data manipulation and hypothesis confirmation. In a manner similar to job satisfaction researchers (as charged by Locke, 1969), absence investigators have "measured and correlated" absence with whatever other variables are available and avoided the more fundamental questions about what it is they are measuring.

Our counterpropositions are thus intended as antidotes to this tradition. We are not trying to level one set of deities to erect another, but seeking to enlarge the possibility for useful future research by bringing to the fore some little considered alternative perspectives on absence.

SOME VIABLE COUNTERPROPOSITIONS

In this section we present six counterpropositions regarding the nature of absence that are intended to demonstrate that new approaches to research are possible. These CPs avoid, but do not preclude, a managerial orientation toward the control of absence.

CP 1: *Absence events are phenomenologically unique.*

The personal significance of each absence event has distinctive properties according to the shifting interaction of personal factors and environmental constraints. Put another way, absence means different things to different people at different times in different situations. We do not deny that valid generalizations may be made about absence behavior, as there are numerous regularities in personal and organizational life. However, there is no law of permanence for such regularities, and we should expect generalized predictions to be unreliable—as indeed they are. This is reflected in small amounts of variance in absence behavior that studies have usually been able to predict, and the instability of these relationships (as is the case of job satisfaction and absence). In order to better explain absence, this more closely contingent approach is needed, in which we attempt to uncover the specific contextual conditions that apply to individual absence episodes. This demands more painstaking investigation, in which idiographic techniques are used to correctly specify the boundaries that are appropriate to explaining episodes and which will enable us to judge when similar explanations are valid for individual actors and episodes. Phenomenological strategies that explore the significance of absence events within the life-space of individuals are an essential prerequisite for the development of grounded theory about individual absence causation.

CP 2: *Much absence is not the result of conscious choice but is the result of nonvolitional forces.*

It is evident that absence is often purposive and environmentally adaptive. Morgan and Herman (1976) have shown how absence can be seen as constructive goal-seeking behavior, directed at fulfilling aspirations and obligations outside the sphere of the organization rather than simply fulfilling a need to escape the discomforts of work. However, this does not constitute confirming evidence for the assertion that most absence is a conscious and calculated act. Even when workers take advantage of a sick pay scheme or take a day off to attend to pressing business affairs, the decision may take place within a "bounded rationality" (Simon, 1957) of rules, constraints, and introjected norms whose potency as guiding forces is largely unseen by the person. More common is the attribution of absence to involuntary factors—usually illness. The pervasiveness of medical criteria for absence legitimation and the extensive penetration of medical etiology into everyday thought and language has meant that the purposive nature of absence is often disguised from the consciousness of the absentee and those close to him or her. Psychological medicine has established that a great deal of common illness has strong psychogenic elements, an insight that has consistently eluded the consciousness of industrial and organizational psychologists! By the same token, most *attendance* is not the result of a daily "decision" of any conscious kind but is behavior executed in accordance with established norms, routines, customs, and habits. The attendance behavior of most employees is effectively on "automatic pilot," and indeed their conscious decisional processes will probably have played only a small part in the original setting of the normative controls that thereafter guide their behavior. A corollary of this view is the suggestion that some individual differences in absence will be due to variations in personal "habit strength." Such strength is probably a function of both the degree of compulsive "attachment" to work (Nicholson & Payne)[8] and external constraints on perceived decisional freedom.

CP 3: *Valid generalizations about absence often require a sociocultural perspective.*

There is increasing recognition in the field of organizational behavior that different work environments may provoke different psychological reactions, often researched under the heading of "organizational climate" (Payne & Pugh, 1976). The psychological environment that is created by structural conditions, by the framework of rules, norms, and customs, and by the values of influential organizational members may be pervasive in its impact on employee thought and action. Comparative research has shown that the absence profiles of individual organizations are indeed highly distinctive, and that the correlates of absence vary widely from plant to plant (Chadwick-Jones, Brown, & Nicholson, in press). We may learn significantly more about absence behavior by moving our focus to encompass absence "cultures," that is, the set of shared understandings about absence legitimacy in a given organization and the established "custom and practice" of employee absence behavior and its control (e.g., predominant supervisory styles and worker beliefs about co-workers' attendance behavior). If one accepts that behavior is mediated by the sociopsychological environment, then it is necessary to establish as a baseline for causal analysis the unique normative constraints that distinguish absence patterns across organizations and their subunits.

CP 4: *Absence is temporal behavior and continually subject to dynamic change.*

By definition, absence reallocates the distribution of time from work to nonwork. Thus, the meaning of absence events to both absentees and others in their social framework may be distinguished by duration as well as perceived causes. Given that absence *a priori* restructures the work week, it follows that this may be the primary outcome for which absence is instrumental; i.e., to autonomously change the schedule of working hours. In expectancy theory terms, the valence of this outcome will derive from the valences of the uses of reallocated time. This compels us to view absence causation as a recursive learning process, and in the words of Hulin and Rousseau[5], to expect "lawful changes" in absence behavior over time and from episode to episode. The longitudinal "dialectic" of attendance behavior has been neglected by research, apart from those studies that have looked for changes in employee attendance following organizational changes. The implication of this CP is that research should attempt more continuous monitoring of feedback and change in employee absence behavior and not merely view such change as a source of unwanted error variance.

CP 5: *Absence represents nonwork behavior and is subject to major causal influences from variables that transcend the workplace.*
By defining the behavior in terms of its obvious organizational impact, the word "absence" involves the same conceptual snare as the term "withdrawal." This perspective neglects the fact that when a person is absent from work he or she is *present* somewhere else, and far too little attention has been paid to the impact of forces outside the workspace. When studies have incorporated work-transcending variables, such as domestic circumstances, they have contributed significantly to absence prediction (e.g., Morgan & Herman, 1976). Staw and Oldham (1978) make a similar point when they charge that too little attention is paid to the complex meaning of our dependent variables in organizational research, and, in the case of absence, how its maintenance functions for individual adjustment should be considered in addition to its more common construal as dysfunctional performance. In short, we need to know more about the barriers to attendance and the incentives to absence that exist beyond organizational boundaries and outside the purview of management controls.

CP 6: *Absence occurs throughout the world of work, and research should reflect this fact.*
Wherever people are subject to the quasi-contractual exchange of time and effort for rewards, there will be occasions when they seek to unilaterally effect a temporary change in their side of the bargain. In short, managers and other higher level organizational members are not immune from the need or desire to take time off work in addition to that scheduled in the work contract. Whether this is viewed as unproblematic or defensible is irrelevant to the fact that such behavior is generically identical to what is considered problematic at lower organizational levels. It only shows that different assumptions, attributions, and controls are thought to be applicable. Researchers' neglect of managerial absence (and that of the self-employed) may be attributable to the paucity of data available in readily analyzable form, though this must be considered a poor excuse for scientific omissions and should only serve as a spur to fresh initiatives. Unfortunately, it has not. In particular, we do not know to what extent absence has common costs, causes, and controls at different organizational levels or in different occupational settings. There is good reason to expect that people who occupy different roles and hold different statuses will differ systematically in motive structures, habits, normative imperatives, and external constraints. A comparative approach that captures the variance in these factors may be an especially effective strategy for exploring the various meanings of absence.

These six CPs do not constitute a more coherent "theory" of absence than the PIUs that they are intended to supplant. However, in our view, they do suggest more complex, realistic explanations of absence and invoke more challenging methodologies than their well-worn predecessors. These methods include phenomenological approaches to dispositions toward absence (e.g., illness behaviors); ethnogenic strategies at various levels of analysis (e.g., work group interpretations of member behavior); longitudinal analyses of cause-effect relationships; the investigation of new variables that surface as a result of the previous techniques. There is growing recognition (among social psychologists in particular) that strategies of this nature are necessary to cope with the historical complexity of social behavior and to encompass the subjective meanings that link it with its context (cf. Gergen, 1973; Harré & Secord, 1972; Pepitone, 1976).

In the sections that follow we consider seven research areas that are suggested by the selective joint application of the CPs. Juxtaposed as they are, it will be apparent that there is some overlap among them, with the consequent potential for eventual theoretical synthesis. First, some basic issues regarding absence are considered. Second, absence as a form of personal control is explored. In conclusion, the social aspects of absence are examined.

SOME BASIC ISSUES

This section considers three fairly basic research issues that stem from the adoption of the CPs. In a sense, work in these areas should "clear the decks" and generate needed information for investigating other substantive topics regarding absence. In two cases (absence proneness and absence and alternative behaviors), we take a new look at old issues. In the other case (the attribution process and absence), we examine a basic issue that has been neglected by previous research.

A Fresh Look at Absence Proneness

Although absence is a universal organizational phenomenon and is exhibited wherever people are employed, it is also a low base rate phenomenon (i.e., a relatively small number of instances are distributed among work forces). At very low levels, the distribution of absence takes the form of the *J*-curve or Poisson distribution (Walker, 1947), with "the many" having few or no spells of absence and "the few" accounting for the remainder. From an observer's point of view, this may have two consequences. First, the visibility of the few is accentuated by figure–ground contrast. Second, a dispositional explanation of absence is invited. These consequences circumscribe what might be called the classical view of absence proneness. Were absence more or less common than it is, it could be accepted as normal or dismissed as aberrant. But absence, being a phenomenon that is readily observable and measurable in all industries but not among all workers, is optimally visible, thus arousing attention and concern.

It is often argued that a small core of workers accounts for a disproportionate share of absenteeism, with 10 to 20 percent of the work force accounting for 80 to 90 percent of time lost (Robinson, 1980; Yolles, Carone, & Krinsky, 1974). Indeed, careful empirical studies provide support for the disproportionate occurrence of absence, although the magnitude of the effect appears to vary with the time frame over which data are aggregated and the specific absence measure used. In a Cardiff, Wales, study of 16 organizations (Chadwick-Jones et al., in press) it was found that 10 percent of the workers were responsible for 25 to 40 percent of 1 year's total absence frequency. This finding was remarkable for its consistency across quite disparate employee populations and quite independent of wide variations in absolute levels of absence. On the other hand, Garrison and Muchinsky (1977), using a 3-month time frame, found that 17 percent of the work force accounted for 90 percent of paid time lost whereas 31 percent accounted for 90 percent of unpaid time lost.

Such findings tend to fuel the common supposition that absence is due to some malaise in disposition or malignancy of constitution on the part of the offenders. Once set apart from their fellow workers in this manner, it is logical to try to "normalize" the distribution by means of various sanctions. In this common managerial strategy we see several of the PIUs exhibited: equivalent meaning among the absences of the core; the assumption that absence reflects a static, volitional personal property; and the notion that absence is widely susceptible to organizational control.

Our CPs suggest that the PIUs are loaded in favor of discovering proneness but ill-suited to explore its nature once identified. Where this reasoning prevails, there is a need to examine empirically the premises upon which it rests and then look at the whole question of proneness afresh. First, there is a need to establish whether absence occurs among the few *more often* than might be expected. The Poisson distribution is, after all, the normal distribution writ small, and the laws of chance alone predict a core at the upper asymptote. Second, it must be established that the core remains *constant,* for there are two alternatives to the attribution of proneness to people. One is that there is a different core each time behavior is sampled. This would be expected if a small number of absences were allocated totally randomly each year across a work force. The other is that apparent proneness is a function of some fairly constant factor such as personal attributes or role requirements.

There have been studies that shed light on these issues. Arbous and Sichel (1954) and Froggatt (1970) have found that statistical proneness clearly exceeds chance expectations. However, even when one accepts this point, it may be reasoned that only a proportion of those who are statistically prone are prone by disposition or constitution. Many of those at the high extreme can still be viewed as merely unlucky rather than culpable, because although curve-fitting reveals significant deviations from chance, these are not sufficiently dramatic to support a dispositional explanation for *all* absence-prone persons. A secondary source of evidence regarding proneness is the incidence of "repeaters." Few studies have quantified this, although it does seem that one of the best predictors of a person's absence spell frequency for one time period is his or her spell frequency for an adjacent period: interyear correlations between .5 and .7 are typical (Froggatt, 1970; Morgan & Herman, 1976; Nicholson & Goodge, 1976; Waters & Roach, 1979). A more differentiated approach has been taken by Garrison and Muchinsky (1977), who showed that proneness was a relatively short-range phenomenon because interperiod correlations declined over time until returning to chance levels. Thus, the core may change, but slowly. However, this does not tell us *what* determines absence proneness, for the factors that lead to a shifting core of prone persons in one setting may not be found in others, e.g., changes in job content, payment systems, supervisory regimes, and the like. In a stable environment, the only predictable changes are in personal characteristics: the effects of aging, increasing job tenure, and variations in domestic circumstances. Relative stability in such factors is the norm, and hence changes in them causing increases or decreases in susceptibility to high levels of absence will be uncommon or very gradual. It would seem then that in most industrial settings proneness will be demonstrable for a given time period, but its immutability cannot be assumed.

Let us now turn to a brief examination of the possible causes of proneness, for ultimately it is upon knowledge of these that inferences about its generality must rest.

Walker's (1947) explanation of the *J*-curve was social. Its clearest manifestation at the subunit level was interpreted as symptomizing emergent patterns of conformity and deviance. There are at least three explanations for deviance: constitutional or character traits, environmental circumstances, or interactions reflecting person–environment mismatches. Conventional correlational studies have implicated all three; though not surprisingly (in view of the highly skewed distribution of absence frequency), they have failed to account for much variance. Neither is this approach able to tell us specifically about the "hard core" absentees. It is plausible that their absence is generated by causes that are different from the majority of absentees who have only one, two, or three spells a year. Cross-sectional correlational studies may confound these different causes, with the very small number of high level absentees submerged in the general mass and with predictions statistically geared to distinguishing the "lows" from the "zeros."

Clearly there is considerable scope for a fresh approach to the question of proneness, for example, by deliberately setting out to analytically isolate the chronic repeaters or employees who deviate radically from subunit norms and *then* commencing the search for causes. However, it is unlikely that research strategies that treat the prone as homogeneous will succeed. As a group they may be few relative to the employee population, but there is good reason to assume that individual differences will distinguish them from each other in as many ways as from their less prone colleagues. For example, if prone workers are deviant relative to low absence norms because of personality characteristics, they are in all probability an aggregate of highly differentiated "characters." In addition, given the multiplicity of potential causes of absence, prone individuals are likely subject to the interactive influence of several factors, and for each person this subset of causes will be unique (e.g., work dissatisfaction × susceptibility to minor illness; domestic anxieties × transportation problems; poor co-worker relations × strong external leisure interests). In short, in most of the directions one may speculatively search for causes of proneness, it would seem advisable to commence by treating the prone as unique cases, searching for the singular meaning of their proneness, and relating affect and behavior to singular contextual characteristics. Much of this work could be accomplished by using timely interviews and diary techniques.

As we have noted, there is no reason to believe that the causes of absence are unvarying over time (CP 4). The Garrison and Muchinsky (1977) findings suggest that investigators should pay particular attention to characteristics that change gradually or continually, such as domestic circumstances, which may give rise to a shifting core of prone workers. Thus, a joint phenomenological and historical approach is needed to decompose the absence patterns of the prone. Only when this has been achieved can individual histories be collated into more general accounts of proneness. Such collation should avoid regenerating a static vision of proneness, one which effectively ignores "time and space." Specifically, the broader concern of proneness research should be the extent of its spatiotemporal stability, its propensity to endure as people move from setting to setting. Are those who are prone in school also prone in subsequent employment settings? Are those who are absent from work also absent from other social obligations? Principally and initially, however, it remains to be discovered whether transituational proneness is normal or whether it is more useful to conceive of proneness within the context of specific absence climates or cultures (to be discussed later).

In summary, we know little about absence proneness, and its examination from the perspective of our CPs may enable us to better understand the behavior of those who contribute disproportionately to the total volume of absence.

Attributional Processes and Absence

In line with CP 2, Nicholson (1977) has argued that there is far less rational calculus preceding most absence events than a process of succumbing to potential risks or barriers deflecting the person from the norm of habitual attendance. In that paper Nicholson described how researchers might develop risk profiles based on objective characteristics such as age, work setting, and family circumstances. Each profile would quantify how employees differ in their susceptibility to proximal causes of absence, such as injury, illness, fatigue, family demands, and personal business. In this section, we take this argument a step further by exploring individual differences in the *interpretation* of these proximal causes. For example, how is it that one worker with a mild head cold manages to come to work whereas another finds this an adequate reason to remain at home?

The preceding suggests that conventional attitudinal and motivational constructs may serve less as direct predictors of absence than as mediators of potential proximal causes. Support for this can be found in an ingenious study by Smith (1977), who showed that job satisfaction predicted absence among managers on the day of a heavy snowfall in Chicago but did not do so on the same day in snow-free New York. The point here is that psychological processes may create individual differences in, the threshold of susceptibility to causes lying more or less outside the employee's control. In order to explore this, we advocate the investigation of the attributional process behind absence from the perspective of both absentees and observers.

Attribution is the process of imputing motives or explanations for observed behavior. Attribution theory has been applied to the analysis of various forms of organizational behavior, including leadership (Calder, 1977), performance (Mitchell, Green, & Wood, 1981), and turnover (Steers & Mowday, 1981).[8] However, we are not merely jumping on the bandwagon. Because absence is a particularly public behavior and because it is frequently viewed as significant behavior by both actors and observers, it seems especially likely to provoke attributed explanations. In many cases, absence is a behavior that *demands* explanation or justification. Additional interest in an attributional analysis of absence stems from CP 1, which suggests that absence may have a variety of meanings for individuals. Insight into these meanings seems accessible through the explanations given for absence. Although such explanations may not be directly predictive of absence, and may indeed be manifestly inaccurate, they should provide a picture of the phenomenal field within which absence occurs.

There are several key questions to be answered regarding the attribution of causes of absence behavior: What are the processes that individuals use to explain discrete episodes of their own absence behavior? What are the processes that observers (superiors, co-workers, family) use to explain discrete episodes of absence on the part of others? To what extent do people harbor *generalized* attributions about the "typical" causes of absence, and when might such attributions be employed? Under what conditions might attributions regarding absence be more or less accurate? How do attributions change over time? Although no single theory of attribution provides the answers to these questions, we hope to demonstrate that the eclectic utilization of several extant theories (Bem, 1972; Jones & Davis, 1965; Kelly, 1972) can provide a good starting point.

There are at least three sources or formats for the exploration of explanations for one's own absence behavior. The first of these involves having organizational officials accurately and completely record the stated explanations provided by absentees. It is reasonable to expect that such reports will be distorted by ego-defensiveness, social desirability, and general self-interest. In fact, exit interview evidence suggests that such motives affect explanations for turnover (Hinrichs, 1975; Lefkowitz & Katz, 1969), and there is every reason to believe that similar forces would be at work in the case of absence. However, such reports should reveal workers' beliefs about what the organization considers to be legitimate reasons for absence. These reasons provide input for the attributions made by organizational observers of absence, including those found officially categorized in personnel records.

It would also be useful to have workers explain in general terms, under research conditions, why they are usually absent from work. As will be discussed later, Nicholson and Payne[9] have done this. Retrospective accounts of "typical" reasons for one's usual absence seem especially likely to reveal what Nisbett and Wilson (1977) have termed *a priori causal theories*. That is, such explanations, removed in time and context from actual proximal stimuli, may invoke accepted cultural or subcultural notions about why absence is likely to occur. Although such theories may be probabilistically accurate, they should inadequately analyze the causes of distinct absence episodes. Yet, as will be pointed out shortly, there may be conditions under which individuals adopt such theories to explain a series of ostensibly poorly justified absences to themselves.

The third and most interesting manner of gathering data to study self-attribution would be to have workers keep diaries of the proximal causes of discrete absence episodes. Alternatively, timely interviews might be arranged with persons who fail to report for work. While there is currently a debate raging in the literature concerning the accuracy of introspective verbal reports (Nisbett & Wilson, 1977; Smith & Miller, 1978; White, 1980; Ericsson & Simon),[10,11] there is apparent consensus that data collection methods that are closer to "real time" should reduce distortions due to the passage of time. If this is so, timely accounts of reasons for absence should have more variance than generalized retrospective reports and relevant context effects should be more readily accessible.

Aspects of extant attribution theories could be incorporated into timely studies of absenteeism. The theories proposed by Kelly (1972) and Jones and Davis (1965) are complementary, because the former involves the temporal and contextual cues that precede a given absence episode, whereas the latter involves cues derived from the consequences of the episode. Thus, perceptions of the consistency, consensus, and distinctiveness of absenteeism could be measured (Kelly, 1972), and the perceived work and nonwork (CP 4) consequences of absence episodes could be obtained (Jones & Davis, 1965).

Just what could the preceding three types of analyses be expected to demonstrate? First, it is reasonable to expect the reversal of the well-established "fundamental attribution error" (Ross, 1977). That is, self-attributions should reveal a disproportionate tendency to invoke circumstantial, rather than dispositional, causes for absenteeism. Such attributions should be supported by the relevant consensus, consistency, and distinctiveness cues. Of course, the circumstances invoked to explain an absence episode to company representatives would often differ from those marshaled to explain the episode to oneself.[12] Obviously, none of this is very surprising. However, there are conditions under which the timely longitudinal study of self-attributions may reveal the tendency to adopt dispositional explanations for one's absence. We now turn to this issue.

There is one type of introspective tendency that may be especially prevalent in probing absence: the unlikely attribution of "large" effects to "small" causes (Nisbett & Wilson, 1977). If this is so, relatively trivial proximal stimuli (the alarm clock failing to go off, an interesting program on television, a slight hangover, a mild cold) may be reinterpreted even under conditions favoring accurate reportage. This situation corresponds to the well-known "insufficient justification" paradigm, especially if the perceived consequences of absence are strongly negative. In this case, Bem's (1972) self-perception theory suggests that actors are likely to adopt the attribution process of external observers and infer that some intrinsic, dispositional motive prompted their behavior. Such an attribution is especially likely if unjustified absence is repeated over time (Jones and McGillis, 1976; Kelly, 1972). For example, the individual who is frequently absent in response to a series of disconnected minor ailments, especially at the expense of negative consequences, may come to perceive himself or herself as constitutionally unfit, effectively adopting a "sick role" (cf. Levine & Kozloff, 1978). Thus, the criteria by which one judges one's fitness to attend work may be altered over time. This attribution may be "borrowed" from an *a priori* causal theory that is approved by the culture or subculture. In fact, this scenario synchronizes nicely with Nicholson and Payne's[8] study of retrospective reports of reasons for typical absence events; this study showed a strong tendency for individuals to invoke medical explanations. Different individuals encountering different proximal stimuli should develop different attributions. For example, a more culturally independent person who experiences a series of hangovers and alarm clock failures may adopt a "deviant" role to account for his or her absence. In fact, these kinds of attributional processes may be characteristic of certain classes of proneness, as discussed earlier.[13]

Before leaving the topic of self-attribution, it is worthwhile to consider another example of the value of this approach. There has been a surprising neglect of a decision with which every absentee is faced: when to *return* to work. We are in agreement with Smulders (1980) that conventional research has been more oriented toward predicting the *inception* of absence rather than its *duration* (consistent with the "withdrawal *from*" argument: PIU 2). Thus, it may be no accident that predictions of frequency of absence (literally, number of inceptions) are consistently stronger than those for time lost (loading on duration) (Johns, 1978; Metzner & Mann, 1953; Nicholson, Brown, & Chadwick-Jones, 1977). While the argument that time lost is "contaminated" by serious sickness may have some validity, such a position ignores the determinant nature of the chosen predictors and ignores the fact that the seriousness of sickness is itself a relative, interpreted, and attributed matter (Smulders, 1980). In his current doctoral research at the University of Sheffield, Chris Brewin is examining the duration of absence following industrial accidents. Preliminary results indicate that individuals who are high on internal locus of control (Rotter, 1966) are more likely to accept a measure of self-blame for their difficulties and return to work earlier than externals, who are less ready to accept such blame. These fascinating results are exactly in line with the earlier arguments concerning the mediation of proximal causes via psychological states through the attribution process. That is, two individuals with objectively similar injuries (proximal cause) who differ in locus of control (psychological state) attribute the reasons for their absence to different causal factors.

In addition to self-attributions, the attribution processes used by observers of absence episodes should be examined. Such observers may include friends and family members, as well as organizational members. The attributions of observers are important because they determine in part the consequences that absence will have for the actor. Again, the theories proposed by Kelly (1972) and Jones and Davis (1965) provide helpful guidelines for such research. Presumably, because observers will usually be in possession of fewer relevant cues than actors, their explanations should reveal more stereotyping. The form of this stereotyping may depend, however, on the location of the observer. Specifically, observers inside and outside of the organization should possess substantially different cues regarding the circumstances of a specific absence episode. These cues should often lead them to provide substantially different explanations for absence. In particular, organizational observers may be especially likely to commit the "fundamental attribution error" (Ross, 1977) of overemphasizing dispositional motives for absence. This may occur because such observers will be unaware of mitigating off-the-job circumstances that preceded an absence event. Furthermore, if these observers are superiors of the absentee, a dispositional attribution enables the superior to discount his or her own role in provoking or preventing absence. Such dispositional explanations should be especially likely when strong sanctions against absence exist, when absence is exhibited steadily (high consistency), when co-workers are seldom absent (low consensus), and when the person is known to have exhibited high absence on previous jobs (low distinctiveness). In fact, this may be just the case in which proneness is most likely to be invoked to "explain" absence.

Some important questions regarding attribution of the absence behavior of others include: What other cues do observers use to explain or classify absence events? Which combinations of cues are associated with "acceptable" and "unacceptable" absence? Is one's explanation of the absence of others related to one's own absence behavior? In addition, CP 6 suggests that it would be illuminating to examine such attributions under systems that differ in expectations regarding attendance or that differ in the extent of formal sanctions against absence (e.g., university professors, the self-employed, and factory workers).

In concluding this section, it seems worthwhile to reverse the coin, as it were, and mention observers' attributions regarding *attendance*. Specifically, it might be hypothesized that a certain proportion of good attendance represents an attempt on the part of subordinates to *ingratiate* themselves to their superiors. Ingratiation tactics are employed to enhance one's attractiveness to others, and as Wortman and Linsenmeir (1977, p. 135) point out, "the ingratiator's task is primarily one of manipulating the attributions made by the target person he is trying to impress." If the likelihood of such strategies is dependent upon their probable success, there is ample reason to believe that good attendance is a frequent ingratiation tactic in work settings. Wortman and Linsenmeir (1977) argue that because of the power differential subordinates must avoid obvious ingratiation tactics such as direct praise and slavish opinion conformity. While good attendance fulfills these criteria, it has some other characteristics that are generally associated with successful ingratiation. First, it is nonverbal. Second, it may represent a subtle, indirect form of opinion conformity with the boss. Third, by making the superior look effective as a leader, it may act as a form of favor rendering for which it is difficult to find an ulterior motive. Good attendance would seem to be an especially effective technique for manipulating the superior's attributions when performance criteria are otherwise vague, when there are few formal sanctions against absence, and when peers exhibit a high level of absence.

Absence and Behavioral Alternatives

If we are to accept CP 1 (that absence benefits from being viewed as phenomenally unique), logic compels us to extend the same courtesy to other employee behaviors. A corollary of this is that an individual absence incident may have more in common with an instance of lateness, slacking off on the job, or similar behavior than it does with many other absence incidents. The reasons for absence are likely to change over time as a function of variations in environmental pressures and personal goals. The same is true for other employee behaviors, and the failure of absence to correlate with these other behaviors in aggregated data sets (across time and across persons), as in the case of absence and lateness (Nicholson & Goodge, 1976), does not mean they are unrelated. Rather it suggests that any such relationships will be subtle and individually differentiated. The likelihood of different behaviors may be under the partial control of similar individual dispositions at a given point in time but subject to quite distinct environmental contingencies. For example, lateness or absence may be equally sufficient responses to a nasty hangover. However, differential organizational sanctions may prompt one reaction rather than the other. The point here is that, whatever behavior we choose to examine, it is for the person an adaptive or proactive response to the unique configuration of the life space at that time. It is thus axiomatic that various work and nonwork behaviors are systematically linked via the "personal system" but that the causal history of each will be different. The real nature of relationships among such behaviors can thus only be revealed by a closer focus on individuals and instances. The same arguments apply to both the relationships between different so-called "types" of absence and between different instances of absence that are classified as similar.

It is not surprising that researchers have shunned this methodologically and theoretically thorny path and found it more attractive to assume that absences themselves share a causal unity (PIU 1), albeit a loose one, and that other employee behaviors exhibit parallel or similar causal coherence. This is usually argued under the rubric of PIU 2, that absence is a motivated "withdrawal" from (negative aspects of) the workplace, as are other behaviors such as turnover, lateness, and some accidents. It has been argued elsewhere (Nicholson, 1977) that this reasoning is the product of the logical fallacy of identifying *physical* withdrawal with *motivated* withdrawal and that the attractiveness of this idea is partly ideological, seeking to keep absence within the zone of managerial control (PIU 5). An opposite fallacy can be seen in the contrasting orientation of some social scientists whose ideological stance leads them to view work behavior in conflict terms, with absence portrayed as "unorganized conflict" sharing common causes with the organized conflict of strikes and other protests (cf. Barbash, 1980; Hyman, 1972). For these writers, absence and industrial action are functionally equivalent responses to similar employment circumstances. Both are manifestations of alienation or of divergent employee–employer goals.

There seems to be little empirical support for either proposition. No research has demonstrated the viability of the "withdrawal" hypothesis. Even between such allegedly similar behaviors as absence and turnover, the evidence does not indicate stable interrelationships or consistently common causes (Lyons, 1972). Data purporting to support the "conflict" hypothesis are even more insubstantial, usually deriving from industry-level data aggregations, where all variance is conveniently eliminated, and where a host of mediating influences could be adduced to account for what tenuous relationships are obvious. At a trivial level, absence may be a form of industrial action, as in cases of "blue flu" where clauses in the labor contract prohibit strike action. Where such constraints do not apply, there is no evidence for any kind of reliable relationship between absence and different forms of industrial action at the plant level (Kelly & Nicholson, 1980).

Let us be clear that in making these points we are not arguing that absence and other behaviors are unrelated. However, we are arguing that to advocate such relationships in general terms is meaningless, for there are as many possible relationships as there are shared causes and conditions. To illustrate this, it is useful to consider the case of absence and turnover. First, these variables may be positively correlated because similar conditions of employment induce both, in which case a quasi-cultural analysis of employment "cultures" is prescribed (CP 4). Second, they may be correlated at the individual level because a spate of absences precedes (as it would in job-seeking behavior) the decision to quit (Burke & Wilcox, 1972). Third, in the long term, they may be disjunctively related as absence substitutes for unfavorable opportunities to quit (Hill & Trist, 1955). Which of these possible relationships receives empirical support can be expected to depend upon the salient causes of behavior in the particular circumstances under consideration (personal, occupational, and cultural factors) and the chosen mode of analysis (group or individual level, cross-sectional, or longitudinal). For example, the capacity for absence to substitute for turnover may depend upon perceived opportunities for alternative employment, as reflected in local levels of unemployment. The likelihood of absence preceding the act of quitting will depend partly on job search opportunities in one's present job (e.g., access to a telephone). The correlation of absence and turnover at the plant level will be a product of intraorganizational homogeneity and interorganizational differentiation (e.g., the existence of clear-cut differences in job characteristics between firms). Obviously, the discovery of such relationships requires specifically tailored research strategies, and any given strategy may necessarily preclude the detection of other possible associations.

This does not mean that research should retreat from the linkage issue. Rather, absence and other behaviors should be treated as lenses through which more fundamental processes of employee motivation and work relations can be observed. There are signs in recent work that this is taking place. Gupta and Jenkins[3] have attempted to use the concepts of "binding" and "distancing" forces between the person and the organization to predict a continuum of withdrawal ranging from estrangement and frequent work breaks, to tardiness and alcohol consumption, to chronic absence and turnover. However, their intent to retain a conceptual unity under the rubric of "withdrawal" from "aversive" conditions owes more to our PIUs than our CPs. Thus, we are unoptimistic about the possibility of meaningful research strategies being evolved to test a general withdrawal model or of its finding consistent empirical support. Nonetheless, it may prove useful to draw attention to a wider range of potential behaviors than are commonly studied in organizations, and use them as vehicles for fresh approaches to social and psychological processes in organizations (e.g., deviance, effort–reward relations, and role stress).

In summary, the connection between absence and other behaviors should be studied as a contingency developing from the operation of universal psychological and social processes under *unique* circumstances. It is worth noting that this approach corresponds to recent arguments for more fine-grained analyses of the typical dependent variables used in organizational behavior research (Moore, Johns, & Pinder, 1980; Staw, 1980; Staw & Oldham, 1978). Cognitive consistency needs aside, we have not been well served by the implicit stereotype of the good worker as one who is highly productive and satisfied, never late or absent, and consistently striving for long tenure. Such a stereotype neglects the fact that the expected probabilities of various attitudes and behaviors are differentially responsive to circumstantial constraints.

ABSENCE AS A MECHANISM OF CONTROL

We do not reject the notion that a certain proportion of absence is volitional or calculated. However, past attempts to explain absence from a personal motivational perspective have been extremely general in focus, relying on some version of need theory and investigating the relationship between absence and job satisfaction. Unfortunately, the generality of the notion that workers are motivated to absent themselves from jobs that fail to meet their needs is equivocal at best (Nicholson et al., 1976). Thus, in the following two sections we partially forsake CP 2 in order to examine two specific intentional functions that absence might serve: the manipulation of work versus nonwork time and the fulfillment of implicit contracts of exchange. In each case, the use of absence can be hypothesized as centering on the notion of *control* over the temporal or socioeconomic environment. Also in each case, CP 5 figures heavily as employees strive to balance work and nonwork demands.

Absence and Time Allocation

Absence researchers have made remarkably little use of one of the few incontrovertible associations in organizational behavior: the negative relationship between work and nonwork time. PIUs 1, 4, and 5 have conspired to treat absence as a static property of individuals that is relevant only to what happens behind organizational walls. The approach we adopt here asserts that absence temporarily redraws the boundaries between work and nonwork time. As such, it is a dynamic response (CP 4) that depends on the interplay between work and nonwork experiences (CP 5). In addition, its personal significance (CP 1) for certain workers may be the purposive restructuring of time that is more or less necessary or possible across various populations (CP 6).

At the outset, it should be recognized that many studies confound factors that may be relevant to the association between absence and time allocation strategies. This is especially true of large-scale projects such as national absence surveys and research concerning the relationship between organizational size and absence. Despite this confusion, there are four classes of studies that may bear upon this issue. These include studies of (1) the association between absence and nonwork variables, (2) the occurrence of absence under various formal work schedules, (3) the temporal location of absence in the work cycle, and (4) the nature of absence under systems that vary in discretion between work and nonwork time. As will be seen, the use of absence as an intentional time control mechanism must be *inferred* from this work rather than be accepted as *demonstrated*.

As discussed earlier, researchers have frequently examined the association between absenteeism and personal variables. Reviews indicate that frequency of absence decreases with age (Nicholson et al., 1977), that women exhibit more absence than men (Steers & Rhodes, 1978), and that workers with larger families tend toward more absence (Muchinsky, 1977). Such findings have often been interpreted from a time allocation perspective. It has been argued that older workers have fewer extracurricular demands for their time than younger workers or that women and those with large families must often allocate more time to family needs. Clearly, these interpretations can be challenged by plausible hypotheses that have little to do with purposive time allocation. However, two studies have specifically explored the relationship between absence and off-the-job experiences. Using an expectancy theory framework, Morgan and Herman (1976) found that absence was strongly associated with the anticipated achievement of off-the-job social outcomes and leisure time. On the other hand, absence was unassociated with anticipated organizational deterrents. It should be emphasized that the *quality* of off-the-job experiences may influence the allocation of time between work and nonwork. Rousseau (1978) found that frequency of absence among employees of a radio station and an electronics firm was negatively related to reports of challenge experienced in nonwork activities.[14] Thus, attendance patterns may reflect an attempt to balance the quantity *and* quality of time spent in various endeavors.

If absence is influenced by off-the-job experiences and demands for time, it should also be affected by the manner in which working time is scheduled by the organization. The majority of research in this area involves the incidence of absence within or across various shift systems. Some relationships between absence and shift systems appear to be attributable to differences in the personal characteristics of workers who are attracted to a particular system or to objective differences in job context or content (cf. Taylor, 1967). However, the consensus of research in this area suggests that the temporal boundaries of shift systems themselves exert an independent influence on attendance (Nicholson, Jackson, & Howes, 1978; Pocock, 1973). Nicholson et al. determined that both work and nonwork factors stimulate shift effects. Specifically, the length of the shift cycle was associated with the frequency of absence at different locations within the cycle. This finding implicates the influence of nonwork demands through the scheduling of leisure activities at different times of the day or on different days of the week. Also relevant here are studies of the impact of the shortened work week. One claimed advantage of this schedule is that it enables employees to meet personal obligations and arrange leisure activities in a manner that is less likely to impinge upon working time. The evidence on this is mixed. Nord and Costigan (1973) found reduced absence following the introduction of a shortened week, whereas Ivancevich and Lyon (1977) found no change in absence. Both of these studies were conducted in manufacturing environments, and it is possible that the longer days required by the shorter work week induce fatigue. If so, absence for recuperative purposes may sometimes offset expected attendance gains.

A third group of studies indicates that absences are distributed nonrandomly over time. While less common than work schedule research, these studies provide better evidence for the strategic, calculated use of absence to restructure work and nonwork time. Chadwick-Jones, Brown, and Nicholson (1973b) found that women's absence peaked at calendar points when competing domestic demands were greatest. Similarly, Nicholson and Goodge (1976) found that ostensibly casual absence was clustered around holiday periods, and Nicholson (1976) observed that it fell into numerical multiples of the working week. The strategic scheduling argument received additional support in the latter study, which recorded systematic changes in the *form* rather than *level* of absence following an escalation of management sanctioning procedures. This suggests that the volitional component of absence may relate less to the nature of the work experience than to variations in the personal value of nonwork time. Indeed, Rousseau (1978) found that the scope of off-the-job activities was a better predictor of absence than job scope.

There are no studies that directly explore the relationship between absence and discretionary temporal aspects of the work itself. However, the nature of the work cycle and the autonomy or discretion of the worker have been shown to discriminate strongly among jobs of varying status (Fox, 1974; Jacques, 1957). In occupations where effort–reward relationships are obscure and the boundaries between work and nonwork are highly discretionary or blurred by the nature of the task, absence may have an entirely different meaning from that exhibited by those engaged in typical industrial employment (CP 6). Professors, artists, basic scientists, and self-employed business persons often experience autonomy in goal setting and relative freedom from the employment contract, which should in turn influence their conception of absence. In fact, for many such individuals, failure to show up at the designated workplace may be equated with actually accomplishing a greater amount of work. It might be argued that the autonomy inherent in such jobs finds parallel expression in some of the casual absence exhibited by workers with less freedom. Indirect evidence for this can be found in absence reductions that are claimed to follow increases in opportunities for the autonomous scheduling of work tasks and leisure, as in flex-time systems (Golembiewski & Proehl, 1978). Under flex-time, employees can fulfill personal business and leisure pursuits during traditional working hours and still meet attendance obligations.

Research has barely scratched the surface of the function of absence as a mechanism of time allocation. Macroscopically, there is a need for comparative studies that treat the "shape" of work and nonwork boundaries as an independent variable and as a factor mediating the relationship between absence and work and nonwork time. Particular attention must be paid to the probability that the very *construct* of absence differs across occupational groups. Research in this area will have to come to grips with the admittedly knotty problem of distinguishing attendance from "motivation" or "performance" on jobs that are characterized by fewer organizational constraints to absence. Microscopically, there is a need for longitudinal studies of the specific time usage of individuals and the extent to which the inception and duration of absence represents an attempt to control or redefine the work/nonwork boundary. Such research should incorporate personal and work schedule variables as a means of exploring the conjectures presented earlier.

As society faces the prospect of declining hours of work and the increasing salience of leisure time and its uses, there would appear to be great social value in pursuing these themes. Action-research strategies might be contemplated to determine how working hours can best be structured to meet the goals of production and the needs of the work force.

Absence as Coin of Exchange

Absence might usefully be viewed as an attempt to fulfill or modify a series of implicit social contracts between the worker and the employing organization and the worker and relevant parties external to the organization. This point of view does not exclude the possibility that many instances of absence are responses to job dissatisfaction. Rather, it is congruent with CP 1 that absence has a variety of "meanings" or functions for individuals in various circumstances. Thus, absence as a response to job dissatisfaction may represent an attempt to adjust one's job inputs in response to a perceived inequitable exchange with the organization. On the other hand, a worker who is well satisfied with job circumstances may still exhibit considerable absence in order to fulfill perceived familial obligations. Although the meaning of absence differs radically for these individuals, both are using absence to redress or fulfill certain social contracts.

An exchange perspective suggests a number of alternative research strategies with which absence might be investigated. For one thing, it would be useful to explore employees' perceptions of the nature of the implicit social contracts that exist between themselves and the employing organization and the family, with special emphasis on the role of absence. Such a strategy would be the first step in isolating those situations in which absence is viewed as a *relevant* input to social exchange equations. For example, perceptions of the organization's expectations regarding attendance might be explored. Similarly, perceptions of the legitimacy of family demands on "working time" should be investigated, since there is evidence that the relevance of such demands for absence may be substantial (Morgan & Herman, 1976). In all cases, it would be useful to determine the extent to which absence is viewed from a moral perspective as being deviant behavior, rule-breaking behavior, or behavior that unfairly damages the interests of other persons.

The study of absence could also benefit from the application of equity theory (Adams, 1965). However, as might be imagined, we are not in particular sympathy with the notion that absence simply represents "leaving the field" in response to inequity. Rather, a key hypothesis here is that attendance may be used to modify an individual's input/outcome ratio, bringing it into line with expectations of "fair exchange." In fact, in some routine, structured jobs, variations in attendance may be one of the few readily available means of manipulating input to modify this ratio. One obvious implication of an equity perspective is the probability that the absence process differs considerably under different payment systems. When payment is not a direct function of attendance, absence might serve to redress felt inequity stemming from perceived underpayment or some other factor. In this case, outcomes remain constant while input is reduced. When payment is closely associated with attendance, behavior other than absence may be necessary to achieve "fair exchange." Evidence linking perceived inequitable pay with absence has been reported by Patchen (1960) for oil refinery workers and by Dittrich and Carrell (1979) for clerical personnel. In line with the input reduction argument, Patchen reported that 75 to 80 percent of absences in the refinery were paid absences. Dittrich and Carrell did not report the relationship between pay and attendance.

There is, of course, a caveat to be observed here. Equity theory does not do a particularly good job of specifying the boundaries that define a particular social exchange. Furthermore, most experimental tests of equity theory have severely and artificially restricted these boundaries. However, as indicated earlier, absence behavior may have a simultaneous impact on several exchange systems. Thus, the *net* effect of absenteeism on these systems must be considered in order to obtain optimal predictive power. For example, even when absence does not appear to be the appropriate response to maintain fair exchange in the *job* system, off-the-job outcomes derived from absenting oneself to nurse a sick child or spouse may mandate this response. What research needs to do, then, is determine the complete phenomenal payoff matrix surrounding absence and attendance.

Moving beyond strict equity considerations, there is considerable scope to examine absence from a more abstract notion of socioeconomic exchange. That is, under what conditions do attendance patterns reflect the desire to establish, maintain, or regain a particular economic position? For example, it would be useful to examine attendance patterns before, during, and after the imposition of mandatory shortened work weeks or threatened layoffs and plant closures. In these cases, we might expect attendance to reveal anticipatory economic maximization; that is, employees should respond to economic threats with improved attendance. Steers and Rhodes (1978) review several studies that suggest that regional unemployment is associated with decreased absenteeism but point out that the attendance of individuals threatened with *personal* unemployment may vary with their expectations of finding another job. Thus, those whose skills are in demand may continue their usual attendance behavior, whereas those whose skills are not may absent themselves to engage in job searches. This qualifier corresponds with Hulin and Rousseau's[5] recent caution about inferring individual effects from rates of behavior.

Under more steady economic conditions, there is the distinct possibility that absence may be associated with those conditions that favor economic "satisficing" rather than "maximizing." For example, we have heard anecdotes about workers restricting their income through absence in order to maintain a favorable tax bracket status. Also, the well-established fact that younger workers tend to exhibit more casual absence than older workers (Nicholson et al., 1977) might be partly attributed to a satisficing strategy. Certainly, the response, "I work 4 days a week because I can't earn enough in 3," would seem to reflect this goal.

Other economic factors that may influence absence involve the degree of autonomy in the rate at which income can be earned or the manner in which it can be earned. Evidence from the Cardiff study (Chadwick-Jones et al., in press) suggested that workers under piecerate payment systems exhibited more absence than those under hourly payment. Under piecerate, the autonomy in the rate at which income can be earned may enable workers to maintain a desired level of income while taking off "deserved" time from work. Similarly, there is some evidence to suggest that workers may substitute lucrative overtime work for regular working hours, exhibiting more absence from scheduled work under conditions of readily available overtime (Gowler, 1969; Martin, 1971). Finally, individuals with outside sources of income may be able to justify absence from their primary jobs. Notice that each of these examples may also reflect the operation of a satisficing motive, and in some cases may reflect equity motives. Also, notice here the delicate interplay between economic autonomy and the structuring of work and nonwork time discussed earlier.

In passing, it is worth mentioning that we have chosen to present the relevance of exchange theory to absence research from a personal motivational perspective rather than an explicitly normative perspective. Whereas the same arguments could have been presented in terms of equity norms, fairness norms, and norms of social comparison, the interpretation of exchange theory from a personal motivational perspective corresponds more closely to the way exchange notions have usually been applied to organizational phenomena. However, as will be demonstrated in the next section, an explicit normative perspective can be utilized to sharpen our understanding of the absence process.

ABSENCE AS A SOCIAL PHENOMENON

Thus far we can hardly be accused of ignoring social influences upon absence. However, in the following two sections, the issue is confronted directly by discussing the normative control of absence and the notion of absence "climates" or "cultures." We confess some ignorance about just when norms begin to constitute climates or cultures. Somewhat arbitrarily, this problem is circumvented by examining absence norms in discrete portions of the employee's role set (co-workers, management, off-the-job parties). Then it is argued that, in part, the net interactive effect of these norms may define an absence climate or culture for a particular subset of employees, an organizational subunit, or the organization as a whole.

Normative Control of Absence

This section is concerned with social norms that have as their explicit content the regulation of work attendance. The exploration of absence from such a perspective follows most directly from CPs 3 and 5. Respectively, these CPs suggest that absence is susceptible to collective influence and that nonwork forces may influence attendance.

While we are unaware of any research that conclusively demonstrates the operation of normative constraints on absence behavior, evidence can be marshaled to suggest that this may be a fruitful approach. First, on an intuitive level, absence is among the most public of work-relevant behaviors in typical job settings. Thus, co-workers, official representatives of the organization, and relevant off-the-job parties can easily observe instances of absence. As such, it should be especially susceptible to potential normative sanctions. In contrast, behavior such as low performance may go unnoticed by persons external to the organization and be obscured from organizational members by "make work" or "cooperative" activities. Second, there is research to suggest that absence may be associated with small group experience and organization (Mann, Indik, & Vroom, 1963; Mayo & Lombard, 1944; Walker, 1947). Taken together, this circumstantial evidence points to the explicit normative control of absence.

In order to truly understand normative constraints on absence, it will be necessary to examine the attendance norms that exist in various portions of an individual's role set. As indicated earlier, the most reasonable partitioning of this role set would probably involve co-workers in the primary work group, supervisors and other official organizational representatives, and relevant family members and friends. Consideration of this fairly complete role set should enable researchers to obtain some notion of the ultimate extent to which normative constraints influence attendance. Perhaps more important, such a strategy should enhance our understanding of apparently anomalous absence patterns. For example, good attendance might prevail in spite of a primary work group norm that is supportive of casual absence. This contradiction might be explained by formal organizational norms and norms in the external community that encourage regular attendance. Because such contradictory norms may be the rule rather than the exception, it will be necessary to determine the attendance norms that may exist in each relevant portion of the role set. In each case answers to the following questions should be sought:

1. Under what circumstances are norms regarding attendance likely to develop?
2. Will developed norms encourage attendance or encourage absence?
3. What is the probability that violations of attendance norms will be detected?
4. What punishments are available for norm violation and what rewards are available for conformity?

Clearly, the answers to these questions may be interdependent. Notice, however, that the questions recognize that attendance norms will only develop if attendance behavior is of at least marginal importance to some portion of a role set. In addition, "attendance norms" may *en*courage or *dis*courage attendance. Furthermore, although absence is an especially public behavior, its ease of detection may vary across portions of the role set. Finally, even clear-cut norms whose violation is easily detectable may exert little influence on attendance if they are not backed by adequate punishment and reinforcement.

For that portion of the role set composed of co-workers or the main work group, the development of attendance norms is probably fairly complex. Important variables to be examined here would include the manner in which work is organized and the nature of the payment system. For example, a norm that favors regular attendance would seem likely when a high degree of interdependence is required for task accomplishment, especially under some form of group payment system. In some cases, even without task or economic interdependence, professional or collegial codes of conduct may encourage a similar norm. For example, whatever their other shortcomings, university professors are generally expected by their colleagues to show up to teach their classes.

Under what conditions might co-workers develop a norm that encourages absence? First, even under conditions of interdependence or professionalism, a depressed work ethic or an unfavorable labor climate might lead to the development of norms that condone, yet systematize, absence. Some explicit or implicit consensus may be reached regarding who can be absent and when absence is permissible. In this manner, workers can "cover" for each other without seriously threatening goal accomplishment or professional standards. In work settings where task interdependence, economic interdependence, or professionalism do not exist, a norm that actually encourages unregulated absence might develop if there is consensus concerning mitigating circumstances (poor labor climate, perceived inequity, job dissatisfaction) *and* if there is consensus that absence is an *appropriate* reaction to these circumstances. In this case, regular attenders might be labeled "suckers," whereas those who are frequently absent are esteemed. Of course, absence can be esteemed even when it is not an approved reaction to a negative environment. In some universities, absence incurred to present conference papers or to do consulting is seen as a sign of professional stature.

In the case of co-workers, the mechanics of detecting deviation from attendance norms and enforcing such norms are fairly obvious. Of all the portions of the relevant role set, this portion should be most aware of attendance patterns, with obvious occupational exceptions. In addition, the extraordinary range of norm enforcement mechanisms available to small groups in work settings has been well documented (e.g., Homans, 1950). Thus, it can be concluded that *if* the work group has developed attendance norms its members should be in an especially good position to enforce these norms.

A final point should be raised regarding the probable relationship between work group *cohesiveness* and attendance norms. Two of the best known "facts" regarding cohesive groups are that they are especially effective in developing and enforcing norms and in inducing active participation in group affairs. When other conditions favor the development of a "good attendance" norm, these characteristics are perfectly consonant and should be facilitative of the norm (cf. Mayo & Lombard, 1944). However, when other conditions favor the development of an "absence" norm, the required behavior would seem to be inconsistent with the participative characteristics associated with cohesiveness. In this case, of course, the requirement for participation might be fulfilled by group activities off the job. For example, a cohesive group might absent itself *en masse* to go hunting or fishing.

Let us now turn to attendance norms that might be developed and sent to organizational members by that portion of the role set consisting of supervisors and other organizational officials. It is important to distinguish between these (latent) norms and official rules and policies regarding absence. Although these concepts are by no means independent, there are organizations that "say" one thing about absence (via rules and regulations) and "do" something else (via informal normative mechanisms). This point will be developed shortly.

Official organizational representatives should be especially likely to develop norms that favor attendance in the presence of certain financial, technological, strategic, or moral imperatives. For example, increased concern with attendance is a frequent outcome of cost-cutting programs or escalating labor costs. In addition, technologies that require the presence of key persons or that require workers on one shift to relieve those on the next should prompt a similar outcome. The strict attendance rules seen in military settings probably result from a combination of strategic and moral imperatives. In contrast to these situations, university professors and administrators seldom develop norms regarding the classroom attendance of students because such imperatives are largely irrelevant in the classroom setting.

In theory, official organizational representatives should be in a good position to monitor deviations from developed attendance norms, especially those prompted by technological or strategic concerns, where absence actually affects operations. In fact, however, there is good reason to believe that the monitoring of absence by this portion of the role set is often unreliable. In some cases, workers may be able to "cover" for each other without detection. In any situation, employees may be motivated to disguise the true reason for their absence. This motivation, coupled with the need for organizational representatives to engage in some attributional process to designate a particular absence event as "voluntary," may further threaten the reliability of the monitoring process. Finally, there is considerable variation in the extent to which organizations actually record and study absence data, however collected, especially for salaried jobs (PIU 6). Each of these factors may in practice limit the ability of organizational officials to accurately detect deviations from attendance norms. Of course, when such norms are strongly established, some (often arbitrary) mechanism may be invoked to bolster the monitoring process.

Organizations may systematize a range of control mechanisms such as disciplinary crackdowns and attendance bonuses. The effectiveness of these mechanisms is reviewed by Muchinsky (1977) and Steers and Rhodes (1978). It is at this enforcement stage, however, that the distinction between official rules and regulations and effective norms becomes apparent. The organization that has a "strong policy" against absence but offers its employees liberal "sick days" may be inadvertently encouraging absence. Similarly, the organization that implements strong sanctions against certain forms of absence may be signaling employees to adopt other forms of absence (Nicholson, 1976). Thus, although it is difficult to conceive of a norm held by official organizational representatives that *favors* absence, this may be the latent message sent to employees when the sanctioning system operates in an unintended manner.

Attendance norms that develop in that portion of the role set external to the organization are probably a function of the prevailing work ethic in the family or community and social and economic imperatives that increase the salience of attendance patterns. Put simply, a highly positive work ethic, coupled with strong economic needs and weak off-the-job demands on "working time" should lead this portion of the role set to develop a norm favoring attendance. The reverse of these conditions may lead to a norm supportive of absence. These perfect combinations are probably the product of unusual circumstances. In most cases, the conditions that increase external demands upon working time (e.g., a large family or dependents with chronic sickness) also increase economic needs that can be fulfilled by regular attendance at work. These conflicting demands suggest that the development of clear-cut attendance norms by off-the-job parties may be atypical.

The ability of external parties to monitor attendance varies with the nature of employment and what the absentee does when time is taken off work. If a worker remains home with the family, an absence episode is immediately detectable. However, absence may go undetected if the worker leaves home and "calls off" work. Such an incident may be detected after-the-fact if it affects a subsequent paycheck of if the organization contacts the home to verify the cause. Under normal circumstances, friends would find it more difficult than family members to monitor attendance behavior. In many cases, then, workers can probably disguise their attendance activities from off-the-job parties with greater ease than they can from organizational members.

Members of the external role set have available a full range of social mechanisms for enforcing developed attendance norms. However, the previous discussion suggests that the application of these mechanisms may often be delayed or confounded by the imperfect monitoring of attendance behavior. In addition, in contrast to the enforcement mechanisms of organizational members, there may be little *direct* connection between the reinforcers and punishment available and the specific acts of attendance or absence. In many cases, the worker who conforms to or violates an attendance norm held by a portion of the external role set may fail to understand that the ensuing consequences were specifically due to attendance behavior.

In summary, if the preceding notions are correct, the primary work group should be especially able to monitor attendance and enforce attendance norms if such norms are developed. Except under the imperatives mentioned, official organizational representatives may adopt a strategy of benign neglect in response to moderate levels of absence. If attendance norms are developed, their direct effectiveness is dependent upon the energy and care invested in monitoring and enforcement procedures. Finally, the development of attendance norms by parties external to the organization may often be precluded by competing social and economic motives. If such norms do develop, several weaknesses in monitoring and enforcement capability may reduce their effectiveness.

Absence Climates and Cultures

If the experiences of workers are constrained by common work environments, task interdependence, similar external socioeconomic circumstances, and a relatively uniform absence control system, it may prove unhelpful to restrict the search for explanations of absence to individual differences. More enlightening may be the identification of distinctions between identifiable aggregates (CP 3). As such, an "absence climate" or "absence culture" might be conceived as the net interactive effect of the normative forces that exist in the various relevant portions of employees' role sets and common nonnormative influences. Such an analysis could be applied to particular classes of employees (e.g., women), organizational subunits (e.g., departments or wards), or an entire organization.

This approach is in sharp contrast to the cumulative tradition that has dominated absence research and many other areas of organizational behavior. It has been assumed that one can understand the behavior of social units by aggregating information derived from individuals (PIU 3).[15] While this may be trivially true, it is likely to restrict the choice of predictors to intrapsychic constructs, job characteristics, and personal circumstances on which individuals may be contrasted, and to overlook those that distinguish between collectivities, including rules of conduct, organizational socialization practices, company ethos, and management style. Among such group level variables, one may also include the signal function served by absence levels themselves.

One reason why the individual level approach often accounts for relatively little variation in absence may be the fact that there are many work settings in which there *is* little variation in absence among employees. This restricted variation, of course, is just what one would expect if social norms from various portions of the role set operate to define an absence climate or culture, and absence at the individual level is thus poorly predicted. Where such cultures or climates exist, analyses between groups, subunits, or organizations, using predictors relevant to collectivities, might account for substantial variance between social units.

A complementary perspective suggests that the restricted variance of a low base rate behavior such as absence gives it by chance alone a spuriously normative appearance (the Poisson distribution). This appearance itself becomes part of the absence culture by providing normative grist. According to this view, the absence culture is the self-attribution by groups about the characteristics of their attendance that they infer from its configuration. Such a phenomenon is open to at least two interpretations, neither of which is exclusive of the other. From a sociological perspective, characteristic absence rates may be indicative of collective behavior that functions to clarify a situation in which there are few objective cues available concerning what is proper. Strike activities have often been interpreted from this collective perspective, and absence may be equally susceptible to collective social forces and definitions of behavior. From a more social psychological angle, we may find group-induced polarization (Lamm & Myers, 1978), in which employees act collectively to exaggerate and regularize their individual attendance patterns. Such a reaction may be reinforced by managers who claim that "most employees are responsible, but we have a core of malingerers" on the basis of absence distributions that do not actually deviate from chance. (In fact this *attitude* toward employee absence may itself be a product of group-induced polarization among managers). Here, we see the convergence of co-worker and management norms that would characterize an absence climate or culture.

Sex differences in absence may illustrate these points. Gender, a surrogate for a veritable stew of individual and social differences, reliably differentiates absence at the group level (Steers & Rhodes, 1978). It does not advance our understanding to attribute this to inherent differences in the susceptibility of the sexes, when our attention can more profitably turn to the convergence of community, work group, and supervisory norms and their effect on attributed legitimacy. For example, family, friends, and female co-workers might support a norm that encourages womens' absence based on a common belief that such work is "only temporary" or that the organization treats women inequitably. Convinced that female absence is a "special case," supervisors may then apply existing sanctions less rigorously, implicitly sending a similar normative message. As a culmination of this process, women employees acquire empirical evidence of the attendance behavior that is expected of them via the resultant absence level and proceed to polarize their behavior against this baseline.

The subcultural dimensions of absence at the organizational level have been revealed in several research investigations. One intriguing illustration is found in the study of epidemics. Colligan and Murphy (1979) have shown how environmental "triggers," such as the appearance of symptoms among workers involved in processes they don't fully understand (such as chemical processes), can lead to contagious mass psychogenic illness. This is characterized by the diffusion of symptoms and pseudo-symptoms across employee populations. Clearly, the capacity for such contagion is dependent upon the existence of intraorganizational networks of communication, as well as shared beliefs and values.

One of the principal general findings of Chadwick-Jones et al. (in press) was that the predictability of absence from work attitudes varied considerably across 16 investigated plants. In most they were unrelated, but in a few, attitudes were viable predictors. This seems to suggest that the plants differed in their "causal climates." Further analysis at the interplant level revealed that differences *between* organizations were often more interesting than differences *within* them and were predictable from a quite different range of variables, such as the role of unions, management sanctioning strategies, and spans of control.

Within most complex organizations, differences in subunit climate are likely to prove an important source of absence variation. In the Cardiff study cited above (Chadwick-Jones et al., in press), it was found in one plant that different shifts of workers on a Continental rotation system had significantly different absence levels. There were no objective differences in job content or personal characteristics, but workers did differ in attitudes toward supervision, with the high absence shift expressing *more* satisfaction. This ostensibly anomalous result is clearly open to a climatic explanation (Nicholson, 1975). The relative social isolation of shifts and their supervisors on continuous rotation systems constitutes an ideal condition for the development of a group climate. Similar conditions obtain in hospitals, where a system of relatively autonomous wards is operated. Under these circumstances it has been shown that objectively similar wards can generate markedly different climates, which are reflected in pronounced differences in absence patterns and levels (Clark, 1975).

It should prove especially valuable to examine the process by which new entrants are socialized into the ambient absence culture. That is, how does the new member learn just what constitutes "legitimate" expected attendance behavior? The sociological literature provides some useful perspectives here. For example, it was the study of interward differences in psychiatric care that led Strauss (1978) to develop the idea of "negotiated order" to describe the dynamic interplay of norm-inducing forces. This notion may be helpfully applied to understanding how norms that legitimate absence are communicated to new members and effectively enforced. Bensman and Gerver's (1963) participant observation study of the social rituals involved in inculcating deviant work behavior in an aircraft plant is also instructive. In the face of pressure for high productivity, experienced workers, supervisors, and government inspectors conspired to encourage the regulated use of shortcut techniques and teach them to novices. Absence, conceived as a deviant behavior, may be influenced through similar processes. Such a perspective suggests that qualitative observational techniques may be especially valuable in probing the nature of absence climates or cultures. This approach may permit an understanding of the complexity of normative forces operating in a situation that may be threatening or sensitive to those involved.

Socialization into an absence culture could also be explored quantitatively. CP 4 indicates that absence should be recognized as temporally structured behavior responsive to feedback over time. As such, the presence of differential absence cultures should be revealed by changes in the absence patterns of new recruits and in the regularization of absence over time. Furthermore, the new worker's first experiences with absence are seldom personal, but instead are observational: the contexts and consequences of co-workers' absences are observed. Relatively straightforward studies in the attributional tradition would be useful to explore this early learning process.

Over 25 years ago, Hill and Trist (1955) argued that at different stages of organizational careers there may be systematic variations in subcultural expectations and limitations surrounding the legitimacy of different forms of absence and alternative behaviors. Now seems like an appropriate time to explore these arguments empirically.

CONCLUSION

In this chapter we have argued for a number of new approaches to conceiving of and studying the meanings of absence. We have chosen the plural term "meanings" carefully in order to emphasize two points about past absence research.

In our opinion, most absence research has been essentially descriptive in nature rather than explanatory. Correlating absence with job satisfaction, job content, and personal characteristics simply has not told us much about what absence *means* nor has it accounted for much variance. For example, although dozens of studies have reported significant associations between absence and age and absence and sex, the *reasons* for these associations remain uncharted. We have emphasized the plurality of the meanings of absence in order to counteract some biases that appear to be held by both researchers and managers. For researchers, absence appears to be seen simply as "one more criterion variable" usually signifying individual withdrawal from aversive work conditions. For managers, absence is often seen merely as a threat to organizational effectiveness, motivated by something that is circularly labeled "proneness." These restricted meanings ascribed to absence by researchers and managers have unduly limited our understanding of the phenomenon.

Just what is new about what we have proposed? First, on the basis of various circumstantial evidence and the limitations of previous research, we advocate the adoption of a fresh series of propositions about the nature of absence behavior. In combination, these premises suggest a series of new research areas. In some cases, these new research areas require the adoption of methods not commonly used in investigations of absence. Let us review two examples of this process.

If absence events can be viewed as phenomenologically unique (CP 1), some way is needed to penetrate this phenomenology. One way to effect this penetration is to use attribution theory to explore the reasons individuals give for their own absence behavior. Such an approach may help us understand why objectively equivalent proximal stimuli (such as sickness, family demands, or bad weather) are differentially interpreted as just causes for absence. If absence is responsive to feedback over time (CP 4), such attributions should depend in part on the successive reactions of relevant observers of absence episodes. In turn, these reactions depend upon *their* attributions of the reasons for a particular episode. There is reason to believe that the details of these attributional processes will differ across occupational groups because of objective differences in the constraints and opportunities regarding absence (CP 6). In this example, we see several CPs marshaled to suggest a particular research area, namely, the study of attributions that underlie absence episodes. In turn, several particular research methods are indicated, including (1) the use of absence diaries, (2) the longitudinal application of conventional attribution theory methods, (3) the incorporation of multiple observers, and (4) comparisons of processes across populations.

Turning to another example, we have argued that absence may often be influenced by social mechanisms and that the study of absence may profit from an explicitly collective perspective (CP 3). In addition, there is reason to believe that some of the social forces that affect attendance behavior stem from parties external to the organization (CP 5). In order to pursue these themes, we have advocated the examination of attendance norms in various relevant portions of employees' role sets. In addition, it is necessary to understand the conditions that favor the development of such norms and the factors that contribute to their enforcement. In many cases, the net effect of a set of attendance norms may be the development of an absence climate or culture that varies across work populations, organizational subunits, or entire organizations (following in part from CP 6). Here, again, we see several CPs marshaled to suggest two new areas of study. In turn, several novel research strategies are indicated, including (1) the collection of data from a variety of source persons, (2) participant observation of absence cultures in action, and (3) longitudinal studies of the absence patterns exhibited by new members of a particular absence culture.

To be realistic in our aspirations, we are aware that it is easier to prescribe change than to bring it about. The paradigms of the PIUs continue to be reinforced by the terms under which researchers gain access to organizations, the methodologies with which we feel most competent, and the criteria by which scientific communication is evaluated. But change is necessary if we are to have any hope of gathering empirical data that will help to systematize the scattered insights about absence that are currently available. More importantly, we will stop doing violence to the experiential reality of the behavior and will achieve a clearer and yet more differentiated view of its personal and social meanings.

ACKNOWLEDGMENTS

The support of a Social Sciences and Humanities Research Council of Canada leave fellowship and research grant is gratefully acknowledged. We wish to thank Richard Mowday for valuable comments on an earlier version.

NOTES

1. This chapter was drafted while the first author was Visiting Research Fellow at the Medical Research Council Social and Applied Psychology Unit, University of Sheffield, and completed while he was Visiting Associate Professor of Management at the University of Oregon.

2. Rhodes, S. R., & Steers, R. M. *Summary tables of studies of employee absenteeism.* Technical Report No. 13, University of Oregon, 1977.

3. Gupta, N., & Jenkins, G. D., Jr. *Employee withdrawal: An expanded definition and conceptual framework.* Unpublished manuscript, The University of Texas at Austin, 1980.

4. For other examples of the interpretation of group-level data at the individual level of analysis, see Rhodes and Steers (Note 2). Also see Muchinsky's (1977) discussion of the association between absence and turnover at the individual and group level.

5. Hulin, C. L., & Rousseau, D. M. *Analyzing infrequent events: Once you find them your troubles begin.* Technical report 80-3, Department of Psychology, University of Illinois at Urbana-Champaign, 1980.

6. Rousseau, D. M. *Measuring exceptional behavior in organizations: Problems in aggregating low base rate phenomena.* Paper presented at the annual meeting of the American Psychological Association, Toronto, 1978.

7. These breakdowns actually represent conservative estimates of the attention that has been paid to the organizational correlates of absence. Both Porter and Steers (1973) and Rhodes and Steers (Note 2) include organizational tenure in categories that otherwise concern extraorganizational "personal factors."

8. Because absence and turnover are so often linked under the rubric of "withdrawal," it is instructive to compare our application of attribution theory to absence with Steers and Mowday's (1981) application to turnover. First, Steers and Mowday correctly point out that the resignation of a particular employee from a particular organization is a one-shot event. The singular nature of such an occurrence, of course, does not preclude an attributional analysis. It does, however, obviate the literal use of consistency cues (Kelly, 1972) by observers. On the other hand, the absence behavior of a particular person in a particular organizational setting may be recurrent, and consistency cues are thus available for use by observers. Steers and Mowday also point out that other perspectives on the attribution of turnover allow for the observation of recurrent behaviors. First, every turnover incident is preceded by a series of job behaviors on the part of the incumbent that may serve as attributional cues regarding the cause of resignation. Second, the observation of several incidents of turnover over some period of time may provide a basis for the explanation of a subsequent specific incident. In the case of attributions by observers, these perspectives are equally applicable to explanations of absence. However, we would point out that because turnover usually occurs less frequently than absence, and because relevant behavioral cues for turnover probably occur over a longer time period, a greater degree of retrospection may be necessary to isolate relevant turnover cues. This may cause turnover attributions to reflect more stereotyping, more ego-defensive bias, and more aspects of cultural approval than absence attributions. Steers and Mowday restrict their discussion of turnover to attributions made by observers, whereas we additionally emphasize the important role of self-attributions of absence. Their perspective would seem to reflect the one-shot nature of turnover. Our perspective stems from the notion that the personal meanings of absence can be partially understood by self-attributions and that these attributions are shaped over recurrent absence events by the consequences provided by observers. These consequences depend upon the attributions that are made by these observers.

9. Nicholson, N., & Payne, R. *Attachment to work and absence behaviour.* Medical Research Council Social and Applied Psychology Unit Memorandum No. 223, University of Sheffield, 1978.

10. Ericsson, K. A., & Simon, H. A. *Retrospective verbal reports as data.* C.I.P. Working Paper No. 388, Carnegie-Mellon University, 1978.

11. Ericsson, K. A., & Simon, H. A. *Thinking-aloud protocols as data: Effects of verbalization.* C.I.P. Working Paper No. 397, Carnegie-Mellon University, 1979.

12. Specifically, explanations given to organizational officials seem likely to involve "motivated" biases of an ego-defensive nature whereas those provided for oneself may

reveal "informational" biases (cf. Ross, 1977). Both phenomena are covered by Green-wald's (1980) neatly coined term "beneffectance"—the tendency to accept personal re-sponsibility for positive outcomes and to reject such responsibility for negative outcomes.

13.   It may be useful to describe how the adoption of such dispositional roles could be detected. Suppose workers A and B exhibit typical absence behavior for their organizations at the beginning of our research. When they are absent, both tend to provide unelaborate medical reasons for organizational officials. Similarly, both tell us retrospectively that they are usually absent due to minor disconnected medical reasons. During this period, their timely introspective reports indicate a mixture of head colds, mild depression, family demands, hobby pursuits, alarm clock failures, and hangovers. In addition, their reports of consistency, consensus, and distinctiveness cues point to circumstantial attributions. Gradually, the timely reports of worker A begin to reveal more and more medical reasons for absence, whereas those for worker B reveal more and more alarm clock failures and hobby pursuits. Simultaneously, their cue utilization shifts from circumstantial to dispo-sitional, and the absence of each begins to increase. In explaining his absence to orga-nizational officials, worker A, adopting a "sick role," begins to provide elaborate medical reasons backed up by vague but supportive physicians' certificates. Worker B, adopting a "deviant" role, provides flippant reasons or simply reports that her absences can be considered unexcused.

14.   Rousseau's (1978) discovery of a negative correlation between off-the-job challenge and absence is open to several causal interpretations. One assumes that high quality nonwork experiences substitute for the quantity of such experiences and thus lead to better attendance. Another assumes that attendance behavior influences the descriptions of non-work experiences, perhaps via dissonance mechanisms.

15.   This is an example of what Roberts, Hulin, and Rousseau (1978) refer to as con-ceptual aggregation in that the theory used to explain the observations is "relatively distant from the observations" (p. 87).

REFERENCES

Absenteeism: The dimensions of the problem. *IR Research Reports*, 1980, *4*, 1–2.

Adams, J. S. Inequity in social exchange. In L. Berkowitz (Ed.), *Advances in experimental social psychology* (Vol. 2). New York: Academic Press, 1965.

Arbous, A. G., & Sichel, H. S. New techniques for the analysis of absenteeism data. *Biometrika*, 1954, *41*, 77–90.

Argyle, M. *The social psychology of work.* London: Penguin, 1972.

Argyris, C., & Schon, D. *Theory in practice.* San Francisco: Jossey-Bass, 1974.

Barbash, J. Collective bargaining and the theory of conflict. *British Journal of Industrial Relations*, 1980, *18*, 82–90.

Beehr, T. A., & Gupta, N. A note on the structure of employee withdrawal. *Organizational Behavior and Human Performance*, 1978, *21*, 73–79.

Behrend, H. Voluntary absence from work. *International Labour Review*, 1959, *79*, 109–140.

Bem, D. J. Self-perception theory. In L. Berkowitz (Ed.), *Advances in experimental social psychology* (Vol. 6). New York: Academic Press, 1972.

Bensman, J., & Gerver, I. Crime and punishment in the factory: The function of deviancy in maintaining the social system. *American Sociological Review*, 1963, *28*, 580–598.

Bernardin, J. H. The relationship of personality variables to organizational withdrawal. *Personnel Psychology*, 1977, *30*, 17–27.

Burke, R. J., & Wilcox, D. S. Absenteeism and turnover among female telephone operators. *Personnel Psychology*, 1972, *25*, 639–648.

Calder, B. J. An attribution theory of leadership. In B. M. Staw & G. R. Salancik (Eds.), *New directions in organizational behavior*. Chicago: St. Clair, 1977.

Campbell, J. P., & Pritchard, R. D. Motivation theory in industrial and organizational psychology. In M. D. Dunnette (Ed.), *Handbook of industrial and organizational psychology*. Chicago: Rand McNally, 1976.

Chadwick-Jones, J. K., Brown, C. A., Nicholson, N., & Sheppard, C. Absence measures: Their reliability and stability in an industrial setting. *Personnel Psychology*, 1971, *24*, 463–470.

Chadwick-Jones, J. K., Brown, C. A., & Nicholson, N. Absence from work: Its meaning, measurement, and control. *International Review of Applied Psychology*, 1973a, *22*, 137–156.

Chadwick-Jones, J. K., Brown, C. A., & Nicholson, N. A-type and B-type absence: Empirical trends for women employees. *Occupational Psychology*, 1973b, *47*, 75–80.

Chadwick-Jones, J. K., Brown, C. A., & Nicholson, N. *The social psychology of attendance motivation*. New York: Praeger, in press.

Clark, J. *Time out?* London: Royal College of Nursing, 1975.

Colligan, M. J., & Murphy, L. R. Mass psychogenic illness in organizations: An overview. *Journal of Occupational Psychology*, 1979, *52*, 77–90.

Confederation of British Industry. *Absenteeism*. London: Author, 1970.

Dennett, B. How to minimize malingering. *Personnel Management*, 1978, *10*, 5, 30–32.

Dittrich, J. E., & Carrell, M. R. Organization equity perceptions, employee job satisfaction, and departmental absence and turnover rates. *Organizational Behavior and Human Performance*, 1979, *24*, 29–40.

Fletcher, B., Gowler, D., & Payne, R. Exploding the myth of executive stress. *Personnel Management*, 1979, *11*, 5, 30–34.

Fox, A. *Beyond contract: Work, power and trust relations*. London: Faber and Faber, 1974.

Fox, J. B., & Scott, J. F. *Absenteeism: Management's problem*. Cambridge, MA: Harvard Business School, 1943.

Froggatt, P. Short-term absence from industry. III. The inference of "proneness" and a search for causes. *British Journal of Industrial Medicine*, 1970, *27*, 297–312.

Garrison, K. R., & Muchinsky, P. M. Evaluating the concept of absentee-proneness with two measures of absence. *Personnel Psychology*, 1977, *30*, 389–393.

Gaudet, F. J. *Solving the problems of employee absence*. New York: American Management Association, 1963.

Gergen, K. J. Social psychology as history. *Journal of Personality and Social Psychology*, 1973, *26*, 309–320.

Golembiewski, R. T., & Proehl, C. W. A survey of the empirical literature on flexible workhours: Character and consequences of a major innovation. *Academy of Management Review*, 1978, *3*, 837–853.

Gowler, D. Determinants of the supply of labour to the firm. *Journal of Management Studies*, 1969, *6*, 73–95.

Greenwald, A. G. The totalitarian ego: Fabrication and revision of personal history. *American Psychologist*, 1980, *35*, 603–618.

Harré, R., & Secord, P. F. *The explanation of social behaviour*. Oxford: Blackwell, 1972.

Hedges, J. N. Absence from work—measuring the hours lost. *Monthly Labor Review*, 1977, *100*, 10, 16–23.

Hill, J. M. M., & Trist, E. L. Changes in accidents and other absences with length of service. *Human Relations*, 1955, *8*, 121–152.

Hinrichs, J. R. Measurement of reasons for resignation of professionals: Questionnaires versus company and consultant exit interviews. *Journal of Applied Psychology*, 1975, *60*, 530–532.

Homans, G. C. *The human group.* New York: Harcourt, Brace and World, 1950.

Huse, E. F., & Taylor, E. K. Reliability of absence measures. *Journal of Applied Psychology,* 1962, *42,* 159–160.

Hyman, R. *Strikes.* London: Fontana, 1972.

Ilgen, D. Attendance behavior: A reevaluation of Latham and Pursell's conclusions. *Journal of Applied Psychology,* 1977, *62,* 230–233.

Ivancevich, J. M., & Lyon, H. L. The shortened workweek: A field experiment. *Journal of Applied Psychology,* 1977, *62,* 34–37.

Jacques, E. *Measurement of responsibility.* London: Heinemann, 1957.

Johns, G. Attitudinal and nonattitudinal predictors of two forms of absence from work. *Organizational Behavior and Human Performance,* 1978, *22,* 431–444.

Jones, E. E., & Davis, K. E. From acts to dispositions: The attribution process in person perception. In L. Berkowitz (Ed.), *Advances in experimental social psychology* (Vol. 2). New York: Academic Press, 1965.

Jones, E. E., & McGillis, D. Correspondent inferences and the attribution cube: A comparative reappraisal. In J. H. Harvey, W. J. Ickes, & R. F. Kidd (Eds.), *New directions in attribution research* (Vol. 1). Hillsdale, NJ: Lawrence Erlbaum Associates, 1976.

Kelly, H. H. Attribution in social interaction. In E. E. Jones, D. E. Kanouse, H. H. Kelly, R. E. Nisbett, S. Valines, & B. Weiner (Eds.), *Attribution: Perceiving the causes of behavior.* Morristown, NJ: General Learning Press, 1972.

Kelly, J., & Nicholson, N. Strikes and other forms of industrial action. *Industrial Relations Journal,* 1980, *11,* 5, 20–31.

Kerr, W. A., Koppelmeier, G. J., & Sullivan, J. Absenteeism, turnover and morale in a metals fabrication factory. *Occupational Psychology,* 1951, *25,* 50–55.

Lamm, H., & Myers, D. G. Group-induced polarization of attitudes and behavior. In L. Berkowitz (Ed.), *Advances in experimental social psychology* (Vol. 11). New York: Academic Press, 1978.

Latham, G. P., & Pursell, E. D. Measuring absenteeism from the opposite side of the coin. *Journal of Applied Psychology,* 1975, *60,* 369–371.

Lefkowitz, J., & Katz, M. Validity of exit interviews. *Personnel Psychology,* 1969, *22,* 445–455.

Levine, S., & Kozloff, M. A. The sick role: Assessment and overview. In R. H. Turner, J. Coleman, & R. C. Fox (Eds.), *Annual review of sociology* (Vol. 4). Palo Alto, CA: Annual Reviews, 1978.

Locke, E. A. What is job satisfaction? *Organizational Behavior and Human Performance,* 1969, *4,* 309–336.

Lyons, T. F. Turnover and absenteeism: A review of relationships and shared correlates. *Personnel Psychology,* 1972, *25,* 271–281.

Mann, F. C., Indik, B. P., & Vroom, V. H. *The productivity of work groups.* Ann Arbor: Survey Research Center, Institute for Social Research, University of Michigan, 1963.

Martin, J. Some aspects of absence in a light engineering factory. *Occupational Psychology,* 1971, *45,* 77–89.

Mayo, E., & Lombard, G. *Teamwork and labor turnover in the aircraft industry in Southern California.* Cambridge, MA: Harvard University Press, 1944.

Metzner, H., & Mann, F. C. Employee attitudes and absences. *Personnel Psychology,* 1953, *6,* 467–485.

Mitchell, T. R., Green, S., & Wood, R. An attributional model of leadership and the poor performing subordinate. In L. L. Cummings & B. M. Staw (Eds.), *Research in organizational behavior* (Vol. 3). Greenwich, CT: JAI Press, 1981.

Moore, L. F., Johns, G., & Pinder, C. C. Toward middle range theory: An overview and perspective. In C. C. Pinder & L. F. Moore (Eds.), *Middle range theory and the study of organizations.* Boston: Martinus Nijhoff, 1980.

Morgan, L. G., & Herman, J. B. Perceived consequences of absenteeism. *Journal of Applied Psychology*, 1976, *61*, 738–742.

Muchinsky, P. M. Employee absenteeism: A review of the literature. *Journal of Vocational Behavior*, 1977, *10*, 316–340.

Nicholson, N. *Industrial absence as an incident of employee motivation and job satisfaction.* Unpublished doctoral dissertation, University of Wales, Cardiff, 1975.

Nicholson, N. Management sanctions and absence control. *Human Relations*, 1976, *29*, 139–152.

Nicholson, N. Absence behaviour and attendance motivation: A conceptual synthesis. *Journal of Management Studies*, 1977, *14*, 231–252.

Nicholson, N., Brown, C. A., & Chadwick-Jones, J. K. Absence from work and job satisfaction. *Journal of Applied Psychology*, 1976, *61*, 728–737.

Nicholson, N., Brown, C. A., & Chadwick-Jones, J. K. Absence from work and personal characteristics. *Journal of Applied Psychology*, 1977, *62*, 319–327.

Nicholson, N., & Goodge, P. M. The influence of social, organizational, and biographical factors on female absence. *Journal of Management Studies*, 1976, *13*, 234–254.

Nicholson, N., Jackson, P. J., & Howes, G. Shiftwork and absence: An analysis of temporal trends. *Journal of Occupational Psychology*, 1978, *51*, 127–137.

Nisbett, R. E., & Wilson, T. D. Telling more than we can know: Verbal reports on mental processes. *Psychological Review*, 1977, *84*, 231–259.

Nord, W. R. Job satisfaction reconsidered. *American Psychologist*, 1977, *32*, 1026–1035.

Nord, W. R., & Costigan, R. Worker adjustment to the four-day week: A longitudinal study. *Journal of Applied Psychology*, 1973, *58*, 60–66.

Patchen, M. Absence and employee feelings about fair treatment. *Personnel Psychology*, 1960, *13*, 349–360.

Payne, R., & Pugh, D. S. Organizational structure and climate. In M. D. Dunnette (Ed.), *Handbook of industrial and organizational psychology.* Chicago: Rand McNally, 1976.

Pepitone, A. Toward a normative and comparative social psychology. *Journal of Personality and Social Psychology*, 1976, *34*, 641–653.

Pocock, S. J. Daily variations in sickness absence. *Applied Statistics*, 1973, *22*, 375–392.

Porter, L. W., & Steers, R. M. Organizational, work, and personal factors in employee turnover and absenteeism. *Psychological Bulletin*, 1973, *80*, 151–176.

Roberts, K. H., Hulin, C. L., & Rousseau, D. M. *Developing an interdisciplinary science of organizations.* San Francisco: Jossey-Bass, 1978.

Robinson, J. Goof-off champs! *Montreal Gazette*, July 5, 1980, p. 17.

Ross, L. The intuitive psychologist and his shortcomings: Distortions in the attribution process. In L. Berkowitz (Ed.), *Advances in experimental social psychology* (Vol. 10). New York: Academic Press, 1977.

Rotter, J. B. Generalized expectancies for internal versus external controls of reinforcement. *Psychological Monographs*, 1966, *80*, (Whole No. 609).

Rousseau, D. M. Relationship of work to nonwork. *Journal of Applied Psychology*, 1978, *63*, 513–517.

Simon, H. A. *Administrative behavior.* New York: The Free Press, 1957.

Smith, E. R., & Miller, F. D. Limits on perception of cognitive processes: A reply to Nisbett and Wilson. *Psychological Review*, 1978, *85*, 355–362.

Smith, F. J. Work attitudes as predictors of attendance on a specific day. *Journal of Applied Psychology*, 1977, *62*, 16–19.

Smulders, P. G. W. Comments on employee absence/attendance as a dependent variable in organizational research. *Journal of Applied Psychology*, 1980, *65*, 368–371.

Staw, B. M. The consequences of turnover. *Journal of Occupational Behaviour*, 1980, *1*, 253–273.

Staw, B. M., & Oldham, G. R. Reconsidering our dependent variables: A critique and empirical study. *Academy of Management Journal,* 1978, *21,* 539–559.

Steers, R. M., & Mowday, R. T. Employee turnover and post-decision accommodation processes. In L. L. Cummings & B. M. Staw (Eds.), *Research in organizational behavior* (Vol. 3). Greenwich, CT: JAI Press, 1981.

Steers, R. M., & Rhodes, S. R. Major influences on employee attendance: A process model. *Journal of Applied Psychology,* 1978, *63,* 391–407.

Strauss, A. *Negotiations: Varieties, contexts, processes, and social order.* San Francisco: Jossey-Bass, 1978.

Taylor, P. J. Shift and day work: A comparison of sickness absence, lateness, and other absence behaviour at an oil refinery from 1962 to 1965. *British Journal of Industrial Medicine,* 1967, *24,* 93–102.

Turner, A. M., & Lawrence, P. R. *Industrial jobs and the worker.* Boston: Harvard University Graduate School of Business Administration, 1965.

Walker, K. The application of the J-curve hypothesis of conforming behavior to industrial absenteeism. *Journal of Social Psychology,* 1947, *25,* 207–216.

Waters, L. K., & Roach, D. Relationship between job attitudes and two forms of withdrawal from the work situation. *Journal of Applied Psychology,* 1971, *55,* 92–94.

Waters, L. K., & Roach, D. Job-satisfaction, behavioral intention, and absenteeism as predictors of turnover. *Personnel Psychology,* 1979, *32,* 393–397.

White, P. Limitations on verbal reports of internal events: A refutation of Nisbett and Wilson and of Bem. *Psychological Review,* 1980, *87,* 105–112.

Wortman, C. B., & Linsenmeier, J. A. W. Interpersonal attraction and techniques of ingratiation in organizational settings. In B. M. Staw & G. R. Salancik (Eds.), *New directions in organizational behavior.* Chicago: St. Clair, 1977.

Yolles, S. F., Carone, P. A., & Krinsky, L. W. (Eds.), *Absenteeism in industry.* Springfield, IL: Charles C. Thomas, 1974.

EMPLOYEE TURNOVER AND POST-DECISION ACCOMMODATION PROCESSES

Richard M. Steers and Richard T. Mowday

ABSTRACT

Based on a review of existing research on employee turnover, this paper suggests a comprehensive model of the processes leading up to voluntary employee termination. The model includes several factors found in research but not heretofore included in previous turnover models. Following this, the paper focuses on the psychological and behavioral mechanisms used by employees to accommodate the decision to stay or leave once this decision has been made. Drawing heavily on attribution theory, a variety of post-decision accommodation processes are suggested. Finally, suggestions for future research are identified to guide additional work in the area.

Studies of employee turnover from work organizations abound in the literature on organizational behavior and industrial psychology. Beginning with the early studies of Bernays (1910) and Crabb (1912) and continuing to the present, well over 1,000 separate studies on the subject can be identified. Moreover, over the last twenty-five years, at least thirteen review articles on turnover have appeared (Brayfield and Crockett, 1955; Forrest, Cummings, and Johnson, 1977; Herzberg, Mausner, Peterson and Capwell, 1957; Lefkowitz, 1971; March and Simon, 1958; Mobley, Griffeth, Hand and Meglino, 1979; Muchinsky and Tuttle, 1979; Pettman, 1973; Porter and Steers, 1973; Price, 1977; Schuh, 1967; Stoikov and Raimon, 1968; Vroom, 1964). Clearly, the subject has not been neglected by researchers.

What does appear to have been neglected, however, are serious, comprehensive attempts to develop useful models of the turnover process. Although several models exist (e.g., March and Simon, 1958; Price, 1977; Mobley, 1977), their eloquence does not seem to match our current level of knowledge on the subject, probably because of the sheer amount of information available. In our efforts at parsimony, we have a natural tendency to simplify, often resulting in propositions for which contradictory data exist.

Due to the abundance of turnover studies and reviews of turnover studies, it hardly seems appropriate to offer another review. It is our opinion that a far more fruitful area of endeavor is to venture further into the morass of turnover modeling and to attempt to extend our theoretical knowledge of the processes by which individuals decide whether to stay or leave. Such an attempt is made here. That is, instead of a review, we shall attempt to piece together the available data and summarize earlier modeling attempts into a (hopefully) fairly comprehensive process model of employee turnover.

In addition, we wish to consider the consequences of the participation or withdrawal decision. Very little is known about how individuals accommodate or learn to deal with this decision once it has been made. As such, we shall draw considerably on the social psychological literature and offer a model of the accommodation process vis-à-vis the participation decision. By doing so, we hope the materials presented here will be interpreted as a series of propositions suitable for subsequent testing. In this way, more will be learned concerning why people choose to remain with or leave an organization as well as how they adjust to such decisions once made.

This paper consists of five parts. First, we shall provide a short synopsis of our current level of knowledge. Second, based on available information, we shall present a process model of employee turnover. Third, we shall extend consideration of the turnover model to consider how individuals accommodate the decision to stay or leave. Fourth, the manner in which individuals interpret the causes of turnover is reviewed. Finally, the implications for future research will be considered.

BACKGROUND AND PROBLEMS OF TURNOVER RESEARCH

Our progress toward a better understanding of employee turnover in organizations can be traced by examining the various reviews that have appeared over time. A careful reading of these reviews reveals that, while some progress has been made, much remains to be learned concerning turnover and its outcomes in work organizations.

We have attempted in Exhibit 1 to summarize several of the more important findings of the various reviews of the turnover literature. Several of these reviews have pointed to the importance of job attitudes as a factor in turnover (Brayfield and Crockett, 1955; Herzberg *et al.*, 1957; Porter and Steers, 1973). In addition, some evidence exists that personality and biodemographic data can predict turnover to some extent (Schuh, 1967). The importance of economic factors has also been shown (Stoikov and Raimon, 1968). Finally, several of the more recent reviews have pointed to the wide diversity of factors (e.g., personal factors, job characteristics, reward systems, supervisory and group relations) that combine to influence the decision to stay or leave (Lefkowitz, 1971; Porter and Steers, 1973; Price, 1977; Mobley *et al.*, 1979; Muchinsky and Tuttle, 1979).

Beyond simple reviews, however, several investigators have attempted to propose conceptual models of the turnover process based on existing literature (March and Simon, 1958; Vroom, 1964; Price, 1977; Mobley, 1977). Although the details of the models differ, turnover is generally thought to be a function of negative job attitudes combined with an ability to secure employment elsewhere. Mobley (1977) goes further here in suggesting several intermediate linkages that intercede between attitudes and actual turnover, noting in particular the importance of behavioral intentions (after Fishbein, 1967).

Despite this long history of research on employee turnover, several issues remain unanswered. At least nine shortcomings of many of the existing models can be identified that need to be taken into account in any comprehensive model of voluntary employee turnover:

1. Many current models ignore the role of available information about one's job or prospective job in an individual's participation decision.

Exhibit 1. Summary of Empirical Reviews of Turnover Literature

Investigator(s)	Focus	Major Findings	Formal Model Presented
Brayfield and Crockett (1955)	Effects of job satisfaction on turnover	Significant if modest relation between dissatisfaction and turnover	No
Herzberg et al. (1957)	Comprehensive review	Significant if modest relation between dissatisfaction and turnover	No
March and Simon (1958)	Comprehensive review	Turnover largely influenced by desirability of leaving plus ease of movement	Yes
Vroom (1964)	Limited review	Turnover influenced by force to remain vs. force to leave	Yes
Schuh (1967)	Personality and biodemographic predictors of turnover	Modest evidence that vocational interest inventories and scaled biographical information blanks predicted some turnover	No
Stoikov and Raimon (1968)	Economic factors in turnover	Money and labor market factors have sizable influence on industry-wide turnover rates	No
Lefkowitz (1971)	Comprehensive review	Turnover influenced by job expectations, satisfaction, work environment, compensation, job itself, and supervisory style	No

Porter and Steers (1973)	Comprehensive review	Satisfaction modesty related to turnover; major influences on turnover can be found in person, job, work environment, and organization-wide factors; importance of met expectations	Partial
Pettman (1973, 1975)	Test of March and Simon model	Modest support for model based on review of literature	Yes
Price (1977)	Comprehensive review	Turnover influenced by dissatisfaction plus opportunity to leave; also considers organizational outcomes of turnover	Yes
Forrest et al. (1977)	Effort to integrate psychological and economic influences on turnover	Based on Vroom model, both psychological and economic factors shown to influence turnover	Yes
Mobley (1977; Mobley et al., 1979)	Comprehensive review	Model of intermediate linkages between satisfaction and actual turnover presented (1977); review of literature (1979) supports expanded version of model	Yes
Muchinsky and Tuttle (1979)	Comprehensive review	Major influences on turnover can be found in attitudes, person, work, and biographical sheets; support for met expectations proposition	No

Recent research on realistic job previews clearly demonstrates how prior knowledge concerning the actual job environment can ultimately affect turnover (Wanous, 1977).

2. The extent to which an individual's expectations and values surrounding a job are met by one's organizational experiences have also been shown to be an important factor in turnover (Porter and Steers, 1973; Muchinsky and Tuttle, 1979). These factors have likewise received scant attention in comprehensive models of employee turnover.

3. The role of job performance level as a factor influencing desire or intent to leave has also been overlooked. High job performance may heighten one's expectations concerning organizational rewards, while poor performance may cause lower attitudes concerning the intrinsic worth of the job. In both cases, performance must be recognized in the turnover process (Marsh and Manari, 1977).

4. Most models of turnover focus exclusively on one job attitude (namely, job satisfaction) and ignore other attitudes (like organizational commitment) that may also be relevant. In view of recent studies indicating that commitment (rather than satisfaction) represents a better predictor of turnover (Porter, Steers, Mowday, and Boulian, 1974; Mowday, Steers and Porter, 1979), this omission appears serious

5. Current models ignore a host of nonwork influences on staying or leaving. When one's spouse is transferred—or when one's spouse cannot transfer—the employee's mobility is affected.

6. Current models assume that once an employee has become dissatisfied, the wheels are set in motion for eventual termination. This assumption ignores the fact that the employee may be able to change his or her current work situation (perhaps through bargaining with the supervisor, threats to quit, etc.) Ironically, March and Simon (1958) did point to this factor over two decades ago, but most subsequent efforts have dropped it from consideration.

7. It would be useful if models of employee turnover would clarify the role of available alternative job opportunities, both in terms of which factors influence such availability and in terms of the consequences for employees of having no alternatives.

8. Current models of turnover assume a one-way flow process and ignore important feedback loops that serve to enhance or ameliorate one's desire to leave.

9. Very little thought has been given to how people accommodate the participation decision. What happens to those who want to leave but cannot or to those who choose to stay when their friends and associates are leaving? Alternatively, how do people adjust psychologically to the act of leaving one organization and joining a second? This accommodation process is perhaps the most fruitful area for future research on the

turnover process since it has significant implications for the attitudes and behavior of both stayers and leavers.

Clearly, there is a need for more comprehensive process models of employee turnover that take such factors as these into account. Such a model is presented here in the hopes that it will stimulate more comprehensive, multivariate efforts to study employee turnover and its outcomes. The model is largely inductive in nature and has been developed from the existing literature on the topic. The model is presented in two parts: 1) the procedures by which employees decide to stay or leave (turnover); and 2) the procedures by which employees learn to cope with their participation decision once it has been made (accommodation). While a good deal of research (albeit of a limited nature) has been carried out on the first of these two areas, the second area has received virtually no consideration.

A MODEL OF EMPLOYEE TURNOVER

In this section, we shall build upon earlier theoretical and empirical work and propose a largely cognitive model of employee turnover that focuses on the processes leading up to the decision to participate or withdraw. This model is meant to summarize and integrate earlier work and to extend such efforts by incorporating the points mentioned above. The model is schematically represented in Exhibit 2. It will provide a basis for the subsequent discussion on accommodation of the participation decision. In order to clarify the dynamics of the model, it will be described in three sequential parts: (1) job expectations and job attitudes; (2) job attitudes and intent to leave; and (3) intent to leave, available alternatives, and actual turnover. Relevant research will be cited as we proceed.

Job Expectations and Job Attitudes

Job Expectations and Values. A model of employee turnover could start in many places. We could begin with the nature of the job or work environment, the job market and economic factors, and so forth. We chose to begin with the individual and his or her expectations and values since it is the individual who must ultimately decide whether to stay or leave. All individuals have expectations upon entering a new organization. These expectations may involve beliefs about the nature of the job, the rewards for satisfactory performance, the availablility of interpersonal contacts and interactions, and so forth. It would be expected that each employee would have a somewhat different set of expectations depending upon his or her own values and needs at the time.

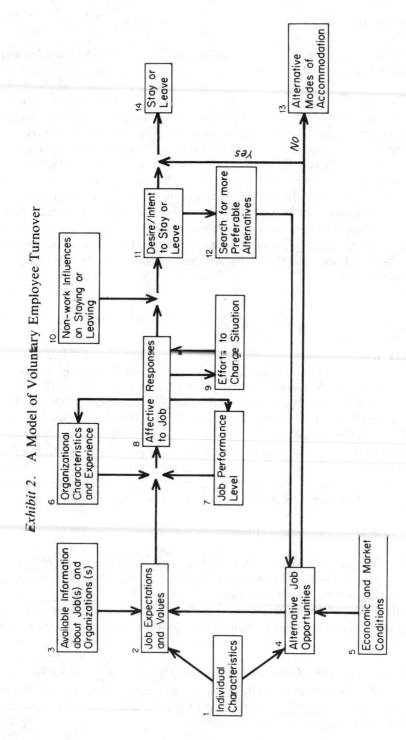

Exhibit 2. A Model of Voluntary Employee Turnover

These expectations (shown in box 2 of Exhibit 2) are believed to be influenced by three categories of variables: (1) individual characteristics; (2) available information about job and organization; and (3) alternative job opportunities. Several individual characteristics (see box 1) can influence job expectations and ultimately turnover. These include one's occupation, education, age, tenure; family responsibilities, family income level, personal work ethic, previous work experiences, and personality (Federico *et al.*, 1976; Mangione, 1973; Mobley *et al.*, 1978; Waters *et al.*, 1976; Porter and Steers, 1973; Hines, 1973; Mowday *et al.*, 1978). As a result of such factors, people determine consciously or unconsciously what they expect from a job: what they feel they must have, what they would like to have, and what they can do without.

A second influence on the determination of job expectations is the available information about the job and organization both at the time of organizational choice and during reappraisal periods throughout one's career (box 3). The basic argument here follows from the literature on "realistic job previews" (Wanous, 1977). It has been fairly consistently found that when people are provided with more complete or more accurate information about prospective jobs, they are able to make more informed choices and, as a result, are more likely to develop realistic job expectations that are more easily met by the organization. Modest support for the ultimate impact of unmet expectations on turnover can be found in studies reviewed by Porter and Steers (1973), Wanous (1977), Muchinsky and Tuttle (1979), and Mobley *et al.* (1979).

Such information about one's job or organization can also be important later in one's career. That is, if an accountant, for example, joins one of the major CPA firms in the hopes of eventually becoming a partner but later learns that the probability of attaining such status is minimal, the accountant may change his or her expectations and may decide to set off on a different course (e.g., corporate accounting).

A third influence on job expectations is the extent to which an individual has alternative job opportunities (box 4). Simply put, the greater the number of attractive job alternatives, the more demanding an individual may be when evaluating his or her current job or job offer. Pfeffer and Lawler (1979) found availability of alternative jobs was negatively related to job attitudes among a large sample of university faculty. However, Mowday and McDade (1979) found that the mere availability of alternative jobs was a less important influence on job attitudes than the relative attractiveness of the alternatives. In addition, they found that the influence of attractive alternative jobs on attitudes changed over time. In a longitudinal analysis, attractiveness of alternative jobs was negatively related to organizational commitment on the first morning a new employee reported for work. After one month on the job, however, attractiveness of alternative job offers the individual did not take advantage of was positively related to organizational commitment. Hence, on the first day at work, information about alternative jobs may be very salient since information about the chosen job is limited. After a period of time at work, however, the individual must justify his or her choice of the job and this may result in more positive attitudes for those who have given up an opportunity to take a relatively attractive alternative job.

Given the salience of alternative jobs during the early employment period, it is not surprising to discover that expectation levels of employees are quite high at the point of organizational entry (Porter and Steers, 1973). Once in a given job for a period of time, however, expectations tend to become more realistic as one develops greater behavioral commitments that make it less attractive to go elsewhere (Salancik, 1977). (We shall say more about the role of alternative job opportunities shortly.)

Affective Responses to Job. The next link in our proposed model relates job expectations and values to subsequent job attitudes (box 8). Following the literature on job attitudes, it is proposed that affective responses (including job satisfaction, organizational commitment, and job involvement) result from the interactions of three factors: (1) job expectations; (2) organizational characteristics and experiences; and (3) job performance level. (A discussion of the relative impact of the various affective responses on turnover goes beyond the scope of this paper—see Hom *et al.*, 1979; Cooper and Payne, 1978; Porter *et al.*, 1974).

The major thrust of the argument here deals with the interaction between job expectations (box 2) and organizational characteristics and experiences (box 6). Again, following from the literature on realistic job previews (Wanous, 1977), the more one's experiences in the organization are congruent with what one expects, the greater the propensity that an individual would be satisfied and would wish to remain with the organization (Muchinsky and Tuttle, 1979; Porter and Steers, 1973; Vroom, 1964). Such experiences have also been shown to be related to organizational commitment (Buchanan, 1974; Steers, 1977).

It should be noted here that the impact of expectations on subsequent job attitudes is a point open to dispute. Locke (1976) has argued that when expectations are not met, the reaction by individuals is surprise, not dissatisfaction. Instead, he argues that it is the extent to which valued attributes (instead of expected attributes) are present in a job that influences satisfaction. Although values and expectations are conceptually distinct, available evidence suggests that they are highly related in practice. [Bray, Campbell, and Grant (1974) found the two to be correlated at $r = .87$]. Perhaps employees develop higher expectations about those aspects of the job that are most highly valued and, hence, both concepts may be related to subsequent attitudes (see also Ilgen and Dugoni, 1977).

Other aspects of organizational life that could influence the extent to which one's expectations are met include the organization's pay and promotion policies, one's actual job duties, co-worker relations, work group size, supervisory style, organization structure and opportunities for participation in decision making, geographic location, and organizational goals and values. (Marsh and Mannari, 1977; Ilgen and Dugoni, 1977; Dansereau *et al.*, 1974; Koch and Steers, 1978; Waters *et al.*, 1976; Krackhardt, McKenna, Porter and Steers, 1978). Variables such as these, when taken together, constitute a form of experienced organizational reality that signal the individual as to whether his or her expectations are being (or are likely to be) met.

In addition, recent research suggests that job performance level (box 7) may also influence job attitudes and ultimate turnover. Poor performance has been shown to lead to poor attitudes about the job, possibly in an attempt to rationalize the poor performance ("This is a crummy job anyway.") Poor performance has also been shown to lead to increased anxiety and frustration (Cooper and Payne, 1978). Finally, two recent studies have shown that poor job performance represented an important influence on voluntary turnover (Marsh and Mannari, 1977; Wanous, Stumpf, and Bedrosian, 1978).

The resulting job attitudes, in turn, influence several other apsects of behavior. First, attitudes can feed back and influence both organizational experiences (box 6) and job performance (box 7), as shown in Exhibit 2 (see, for example, Forrest *et al.*, 1977). Poor job attitudes often color an employee's perceptions of organizational actions (e.g., promotion decisions, pay raises, supervisory behavior). Support for this position can be found in the recent attribution theory literature (Salancik and Pfeffer, 1978) and in studies of selective exposure to information (Janis and Mann, 1977).

Poor attitudes may in fact lead supervisors to take certain (punitive) actions which, in turn, lead to further reduced job attitudes. Likewise, negative affective responses to one's level of job performance can lead to further reductions in performance level (a "who cares?" attitude). This degenerative, self-reinforcing cycle can significantly enhance an employee's desire and interest to leave.

In addition, poor job attitudes may cause individuals to engage in efforts to change the situation (box 9). It is logical to assume that before actually deciding to leave, an individual would in many cases attempt to change or eliminate those aspects of the work situation that are compelling the ˙individual to leave. Such efforts may take the form of attempted intraorganizational transfer (March and Simon, 1958) or, alternatively, attempts to act on the work environment. Efforts to change the situation by acting on the environment can include attempts to restructure one's job or job responsibilities, changing the payoffs for continued participation, unionization efforts, threatening to leave, or forcing someone else to leave. Through mechanisms such as these, the work environment hopefully becomes more tolerable, thereby improving one's job attitudes and desire to stay. On the other hand, where an employee finds it impossible to alter the situation, poor job attitudes would be expected to remain the same (or possibly decrease), thereby strengthening one's resolve to leave. The potential effects of efforts to change the situation (whether successful or unsuccessful) on intent to leave and actual turnover represents a major area in need of serious study.

Job Attitudes and Intent to Leave

The second phase of the model focuses on the linkage between one's job attitudes and one's desire and intent to stay or leave. In brief, it is suggested that desire/intent to leave is influenced by: (1) affective responses to job; and (2) nonwork influences on staying or leaving.

Following from the work of Fishbein (1967) and others on attitude theory, it is assumed that one's affective responses to the job lead to behavioral intentions. In the case of employee turnover, we would expect reduced levels of job satisfaction and organizational commitment (box 8) to result in an increased desire or intent to leave (box 11; Mobley, 1977; Price, 1977; Steers, 1977; Koch and Steers, 1978). Such an assertion is common throughout the literature on turnover.

What is often overlooked in determining desire/intent to leave, however, is a constellation of nonwork influences on staying or leaving (box 10). There are many instances in which one may not like a particular job but still does not desire or seek termination. Such instances include situations where (1) an individual tolerates an unpleasant job (e.g., an apprenticeship) because of its instrumentality for future career considerations (e.g., a master craftsman); (2) a spouse is limited geographically to a certain region and alternative employment is scarce; (3) an individual's central life interests lie outside of work; and (4) family considerations (Dubin, Champoux and Porter, 1975; Porter and Steers, 1973; Schneider and Dachler, 1978).

In fact, following a review of relevant work, Sussman and Cogswell (1971, p. 485) suggested that "there is a direct relationship between the supply and demand of workers in any occupational system and the consideration of noneconomic factors in job movement; the greater the demand for workers in any occupational system the greater is the consideration given to familial concerns such as work aspirations of spouses, special needs of children, community activities, linkages with kin, friends, and voluntary associations; physical and social environments." Included here too would be Fishbein's (1967) notation of subjective normative beliefs, or how those around an individual would feel about his or her leaving. These nonwork factors are often overlooked in turnover research but may, in fact, explain a greater proportion of the turnover variance than job attitudes.

Parenthetically, it should be noted here that in our proposed model, we have combined desire and intent to leave. This has been done for the sake of parsimony and because we wished to focus our attention on the processes leading up to one's behavioral intentions. It was felt that these early influences were perhaps the least understood segment of the participation decision. It should be noted that more elaborate distinctions between desire to leave and intent to leave are presented by Mobley (1977; Mobley, Horner and Hollingsworth, 1978) and Fishbein (1967). Fishbein introduces the term "attitude toward the act," which is similar to our use of "desire to leave." Fishbein and others (e.g., Hom *et al.*, 1979) argue that an individual's feelings toward the act of quitting (desire) represent a more immediate determinant of intent to leave than feelings about the job.

Intent to Leave, Available Alternatives, and Turnover

Finally, the third segment of the proposed model focuses on the link between behavioral intent to leave and actual turnover. Following from the earlier work of March and Simon (1958), it is argued that employee turnover is ultimately determined by a combination of behavioral intent to leave (box 11) and the availability of alternative job opportunities (box 4). Although research support for this contention is mixed, much of the discrepancy appears to result more from inadequate methodology than from any repudiation of the basic hypothesis (Pettman, 1973; Schwab and Dyer, 1974; Schneider, 1976; Dansereau, Cashman and Graen, 1974).

Intent to leave apparently influences actual turnover in at least two ways. First, it may lead fairly directly to turnover (Muchinsky and Tuttle, 1979). Some people decide to leave their jobs even when alternative jobs are not available. Recent changes in the social welfare system aimed at providing unemployed people with minimal support levels may serve to enhance this direct relationship by providing an economic cushion to leavers.

Intent to leave may further influence actual turnover in an indirect fashion by causing the individual to initiate search behavior for more preferable alternative jobs (box 12). Research suggests that less satisfied people are more likely to be sensitive to job market changes (March and Simon, 1958). Such search behavior serves to open up to an individual a greater number of job possibilities, thereby increasing the likelihood of leaving.

In addition, however, alternative job opportunities (box 4) are also influenced by individual characteristics (box 1) and economic and market conditions (box 5). Individual characteristics such as age, sex, and occupation often constrain one's opportunities for jobs (Porter and Steers, 1973). Moreover, economic and market conditions also influence the availability of jobs (Forrest, Cummings and Johnson, 1977).

If an individual has no (or few) alternative job opportunities, he or she would be less likely to leave the organization. Instead, however, the individual may engage in alternative forms of withdrawal or accommodation in order to reduce the anxiety or frustration that results from not being able to leave (box 13). These alternatives may include absenteeism, drug abuse or alcoholism, sabotage, slowdowns, and so forth. Or, alternatively, they may take the form of rationalizing why it is in one's best interest to remain after all, as we shall see in the next section. In any case, where an individual wishes to leave but is unable to do so, some form of accommodation process can be expected. Where the individual wishes to leave and is able to do so, the probability of actual turnover (box 14) is markedly increased (Dansereau et al., 1974; Mobley et al., 1978; Woodward, 1976).

With regard to the availability of alternative job opportunities, we can see a further feedback loop in operation. Specifically, when an employee is presented with a new and attractive alternative position, perhaps because of changes in market conditions, his or her expectations on the current job are likely to be increased, making it more difficult for the organization to meet these expectations. As a result, job attitudes may suffer which cause heightened desire and intent to leave. This, in turn, sensitizes the individual to the possibility of changing jobs. Again, this self-reinforcing cycle can ultimately hasten the decision to leave.

Relationship to Earlier Models

As noted above, the model suggested here attempts to summarize and integrate much of the earlier theorizing on the topic of employee turnover. Even so, while many aspects of the model have appeared earlier, other aspects are somewhat unique.

To begin with, the role of available information about the prospective job and organization is explicitly recognized (box 3). Second, job performance level as a factor in affective responses to the job is also noted (box 7). Third, like Mobley et al.'s (1979) model, but unlike others, several attitudes (not simply job satisfaction) are considered as they related to turnover (box 8). Fourth, major emphasis is placed on a series of nonwork factors that have been shown to influence desire to leave and/or actual termination (box 10). Fifth, recognition is also given to the fact that when an employee is dissatisfied he or she may engage in attempts to change the situation or work environment prior to deciding upon termination (box 9). Finally, special emphasis is given to the accommodation processes used by individuals who leave a positive situation or remain in a negative one (box 13), as well as those used by individuals left behind when someone else leaves.

In all, then, it is our belief that the model presented here does suggest several new avenues for future research on the turnover decision that should aid in our understanding of the process. Based on this model, we now turn to a consideration of the processes by which individuals accommodate the decision to participate or withdraw.

ACCOMMODATING THE DECISION TO PARTICIPATE OR WITHDRAW: ATTITUDINAL AND BEHAVIORAL CONSEQUENCES OF TURNOVER

The primary analytical focus in previous research on turnover in organizations has been concerned almost exclusively with understanding the psychological processes leading up to the decision to stay or leave and identifying factors which may influence these processes. Numerous investigations have attempted to determine the extent to which characteristics of the individual employee, task, work environment, and larger organization predict subsequent turnover behavior (Mobley *et al.*, 1979; Porter and Steers, 1973). In the previous section a number of such antecedent factors were identified and integrated into a comprehensive model of the processes leading up to the decision to stay or leave. Important questions still remain, however, concerning the *consequences* of turnover behavior for both individuals and organizations. In this section we will consider the turnover decision of an individual in terms of its consequences. Relatively little empirical or theoretical attention has been given to the consequences of turnover for either individuals or organizations. As a result, much of the discussion that follows remains somewhat speculative. Our intent in this section is not to provide definitive answers concerning the consequences of turnover, but rather to stimulate research interest in this area and to suggest several tentative conceptual models that can be used to guide future inquiry.

The consequences of turnover can be viewed from at least four perspectives. The first three perspectives concern the consequences for several types of organizational participants at an individual level of analysis, while the fourth represents the consequences of turnover for organizations.

First, the decision to stay with or leave an organization is clearly likely to have consequences for the person making the decision. Although previous research in organizational behavior has concentrated on the implications of job attitudes for subsequent behavior (e.g., job satisfaction as a predictor of turnover), there is considerable evidence that behavior also has important implications for subsequent attitudes (Salancik and Pfeffer, 1978). Research on job choice, for example, has shown that individuals who select among alternative jobs often systematically re-evaluate both the chosen and unchosen jobs following the choice (Lawler, Kulick, Rhode and Sorenson, 1975; Vroom and Deci, 1971). From the perspective of the individual leaving the organization, the act of turnover may therefore have important implications for attitudes toward the job the individual is leaving, as well as the new job he or she is taking.

A second perspective from which to view the consequences of turnover concerns the co-workers of the individual who leaves the organization. Turnover by an individual can be interpreted by his or her former co-workers as a rejection of the job and/or as an implicit, if not explicit, recognition that better job opportunities exist elsewhere. Those who remain in the organization may have to reconcile their decision to stay in light of evidence from the behavior of another individual that the job may not be all that desirable. Turnover may therefore cause former co-workers to re-evaluate their present position in the organization and possibly lead to the development of more negative job attitudes. Furthermore, it may cause former co-workers to initiate a search for a more attractive job.

A third perspective from which to view the consequences of turnover is from the perspective of the supervisor of the individual who has left the organization. This may be the most important perspective from an organizational standpoint since it is the supervisor who must take steps to prevent turnover in the future. Since turnover is most often viewed as a problem in organizations, a high rate of turnover by subordinates may adversely reflect on the effectiveness of the supervisor, particularly when it is the best employees who leave. Turnover by subordinates may be perceived as threatening by the supervisor. Moreover, supervisors in organizations experiencing high rates of turnover must diagnose the reasons why employees leave and make decisions about appropriate courses of action to reduce turnover. The ability of supervisors to accurately determine the reasons why employees leave has important implications for the effectiveness of subsequent efforts designed to remove the causes of turnover. Despite the importance of understanding how supervisors interpret the reasons for subordinate turnover, very little is known about this process or the factors which may influence it.

The fourth and final perspective from which to view the consequences of turnover concerns the impact of turnover on overall organizational effectiveness. A number of writers have developed methods for identifying and measuring the costs associated with replacing employees who leave the organization (e.g., Jeswald, 1974; Macy and Mirvis, 1976). In addition, Price (1977) has suggested that turnover has implications for such organization-wide variables as size of administrative staff, formalization, integration, innovation, and centralization. Since the consequences of turnover for organizations have already received some attention in the literature, this section will focus only on the consequences of turnover from the perspective of individuals.

In the discussion that follows, the consequences of turnover behavior will be considered from the perspective of both the person leaving the organization and observers of the behavior (i.e., co-workers and supervisors). The discussion in this section will focus on the attitudinal and behavioral consequences of turnover. Particular attention in this discussion will focus on the consequences of turnover for the individual making the decision to leave the organization, although the attitudinal and behavioral consequences of turnover for observers of the action will also be briefly considered. In the next section, a theoretical model of the processes through which the causes of turnover are identified will be presented and the factors which influence this process will be discussed. This discussion will draw heavily upon the work of social psychologists in the area of attribution theory.

General research interest in the consequences of choice behavior for subsequent attitudes has increased in recent years among those interested in investigating behavior in organizations (cf. Salancik and Pfeffer, 1978). Research on the implications of behavior for attitude change has a long history in social psychology. The important work of Festinger (1957) and Brehm and Cohen (1962) on cognitive dissonance and Bem (1967) on self-perception theory provide theoretical frameworks within which attitude change on the part of the person behaving can be predicted from a knowledge of the circumstances under which behavior took place. Although primary interest has been focused on attitude change on the part of the person behaving, research evidence also suggests that an individual's behavior may have implications for the attitudes of those who observe it (Nisbett and Valins, 1972).

Consequences for the Person Staying or Leaving

From an analytical standpoint, the decision to remain on a job that is satisfying or leave one that is dissatisfying is less interesting with respect to its consequences than cases in which satisfied employees leave or dissatisfied employees stay (i.e., "off-quadrant" behavior). When behavior is consistent with prior attitudes (e.g., a dissatisfied employee leaves) there would appear to be little need to change subsequent attitudes as a consequence of the decision. Although, in cases where behavior is consistent with prior attitudes, the individual may strengthen preexisting positive or negative feelings in the process of justifying his or her decision, it is doubtful whether attitudes would dramatically change (e.g., shift from positive to negative). When behavior is inconsistent with prior attitudes (e.g., a dissatisfied employee remains in the organization), however, there is reason to believe that a dramatic shift in attitudes may take place under certain circumstances.

Festinger's (1957) theory of cognitive dissonance is relevant to understanding the consequences of behavior (staying or leaving) which is inconsistent with prior attitudes.[1] Briefly stated, the theory suggests that dissonance is aroused whenever two cognitions psychologically stand in obverse relation to each other. The existence of dissonance is viewed as creating tension within the individual and motivating actions designed to reduce the dissonance (cf. Zanna and Cooper, 1976). The motivation to reduce dissonance is a function of the magnitude of the dissonance created; the greater the dissonance, the greater the motivation to reduce it. Applied to the turnover decision, the theory clearly suggests that the decision to leave a job which is satisfying or remain on a job which is dissatisfying will, under certain conditions, create dissonant cognitions in the mind of the employee. In the former case, the "satisfied-leaver" may hold the two dissonant cognitions, "I am satisfied with my job" and "I am leaving my job." The "dissatisfied-stayer," on the other hand, holds the two dissonant cognitions, "I am dissatisfied with my job" and "I am remaining on the job." When such dissonant cognitions exist, the theory predicts individuals will be motivated to reduce dissonance through either behavioral or cognitive means (Brehm and Cohen, 1962; Festinger, 1957; Wicklund and Brehm, 1976). Since it is usually difficult to change or deny a decision once it has been made, this generally suggests that the individual will change his or her attitudes or perceptions to be more consistent with the choice.

Recent research on dissonance theory has been directed toward the problem of explicating the conditions under which predictions of the theory will hold (Kiesler and Munson, 1975; Wicklund and Brehm, 1976). Several situational factors surrounding choice processes are thought to be necessary to produce dissonance. First, the decision must involve a behavioral commitment on the part of the individual and/or the action taken must be difficult to change or revoke (Brehm and Cohen, 1962; Staw, 1974). In other words, a definite choice must be made between two or more alternatives and the decision may not be easily changed. Second, the decision must have important consequences for the individual in order to produce dissonance (Festinger, 1957; Staw, 1974). Third, the individual must feel personal responsibility for the decision (Collins and Hoyt, 1972;

Staw, 1974). In other words, the decision situation must be perceived as one in which the individual had freedom of choice among the alternatives. Finally, there must be an element of inadequate justification associated with the choice between alternatives (Brehm and Cohen, 1962; Freedman, 1963). This requirement suggests that there must be some characteristic of the unchosen alternative which, when considered alone, would have led the individual to select that alternative. In general, we would expect dissonance to be greatest when the alternatives are similar in terms of their overall attractiveness but differ with respect to the attractiveness of specific characteristics associated with each alternative.

Since the turnover decision involves a definite choice, is a decision that is most often difficult to revoke or change, and is of considerable importance to most individuals, the first two conditions necessary to produce dissonance can be assumed to exist in most, if not all, turnover decisions. Consequently, the third and fourth conditions (perceived choice and inadequate justification) appear to be most crucial in determining the attitudinal consequences of the decision to stay or leave. More specifically, for purposes of the discussion below the presence or absence of perceived choice and inadequate justification will be viewed as determining whether or not an individual reacts to the decision in a manner predicted by dissonance theory.

When a turnover decision is characterized by both perceived choice and inadequate justification, dissonance theory predicts several possible behavioral or attitudinal consequences. In any given situation, a number of alternative methods of reducing dissonance may be available to the individual. It is difficult, however, to make precise predictions about how individuals will reduce dissonance (Wicklund and Brehm, 1976). Festinger (1957) originally proposed that the method of dissonance reduction chosen would be sensitive to the "reality" of the situation. In a test of this proposition, Walster, Berscheid, and Barclay (1967) found that subjects chose a method of dissonance reduction that was unlikely to be challenged by future events. Considerable ambiguity still remains, however, about what method of dissonance reduction will be chosen in a particular situation. As a consequence, the discussion in this section remains somewhat speculative.

In considering the consequences of turnover for the individual making the decision, a distinction will be drawn between: 1) whether a person is a "satisfied-leaver" or a "dissatisfied-stayer"; and 2) whether or not the conditions necessary to produce dissonance are present. To simplify the discussion, only decision situations in which *both* perceived choice and inadequate justification are present or where at least one or both of the conditions are absent will be considered. When both conditions are present, it is assumed that dissonance may result from the turnover decision.

If one or both of the conditions are absent, no dissonance is predicted since external justification for the behavior will exist in the situation. This distinction results in the fourfold classification of cases presented in Exhibit 3.

1. Satisfied-Leaver/Dissonance Present. In this situation the employee has voluntarily resigned from a job (i.e., high personal responsibility and choice) which he or she found satisfying. Inadequate justification exists in that a trade-off was made between attractive elements of the old and new job. When this situation exists, it is predicted that post-decision dissonance will result and that the employee will be motivated to reduce this dissonance.

Several alternative modes of dissonance reduction would be available in this situation, as shown in Exhibit 3. First, dissonance may be reduced by denying personal responsibility for the decision (Cooper, 1971). The employee may, for example, cognitively distort the circumstances surrounding the decision in a manner which suggests the organization was subtly urging him or her to leave. Such a strategy is equivalent to cognitively manipulating the attribution of the reason for leaving. (Attribution processes surrounding the turnover decisions are discussed in the next section.) The fact that people are more likely to attribute the causes of their own behavior to characteristics of the environment (Jones, 1976) suggests that this may be a common strategy. This strategy may be difficult to reconcile with reality, however, when the organization has made attempts to retain the employee (e.g., promised a raise or promotion).

A second plausible method of reducing dissonance is to cognitively distort the characteristics of the old and new job. This strategy can be seen in research on job choice which has found that people systematically re-evaluate the alternatives after a choice has been made (Lawler *et al.*, 1975; Vroom and Deci, 1971). It has been found, for example, that people reduce dissonance by increasing their positive evaluation of the chosen (new) job while at the same time magnifying the negative aspects of the unchosen (old) job. In the turnover decision, this is likely to result in a third consequence which is a rapid shifting of loyalties and commitment from the old to new job. The generally high levels of commitment found among newly hired employees on the first day at work may be evidence of this phenomenon (Porter, Crampon and Smith, 1976; Van Maanen, 1975).

Fourth, and consistent with the process of systematically re-evaluating the old and new job, it is probable that individuals will avoid information that is inconsistent with their choice and selectively seek information which confirms the choice (Festinger, 1957; Janis and Mann, 1977). This may result in selective perception as the employee experiences the new

Exhibit 3. Possible Attitudinal and Behavioral Consequences for the Decision Maker of the Decision to Participate

Situational Characteristics	Emergent Condition	Attitudinal and Behavioral Consequences	
		Satisfied-Leaver	Dissatisfied-Stayer
High personal responsibility and inadequate justification	High dissonance	1. Denial of responsibility for decision to change jobs.	1. Denial of responsibility for decision to remain.
		2. Systematic distortion of characteristics of old and new job.	2. Systematic distortion of characteristics of current and alternative jobs.
		3. High organizational commitment and satisfaction on new job.	3. Shifting valence of inducements for membership in present organization.
		4. Selective perception of new job.	4. Increased satisfaction and commitment on present job.
		5. Reduced social contacts with former co-workers.	5. Deliberate increase in dissonance.
Low personal responsibility and/or adequate justification	Low dissonance	1. Pleasant memories of old job.	1. Change job situation.
		2. Willingness to maintain social contacts with former co-workers	2. Continued job search behavior.
			3. Lowered self-esteem and self-confidence.
			4. Alternative forms of withdrawal.
			5. Shifting central life interests.

job environment. Finally, employees may reduce social contacts with co-workers on the previous job and develop new social relationships based on the chosen job, since association with previous co-workers may make salient information inconsistent with the choice. Caplow (1964) has cited the termination of social relationships based on past organizational memberships as an important part of socialization into a new organization. This socialization requirement may in part serve to reconfirm the job choice of the individual.

2. *Dissatisfied-Stayer/Dissonance Present.* This situation describes an employee who perceives that alternative jobs are available but who voluntarily turns down a job to remain in a relatively dissatisfying position. Inadequate justification for the decision to remain may be created when the alternative job was at least in some respect more attractive than the current job. The decision to remain would be predicted to create dissonance.

One method of reducing dissonance in this situation is to deny responsibility for the decision. In other words, the circumstances surrounding the choice can be cognitively distorted to eliminate the perceived voluntary nature of the decision (i.e., low perceived choice or personal responsibility). For example, the employee may attribute the causes for his or her behavior to environmental factors beyond his/her control (e.g., "I can't leave while my children are still in school"). As noted earlier, the attribution of causes of behavior to environmental factors may be a common strategy since there is a natural tendency for this to occur (Jones, 1976) and it may be successful since a multiplicity of such factors are likely to exist in any decision situation. When this occurs, the individual may remain dissatisfied with the job and react in a manner described in Case #4 below.

When it is impossible to deny personal responsibility for the choice, the employee may distort perceptions of the existing job to magnify its positive features. For example, the individual may re-evaluate the inducements associated with the job and place a higher valence on those inducements previously considered unattractive (an employee may come to value aspects of the current job such as seniority, pension benefits, and job security more highly than before to reduce dissonance). In addition, the individual may "discover" features of the job which cast it in a more favorable light. For example, the individual may perceive greater opportunities for promotion in the future than were previously thought to exist. Alternatively, the employee may cognitively redefine the nature of the job itself to make it more attractive and satisfying (Porter, Lawler and Hackman, 1975).

In general, it can be predicted that many "dissatisfied-stayers" will not be likely to remain dissatisfied for long. This condition can be viewed as unstable when perceived choice and inadequate justification are present. The process of reducing dissonance through a cognitive re-evaluation of the job is thus likely to result in movement from a "dissatisfied-stayer" to a "satisfied-stayer."

When dissatisfaction with the job is very high there is one additional method through which dissonance can be reduced. This would involve a temporary increase in the level of dissonance associated with the decision to remain to a point greater than the resistance to changing jobs (Festinger, 1957). Once the level of dissonance met or exceeded the resistance to change, the individual would be predicted to leave the organization (i.e., become a "dissatisfied-leaver"). This may be a less common form of dissonance reduction. However, some employees never seem to find anything right on the job and continually express a high degree of dissatisfaction with relatively minor irritations at work. Such employees may be following a more or less deliberate, albeit unconscious, strategy designed to increase dissonance associated with remaining on a job to a point where they have little choice but to leave (or be asked to leave). The negative consequences of this strategy for the organization in terms of potential work disruptions, discipline incidents, and low morale are apparent.

3. Satisfied-Leaver/Dissonance Absent. When an employee has little control over the decision to leave a job or when the decision is voluntary but clearly the "right" choice (i.e., adequate justification), there is little reason to believe the individual will experience dissonance. Based on theory, there is little reason to believe the individual will engage in the systematic cognitive distortion described in Case #1 since there is no need to psychologically justify the decision. The employee may, depending on the circumstances under which he or she left, retain pleasant memories about the old job and positively evaluate the time spent in the organization. In addition, the individual may wish to maintain active social contacts with former co-workers and take an active interest in the work-related affairs. From the perspective of the leaver's former co-workers, however, these social contacts may become increasingly less attractive for reasons discussed below.

When a person voluntarily leaves the job for what is clearly a more attractive alternative, however, it is possible to question whether the concept of a "satisfied-leaver" is really viable. Although an employee may be satisfied with his or her current job, receipt of information about an attractive alternative should cause the person to re-evaluate his or her current position. Comparing the current job to the attractive alternative may result in dissatisfaction and thus the person would become a "dissatisfied-leaver." Although there may be little dissonance associated with this situation, the dissatisfaction which results from comparing the current job with the alternative may appear to be the consequence of dissonance reduction processes. In other words, the employee may express increasing dissatisfaction with the job he or she is leaving both when conditions producing dissonance are present or absent. When the conditions producing dissonance are absent, however, dissatisfaction should increase *prior* to the decision to leave the organization since it is at this time that comparisons are made between the present and alternative job. In contrast, dissatisfaction should theoretically *follow* the decision to leave when the conditions producing dissonance are present. Although this distinction follows from theory, it may be difficult in actual practice to distinguish between these two conditions since it is often impossible to determine when the actual decision to leave has been made.

4. *Dissatisfied-Stayer/Dissonance Absent.* In this situation the employee is dissatisfied with the job but, for a number of possible reasons, finds it impossible to leave (i.e., low perceived choice). Such reasons may include economic constraints (e.g., investments in the pension system), family constraints (e.g., dual career families), or no available alternatives. In contrast to the situation where the conditions producing dissonance are present, employees in this situation may pose serious problems of an unexpected nature to the organization. In considering the possible actions of employees in this situation, it should be remembered that these actions are motivated by a desire to deal with the dissatisfying job situation and not by an attempt to reduce dissonance associated with the decision to remain in the organization.

First, as suggested previously, employees may engage in attempts to change the job situation (see Exhibit 2, box 9). Dissatisfied employees who are forced to remain in the organization may be motivated to remove the source of dissatisfaction through such means as restructuring the job, efforts to obtain a transfer within the organization, unionization, and so forth. Although little is currently known about how employees accommodate dissatisfying jobs by attempting to restructure the work environment, it is likely that such attempts are made.

Second, when attempts at changing the job are unsuccessful or when the reason for remaining in the organization is the lack of alternative jobs, employees may be likely to continue to engage in search behavior designed to find another position (March and Simon, 1958; Mobley, 1977). In other words, dissatisfaction may remain high and the individual will continue to look for any reasonable way to leave the organization. From the perspective of reactance theory (Brehm, 1966), heightened and continued search behavior would be predicted as a way for employees to reassert their freedom of action.

When continued search activity remains unsuccessful, several potentially negative consequences may result (cf. Wortman and Brehm, 1976). For instance, the employee may experience decreased self-esteem and self-confidence as a result of his or her failure to find another job. This decreased self-esteem may ultimately influence performance on the job (Korman, 1977). Furthermore, the employee may engage in alternative forms of withdrawal behavior such as absenteeism and tardiness (Porter and Steers, 1973). Alternatively, the employee may turn to more severe forms of withdrawal such as alcoholism or drugs when other means of withdrawal are unavailable (cf. Staw and Oldham, 1978). Several authors (e.g., Kornhauser, 1965) have suggested that job-related frustrations may be related to mental and physical illness as well as other problems off-the-job. These individuals are likely to present severe problems for the organization and it may be useful for organizations to consider making available periodic forms of withdrawal (e.g., "mental health" days) as a method of countering these problems.

Finally, a somewhat less severe reaction under these circumstances has been suggested by the work of Dubin (1956). His research on the "central life interests" of employees suggests that many employees cope with dissatisfying jobs by shifting their central life interests from work to nonwork areas of their life. For example, the employee may become highly involved in family activities, church or civic groups, and so forth. Employees with non-work central life interests have little psychological investment in the work place. Their orientation toward the job is likely to be of an instrumental nature in which work is seen as a means to the attainment of more highly valued outcomes off-the-job. From the organization's perspective, these employees may remain productive and contributing members of the work force, although their commitment to the organization and involvement in the job are likely to remain low (Dubin, Champoux, and Porter, 1975).

Consequences for Observers of Turnover by Another Person

From an objective standpoint, the consequences of turnover by another individual appear fairly straightforward. The fact that another individual has resigned from his or her job in the organization provides potentially valuable information and may serve as a stimulus for future action. Former co-workers of the person who resigned, for example, may analyze the reasons why the individual left for purposes of re-evaluating their own position in the organization. Turnover by another individual may also provide new information about attractive alternative job opportunities.

Similarly, the supervisor of the person leaving may analyze the reasons for turnover and use this information to solve any problems in the work place that may be causing employees to resign.

Although the consequences for observers of turnover by another individual can be approached from a rational information processing perspective, it is likely that a number of motivational factors may influence the interpretation of why another person leaves the organization. Dissonance theory can also be used to understand why observers may be motivated to distort the reasons why other people leave. In the case of a supervisor, for example, his or her self-image as a good manager may be threatened by the belief that an employee left the organization because of poor supervision. Rather than change his or her self-image, the supervisor may find it easier to reduce dissonance in this situation by distorting the reasons why the individual left the organization. This may involve cognitively distorting the individual's prior job behavior (e.g., the person frequently complained about the pay in the organization) or the nature of the new job to which the individual is moving (e.g., the new job provides much better opportunities for promotion and career advancement). Reassessing the person's prior job behavior or the characteristics of the new job to which the person is moving would shift the blame for turnover from poor supervision to other factors in the work environment or characteristics of the person leaving (e.g., he or she was not very reliable or loyal). As a result, the supervisor may come to believe that changes in supervisory practices are unnecessary while changes in selection practices or other aspects of the work environment are desirable. Distorting the reasons why the person left the organization may result in both more negative attitudes toward the person and actions designed to reduce future turnover that do not address the real reason why the employee left.

Co-workers may also find that the knowledge that an individual has left the organization for a better position is a source of dissonance and psychological discomfort. The fact that another individual found the job dissatisfying may be dissonant with the co-worker's implicit decision to stay in the organization. It may be easier for the co-worker to cognitively distort the reasons why an individual resigned from the job rather than raise serious questions about his/her own decision to remain in the organization. As with the case of supervisors, this process may involve distorting information about the former co-worker's job behavior before resignation or the nature of the co-worker's new job. Changing perceptions about the reasons why the individual has left the job may make the act of turnover less threatening to employees who remain.

Although motivational factors are likely to have an impact on beliefs about why other people leave and subsequent attitudes toward the individual, the extent of this influence may be greater under certain conditions and for some individuals than for others. From the perspective of former co-workers, the knowledge that another person has left because they found the job to be dissatisfying is likely to be most threatening when the person remaining has the same freedom to leave but chooses not to do so. It follows that the co-worker could also reduce dissonance associated with another person leaving by denying that they have the same freedom of action. It might also be hypothesized that the motivation to distort the reasons why others leave would be greatest for individuals with a poor self-concept or a lack of confidence in their own judgment (Bradley, 1978). More will be said about this in the next section on attribution processes.

Beliefs about the reasons why an individual has left the organization have been found to play an important role in determining the attitudinal and behavioral consequences of turnover. Little is currently known, however, about how such beliefs concerning the reasons for turnover are formed. In the next section the processes through which people develop beliefs about the causes of turnover will be discussed and a conceptual model of this process will be presented.

INTERPRETING THE CAUSES OF TURNOVER BEHAVIOR

The manner in which individuals react to turnover behavior, whether their own or that of other employees, may largely depend upon the reasons why they believe turnover took place. As suggested earlier, the consequences of turnover may be quite different if co-workers believe that a dull and uninteresting job was the cause of turnover rather than the fact that the leaver was a malcontent or was unreliable. A knowledge of the processes through which individuals determine the causes of turnover behavior therefore appears to be an important element in understanding the larger consequences of turnover behavior.

The processes through which individuals attempt to understand the causes of events they observe have been the province of social psychologists interested in attribution theory. Attribution theorists view individuals as "intuitive scientists" who observe events in their environment and attempt to provide explanations for these events by identifying their causes (Ross, 1977).

Current research on attribution processes has been greatly influenced by two important theories. Jones and Davis (1965) developed a theory of correspondent inferences to describe how personal characteristics of an actor could be inferred from the consequences of their action. Their primary interest was in explaining how attributions to the traits and dispositions of the person could be made by ruling out environmental explanations (Jones, 1976). A complimentary theory of attribution processes developed by Kelley (1967, 1972, 1973) focuses on how multiple occurrences of a behavior are attributed to characteristics of the person, environment, or the circumstances under which the behavior took place. Unlike the approach of Jones and Davis (1965), which examines consequences of the behavior, Kelley's theory focuses attention on factors which covary with behavior for purposes of making attributions. A fundamental assumption of Kelley's theory is that the processes used by observers to determine the cause of behavior are similar to those used by the actor to determine the cause of his or her own behavior (cf. Bem, 1967).

The attribution theories of Jones and Davis (1965) and Kelley (1973) focus attention on different types of information that can be used to form beliefs about the causes of turnover behavior (i.e., information about the consequences of turnover vs. information about job-related behavior prior to the point of turnover). Although the two theories have generally been viewed as distinct, it is possible to integrate both approaches in developing a more comprehensive model of the processes through which individuals attribute the causes of turnover behavior (cf. Jones and McGillis, 1976). Such an effort is presented here in a model of the processes associated with forming beliefs about the reasons why people leave an organization. Before presenting the model, however, it is first necessary to briefly consider the nature of turnover as a category of behavior.

Nature of Turnover as a Behavior

Unlike attribution processes associated with behaviors such as job performance (Green and Mitchell, 1979), it should be recognized that turnover is a behavior that occurs at one point in time and seldom, if ever, more than once for the same individual in a particular organization. Turnover behavior therefore differs from job performance in that it is most often characterized by a single rather than multiple occurrence. This has important theoretical implications since previous theory suggests that the attribution processes involved in analyzing the single occurrence of a behavior may differ from those used to analyze a behavior which is repeated over time (Kelley, 1973). Attribution processes associated with assessing the causes of turnover behavior are complicated, however, by the fact that individuals may analyze it as a single occurrence of behavior, a multiple occurrence of behavior, or both.

The view that turnover behavior can be analyzed as a single occurrence of behavior is obvious from the nature of the act itself. Although a person may change jobs many times in his or her career, the attribution processes of interest here are those associated with the resignation of an individual from a particular organization. Jones and Davis' (1965) theory suggests that the causes of an action can be determined from an analysis of its consequences. When behavior and its associated consequences are observed, it is possible to make inferences about its causes with no prior knowledge about the behavior. Turnover behavior can therefore be treated as a single occurrence of a behavior for purposes of making attributions.

The reasons for assuming that turnover can also be analyzed as if it were multiple occurrences of behavior may be less obvious. Several considerations are relevant in this regard. First, individuals frequently possess historical information about a number of turnover incidents and this information can be used in identifying why, in a particular instance, an individual left the organization. The turnover of a particular individual is a single occurrence of behavior. The knowledge that the previous three people performing the same job also quit, however, may be viewed as multiple occurrences of the same behavior for analytical purposes of identifying the cause that made a particular individual leave the job.

Second, job behavior prior to the point of termination may be considered in identifying the reasons why an individual has left the organization. For purposes of analyzing the causes of turnover behavior, for example, expressions of dissatisfaction with a particular facet of the job prior to the point of termination may be viewed as consistent with the subsequent turnover and thus multiple occurrences of the same underlying behavior. It should be recognized that linking prior expressions of dissatisfaction with subsequent turnover involves a second causal inference that dissatisfaction causes turnover. Although there is little evidence available on this point, it is probable that most employees believe a strong relationship exists between job dissatisfaction and turnover.

Recognizing that turnover behavior, although it occurs at one point in time, can be analyzed as either a single or multiple occurrence of behavior suggests that people may use different processes in making attributions about the causes of turnover. The nature of these processes is discussed in the model suggested below.

A Model of Attribution Processes Associated with Turnover Behavior

The proposed model of the processes through which people may infer the causes of turnover behavior is presented in Exhibit 4. The model is an integration of earlier work on attribution processes by Jones and Davis (1965) and Kelley (1967, 1973). It suggests that people perceive different categories of causal agents (i.e., characteristics of the person, job and external environment, or circumstances) as causing an individual to leave the organization and that turnover, in turn, results in certain unique effects or consequences to the individual. Although the model suggests a causal process proceeding from cause to turnover behavior to conse-

Exhibit 4. A Model of Factors Influencing Attributions of the Causes of Turnover Behavior

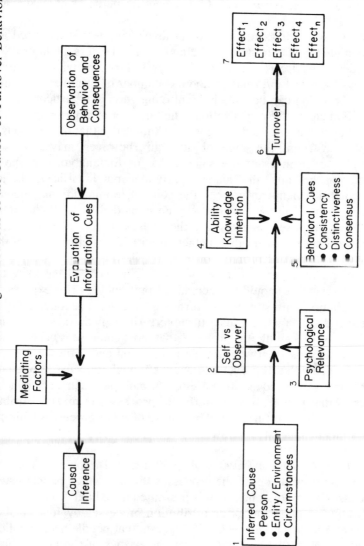

quences of turnover behavior, it is important to recognize that people are assumed to reason backwards from the observation of turnover and its effects to an inference about the cause of turnover. In other words, the logical flow of an individual's cognitive processes is from turnover behavior to the causes of turnover.

Three broad categories of possible causes of turnover behavior are identified in Exhibit 4 (box 1): characteristics of the individual employee, environmental factors (including both the job and external environment), and the circumstances under which the behavior took place. The important issue dealt with in the model concerns identifying the types of information people use in making inferences about which of these three categories of causes actually led to turnover (box 6). Two types of information are considered relevant to making inferences about the reasons for turnover.[2] First, following Jones and Davis (1965), beliefs about the causes of turnover can be derived from an analysis of the effects or consequences of turnover (box 7). These effects may include increased pay or a more challenging job. Second, the causes of turnover may, as suggested earlier, be inferred from analysis of the individual's behavior on the job prior to the point of termination. This latter analysis is more closely associated with the work of Kelley (1973) and involves consideration of the behavioral cues of consistency, distinctiveness, and consensus (box 5). The extent to which either approach leads to the identification of a specific cause of turnover, however, is thought to be mediated by several additional factors: whether an individual is analyzing his or her own behavior or that of another employee (box 2), the psychological relevance of the observed behavior for the person making the attribution (box 3), and beliefs about the ability, knowledge, and intention of the person leaving to achieve the observed effects of turnover (box 4).

For purposes of discussion it is convenient to consider the two sources of information about the causes of turnover (i.e., prior job behavior vs. consequences of turnover) separately. It should be apparent, however, that the two sources of information are not entirely independent. In the discussion below, the two approaches to making causal attributions about the reasons for turnover will be presented separately and then consideration will be given to the relationship between the two approaches.

Analysis of Effects. The major premise underlying the approach of Jones and Davis (1965) to attribution theory is that people who have freedom of choice will attempt to achieve positive outcomes by their behavior. It follows that a great deal can be learned about the reasons for an action by examining its effects or consequences.

Jones and Davis (1965) suggest that the first step in such an analysis is to compare the characteristics of the job an individual has left with characteristics of the new job he or she has taken. The characteristics that the two jobs share in common are separated from the characteristics that are unique to each job. Two hypothetical examples of such comparisons are presented in Exhibit 5 for purposes of illustrating the discussion.

In example A in Exhibit 5, it can be seen that the old and new jobs are similar in pay, job security, and desirability of geographic location. The old and new jobs differ, however, in terms of the nature of the task (routine vs. challenging). Few clues about the reasons why an individual left the job are contained in the characteristics the old and new jobs share in common. Information about the causes of turnover is therefore more likely to be found among characteristics of the jobs that differ.[3] When there are a large number of unique effects, the task of determining which may have caused turnover is more difficult, if not impossible. When a large number of unique effects are present we would have little confidence in asserting which particular effect was the actual reason for turnover since any one of them may have been a sufficient cause. This situation appears similar to Kelley's (1973) discussion of multiple sufficient causes and the discounting principle (i.e., the role of any particular cause of behavior will be discounted when other plausible causes for the behavior also exist in the situation).

An attribution to characteristics of the person is most likely to occur when the unique effect associated with the new job is one that is not widely valued by most people or has some undesirable aspect that would not have been expected to be valued by the person leaving (cf. Jones and McGillis, 1976).[4] When an action such as turnover disconfirms our expectations about what the person was likely to do in that situation (i.e., leads to consequences we would not have expected the person to value), unique information is gained about the person. For instance, in example A in Exhibit 5 it is suggested the person left an interesting and challenging job for one that is routine and uninteresting. Since we would assume that most people would want an interesting and challenging job, Jones and Davis (1965) suggest this situation is more likely to lead to an attribution to the unique characteristics of the person as a cause for turnover. Although not explicitly considered in the theory, it also seems possible that the existence of undesirable unique effects associated with the new job would lead observers to continue to search for additional information until a more plausible explanation for turnover is found. In the absence of additional plausible explanations, however, undesirable effects associated with the new job are likely to be viewed as providing unique information about the individual and thus lead to an attribution to personal characteristics as the cause for turnover.

In contrast, an attribution to environmental characteristics as the cause for turnover would appear most likely when the effects achieved by

Exhibit 5. Inference Processes of the Causes of Turnover from an Analysis of its Consequences

Example A

Characteristics of Old Job	Characteristics of New Job
Good pay	Good pay
Average job security	Average job security
Challenging and interesting job	Routine and uninteresting job
Desirable geographic location	Desirable geographic location

Non-Common Effects

Challenging and interesting job	Routine and uninteresting job

Inference

Cause of turnover is related to characteristics of the person (e.g., cannot take demands associated with challenging task).

Example B

Characteristics of Old Job	Characteristics of New Job
Good pay	Good pay
Average job security	Average job security
Routine and uninteresting job	Challenging and interesting job
Desirable geographic location	Undesirable geographic location

Non-Common Effects

Routine and uninteresting job	Challenging and interesting job
Desirable geographic location	Undesirable geographic location

Inference

Cause of turnover is attractiveness of new job. Most people assumed to want an interesting job but not an undesirable geographic location. Undesirable geographic location viewed as inhibitory cause (cost) that strengthens attribution to positive feature of new job.

turnover are ones that most people would be expected to value. In example B in Exhibit 5 an individual has left a routine and uninteresting job for one that is challenging and interesting. Moreover, the individual has left a job in a desirable geographic location for a job that is in a less desirable geographic location. Since most people would be assumed to want an interesting job, the challenging nature of the new job provides a sufficient explanation for turnover. The attribution in this case may be complicated, however, by the fact that the new job also has an undesirable unique effect (i.e., geographic location). In this case the challenging nature of the new job provides a sufficient explanation for turnover and the role of geographic location may be discounted as a reason for leaving. The undesirable geographic location may be viewed as a cost associated with turnover and therefore strengthen the attribution to the challenging nature of the new job [cf. see Kelley's (1973) discussion of facilitory and inhibitory causes].

Some ambiguity may remain in this situation as to whether it was really the characteristics of the old job which "pushed" the individual out of the organization or the characteristics of the new job that exerted an attraction or "pull." How this ambiguity is resolved may depend upon the knowledge possessed about the person's behavior on the old job (e.g., did he or she frequently express dissatisfaction with the job?). In addition, Newtson (1974) found that attributions are more highly influenced by characteristics of the chosen alternative (new job) than characteristics of the alternative foregone (old job).

Jones and Davis (1965) suggest that several additional aspects of the situation must be considered in making attributions about the causes of turnover from an analysis of its effects. First, the individual leaving must be assumed to have had freedom of choice in leaving the job. Second, the individual must be assumed to have had a knowledge of the effects of their action and the intention and ability to achieve these effects. When the effects of turnover are unknown to the individual at the time he or she left or the effects are unintended (e.g., lucky coincidence), it would be difficult to make attributions to characteristics of either the person or environment as a cause of turnover.

Analysis of Prior Job Behavior. The attribution theory suggested by Kelley (1973) provides a framework within which to understand how the causes of turnover can be inferred from knowledge about the leaver's *prior* job behavior. Since Kelley's theory is better known among organizational researchers than the work of Jones and Davis (1965) and is reviewed elsewhere in this volume (see Mitchell's paper), it will only be briefly discussed here.

The principle of covariance states that a behavior will be attributed to a cause with which it covaries over time. Kelley (1973) identified three sources of information that are used to analyze covariation and make causal inferences about behavior: information from observations of people, entities, and across time. These three sources of information provide specific types of information relevant to considering the cause of a behavior: the consistency, consensus, and distinctiveness of a response. Information from observations of people leads to knowledge of consensus or the extent to which the individual behaves in a manner similar to that of other people in the same situation. Information from observations of entities provides clues about the distinctiveness of a response. Does the individual behave this way toward all entities or stimuli (e.g., supervisor, task, co-worker) or just one particular entity? Finally, information from observations across time provides clues about the consistency of a behavior or response. Does the individual respond this way to a particular entity each time it is encountered or was the response unique to just one occasion? Consistency information can also be over modality (i.e., does the person respond to the entity in the same way regardless of the situation in which it is presented?).

Consensus, consistency, and distinctiveness information are combined to make attributions about the cause of turnover. Kelley (1973) suggests this is done as if the different types of information are combined in the form of a 2 × 2 × 2 analysis of variance framework. To simplify the analysis, each type of information is thought to take on either a high or low value (e.g., high or low consistency). This framework leads to eight cells or unique combinations of consensus, consistency, and distinctiveness information. Each unique combination or cell leads to a specific attribution about the cause of a behavior.

Based on earlier work (Kelley, 1973; McArthur, 1972; Orvis, Cunningham and Kelley, 1975), it is possible to predict attributions for various combinations of information. An attribution to characteristics of the person as the cause of behavior is most likely when consistency information is high and consensus and distinctiveness information are low. Attributions to an entity or stimulus are most likely when consensus, consistency, and distinctiveness information are high. Finally, an attribution to the circumstances within which behavior took place is likely to occur when distinctiveness information is high and consensus and consistency information are low. The attributions resulting from other information combinations are more complex and less easily predicted on an intuitive basis. However, Orvis *et al.* (1975) found that people tend to limit their attributions to the three information combinations mentioned above (i.e., make attributions to characteristics of the person, entity or environment, or circumstances as the cause for an observed behavior). In fact, their research suggests that people look for information that is consistent with one of these three attributions and will "fill in" missing information to be consistent with one of the combinations.

Applying Kelley's (1973) theory to the analysis of the causes of turn-over behavior requires a less rigid interpretation of the covariance principle than originally implied by the theory. That is, attributions about the causes of turnover do not require that the behavioral cues of consensus, consistency, and distinctiveness occur at the same point in time as turn-over. Rather, what is likely to be examined is the individual's past job behavior that is consistent with the act of turnover. For example, an entity attribution would result if in the past the individual leaving consistently expressed dissatisfaction with a particular aspect of the job (e.g., supervisor) and other employees also expressed dissatisfaction with this aspect. Analyses of prior job behavior can also be utilized to assess the credibility of public statements about why a person is leaving.

Mediating Influences on Attributions. Although the attribution theories presented suggest rational procedures for processing information to make attributions about the causes of turnover, research suggests that people may deviate from the model under several circumstances. First, Jones and Nisbett (1972) have suggested that actors and observers may process the same information differently. The fundamental attribution error has been described by Jones (1976, p. 300) "whereas the actor sees his behavior primarily as a response to the situation in which he finds himself, the observer attributes the same behavior to the actor's dispositional characteristics." Second, individuals may be motivated to deviate from attributions prescribed by the model when the attribution made has nega-tive consequences for the individual's self-image. Jones and Davis (1965) introduced the concept of "hedonic relevance" to refer to the motiva-tional significance of an action for the observer with respect to promoting or undermining the observer's values, beliefs, or purposes. A commonly studied manifestation of hedonic relevance is the ego-defensive bias in attributions (Bradley, 1978; Miller and Ross, 1975; Ross, 1977; Stevens and Jones, 1976). For example, a supervisor may be more likely to take credit for the good performance of a subordinate while blaming poor performance on the employee's personal characteristics. The ego-defensive bias often influences attributions in a manner opposite from what might be predicted from the fundamental attribution error.

Integrating the Two Approaches to Attributions. The two attribution theories incorporated in the model presented in Exhibit 4 suggest that different types of information may be employed in causal inferences about turnover. Attributions about the causes of turnover can be made from either an analysis of its effects or an analysis of prior job behavior. The existence of two distinct sources of information that can be used in making inferences raise questions about which of the two is most likely to be used and under what circumstances.

The particular approach adopted by an individual is likely to depend upon the type of information he or she has available. For the former supervisor or co-worker of an employee, for example, job-related behavior prior to turnover is likely to be most salient. Nonwork friends of the individual leaving, however, may only have information about the consequences of the action (e.g., information about the pay, security, and location of the old and new job). As a result, former supervisors and co-workers may be more likely to utilize the approach described by Kelley (1973) while nonwork friends may process information in the manner described by Jones and Davis (1965).

The type of information which becomes salient in making attributions about the causes of turnover may also be sensitive to environmental considerations. For example, when economic conditions are good it may be more reasonable to assume that turnover was caused by a "pull" from attractive alternative jobs. This would be likely to lead to an analysis of the consequences of turnover for purposes of determining the specific cause. In contrast, when economic conditions are poor and few alternative jobs are available, it may be more reasonable to assume that turnover was caused by a "push" from the job (e.g., by dissatisfaction). In this situation, prior job-related behaviors may become more salient in making inferences about the causes of turnover.

In addition, the concept of hedonic relevance or ego-defensive bias suggests that individuals may be motivated to selectively process information in a way that reinforces existing beliefs and attitudes. Although evidence on this is limited, Mowday (in press) found that employees who were themselves dissatisfied with the job and uncommitted to the organization were more likely to believe that others left the organization because of job dissatisfaction than were employees with positive job attitudes. The influence of job attitudes on causal inferences about the reasons why employees leave the organization would be consistent with the ego-defensive bias, although it is also consistent with the egocentric or false consensus bias (see Ross, 1977).

The existence of at least two sources of information upon which to base attributions about the causes of turnover suggests that the attributions resulting from different information sources may differ or be in conflict. The possibility that the two approaches discussed above will lead to conflicting attributions appears less likely, however, when it is considered that the theories of Kelley (1973) and Jones and Davis (1965) overlap in terms of the information used to make attributions.[5] The expectation that an individual intended to achieve a particular effect through turnover, for example, may be influenced by observations of the behavioral cues associated with on-the-job behavior. The possibility still remains, however, that analyses of effects vs. job behavior may result in conflicting conclusions about the causes of turnover. It is difficult at this point to do little more than speculate about how such conflicts will be resolved.

There is little doubt that employees develop beliefs about the reasons why their co-workers leave the organization and that these beliefs may have important attitudinal and behavioral consequences. At present the attribution theories developed by social psychologists provide one of the clearest indications of the processes employees may use in developing such beliefs. To place the discussion in this section in perspective, however, it should be recognized that these theories have been developed in well-controlled environments in which relatively simple, well-structured problems have been studied. In contrast, organizations are complex environments that present employees with a wide variety of information and stimuli. The cognitive limitations of individuals suggest that employees may be ill-equipped to cope adequately with the complex environment they face. The model presented in this section provides a starting point for research in organizations designed to understand how employees cognitively process information about turnover and the implications of resulting beliefs for attitudes and behavior. As research in this area is undertaken, however, it is likely to be found that employees use additional sources of information in making causal judgments and employ heuristics to assist them in the judgment process. What is crucial at this point in time is to recognize the importance of causal inferences made by employees so that research will be undertaken to further refine and extend our understanding of the consequences of turnover.

CONCLUSIONS AND DIRECTIONS FOR FUTURE RESEARCH

Even though it is possible to identify over 1,000 studies of turnover which have been conducted since the turn of the century, our understanding of how employees decide whether to stay with or leave organizations and the consequences of such decisions remains limited. It should be apparent that the problem is not that turnover in organizations has suffered from a lack of research attention. Rather, the problem appears to be attributable to the rather narrow range of issues associated with turnover that researchers have chosen to study and to the methods which have been used in studying these issues.

It is our contention that the level of understanding of turnover processes can best be increased in at least two general ways. First, greater attention needs to be given in research to testing comprehensive models of the turnover process. Although recent research has moved in this direction, there is still a need to move beyond studies focusing on a limited number of variables and/or a limited perspective with respect to the turnover process. Toward this end a comprehensive model of the turnover process has been proposed here. Although the model is generally consistent with existing albeit piecemeal research, it should be considered a series of propositions requiring further study.

Second, it has been argued that future research needs to move beyond consideration of the processes leading up to turnover and consider its consequences. Although it is often recognized that turnover has important consequences for both individuals and organizations, these consequences remain virtually unstudied. A model of the consequences of turnover for individuals was proposed here to complement the earlier work of Price (1977), who considered the problem at the organizational level of analysis. Our model focuses particular attention on how individuals form beliefs about the causes of turnover and the implications of these beliefs for subsequent attitudes and behavior. In this regard the model is not all-encompassing in that it does not consider several possible consequences for individuals of the decision to leave organizations (e.g., stress associated with changing jobs). However, it does suggest a variety of areas for future research that should increase our understanding of the consequences of turnover.

In addition to these two general directions for future research, a number of specific research needs can also be identified. These are briefly presented below.

1. We are still in need of research focusing on the role of job performance in the turnover process. The turnover model proposed here incorporates performance as a factor in turnover decisions, but research is clearly needed in this area. Specifically, do high performers leave for different reasons than poor performers? What is the effect of poor performance on subsequent job attitudes and desire to stay? Do high performers raise their level of job expectations thereby making it more difficult for the organization to satisfy (and perhaps retain) them?

2. March and Simon (1958) noted long ago that dissatisfied employees may make efforts to change the work situation and reduce or eliminate the more distasteful aspects of it. There is no research to date, however, to suggest whether this hypothesis is in fact correct. If employees do undertake systematic efforts to change the work situation, it is necessary to identify the more common change mechanisms used by individuals and groups in this regard. It is also necessary to examine the conditions under

which such efforts are likely to be successful. When efforts to change the work environment are unsuccessful, are negative job attitudes strengthened or do they remain unchanged?

3. We are just beginning to acknowledge the existence of a host of nonwork factors than can influence staying or leaving. Most of these factors are related to matters of personal goals and values and family considerations. Yet few studies have examined these factors in a systematic way as they relate to the decision to participate. In view of the considerable amount of turnover variance probably explained by such factors, it represents a rich area for future research.

4. Most models of employee turnover include the notion of search behavior for more preferable job alternatives. This notion is typically coupled with economic considerations or actual alternative job opportunities. What appears lacking here, however, is a systematic examination of how people initiate search processes, the quality of information they receive, and how they process such information in arriving at a participation decision. This topic lends itself particularly well to laboratory experimentation, a method of research typically not used in the study of turnover. Information gained in the laboratory could then be used to guide field investigations.

5. The literature on withdrawal behavior in general suggests that some forms of withdrawal may at times act as a substitute for other forms. When an individual is unable to quit an undesirable job, for example, he or she may use absenteeism as a temporary form of escape (Porter and Steers, 1973). Alcoholism and drug abuse also represent possible substitutes, as do sabotage and work slowdowns. Although psychiatrists have studied alcoholism and drug abuse and labor economists have looked at sabotage and slowdowns, few systematic attempts have been made by organizational psychologists to examine the substitutability of these forms of behavior for turnover. That is, when an employee cannot leave an undesirable job, how likely is he or she to find alternative modes of accommodation that may be dysfunctional both to the employee and the organization? Moreover, are certain types of employees more likely to engage in these behaviors than others? Finally, is there a generalizable sequencing of substitute behaviors, perhaps beginning with increased absenteeism and then proceeding to alcoholism and drug abuse, or do different employees simply select different modes of accommodation?

6. Researchers have generally been quite skilled at developing elaborate statistical models designed to identify the reasons why employees leave an organization. What we have neglected to consider, however, is that people also develop cognitive models to explain turnover behavior. The inferences people make about the causes of turnover represent a relatively unexplored area for future research. Although some work has been

done asking employees who leave an organization the reasons for their action (e.g., exit interviews), few studies have attempted to explore the beliefs of former co-workers or supervisors about the causes of turnover. Virtually no research has examined how such beliefs are formed and the factors that may influence this process. Even so, it is highly likely that people in organizations do form beliefs about why others leave and that these beliefs influence subsequent attitudes and behavior. This is particularly true for supervisors who may have the responsibility for taking steps to reduce turnover. The effectiveness of organizational attempts to reduce turnover is likely to be vastly improved if a greater understanding can be achieved of how supervisors intuitively develop causal models to explain turnover and the extent to which these models are linked to subsequent changes.

7. It is important to recognize that the attribution model presented earlier is a rational model of how certain types of information should be processed to determine the causes of turnover. Comprehensive empirical tests of the model suggest that people actually infer the causes of behavior as the model predicts (McArthur, 1972; Orvis *et al.*, 1975), although the model remains largely untested among managers. Research is therefore needed to determine whether managers actually use the systematic information processing strategies described in the model or whether the demands inherent in managerial positions force managers to follow a less systematic approach designed to identify a sufficient if incomplete explanation for turnover. Managers may limit their search for explanations to highly salient sources of information while ignoring more subtle and less readily accessible information relevant to determining why employees leave the organization (Taylor and Fiske, 1978).

In addition, it was suggested that motivational factors may cause individuals to deviate from attributions predicted by the model. Several such factors were discussed, but it is likely that future research in organizations will identify additional motivational influences on attributions. Such motivational factors are likely to be particularly salient in organizational settings where the manager's performance and career advancement may in part depend upon how the causes of employee behavior such as turnover are assessed. Finally, the attribution model presented suggests that managers will rely on certain types of information in making causal inferences (e.g., behavioral cues and consequences of the action). It is important to determine the extent to which managers actually rely on these sources of information and if additional types of information are utilized. In addition, how do managers make attributions and thus take action when imperfect or limited information is available?

These areas for future research represent only a few of the ones that might have been mentioned. It is customary to end a paper of this type by expressing the need for additional research in this area. Such a statement would appear to be particularly appropriate with respect to turnover and its consequences. Our understanding of turnover processes is less likely to depend on the quantity of future research, however, than its quality. We simply do not need more studies of turnover (or reviews of studies, for that matter). Rather, what is needed are rigorous investigations of a *comprehensive* nature designed to test existing theories and which offer the promise of improving our current level of understanding of the processes preceding and following an employee's decision to leave.

ACKNOWLEDGMENT

Support for the preparation of this chapter was provided by the Office of Naval Research, Contract N00014-76-C-0164, NR 170-812. The authors wish to express their appreciation to Thomas W. McDade for his valuable contributions to our thinking about attribution theory as it applies to the consequences of turnover and to Larry Cummings, Daniel Ilgen, Terence R. Mitchell, Charles O'Reilly, and Barry Staw for their insightful and useful comments on an earlier draft.

NOTES

1. Bem's (1967, 1972) self-perception theory is also relevant to understanding the implications of behavior for subsequent attitudes. However, a central postulate of Bem's (1972, p. 5) theory suggests that the self-perception processes he has described are most likely to occur in situations where internal cues (i.e., attitudes) associated with a behavior are weak or ambiguous. This is unlikely to be the case in most turnover decisions. As indicated in the model presented in Exhibit 2, affective reactions to the job are an important antecedent of turnover behavior. As a result, self-perception theory appears less useful for understanding the attitudinal consequences of most decisions to remain or leave an organization than Festinger's (1957) theory of cognitive dissonance. In the case of impulsive decisions to leave the organization, however, the attitude change processes associated with turnover may be similar to the self-perception processes described by Bem (1972).

2. A third source of information about the causes of turnover is available from the individual's publicly stated reasons for leaving. Although the stated reasons for leaving may provide the most straightforward information about the causes of turnover, this information may not always be regarded as credible. It is commonly recognized that employees leaving an organization may feel constrained in candidly discussing their reason for leaving in conversation with others. It has been found, for example, that the exit interview is not a valid source of information about the reasons why employees leave (Lefkowitz and Katz, 1969). As a result, those who remain in the organization may discount stated reasons for leaving and still use the processes described in the model for inferring the causes of turnover and as a method for verifying whether the stated reasons for leaving are consistent with information available from other sources (e.g., prior behavior on the job).

3. While Jones and Davis (1965) are primarily concerned with existence of unique effects or differences between the old and the new job, it is also apparent that the magnitude of such differences are also important. The degree of difference between the old and new job can be interpreted in two ways. First, the greater the difference between the old and new job with respect to *one* particular effect, the more confidence that can be placed in the attribution to this as a cause for turnover. Second, the greater the number of unique effects associated

with the old and new job, the larger the overall difference between the jobs. In this latter case, the existence of a large number of unique effects will make it more difficult to confidently assess which particular unique effect caused turnover.

4. Jones and Davis (1965) and Jones and McGillis (1976) dicuss factors which are likely to influence the development of expectations about the values and behavior of others. In addition, attribution theorists have discussed the egocentric or false-consensus bias which suggests there is a tendency to assume that others hold the same values as we do and thus would possess behavioral intentions similar to our own.

5. Jones and McGillis (1976) provide an excellent integration of current attribution theories.

REFERENCES

Bem, D. J. (1967) "Self-Perception: An Alternative Interpretation of Cognitive Dissonance Phenomena," *Psychological Review* 74: 183–200.

—— (1972) "Self-Perception Theory." In L. Berkowitz (ed.). *Advances in Experimental Social Psychology*. New York: Academic Press.

Bernays, J. (1910) *Auslease und Anpassung der Arbeiterschaft der Geschlossenen, Grossindustri, Schriften des Verein Für Sozialpolitik*. Leipzig: Verlag von Dunder und Humblot.

Bradley, G. W. (1978) "Self-Serving Biases in the Attribution Process: A Reexamination of the Fact or Fiction Question," *Journal of Personality and Social Psychology*, 36: 56–71.

Bray, D. W., Campbell, R. J., and Grant, D. L. (1974) *Formative Years in Business*. New York: Wiley-Interscience.

Brayfield, A. H., and Crockett, W. H. (1955) "Employee Attitudes and Employee Performance," *Psychological Bulletin*, 52: 396–424.

Brehm, J. W. (1966) *A Theory of Psychological Reactance*. New York: Academic Press.

Brehm, J. W., and Cohen, A. R. (1962) *Explorations in Cognitive Dissonance*. New York: Wiley.

Buchanan, B. (1974) "Building Organizational Commitment: The Socialization of Managers in Work Organizations," *Administrative Science Quarterly*, 19: 533–546.

Caplow, T. (1964) *Principles of Organization*. New York: Harcourt, Brace & World.

Collins, B. E., and Hoyt, M. F. (1972) "Personal Responsibility-for-Consequences: An Integration and Extension of the 'Forced Compliance' Literature," *Journal of Experimental Social Psychology*, 8: 558–593.

Cooper, C., and Payne, R. (1978) *Stress at Work*. London: Wiley.

Cooper, J. (1971) "Personal Responsibility and Dissonance: The Role of Unforeseen Consequences," *Journal of Personality and Social Psychology*, 18: 354–363.

Crabb, J. T. (1912) "Scientific Hiring," *Efficiency Society Transactions*, 1: 313–318.

Dansereau, F., Cashman, J., and Graen, G. (1974) "Expectancy as a Moderator of the Relationship Between Job Attitudes and Turnover," *Journal of Applied Psychology*, 59: 228–229.

Dubin, R. (1956) "Industrial Workers' Worlds: A Study of the 'Central Life Interests' of Industrial Workers," *Social Problems*, 3: 131–142.

Dubin, R., Champoux, J. E., and Porter, L. W. (1975) "Central Life Interests and Organizational Commitment of Blue-Collar and Clerical Workers," *Administrative Science Quarterly*, 20: 411–421.

Federico, J. M., Federico, P., and Lundquist, G. W. (1976) "Predicting Women's Turnover as a Function of Extent of Met Salary Expectations and Biodemographic Data," *Personnel Psychology*, 29: 559–566.

Festinger, L. (1957) *A Theory of Cognitive Dissonance*. Evanston, Ill.: Row, Peterson.

Fishbein, M. (1967) "Attitude and the Prediction of Behavior." In M. Fishbein (ed.). *Readings in Attitude Theory and Measurement.* New York: Wiley.

Forrest, C. R., Cummings, L. L., and Johnson, A. C. (1977) "Organizational Participation: A Critique and Model," *Academy of Management Review,* 2: 586–601.

Freedman, J. L. (1963) "Attitudinal Effects of Inadequate Justification," *Journal of Personality,* 31: 371–385.

Green, S. G., and Mitchell, T. R. (1979) "Attributional Processes of Leaders in Leader-Member Interactions," *Organizational Behavior and Human Performance,* 23: 429–458.

Herzberg, F., Mausner, B., Peterson, R. O. and Capwell, R. (1957) *Job Attitudes: Review of Research and Opinions.* Pittsburgh: Pittsburgh Psychological Services.

Hines, G. H. (1973) "Achievement Motivation, Occupations, and Labor Turnover in New Zealand," *Journal of Applied Psychology,* 58: 313–317.

Hom, P. W., Katerberg, R., and Hulin, C. L. (1979) "Comparative Examination of Three Approaches to the Prediction of Turnover," *Journal of Applied Psychology,* 64: 280–290.

Ilgen, D., and Dugoni, I. (1977) "Initial Orientation to the Organization: Its Impact on Psychological Processes Associated with the Adjustment of New Employees." Paper presented at the National Meeting of the Academy of Management, Kissimee, Florida (August).

Janis, I. L., and Mann, L. (1977) *Decision Making.* New York: Free Press.

Jeswald, T. A. (1974) "The Cost of Absenteeism and Turnover in a Large Organization." In W. C. Hamner and F. L. Schmidt (eds.), *Contemporary Problems in Personnel.* Chicago: St. Clair Press, pp. 352–357.

Jones, E. E. (1976) "How Do People Perceive the Causes of Behavior?" *American Scientist,* 64: 300–305.

Jones, E. E., and Davis, K. E. (1965) "From Acts to Dispositions: The Attribution Process in Person Perception." In L. Berkowitz (ed.). *Advances in Experimental Social Psychology.* New York: Academic Press.

Jones, E. E., and McGillis, D. (1976) "Correspondent Inferences and the Attribution Cube: A Comparative Reappraisal." In J. H. Harvey, W. J. Ickes, and R. F. Kidd (eds.), *New Directions in Attribution Theory,* Vol. 1. Hillsdale, N.J.: Lawrence Erlbaum.

Jones, E. E., and Nisbett, R. E. (1972) "The Actor and the Observer: Divergent Perceptions of the Causes of Behavior." In E. E. Jones, D. E. Kanouse, H. H. Kelley, R. E. Nisbett, S. Valins, and B. Weiner (eds.), *Attribution: Perceiving the Causes of Behavior,* Morristown, N.J.: General Learning Press.

Kelley, H. H. (1967) "Attribution Theory in Social Psychology." In D. Levine (ed.), *Nebraska Symposium on Motivation.* Lincoln: University of Nebraska Press.

―――― (1972) "Attribution in Social Interaction." In E. E. Jones, D. E. Kanouse, H. H. Kelley, R. E. Nisbett, S. Valins, and B. Weiner (eds.), *Attribution: Perceiving the Causes of Behavior.* Morristown, N.J.: General Learning Press.

―――― (1973) "The Process of Causal Attribution," *American Psychologist,* 28: 107–128.

Kiesler, C. A., and Munson, P. A. (1975) "Attitudes and Opinions," *Annual Review of Psychology,* 26: 415–456.

Koch, J. L., and Steers, R. M. (1978) "Job Attachment, Satisfaction, and Turnover among Public Employees," *Journal of Vocational Behavior,* 12: 119–128.

Korman, A. K. (1977) *Organizational Behavior.* Englewood Cliffs, N.J.: Prentice-Hall.

Kornhauser, A. (1965) *Mental Health of the Industrial Worker.* New York: Wiley.

Krackhardt, D., McKenna, J., Porter, L. W., and Steers, R. M. (1978) "Goal-Setting, Supervisory Behavior, and Employee Turnover: A Field Experiment." Technical Report No. 17. Graduate School of Management, University of Oregon (November).

Lawler, E. E., Kulick, W. J., Rhode, J. G., and Sorenson, J. E. (1975) "Job Choice and Post-Decision Dissonance," *Organizational Behavior and Human Performance*, 13: 133–145.

Lefkowitz, J. (1971) "Personnel Turnover," *Progress in Clinical Psychology:* 69–90.

Lefkowitz, J., and Katz, M. (1969) "Validity of Exit Interviews," *Personnel Psychology*, 22: 445–455.

Locke, E. A. (1976) "The Nature and Consequences of Job Satisfaction." In M. D. Dunnette (ed.), *Handbook of Industrial and Organizational Psychology*. Chicago: Rand McNally.

Macy, B. A., and Mirvis, P. H. (1976) "A Methodology for Assessment of Quality of Work Life and Organizational Effectiveness in Behavioral-Economic Terms," *Administrative Science Quarterly* 21: 212–226.

Mangione, T. W. (1973) "Turnover: Some Psychological and Demographic Correlates." In R. P. Quinn and T. W. Mangione (eds.), *The 1969–1970 Survey of Working Conditions*. Ann Arbor: University of Michigan, Survey Research Center.

March, J. G., and Simon, H. A. (1958) *Organizations*. New York: Wiley.

Marsh, R., and Manari, H. (1977) "Organizational Commitment and Turnover: A Predictive Study," *Administrative Science Quarterly*, 22: 57–75.

McArthur, L. A. (1972) "The How and What of Why: Some Determinants and Consequences of Causal Attributions." *Journal of Personality and Social Psychology*, 22: 171–193.

Miller, D. T., and Ross, M. (1975) "Self-Serving Biases in the Attribution of Causality: Fact or Fiction?" *Psychological Bulletin*, 82: 213–225.

Mobley, W. H. (1977) "Intermediate Linkages in the Relationship Between Job Satisfaction and Employee Turnover," *Journal of Applied Psychology*, 62: 237–240.

Mobley, W. H., Griffeth, R. W., Hand, H. H., and Mezlino, B. M. (1979) "Review and Conceptual Analysis of the Employee Turnover Process," *Psychological Bulletin*, 86: 493–522.

Mobley, W. H., Horner, S. O., and Hollingsworth, A. T. (1978) "An Evaluation of Precursors of Hospital Employee Turnover," *Journal of Applied Psychology*, 63: 408–414.

Mowday, R. T. (in press) "Viewing Turnover from the Perspective of Those Who Remain: The Influence of Attitudes on Attributions of the Causes of Turnover." *Journal of Applied Psychology*.

Mowday, R. T., and McDade, T. W. (1979) "Linking Behavioral and Attitudinal Commitment: A Longitudinal Analysis of Job Choice and Job Attitudes." Paper presented at the 39th Annual Meeting of the Academy of Management, Atlanta (August).

Mowday, R. T., Porter, L. W., and Stone, E. F. (1978) "Employee Characteristics as Predictors of Turnover Among Female Clerical Employees in Two Organizations," *Journal of Vocational Behavior*, 12: 321–332.

Mowday, R. T., Steers, R. M., and Porter, L. W. (1979) "The Measurement of Organizational Commitment," *Journal of Vocational Behavior*, 14: 224–247.

Muchinsky, P. M., and Tuttle, M. L. (1979) "Employee Turnover: An Empirical and Methodological Assessment," *Journal of Vocational Behavior*, 14: 43–77.

Newtson, D. (1974) "Dispositional Influence From Effects of Actions: Effects of Chosen and Effects Foregone," *Journal of Experimental Social Psychology*, 10: 489–496.

Nisbett, R. E., and Valins, S. (1972) "Perceiving the Causes of One's Own Behavior." In E. E. Jones, D. E. Kanouse, H. H. Kelley, R. E. Nisbett, S. Valins, and B. Weiner (eds.), *Attribution: Perceiving the Causes of Behavior*. Morristown, N.J.: General Learning Press.

Orvis, B. R., Cunningham, J. D., and Kelley, H. H. (1975) "A Closer Examination of Causal

Inference: The Roles of Consensus, Distinctiveness, and Consistency Information," *Journal of Personality and Social Psychology*, 32: 605–616.

Pettman, B. O. (1973) "Some Factors Influencing Labour Turnover: A Review of the Literature," *Industrial Relations Journal*, 4: 43–61.

—— (1975) *Labour Turnover and Retention*. London: Wiley.

Pfeffer, J., and Lawler, J. (1979) "The Effects of Job Alternatives, Extrinsic Rewards, and Commitment on Satisfaction with the Organization: A Field Example of the Insufficient Justification Paradigm." Unpublished manuscript, School of Business Administration, University of California, Berkeley.

Porter, L. W., Crampon, W. J., and Smith, F. J. (1976) "Organizational Commitment and Managerial Turnover: A Longitudinal Study," *Organizational Behavior and Human Performance*, 15: 87–98.

Porter, L. W., Lawler, E. E., and Hackman, J. R. (1975) *Behavior in Organizations*. New York: McGraw-Hill.

Porter, L. W., and Steers, R. M. (1973) "Organizational, Work, and Personal Factors in Employee Turnover and Absenteeism," *Psychological Bulletin*, 80: 151–176.

Porter, L. W., Steers, R. M., Mowday, R. T., and Boulian, P. V. (1974) "Organizational Commitment, Job Satisfaction, and Turnover Among Psychiatric Technicians," *Journal of Applied Psychology*, 59: 603–609.

Price, J. L. (1977) *The Study of Turnover*. Ames: Iowa State University Press.

Ross, L. (1977) "The Intuitive Psychologist and His Shortcomings: Distortions in the Attribution Process." In L. Berkowitz (ed.). *Advances in Experimental Social Psychology*. New York: Academic Press.

Salancik, G. R. (1977) "Commitment and Control of Organizational Behavior." In B. M. Staw and G. R. Salancik (eds.), *New Directions in Organizational Behavior*. Chicago: St. Clair.

Salancik, G., and Pfeffer, J. (1978) "A Social Information Processing Approach to Job Attitudes and Task Design," *Administrative Science Quarterly*, 23: 224–253.

Schneider, B., and Dachler, H. P. (1978) "Work, Family and Career Considerations in Understanding Employee Turnover Intentions, Technical Report No. 19, Department of Psychology, University of Maryland (May).

Schneider, J. (1976) "The 'Greener grass' Phenomenon: Differential Effects of a Work Context Alternative on Organizational Participation and Withdrawal Intentions," *Organizational Behavior and Human Performance*, 116: 303–333.

Schuh, A. J. (1967) "The Predictability of Employee Tenure: A Review of the Literature," *Personnel Psychology*, 20: 133–152.

Schwab, D. P., and Dyer, L. D. (1974) "Turnover as a Function of Perceived Ease and Desirability: A Largely Unsuccessful Test of the March and Simon Participation Model." Paper presented at the 34th Annual Meeting of the Academy of Management, Seattle.

Staw, B. M. (1974) "Attitudinal and Behavioral Consequences of Changing a Major Organizational Reward," *Journal of Personality and Social Psychology*, 29: 742–751.

Staw, B. M., and Oldham, G. R. (1978) "Reconsidering Our Dependent Variables: A Critique and Empirical Study," *Academy of Management Journal*, 21: 539–559.

Steers, R. M. (1977) "Antecedents and Outcomes of Organizational Commitment," *Administrative Science Quarterly*, 22: 46–56.

Stevens, L., and Jones, E. E. (1976) "Defensive Attribution and the Kelley Cube," *Journal of Personality of Social Psychology*, 34: 809–820.

Stoikov, V., and Raimon, R. L. (1968) "Determinants of Differences in the Quit Rate Among Industries," *American Economic Review*, 58: 1283–1298.

Sussman, M. B., and Cogswell, B. E. (1971) "Family influences on Job Movement," *Human Relations*, 24: 477–487.

Taylor, S. E., and Fiske, S. T. (1978) "Salience, Attention, and Attribution: Top of the Head Phenomena." In L. Berkowitz (ed.). *Advances in Experimental Social Psychology*. New York: Academic Press.

Van Maanen, J. (1975) "Police Socialization: A Longitudinal Examination of Job Attitudes in an Urban Police Department," *Administrative Science Quarterly*, 20: 207–228.

Vroom, V. H. (1964) *Work and Motivation*. New York: Wiley.

Vroom, V. H., and Deci, E. L. (1971) "The Stability of Post-Decision Dissonance: A Follow-up Study of the Job Attitudes of Business School Graduates," *Organizational Behavior and Human Performance*, 6: 36–49.

Walster, E., Berscheid, E., and Barclay, A. M. (1967) "A Determinant of Preference Among Modes of Dissonance Reduction," *Journal of Personality and Social Psychology*, 7: 211–216.

Wanous, J. P. (1977) "Organizational Entry: Newcomers Moving from Outside to Inside," *Psychological Bulletin*, 84: 601–618.

Wanous, J. P., Stumpf, S. A., and Bedrosian, H. (1978) "Job Survival of New Employees." Unpublished paper, New York University.

Waters, L. K., Roach, D., and Waters, C. W. (1976) "Estimate of Future Tenure, Satisfaction, and Biographical Variables as Predictors of Termination," *Personnel Psychology*, 29: 57–60.

Wicklund, R. A., and Brehm, J. W. (1976) *Perspectives on Cognitive Dissonance*. Hillsdale, N.J.: Lawrence Erlbaum.

Woodward, N. (1975–1976) "The Economic Causes of Labour Turnover: A Case Study," *Industrial Relations Journal*, 6: 19–32.

Wortman, C. B., and Brehm, J. W. (1976) "Responses to Uncontrollable Outcomes: An Integration of Reactance Theory and the Learned Helplessness Model." In L. Berkowitz (ed.), *Advances in Experimental Social Psychology*. New York: Academic Press.

Zanna, M. P., and Cooper, J. (1976) "Dissonance and the Attribution Process." In J. H. Harvey, N. J. Ickes, and R. F. Kidd (eds.), *New Directions in Attribution Research*, Vol. 1. Hillsdale, N.J.: Lawrence Erlbaum, 1976.

THE EFFECTS OF WORK LAYOFFS ON SURVIVORS:

RESEARCH, THEORY, AND PRACTICE

Joel Brockner

ABSTRACT

This chapter describes a program of research exploring the effects of layoffs on the work behaviors and attitudes of the employees who are *not* laid off (i.e., the "survivors"). A conceptual model is presented that focuses on the factors that moderate individuals' reactions to the layoffs of fellow workers; perceived equity and stress are critical mediators in this analysis. Seven studies are then presented that have evaluated various hypotheses derived from the conceptual model. The theoretical and managerial implications of the research findings are discussed. The chapter concludes with a future research agenda, including methodological improvements, refinements of the conceptual model, and the implications of research on survivor reactions for related areas of inquiry in organizational behavior.

Layoffs are a persistent phenomenon in corporate America. Often as a result of generally unfavorable business conditions, organizations "tighten their belts," "downsize," or "prune" their workforce in order to cut labor costs. Mergers and acquisitions—some of the most dramatic developments in business organizations in the past few years—are another precipitating cause of layoffs; the newly formed organization may discover that it needs to reduce duplicated or otherwise unnecessary jobs, and often does so through layoffs. Recently, organizational scholars and practitioners have focused on an important aspect of layoffs: their impact on the work behaviors and attitudes of the "survivors," i.e., the employees who are not laid off.

To be sure, the topic of layoffs has not been entirely neglected by theoreticians. However, such studies have tended to focus on the antecedents of layoffs (e.g., Cornfield, 1983) or the consequences of layoffs for the individuals who were laid off (Jahoda, 1982). In sharp contrast, surprisingly little research has focused on the impact of layoffs on the surviving workforce (Blonder, 1976; Greenhalgh, 1982). The failure to study survivors' reactions is unfortunate, because it is a topic with potentially important implications for both the theory and practice of organizational behavior. At the theoretical level, several existing theories may elucidate, and no less important, be elucidated by, the effects of layoffs on survivors. At the practical level, managers are concerned with the reactions of survivors to the dismissal of co-workers; theory and research may ultimately enable administrators to make more informed decisions about how to manage layoffs so as to elicit the most favorable (or least unfavorable) survivor reactions.

This paper is devoted to further our understanding of the impact of layoffs on survivors' work behaviors and attitudes; it consists of four major sections. First, I describe the conceptual model that has guided our thinking about the reactions of survivors to co-workers' layoffs. Second, empirical research is presented that has explored some of the hypotheses derived from the conceptual model. Third, I discuss the theoretical and practical implications of the research findings. Fourth, the paper will conclude with a section devoted to prospects for future research.

Before we turn to the first section, let me clarify the entity "layoffs." They are a permanent, involuntary separation of individuals from the organization due to the need to cut costs. Thus, layoffs refer to dismissals that are permanent rather than temporary, and involuntary rather than voluntary. Moreover, layoffs are implemented to trim costs, rather than to "fire" employees for inappropriate or inadequate work behavior. This is not to say that other kinds of layoffs do not exist. For example, in certain industries the work is "seasonal"; as a result, some employees fully expect to be laid off and then rehired. Nor is it to say that the ensuing conceptual model is irrelevant to these other types of layoffs; rather, other kinds of layoffs simply have not been the focus of our inquiry.

CONCEPTUAL MODEL

Managerial anecdotes suggest that a wide variety of survivors' work behaviors and attitudes may be influenced by layoffs, including productivity, organizational commitment, and attitudes towards one's co-workers and job, to name a few. Moreover, *within* each of the above dimensions, survivors may respond in very different ways. For example, it has been suggested anecdotally that some layoffs may have a demotivating effect on the surviving workforce; other managerial accounts imply that layoffs may heighten, or have no effect at all on, survivors' work performance. Any comprehensive model of survivor reactions to layoffs, therefore, must be able to explain how various survivor work behaviors and attitudes are affected, as well as the variation in survivors' responses along each of the behavioral and attitudinal dimensions.

The Underlying Conceptual Model that has Guided our Thinking Consists of Three Major Components.

First, layoffs *have the potential* to engender a variety of psychological states in survivors. These include: (a) job insecurity, e.g., if employees perceive that additional downsizings are in the offing, (b) positive inequity, e.g., if employees perceive that they did not "deserve" to remain, relative to their dismissed co-workers, (c) anger, e.g., if survivors believe that the method of the layoff, or even the very existence of the layoff were inappropriate or illegitimate; and (d) relief, e.g., if survivors were worried prior to the layoff that they would be dismissed. This list of survivor psychological states is not exhaustive; it does suggest, however, that layoff survival is the kind of event that can be experienced very differently. Moreover, as highlighted by the fact that some survivors feel relieved, not all such psychological states are phenomenologically aversive.

Second, the psychological states that layoffs evoke *have the potential* to affect survivors' work behaviors (e.g., level of performance, motivation) and attitudes (e.g., satisfaction, commitment). For example, the relationship between job insecurity and performance may be a special example of the anxiety/performance relationship. It could be that very low or very high levels of job-insecurity–produced anxiety lead to impaired performance, but that moderate levels of insecurity actually facilitate performance (Yerkes & Dodson, 1908).

In addition, positive inequity could produce a significant boost in work motivation. Equity theorists (e.g., Adams, 1965) have suggested that a perceived imbalance between workers' outcomes and inputs—relative to those of comparison others—produces an unpleasant state of inequity that must be redressed through behavioral and/or psychological means. More specifically, surviving employees could perceive that their outcome-to-input ratio is greater than that of the laid-off workers. To alleviate this state of positive inequity, survivors may increase their inputs (i.e., work harder), at least in the short run (Mowday, 1979).

Layoff-produced anger or resentment, on the other hand, could have a demotivating effect on survivors. The perceived illegitimacy or unfairness of the layoff could cause survivors to want to "take out" their feelings of hostility towards the organization in the form of reduced productivity and/or other forms of sabotage.

The psychological states of job insecurity, positive inequity, and anger could also mediate survivors' work attitudes. All three reactions could lead to a lessening of organizational commitment and job satisfaction. For example, job insecurity could cause a sharp decrease in the intrinsic appeal of the job; survivors may come to perceive that they are performing their tasks *in order to maintain their job security*. That is, the perception of being extrinsically motivated may make it more difficult for survivors to experience the intrinsic appeal associated with their jobs (e.g., Deci, 1975). Similarly, job insecurity could lead to greater tensions among survivors; they may perceive that in order to remain they need to outperform their remaining co-workers. To the extent that survivors perceive that their relationship with fellow employees is competitive, co-worker relationships may be strained.

Moderator Variables

Thus far we have considered some of the *possible* effects of layoffs on survivors. The third component of the conceptual model that has guided our empirical efforts seeks to delineate the factors that moderate the *actual* impact of layoffs on those who stay. Note that moderator variables are relevant at two places in the conceptual model: (1) the link between layoffs and the survivors' psychological states, and (2) the relationship between the psychological states and survivors' work behaviors and attitudes.

What, then, are the moderator variables that transform potential to actual effects? Organizational scholars (e.g., Nadler & Tushman, 1980) have noted that all work organizations consist of a number of component parts; the nature of the work, the individuals upon whom the organization relies to perform its work, and the formal and informal arrangements that the organization makes to accomplish its objectives. In addition, all organizations perform their tasks in the context of a broader external environment. The moderator variables are thus drawn from these five categories of factors; the categories, as well as an example within each, are discussed in greater detail below.

The nature of the work. One relevant work dimension is degree of task interdependence. Employees who survive the dismissal of co-workers on whom they were interdependent are likely to experience several psychological states to a greater degree than employees whose dismissed co-workers were task independent of them. For example, the interdependent group might feel more job insecure as they contemplate the self-relevance of the dismissal of fellow employees on whom they were interdependent. Or, in having worked interdependently with the dismissed employees, survivors may have developed a strong sense of identity with them; as a result survivors could feel greater anger about the layoffs.

Survivor individual differences. Given that layoffs have the potential to elicit several psychological states, theoretically relevant individual differences between survivors should moderate the impact of the layoff on their thoughts, feelings, and actions. For example, suppose that the layoff aroused job insecurity–produced worry. If so, then survivors low in chronic self-esteem—who have been shown in past research to be highly susceptible to influence by worry cues in general (e.g., Shrauger, 1972)—may experience an even stronger sense of worry then their high self-esteem counterparts.

Formal organization. The formal organization refers to, among other things, the rules, policies, procedures, reporting relationships, grouping, and linking arrangements that the firm has made to accomplish its objectives. For example, subsequent to layoffs the organization may institute a set of official procedures designed to provide for its laid-off workers. Included in such activities are the provision of severance pay, outplacement counseling, and the continuation of health insurance and other benefits. It seems likely that organizations that provide formal programs to "take care of " the separated employees will find its surviving workforce to be experiencing less insecurity, and/or positive inequity, and/or anger.

Informal organization. The informal organization includes, but is not limited to, the values, norms, and interpersonal relationships that emerge as the employees and firm go about accomplishing their tasks. One aspect of the informal organization that could moderate survivors' reactions is the firm's past record of implementing layoffs. In a paternalistic organization, such as Kodak, top management guarantees that it will take care of its workers (e.g., offer them lifetime security). Other firms have developed the informal policy of being far less "nurturant." How might layoffs be experienced by survivors at these two different types of organizations? It seems likely that layoffs will be far more unexpected—and consequently much more apt to arouse anger—among survivors in the former than latter instance. Indeed, in a recent reversal of form Kodak has initiated several layoffs in the past few years, which, at least anecdotally, were reported to have had a profound impact on its surviving workforce. The above example also serves as a more general reminder of the relationship between corporate culture and human resource policy, and how organizational success may partly depend upon the degree of congruence between the two.

Of course, the informal organization can also generate the prior expectation that certain employees and/or groups will be laid off. If—in contrast to their pessimistic expectations—these employees and/or groups are *not* laid off then their reaction is likely to be one of relief.

Environmental conditions. Factors external to the organization can also moderate survivors' reactions to the layoffs. For example, if survivors know that market conditions are such that the laid-off workers will not easily be able to find comparable work elsewhere, then survivors are likely to feel greater job insecurity. To cite yet another example, if survivors perceive that organizations similar to their own are not experiencing layoffs, they are more likely to question the legitimacy of, and thus feel angry about, the layoff taking place within their own organizaton.

Most of the examples above illustrate factors that moderate the impact of the layoff on survivors' psychological states. As stated previously, these five categories of factors also include variables that moderate the relationship between survivors' psychological states and their behavioral and/or attitudinal expressions of those states. For example, suppose that the layoff elicited an ample degree of positive inequity among survivors. If the nature of their work were highly automated, then the effect of the layoff on survivors' work performance may be minimal; simply put, if workers' machines do most of the work for them anyway then the relationship between employees' motivation and performance is apt to be slight at best. Instead of redressing the positive inequity through an increase in work performance, survivors may utilize cognitive adjustments to do so (e.g., convincing themselves that the laid off workers deserved their fate).

Or, suppose that the layoff were one that elicited considerable anger among survivors. In order to "get even" with the organization survivors may wish to withhold their level of motivation. However, several factors could moderate the extent to which survivors act on that wish. In particular, if survivors are also worried about their job security then they may work harder in spite of their underlying desire to act in ways that harm the organization. Similarly, if market conditions are such that the survivors would not easily be able to find comparable work elsewhere then they may continue to work hard in spite of their feelings of anger. These latter two examples also suggest the possibility that the (five categories of) moderator variables may jointly *and* interactively influence the impact of layoffs on survivors.

To be sure, the conceptual model is not a theory *per se;* rather, it draws upon several existing theories in organizational psychology in order to predict and explain the effects of layoffs on survivors. In particular, the literatures on equity theory (e.g., Adams, 1965, Mowday, 1979) and organizational stress (e.g., Jick, 1985; McGrath, 1976) are especially germane, and have guided the empirical research to be presented in the second section of this chapter. Before the research findings are presented, however, it may be useful to describe the relevance of each theory to the analysis of survivor reactions.

Equity Theory. Equity theory (Adams, 1965) posits that employees are highly motivated to attain fairness in their exchanges with their work organizations. In the terminology of the theory, employees' work outcomes (e.g., salary, rank) should be commensurate with their work inputs (e.g., performance, seniority, prestige lent to the organization). Perceived inequity between outcomes and input in relation to some standard—typically the outcome-input relationships of co-workers—is distressing, which motivates employees to redress the inequity through behavioral and/or psychological means. Moreover, the theory posits that the primary nature of the distress differs, depending upon whether the perceived inequity is negative (in which the outcome/input relationship is less than that of the standard of comparison), or positive (in which the outcome/input relationship is greater than the standard of comparison). In the former, employees primarily feel angry; examples of inequity redress take the form of reducing one's actual and/or perceived inputs, and/or increasing one's actual and/or perceived outcomes. In the latter, their predominant reaction is one of guilt; some modes of equity restoration include increasing one's actual and/or perceived inputs, and/or decreasing one's actual and/or perceived outcomes.

Layoffs in work environments may elicit in survivors numerous questions about equitable or fair treatment. These include, but are not limited to: (a) Was the need for the layoff justifiable? (b) Were those to be laid off provided with ample forewarning? (c) Was the decision rule used to lay off certain workers and retain others based on "relevant" inputs (e.g., relative performance)? (d) Were the laid-off workers treated fairly by the organization? For example, did the organization provide "caretaking" activities for the separated employees, such as the opportunity to move to another plant location, outplacement counseling, and severance pay? and (e) In addressing the questions above, did the organization use fair or legitimate *procedures?*

Survivors' perceptions of inequity concerning these and other issues could have implications for their subsequent work behaviors and attitudes. For example, to the extent that survivors perceive that their inputs were no greater than those of dismissed workers, they may experience positive inequity or "survivor guilt." As a result, they may work harder in order to redress the inequity. Or, if survivors perceived that the layoff was unfair, *and if they strongly identified with the laid-off workers,* then they may experience negative inequity (vicariously). Said differently, the predominant psychological reaction could be one of anger or hostility towards management; one possible behavioral manifestation of such a reaction is reduced work motivation.

Organizational Stress. Anecdotal and empirical evidence (e.g., Greenhalgh, 1982) suggest that the postlayoff work environment can be quite stressful, for a variety of reasons. Probably foremost among them is that layoffs often cause workers to worry about their own job security, even if management claims that no additional layoffs are in the offing. Furthermore, the anger associated with many layoffs could be a significant stressor. In the general terminology of stress researchers, survivors are likely to be uncertain about whether they possess the resources and coping strength needed to deal with the demands of a postlayoff work environment.

The onset of stress, in turn, typically leads to numerous significant changes in survivors' work attitudes and behaviors. For example, employees' sense of commitment to the organization and/or satisfaction with their jobs often suffer subsequent to the dismissal of co-workers. Survivors' turnover may also increase, to the extent that the layoffs are perceived to threaten opportunities for advancement and development. Furthermore, survivors' work performance may be altered subsequent to layoffs. Of course, the relationship between layoff-produced stress and survivors' work performance is quite complex. As Jick (1985) and others have pointed out, moderate levels of stress may elicit greater performance than very high or low levels.

Summary

The conceptual model guiding the empirical research suggests that layoffs have the potential to affect survivors' psychological states, which, in turn, have the potential to influence a variety of work behaviors and attitudes. A host of factors—including the nature of the work, individual differences between survivors, formal and informal organizational arrangements, and environmental factors—moderate the actual impact of (a) layoffs on survivors' psychological states, and (b) survivors' psychological states on their work behaviors and attitudes. The conceptual model, moreover, relies on several literatures—equity theory and organizational stress—to predict and explain the ways in which the moderator variables influence the relationships between layoffs and the psychological states, and between the psychological states and survivors' work behaviors and attitudes. See Figure 1 for an overview of the conceptual model.

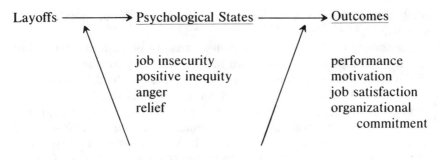

Layoffs ⟶ Psychological States ⟶ Outcomes

job insecurity   performance
positive inequity   motivation
anger   job satisfaction
relief   organizational
                                           commitment

Moderator Variables

nature of work
survivor individual differences
formal organization
informal organization
environment

Note: The examples under each heading are not exhaustive.

Figure 1. Overview of the conceptual model.

EMPIRICAL RESEARCH

This section describes recent research that my colleagues (Mike O'Malley, Jeff Greenberg, and Mauritz Blonder), students (most notably Steve Grover, Jeanette Davy, and Carolyn Carter), and I have conducted on the effects of layoffs on survivors. The conceptual overview suggests that numerous factors may moderate the impact of layoffs. Our choice of factors was guided by two considerations: first, they had to be well-grounded theoretically. Indeed, the literatures on equity theory and/or organizational stress typically enabled us to make predictions about the effects of the moderator (or independent) variables on survivors' work behaviors and/ or attitudes. Second, we wanted to explore the effects of factors chosen from the different categories of moderating variables described in the preceding section.

Moreover, a blend of both laboratory and field methodologies have been employed in our investigations. The initial studies utilized well-controlled laboratory procedures, in which we created an analogue of a layoff situation, and randomly assigned subjects to experimental conditions. Given the sheer volume of potentially relevant moderator variables, and given the early stage of theory building, it seemed appropriate to employ a methodological procedure high in internal validity in our initial investigations.

Laboratory methodologies, of course, tend to be high in internal but low in external validity. Therefore, it was necessary to complement the initial laboratory experiments with field studies. Indeed, several such studies have already been performed and will be discussed in this section; as of this writing, many more field studies are in progress. Organizational psychologists in general have long recognized the need for multi-method approaches to empirical research. Given the specific nature of this research program, it is virtually imperative to ensure that findings derived from an internally valid laboratory procedure are evaluated in more externally valid, field settings; moreover, processes discovered in the field should be examined under controlled experimental conditions.

Study I: Layoffs, Equity Theory, and Survivor Guilt

Our first experiment (Brockner, Davy, & Carter, 1985) sought to determine whether layoffs could elicit a state of positive-inequity–produced survivor guilt. If so, then according to equity theory survivors should engage in behavioral and/or belief change designed to redress the inequity. Each subject and an experimental accomplice worked on two clerical tasks After the first task had been completed, the researchers announced that an unforeseen problem required that one of the two persons present would have to depart; moreover, the "really bad news" was that the person chosen to leave could not receive any compensation (i.e., money or research credit) for having participated up to that point. On a seemingly impromptu basis, the researchers announced that the subject and experimental accomplice would draw lots in order to determine which of the two would have to leave. The lottery procedure was rigged (unbeknownst to the subject, of course) so that the accomplice was always chosen to leave. The accomplice had been instructed to protest mildly prior to departing, saying "making me leave seems unfair. I did do half of the experiment, you know." It is also important to emphasize that the layoff was implemented in such a way that other psychological states that often accompany layoffs (e.g., job insecurity) were minimized.

The results provided strong support for equity theory: compared with those in a no layoff control condition, those who witnessed the dismissal of a co-worker reported feeling more positive inequity and guilt. The layoff also caused "survivors" to exhibit a greater increase in work performance (from the first to the second task) than those in the control condition. In addition, the layoff-produced increase in work performance was moderated by individuals' chronic self-esteem; low self-esteem individuals exhibited a much greater boost in work performance than their high self-esteem counterparts, perhaps because the former group experienced more positive inequity due to their generalized tendency to denigrate their inputs to an exchange relationship. Finally, survivors in general expressed less positive attitudes towards the accomplice if the latter was laid off rather than not; this intriguing finding could be reflective of a "victim-blaming" tendency on the part of survivors. Note that a victim-blaming response may also be explained by equity theory: those who remain may need to redress the inequity elicited by their survival by convincing themselves that the laid-off workers "got what they deserved."

The results of our first experiment provided a promising start to this line of research; the experimentally manipulated layoff elicited a host of behavioral and attitudinal effects, all of which were consistent with equity theory. Utilizing an equity theory framework, the subsequent four studies were designed to explore the moderating impact of several factors on survivors' behaviors and beliefs.[1]

Studies II-IV: The Effects of the Decision Rule on Survivors' Reactions

To reiterate, the layoff decision in the initial study was decided on a random basis. However, most organizations have more clearly defined bases for making decisions about whom to lay off versus retain. For example, the relative merit of employees' performance prior to the layoff could be one criterion. In addition, many organizations make such decisions on the basis of seniority, especially those in which the work force is unionized.

Equity theory predicts that merit and seniority-based layoffs may have different effects on survivors, relative to the random-based layoff in Study I. More specifically, merit and seniority-based layoffs enable survivors' to believe that they were chosen to remain on the basis of their greater inputs (than the laid-off workers'). As a result, survivors of merit and/or seniority-based layoffs may experience less positive inequity or survivor guilt than those who survive random-based layoffs. Or, survivors of merit and seniority-based layoffs may choose to redress the inequity psychologically (i.e., by focusing on their greater inputs) rather than behaviorally (e.g., by working harder, like those in the random-based layoff in Study I).

Study II (Brockner, Greenberg, Brockner, Bortz, Davy, & Carter, 1986) was designed to replicate and extend the initial experiment. As in the prior study, both a random layoff and a no layoff control condition were included in the experimental design. In addition, a third group of participants were assigned to a condition in which they survived the layoff on the basis of having performed better on the first task than the laid-off co-worker (merit condition). As in the earlier study, those in the random layoff condition exhibited a greater increase in productivity than those in the control condition; those in the merit condition performed much like those in the control condition, i.e., exhibiting a significantly smaller increase in productivity than participants in the random layoff condition.

Additional evidence suggested that the merit condition subjects did feel positive inequity and survivor guilt. However, they may have justified the inequity by claiming greater inputs. More specifically, subjects in all conditions were asked to evaluate their performance on the first (i.e., prelayoff) task. Those in the merit condition rated their performance (i.e., inputs) more favorably than participants in both the random and control conditions. Of course, such findings do not prove that subjects in the merit condition *psychologically* justified their survivor status and thus reduced their need to redress the inequity through *behavioral* means (e.g., by working harder). However, the results on the perceived performance measure at least are consistent with the above possibility.

Studies III and IV (Ichniowski, Brockner, & Davy, 1987) investigated the effects of seniority-based layoffs on survivors' work performance. Study III consisted of a laboratory study that was a partial replication and extension of study II. Two conditions paralleled the merit and no layoff control conditions of Study II. A third group survived the "layoff" on the basis of their greater seniority in the study. All three groups exhibited comparable levels of work performance.

Study IV was conducted in a field setting, in which layoffs were decided on the basis of seniority. More specifically, we explored the relationships between layoff severity and subsequent plant performance in nine paper mills. As in the laboratory study, there was no relationship between the presence or absence of a seniority-based layoff and plant performance. Studies III and IV provide converging evidence across multiple methodologies; the former was high in internal but low in external validity. The latter was high in external but low in internal validity. Given the vast procedural differences, the common finding across the two studies is all the more compelling: that seniority-based layoffs had minimal impact on the work performance of survivors.

Study V. The Moderating Effects of Co-Worker Identification and Compensation

The initial laboratory studies explored the impact of layoffs in the context of minimal interaction between the survivors and their laid-off co-workers. In the "real world," however, workers form relationships with one another. For example, fellow employees may come to know one another because of having worked interdependently. Or, on a more informal basis, workers may socialize with one another both during (e.g., lunch hour) and after the work day. In short, employees may develop a sense of attachment to, and psychological identification with, one another to varying degrees; as a result, survivors may become more concerned with whether the organization treats its laid-off workers in an equitable fashion. Deutsch (1985) has proposed the notion of "scope of justice," which refers to individuals' beliefs about the entitlement of others. One factor that heightens party A's perception that party B is entitled to fair treatment is the extent to which party A identifies with party B. Indeed, if party A identifies with party B, and if party B has been treated unfairly by some external agent then party A may seek to redress party B's unfair treatment by retaliating against the external agent.

Studies I-III held constant survivors' degree of identification with their co-workers, and at a low level. In study V (Brockner, Grover, & O'Malley, 1986) subjects' level of attachment to their laid-off co-worker was experimentally manipulated. Half of the participants were led to believe that their attitudes were quite similar to those of the dismissed individual (high identification condition), whereas the remaining half were informed that their attitudes were very different from the dismissed individual's (low identification condition). The random-based decision rule from study I was utilized in all conditions. It was expected that survivors in the high identification condition would respond to the inequity heaped upon their co-worker (i.e., being laid off without compensation) primarily with feelings of anger or resentment. Rather than to respond to the layoff with feelings of survivor guilt and working harder as a result (as in study I), it seems more likely that the layoff-engendered resentment would lead to a *decrease* in the survivors' work performance.

Study V also explored the effect of another factor that was (a) derived from equity theory, (b) present to varying degrees in actual layoff situations, and (c) expected to interact with the identification variable to influence survivors' work performance. In studies I–III the laid-off workers were treated quite unfairly; they were asked to leave without receiving any compensation for the time that they had devoted to the experiment. In layoffs in actual work organizations, however, separated employees often are "taken care of" in a variety of ways (e.g., they receive severance pay, outplacement counseling, and continuation of benefits, to name a few). In essence, the organization often makes efforts to treat the laid-off workers with some sense of fairness.

According to equity theory, survivors' negative reactions to layoffs should be reduced to the extent that their dismissed co-workers have been taken care of or treated fairly in the process; this should be especially so if survivors feel a prior sense of kinship with the dismissed employees. In the layoff conditions of study V, half of the survivors were informed that the laid-off workers received no compensation for their efforts (uncompensated layoff condition), just as in studies I–III. The remaining half witnessed the fact that the laid-off workers were given partial payment for their efforts; in this sense we created a laboratory analogue of severance pay (compensated layoff condition).

Study V thus consisted of a two-factor (3 × 2) design, crossing the layoff variable (uncompensated layoff, compensated layoff, and no layoff control) with the identification manipulation (high or low). As predicted, participants' level of work performance was lowest in the uncompensated layoff/high identification condition; in fact, their work performance was significantly less than that exhibited in each of the compensated layoff/ high identification, no layoff/high identification, and uncompensated layoff/ low identification conditions. In addition, subjects rated the treatment meted out to the other person as least fair in the uncompensated layoff/ high identification condition; such results are consistent with our hunch that perceived inequity mediated work performance.[2]

Summary of Studies I–V.   Taken together, the results of the first five studies provide some insight into the effects of layoffs on survivors. A variety of factors were shown to moderate the impact of layoffs on those who stay; these factors represented some of the categories mentioned in the first section of the chapter, including individual differences (self-esteem), formal organizational arrangements (decision rule, compensation provided to the laid-off workers), and the informal organization (survivors' identification with the dismissed employees). Moreover, a host of "survivor outcome variables" were affected. Our focus of discussion has been on survivors' work performance. However, subsidiary analyses in these studies revealed that numerous attitudes (i.e., towards the laid-off worker, experimenter, and the task itself) were (adversely) affected by the dismissal of the co-worker. The studies also revealed considerable variability in survivors' response *within* a particular outcome dimension. That is, layoffs were shown to increase, decrease, or have no effect on survivors' work performance, depending upon condition. The variance in survivors' work performance thus parallels the variability in managers' "war stories" about the effects of layoffs with which we began this program of research. Perhaps most important, the results across studies I–V were internally consistent, held together by the equity theory framework from which the studies were derived.

Nevertheless, the preceding research suffers from two important limitations, one conceptual and the other methodological. At the conceptual level, we have suggested that perceived inequity is one survivor reaction that can explain some of the variability in their subsequent work behaviors and attitudes. It would be incorrect to assume, however, that equity theory provides a *complete* explanation of the impact of layoffs on survivors.

Simply put, survivors may experience other psychological states that have little to do with equity theory. Most notably, they may feel a profound sense of job insecurity—i.e., wondering whether they are the next to go—which could have numerous effects on their subsequent work behaviors. If so, then prior theory and research on job insecurity (e.g., Greenhalgh & Rosenblatt, 1984) in particular and organizational stress (e.g., McGrath, 1976) in general would seem relevant to the analysis of survivors' reactions. Studies VI and VII draw upon these literatures in order to predict survivors' reactions in a post-layoff work environment.

At the methodological level, the external validity of the previous results are questionable in that four of the five studies were conducted in controlled laboratory settings, far removed from the organizational context in which layoffs actually occur. Study VII was performed in a field setting; the survivors of layoffs in work organizations that recently had gone through layoffs were surveyed, in order to delineate some of the factors associated with their work attitudes and behaviors.

Study VI: The Effects of Layoffs, Job Insecurity, and Self-Esteem on Survivors' Work Performance and Attitudes

The previous laboratory studies explored the effects of "layoffs" that did not threaten the survivors' job security. Many, if not most, naturally occurring layoffs, however, are viewed by survivors as possible threats to their own job security. Thus, study VI examined the impact of layoffs that were or were not accompanied by job insecurity on survivors' work performance and attitudes. Note that predicting the *precise* impact of layoff-induced job insecurity on survivors is no simple matter. Previous research on job insecurity has demonstrated that it can have a negative impact on work performance (Cobb & Kasl, 1977; Greenhalgh, 1982), or have no effect at all (Hershey, 1972).

Moreover, it is even possible that layoff-induced job insecurity will have a motivating effect on survivors under certain conditions. Suppose, for example, that the level of threat to job insecurity posed by the layoff was moderate; that is, the likelihood of survivors being laid off was neither very high nor very low. Furthermore, imagine that survivors perceived that they could enhance their job security by working harder, a belief that many survivors of actual layoffs do entertain, whether accurate or not, probably in order to increase their impoverished sense of control. Under these circumstances it seems likely that layoff-produced job insecurity would heighten survivors' work performance. In fact, these were precisely the circumstances that existed in the insecurity-accompanied layoff condition in study VI.

Study VI (Brockner, O'Malley, Grover, Esaki, Glynn, & Lazarides,

1987) also explored the moderating impact of survivors' self-esteem; recall from study I that low self-esteem individuals were more likely than their higher self-esteem counterparts to work harder after a layoff that was *not* accompanied by job insecurity (a finding consistent with equity theory). It also seems likely that low self-esteem persons will be more influenced than high self-esteem individuals by layoffs that are accompanied by job insecurity, but for reasons very different than in the earlier case. Much research in both the basic personality/social psychology (Brockner, 1983) and applied industrial/organizational psychology (Mossholder, Bedeian, & Armenakis, 1982) literature has demonstrated that low self-esteem individuals are more susceptible to influence by a variety of environmental cues, and in particular, those that elicit worry or insecurity. Therefore, if the insecurity-accompanied layoff does increase survivors' work performance, this tendency should be more pronounced among low than high self-esteem participants.

The results of this laboratory experiment replicated and extended the findings of study I: both the layoff that was not accompanied by job insecurity (replication) and the one that was (extension) elicited an increase in work performance among survivors; moreover, self-esteem was a significant moderator variable in both conditions, such that low self-esteem individuals showed a greater performance enhancement effect than did their high self esteem counterparts. Perhaps most intriguing, subsidiary analyses (garnered from questionnaire data) suggested that the insecurity-accompanied and security-accompanied layoffs produced similar enhancement effects on work performance, but for very different reasons in the two conditions. In the former condition individuals (especially low self-esteem persons) worked harder because they were worried about their job security; by working harder they probably perceived that the threat to their job security could be reduced. In the latter condition the mediator, as in the previous experiments, was positive inequity. In order to redress their feelings of survivor guilt participants, especially those low in self-esteem, exhibited a significant increase in work performance.

Study VI also revealed a number of interesting attitudinal effects. As in several earlier studies, the layoff elicited negative feelings towards the co-worker who was laid off (i.e., the "victim-blaming" effect) as well as the experimenter. In addition, the layoff accompanied by job insecurity caused participants to feel more negatively towards their co-workers who had *not* been laid off. One possible explanation of this finding is that the insecurity-accompanied layoff placed survivors in a competitive relationship with one another; they had been told that if additional layoffs were necessary it would be decided on the basis of the relative work performance of survivors on upcoming tasks. Note that the perception of competitiveness towards fellow survivors could easily occur in the real world, as employees come to perceive job security as a scarce resource. To the extent that survivors perceive that their relationship with one another is more competitive, feelings of interpersonal hostility are likely to develop (e.g., Aronson, 1984; Sherif, Harvey, White, Hood, & Sherif, 1961).

Study VII: Predictors of Survivors' Reactions in a Post-Layoff Environment: A Field Study.

The seventh and final study to be described differs from the previous studies in several important respects. First, the data were collected in a field setting; we (Brockner, Grover, & Blonder, 1987) surveyed a sample of survivors whose organizations had been in the process of laying off employees for the past year or two. Most of the previous research has been conducted under controlled laboratory conditions.

Second, this study did not explore the *effects* of layoffs on survivors per se. Rather, the conceptual model in the first part of this paper and the empirical research in the second part have suggested that survivors' work behaviors and attitudes are quite variable, depending upon a host of moderating variables. All of the participants in study VII were survivors of layoffs, i.e., there was no "control" condition. Given the great variance in survivors' behaviors and attitudes suggested by previous theory and research, our goal was to identify some of the factors that could account for a significant portion of the variance.

Third, the underlying conceptual framework was not derived from equity theory, but rather, the vast literature on organizational stress (e.g., Jick, 1985). The working assumption was that the post-layoff work environment *has the potential* to be quite stressful for a variety of reasons (e.g., survivors' concerns about job insecurity). Stress, in turn, *has the potential* to affect adversely survivors' work attitudes and behaviors. The *actual:* (a) degree of stress experienced, and (b) attitudinal and behavioral consequences of the stress are bound to be determined by a host of factors. As stress researchers have pointed out, two general categories of factors are predictive of employees' degree of, and/or reactions to, stress: (a) the "objective" properties of the stressor (e.g., severity of the layoff, amount of response time), and (b) workers' desires and abilities to cope with the stressor (e.g., self-esteem, social support).

Six independent variables were explored in study VII: one related to an objective property of the layoff (severity) whereas the other five (self-esteem, work ethic, and workers' prior degree of experience in the organization with task variety, participation in decision making, and role ambiguity) were believed to reflect survivors' motivation and/or ability to cope with stress. For example, employees' work ethic seems related to their desire to "get through" the difficulties in a postlayoff environment and their chronic self-esteem is likely correlated with their ability to do so.

In addition to personality variables such as work ethic and self-esteem, characteristics of individuals' past work histories are likely to affect their coping reactions in a high stress environment. For example, the extent to which employees have had task variety, participation in decision making, and possibly other relevant work dimensions in the job characteristics model (Hackman & Oldham, 1976) may influence their commitment to their organization and/or work in a postlayoff environment. A past history of task variety and participation may heighten individuals' involvement with their organization and/or work, which may enable them "tough it out" in the face of the stressors posed by a postlayoff environment. Put differently, the postlayoff environment is likely to threaten survivors' sense of perceived control; therefore, factors that affect employees' sense of control (e.g., personality variables such as self-esteem, past work history factors such as degree of participation, and interpersonal determinants such as social support) are likely to be highly correlated with their work behaviors and attitudes in a postlayoff work environment.

Our predictions concerning the associations between prior experience with role ambiguity and survivors' work behaviors and attitudes were more tentative. On the one hand, it could be that prior experience with role ambiguity will be positively correlated with survivors' involvement with their organization and/or work. After all, having had experience with the stress associated with role ambiguity may prepare one to cope with the stress of a postlayoff environment. On the other hand, it may be that prior experience with role ambiguity negatively affects survivors. Prior role ambiguity is apt to decrease employees' sense of control, which may serve to "lower their resistance" to the demands of a postlayoff setting.

The dependent variables in study VII were survivors' degree of commitment to the organization and their work. Multiple regression analyses revealed that the six independent variables accounted for highly significant portions of the variance in each dependent measure, though more so in the case of organization commitment ($R^2 = .52$) than job commitment ($R^2 = .19$). Individual factors that attained significance (at least at the .05 level) were the severity, work ethic, role ambiguity, and participation variables in the case of organizational commitment, and task variety, and to a marginal extent ($p < .09$) role ambiguity in the case of job commitment. As predicted, severity was negatively associated with organizational commitment, whereas work ethic and prior degree of participation were positively correlated with organizational commitment. Prior degree of role ambiguity was negatively correlated with organizational commitment. Also as expected, prior degree of task variety was positively associated with job commitment; prior degree of role ambiguity was negatively correlated with job commitment.

Further analyses revealed that additional variance in job (but not organizational) commitment could be explained through tests for nonlinear relationships and interaction effects. Specifically, self-esteem was related to job commitment, though in a nonlinear fashion; the top 20% of the distribution expressed greater job commitment than did the bottom 80%. In addition, the severity × work ethic and severity × role ambiguity interaction effects were significant. In both instances it was shown that the individual difference variable was significantly associated with job commitment in the mild, but not in the severe layoff condition; more precisely, work ethic was positively correlated and role ambiguity negatively associated with job commitment in the mild layoff condition only.

Study VII was grounded theoretically in the literature on organizational stress; we hypothesized that survivors' stress levels played key mediating roles in the relationships between the independent and dependent variables. Although perceived stress was not directly measured, several finding support a stress-based interpretation. First, recall the basic prediction: stress in a postlayoff work environment is bound to be affected by (a) the "objective" properties of the layoff (e.g., severity), and (b) workers' desires and abilities to cope with the stress (i.e., the remaining five independent variables). Importantly, the *pattern* of results are consistent with a stress-based interpretation: the objective severity of the layoff was negatively associated with the survivors' organizational commitment. Their desire to cope with the work-related stress (probably correlated with their degree of work ethic) and their ability to do so (probably correlated positively with their self-esteem, prior task variety, and prior participation, and negatively with prior role ambiguity) also was significantly associated with the dependent variables in the expected directions. Clearly, alternative explanations exist for many of the findings; however, the explanation centered on perceived stress has the advantage of parsimony.

Second, layoffs refer to an organizationally induced stressful event. Therefore, it stands to reason that survivors' commitment to the organization should be more strongly correlated with layoff severity (and the other independent variables) than should their commitment to their work. In fact, layoff severity (and the other independent variables) did a far better job in explaining the variance associated with survivors' commitment to the organization than their jobs.

Third, layoff severity referred to the proportion of the workforce that was eliminated. In the mild or low severity organization that proportion was relatively slight (i.e., 2–5%). In the high severity organization the proportion was much greater, ranging from 25–70%. The fact that the layoff rate was *so* much greater in the high than low severity organization makes it reasonable to assume that organizational stress was higher in the former than the latter instance.

In study VII it was shown that high self-esteem survivors were more work-involved than their low self-esteem counterparts; such findings seem contrary to the results in laboratory studies I and VI. The external validity of the laboratory studies must therefore await further research, especially that which explores the different factors between the laboratory and field research, which may be responsible for the different outcomes. Possibly relevant moderator variables include: (a) the decision rule. In the laboratory studies low self-esteem participants worked harder subsequent to the random basis of implementing layoffs. The basis of the decision in the field study was not known, and (b) severity. The laboratory layoff manipulation had to be much milder than the naturally occurring ones in which workers lost real jobs (even in the low severity condition in study VII). It may be that low self-esteem survivors work harder subsequent to mild layoffs, whereas high self-esteem persons do so following more severe layoffs.

To reiterate, the results of study VII are low in internal validity; the methodology employed merely enabled us to delineate some of the predictors of survivors' commitment to the organization and their work in a postlayoff environment. We are by no means implying that the results obtained in study VII cannot be obtained in a "no layoff" environment; in fact, much organizational behavior research suggests quite the contrary. In spite of its shortcomings, however, study VII represents an important extension of the bulk of research presented in this chapter, on both methodological and conceptual grounds. At the methodological level, it is one of the first studies to explore survivors' reactions in an actual postlayoff environment. Conceptually, the findings suggest that in addition to equity theory, the literature on organizational stress may elucidate the reactions of survivors to the dismissal of co-workers.

THEORETICAL AND PRACTICAL IMPLICATIONS

Having described our empirical research, I now will attempt to provide some perspective on the present and possibly future status of this line of research. Taken together, these seven studies provide a much-needed initial impetus to the study of the effects of layoffs on those who survive. As our research suggests, the pertinent conceptual and empirical tasks are not merely to document the effects of layoffs on survivors so much as they are to delineate the factors that *moderate and mediate* the effects of layoffs on survivors. The first two sections of this chapter also suggest that we have only scratched the surface in our quest to elucidate survivors' reactions; from Figure 1 it can be seen that five categories of factors, with numerous variables included within each category, moderate the impact of layoffs on survivors. Studies I–VII merely explored a handful of relevant moderator variables. Nonetheless, even at this relatively early stage the research has several theoretical and practical implications.

Implications for Theory

First and foremost, the studies suggest that several bodies of existing knowledge in organizational psychology may shed light on the reactions of survivors to layoffs. Equity theory (e.g., Adams, 1965) proved helpful in accounting for a number of possible layoff-produced behavioral (i.e., work performance) and attitudinal (e.g., towards the laid-off worker) effects. Moreover, the theory may help explain variability in survivors' reactions *within* one or more behavioral and attitudinal dimension. Consider work performance as a case in point. Studies I, II, and VI demonstrated that layoffs may produce positive inequity that could lead to increased work performance. If survivors' perceived inputs are relatively high (e.g., as in the merit condition of study II, the seniority-based layoffs in studies III and IV, or among high self-esteem persons in the random-based layoffs of studies I and VI), then there should be less of an experience of positive inequity in which survivors feel that they must work harder. Moreover, certain layoffs may elicit in survivors the perception of negative, rather than positive inequity. For example, study V suggested that survivors who strongly identify with laid-off workers may feel a certain sense of illegitimacy about the layoff and resentment towards management, especially when the laid-off workers are not provided for. If so, survivors may redress the inequity not by working harder, but rather, less hard.

In a related vein, the voluminous literature on organizational stress (e.g., McGrath, 1976) identifies various categories of factors that could moderate the effects of layoffs on survivors. Relevant categories include characteristics of the layoff itself (e.g., its severity) as well as determinants of the survivors' motivation and/or ability to cope with stress; included in the latter categories are attributes of the survivors' personalities (e.g., work ethic) and prior work histories (e.g., amount of experience with task variety).

In short, these seven studies make a strong case that survivors' perceptions of fairness and stress play key roles in mediating the behavorial and attitudinal consequences of layoffs. Having identified these mediators, we are on much firmer theoretical ground in generating future research. For example, *The Wall Street Journal* (1/20/84) described the reaction of a woman who was forced to work overtime at her automobile plant when many of her laid-off co-workers had yet to be recalled. "When people find out you're working overtime, they're bitter and they make comments. They feel that people who work overtime shouldn't be working that much." How does this woman ease her conscience? "I've given more to people and the Salvation Army than I can afford," she replies, implying (as a hypothesis for future research) that layoff-induced positive inequity may have behavioral consequences for survivors that extend beyond the work setting.

A sound theoretical understanding of survivors' reactions could encourage future researchers to study additional dependent variables (as in the example above) as well as independent variables. Studies VI and VII, derived from the notion that perceived stress moderates survivors' reactions, explored several predictor variables, but many other possible antecedents of layoff-induced stress still need to be studied. Indeed, our initial research studies have devoted more attention to the mediating role of perceived equity than felt stress. This is not necessarily to suggest that the former is more relevant than the latter; indeed, we fully recognize that the existing evidence for the mediating role of perceived stress is rather thin at this point, and we look forward to further research that evaluates the extent to which stress factors elucidate the effects of layoffs on survivors. For example, the precise extent that the layoff threatens survivors' job security warrants close investigation; as suggested previously, the relationship between insecurity-produced-stress and survivors' work performance may be complex (i.e., nonlinear). In addition, it may be worthwhile to determine the extent to which survivors' layoff-produced stress is influenced by social information processes (Bies, 1987; Salancik & Pfeffer, 1978). That is, subsequent to dramatic (i.e., uncertainty arousing) organizational events such as layoffs employees are highly motivated to make sense of the past, present, and likely future. As a result, they may be keenly sensitive to the social accounts that the organization provides to explain why the layoff has occurred. Also central to survivors' sense-making process is their tendency to seek out significant others (e.g., co-workers, supervisors) in order to construct a socially defined reality of what has happened and what is likely to occur (Festinger, 1954). The extent to which the stress inherent in a postlayoff environment is socially defined may well prove to be a fruitful area for future research.

Not only are the literatures on equity theory and stress potentially useful in elucidating survivors' reactions, but also the study of survivors' reactions may have implications for the underlying theoretical frameworks. For example, the effects of inequity on employees' work performance has been of considerable interest to industrial/organizational psychologists for at least a quarter century (e.g., Adams & Rosenbaum, 1962). Most of these studies have operationalized inequity by changing (either heightening or lowering) the outcomes of *the target person*. Studies I–III and VI operationalized positive inequity by decreasing the outcome of *the comparison person;* moreover, these studies were among the few to have operationalized inequity using non-monetary outcomes (cf. Greenberg & Ornstein, 1983). In spite of the methodological innovations the results were both internally consistent with one another, and with equity theory more generally. Said differently, these studies reinforce previous studies of inequity in demonstrating that perceived inequity, *however induced,* should elicit systematic behavioral and/or attitudinal consequences.

Similarly, theoretical complexities in the literature on organizational stress may be better understood through present and future research on the effects of layoffs on survivors. For example, in study VII the following results were obtained: (a) the predictor variables accounted for a much greater portion of the variance in organizational than job commitment, and (b) layoff severity interacted with several of the individual difference factors to predict job commitment. In coming to understanding these curious findings, future researchers may also reveal something(s) of interest about the nature of organizational stress.

On a related note, the present studies may initiate theoretical development about the nature of survivors' reactions; equity theory and organizational stress are the two key explanatory mechanisms that have guided the research to this point, but they probably are not the only relevant mediators. I hint at some of the other possibilities in the final section of this chapter. More generally, my point is that present and future research on the effects of layoffs on survivors highlight the reciprocal relationship between theory and research; existing theory can be used to guide empirical research, the results of which can be fed back to evaluate (i.e., clarify, modify) the existing theory.

Implications for Practice

This research may provide managers with insights into how to administer layoffs so as to elicit from survivors the most positive (or least negative) behavioral and attitudinal reactions. Clearly, further research is needed before more definitive managerial prescriptions can be offered. Nonetheless, the present research suggests a number of ways in which managers may be able to put to good use the theory and research described herein.

The present studies suggest that many independent variables are associated with survivors' reactions to layoffs. The types of managerial prescriptions to be offered depend upon whether the associations between the independent variable(s) and survivors' reactions (i.e., the dependent variables) are causal or correlational in nature. Let's suppose that an in-

dependent variable was shown to have a causal impact on survivors' reactions. For example, in study V we found that survivors worked less
hard when someone with whom they identified closely was laid off unfarily,
i.e., without receiving compensation. This tendency was eliminated, however, when: (a) the worker with whom survivors identified was treated
fairly, i.e., given compensation, and (b) survivors were led not to identify
with the laid-off worker. On the assumption that future research in more
ecologically valid settings confirms these findings managers may wish to
influence directly the factors that causally affect survivors' reactions, or
at least survivors' *perceptions* of those factors. For example, if a layoff
breaks up a highly cohesive work group, in which group members were
known to identify strongly with one another, then it would seem especially
prudent for managers to treat the laid-off workers in a caretaking (i.e.,
fair) manner. In addition, managers will want to act in ways that reinforce
the survivors' *perceptions* of the fair treatment afforded to the laid-off
workers. For instance, management may *publicize* the ways in which the
laid-off workers have been taken care of, precisely in order to soften the
impact of the layoff on survivors.

Clearly, not all of the variables that moderate survivors' reactions are
under managers' control. For instance, factors external to the work organization can not be influenced by management. However, even in some
of these instances management may be able to influence survivors' per-
ceptions of the external environment and, in so doing, influence the survivors' likely response to the layoff. For example, management may attempt to make survivors aware of the fact that other organizations in the
competitive environment also are undergoing layoffs. Indeed, if appropriate, management could call attention to the fact that the layoff in its
own organization is not as dramatic or severe as those taking place in the
organization's reference group. In these and other ways management may
be able to exert influence over its employees' perceptions of key extraorganizational events, even if they are unable to affect those events themselves.

Let us imagine, however, research findings that merely establish a correlational (rather than causal) association between the independent and
dependent variables. We would not advocate that managers attempt to
influence the actual (or survivors' perceptions of the) independent variables, because doing so would not necessarily lead to the desired changes
in survivors' reactions. Nevertheless, even the establishment of correlational findings has several managerial prescriptions. For instance, study
VII revealed that the following factors were correlated with lower organizational and/or job commitment among survivors: low work ethic, low
self-esteem, little prior experience with task variety and participation in
decision making, and much prior experience with role ambiguity. Such

correlational results may enable managers to identify the survivors who are likely to be "at risk" in a post-layoff work environment; "at risk" refers to the possibility that the survivors' work attitudes and behaviors are likely to suffer.

Moreover, provided that management has some prior knowledge about would-be survivors' likely standing along the independent variable dimensions, they will be able to identify those who are at risk *before* the layoff has begun. Armed with this knowledge, management may be able to implement the layoff more effectively. For example, extra social support may be provided to those who would otherwise be suspected of reacting most unfavorably to the dismissal of co-workers. Or, management may wish to consider the likely reactions of survivors in making decisions about whom to layoff. Of course, I am *not* advocating that such decisions be based solely or even primarily on the results of research findings such as those in study VII. Rather, it is being suggested that this information may be one of the pieces of data that management should consider upon making the difficult and painful decisions about whom to retain vs. dismiss.

The theory and research in the first two sections of this paper also raise more general practical considerations. First, layoffs typically heighten survivors' stress levels (although, as we have seen, the extent to which this is true may be moderated by a variety of situational and dispositional factors). Therefore, managers may need to conduct their affairs in ways different from the way that they do so in a less stressful environment. Barton (1986), for example, has suggested that astute managers of layoffs attempt to get survivors working on "doable" tasks in which they are likely to succeed. In addition, the vast literature on psychological and organizational stress (e.g., Staw, Sandelands, & Dutton, 1981) suggests that resistance to change is apt to be great in a high stress environment; the clear implication is that wherever possible managers should attempt to minimize change, because survivors are not likely to be responsive to them in times of high threat or stress. Perhaps these changes can be more profitably introduced after the layoff-induced stress has dissipated somewhat.

Second, layoff managers should expect survivors to experience a wide variety of psychological states—even some that seem self-contradictory— both across and within persons. Some survivors may be feeling guilty, others angry, others anxious, and still others relieved. Moreover, certain individuals may feel two or more of these states simultaneously. In study I, for example, survivors reported feeling sorry for the laid-off co-worker, but yet they also derogated that person. At first blush, such results seem contradictory; however, they also may reflect the ambivalent feelings that layoffs elicit within individuals.

In order to reduce the possibly interfering effects of these psychological reactions on survivors' work behaviors and attitudes, managers may wish to hold small group meetings in which survivors are encouraged to "get things off their chest." The psychological states that layoffs arouse—especially guilt, anger, and anxiety—may be difficult for survivors to express to one another informally. For example, survivors may experience guilt, but believe that they "should not" be feeling that way (after all, one might reason, "I didn't do anything wrong"). In addition, there may be strong taboos against admitting anger or anxiety. Consequently, survivors may keep such feelings bottled up inside, when it would be far more beneficial, both to themselves and the organization, to air their feelings. Moreover, it may be especially useful to have such meetings shortly after the layoffs occur, when survivors are apt to be highly distracted and therefore not terribly productive anyway. To be sure, such proposed group meetings must be conducted by leaders who are well trained in interpersonal and intrapersonal processes. It is not clear, for instance, that the formal manager would always be the best leader of these group meetings. The possible longer term benefits of a well-run "venting" session, however, could be considerable.

Third, there are important implications embedded in the fact that *numerous* factors moderate the impact of layoffs on survivors. In fact, layoff managers may feel a bit overwhelmed as they contemplate the sheer number of factors over which they need to exert influence. Further complicating matters is that the moderator variables may combine with one another on interactive, rather than additive bases to affect survivors' reactions. For example, suppose that management decided to implement the layoffs on the basis of seniority. If so, they will also need to consider whether this decision rule is congruent with the informal values of the organization (i.e., its corporate culture).

In a more optimistic vein, the conceptual model may also provide insights into the conditions under which certain moderator variables are more or less relevant. For example, workers concerned with their own job security may be less concerned, at least initially, with the fairness with which the laid-off workers were dismissed. Moreover, the conceptual model and associated research may enhance managers' perceived ability to manage layoffs, as they come to realize that many, if not most, of the variables that moderate survivors' reactions can be directly or indirectly influenced by managers' actions. It may be an overstatement to suggest that managers can implement layoffs in ways that have a *positive* impact on survivors' work behaviors and attitudes (relative to prior to the onset of the layoff). However, it is not an exaggeration to assert that managers' handling of layoffs will have a significant effect on the extent to which survivors exhibit *dysfunctional* work behaviors and/or attitudes.

FUTURE RESEARCH DIRECTIONS

The purpose of this chapter is to summarize previous theory and empirical data pertinent to the effects of layoffs on survivors; my goal also is to stimulate further thinking and research on this practically and theoretically important topic. Therefore, this concluding section of the paper outlines three general areas that warrant further attention by those who study the effects of layoffs on survivors: methodological advances, further development of the conceptual model used to study survivors' reactions, and the implications of this line of research for other areas of inquiry in the field of organizational behavior.

Towards Improved Methodology

Any scientific program of research should attempt to maximize both internal and external validity. To achieve these ends our approach thus far has been to use two different methodologies, i.e., laboratory experiments and field studies, in which the two types of validity typically are inversely related to one another. I wholeheartedly believe that both methodologies are important, and that future research on survivors' reactions should take both forms. Moreover, it would also be extremely valuable if internal and external validity could be incorporated into a single methodological procedure. Badly needed are studies conducted in the field setting in which—as in the laboratory procedure—measurement occurs both before and after the layoff event in both the "experimental" (i.e., layoff present) and "control" (i.e., layoff absent) groups. There are at least two ways in which to enact such a research strategy. First, it may be possible to predict the onset of layoffs in certain organizations, well before the possibility is highly salient to the employees who are most apt to be threatened. (Indeed, research on the antecedent conditions of layoffs may prove useful in identifying the likelihood of layoffs across and/or within organizations, e.g., Cornfield, 1983.) If so, then the premeasurement should be administered to the experimental and appropriate control groups. Over time, the layoff "manipulation" should occur, after which it would be necessary to administer the postmeasurement to both groups.

A second possibility is to track the outcome variables (i.e., productivity, satisfaction) over time from actual data bases (as in study IV), utilizing a time series or some other procedure that may enable investigators to draw causal inferences from the data. In any event, future researchers should be prepared to explore not only the effects of layoffs on survivors, but also, as our conceptual model implies, the *factors that moderate and mediate* the effects of layoffs on those who remain.

Towards an Improved Conceptual Model

The conceptual model presented in the first section of the paper (see Figure 1) seems elegantly straightforward; it suggests that layoffs can affect survivors' psychological states, which, in turn, can influence their work behaviors and attitudes. Moreover, a variety of factors, derived from the literatures on equity theory and organizational stress, moderate the actual relationships between layoffs and survivors' psychological states, and between their psychological states and behavioral and attitudinal outcomes. Although this conceptual model is simple, I suspect that the phenomenon it is designed to elucidate is anything but simple. Therefore, in this section it may be useful to make explicit several features of the existing model that could serve to limit its ability to predict and explain survivors' reactions. Such features include the following: (a) it is "multi-theoretical," i.e., it draws upon several theories to explain survivors' reactions, unlike many lines of research which limit themselves to a single perspective, (b) it has not spoken to the process(es) of employees' reactions to layoffs, and (c) it employs the individual as the unit of analysis.

In ways that will soon become apparent, these three features (and possibly others) of the conceptual model probably detract from its ability to provide a comprehensive and accurate account of survivors' reactions. In this section I discuss some of the kinds of conceptual advances that need to occur in these three areas. Such development will have the obvious effect of "complicating" the conceptual model posed in the first section of the paper; however, such advances probably are necessary for the conceptual model to achieve a level of complexity that is congruent with the phenomenon that it purports to elucidate.

The "multi-theoretical" perspective. It has been suggested throughout that at least two literatures may help explain the impact of a wide variety of moderator variables on survivors' reactions: equity theory and organizational stress. If so, then it is important in future research to delineate the conceptual relationship between these two theories. Are they competing theories or complimentary theories? Does one theory subsume the other? In a related vein, is there a prepotency to the arousal of psychological states in survivors? For example, if survivors feel job-insecurity–produced stress, can they also feel positive inequity–produced guilt? A econd set of questions pertains to the ability of these two theories to predict survivors' work behaviors and attitudes. Does one theory account for more of the variance than the other? Moreover, if survivors do simultaneously experience the different psychological states associated with each theory (e.g., job insecurity and positive inequity), how do these states *jointly* mediate the reactions of survivors?

The perspectives offered by the literatures on equity theory and organizational stress do not appear to be in competition with one another. Rather, both might be related derivatives of a more generic "stress hypothesis," which posits that individuals experience stress when they perceive that they may not be able to muster the resources necessary to respond successfully to significant environmental demands. Perhaps the predominant source of stress in a postlayoff environment is job insecurity (Greenhalgh & Rosenblatt, 1984). However, job insecurity is by no means the only source of stress among survivors. The experience of stress may be due to other factors, some having to do with perceived inequity. For example, if survivors experience positive inequity they could feel an intense pressure to perform at a much higher level of performance; the belief that they will be unable to live up to such high standards could evoke stress. In addition, survivors could feel negative inequity–produced anger. The perception that they will not be able to eliminate or reduce the source of the negative inequity also could be quite stress inducing. Thus, it could be that layoff-produced inequities simply give rise to particular stress experiences (e.g., guilt, anger), just as job insecurity elicits a particular type of stress experience (e.g., anxiety). From a stress theory framework, all that may be necessary to know is the extent to which survivors perceive that they will not be able to live up to the stresses in a postlayoff environment, regardless of whether the substance of the stress is job insecurity, positive inequity or guilt, negative inequity or anger, or anything else.

A related matter is whether the different sources of stress are arranged in a "psychologically prepotent" manner. It could be, for example, that the experience of job insecurity makes it difficult for survivors to feel positive inequity. Put differently, if workers are worried about whether they will be able to keep their jobs they might not be able to "indulge" themselves in feeling guilty about their co-workers' dismissal (and their own survival).

The second set of issues deals with the *joint* effects of the various psychological states on survivors' behaviors and attitudes. Poorly understood are the *precise* ways in which survivors may respond to simultaneous sources of pressure. For example, suppose that the layoff elicited both guilt (an impetus to work harder) and anger (an impetus to reduce motivation). Will the net effect of these two mediators on motivation be equal to zero, as if they cancelled each other in an additive relationship? If so, then observers may erroneously conclude that the layoff "had no effect"; in reality, large effects may appear on dimensions in which guilt and anger yield similar (rather than opposing) effects. For example, both guilt and anger may reduce individuals' job satisfaction and/or organizational commitment. Consequently, a layoff that elicited both guilt and anger could have a very large effect on such outcome measures.

Yet another possibility is that the various mediators will combine on an interactive, rather than additive basis. For example, suppose that the layoff elicited guilt and job insecurity (both of which, under certain conditions, can be an impetus to greater performance). It could be that survivors will respond by working much harder than would be expected by the presence of either mediator alone. Or, to cite another type of interactive relationship, it could be that survivors will not be responsive simultaneously to more than one mediator, even though the layoff, in theory, could have elicited more than one process. For instance, in experiment VI we found evidence to suggest that survivors were influenced by perceived insecurity when the layoff threatened their job security, and positive inequity when it did not.

In summary, because layoffs have the potential to elicit a variety of psychological states in survivors (which in turn are believed to mediate survivors' behavioral and attitudinal reactions), it is important for future theorists and researchers to enhance our understanding of (a) the conceptual relationships between the various psychological states, and (b) the joint effects of the psychological states on survivors' reactions.[3]

Viewing survivors' reactions as a process.   Many scientific phenomena lend themselves to complementary, but clearly different, modes of analysis: structure and process. Structural analyses typically focus on the contextual and individual difference factors that make a given phenomenon more or less likely to occur. Process analyses typically attempt to fractionate a phenomenon into its naturally occurring sequence of events, with particular attention devoted to the impact of one event on the next one in the sequence. Several voluminous areas of research in the behavioral sciences have been analyzed at the levels of both structure and process. For example, social psychologists have long been interested in the role of persuasive communications in producing behavioral change. Much of this research, most notably the efforts of the early "Yale School" (Hovland, Lumsdaine, & Sheffield, 1949), has employed a structural approach. Thus, researchers explored the effects on attitude/behavioral change of various categories of factors including characteristics of the communicator, the nature of the communication, audience attributes, and the context in which the communication attempt took place.

The process approach to studying the effects of persuasive communications on behavior change, in contrast, views behavior change as culminating from a series of more micro-level events. For example, McGuire (1972) has suggested that the effect of persuasive communication on behavior change is dependent upon the audience's tendencies to: (1) attend to, (2) comprehend, (3) yield to, and (4) remember the communication; in addition (5), change in attitude may or may not lead to change in behavior. Important advances in understanding behavioral change have been made through both the structure and process approach. Perhaps closer to our organizational homes, theory and research on interpersonal conflict (e.g., Thomas, 1976) and feedback (e.g., Ilgen, Fisher, & Taylor, 1979) have called attention to the utility of exploring workplace–related phenomena at the levels of both structure *and* process.

To be sure, our approach thus far in studying layoffs has had a decidedly structural flavor; we have focused on the *factors that affect* the effects of layoffs on survivors' psychological states, and the *factors that affect* the impact of the psychological states on work behavior and attitudes. In so doing, however, we have overlooked much potentially useful information that can be learned from a process approach.

Therefore, I strongly advocate future researchers to study survivors' reactions as a process. Such an approach could fractionate the effects of layoffs on survivors into three points in time: before, during, and after the layoff has taken place. At each of these three points in time survivors are likely to ask a number of questions about the layoff. Their answers to these questions, i.e., the interpretations that they make about the layoff, are likely to affect a variety of work behaviors and attitudes including job performance, perceptions of justice, interpersonal relationships, and their feelings about the organization.

More specifically, *prior to* the actual announcement of a layoff employees are likely to have the following concerns: Is the layoff really going to happen? If so, how will the organization decide who stay and who goes? Am I likely to be affected, and so on. *During* the days in which the layoff actually is announced, some of the questions employees ask are: Am I going to be laid off (let us assume that the answer is no, thereby making the employee a survivor). How will the nature of my job (scope, responsibilities, co-worker relations) be affected? Is the layoff being handled with a tone of dignity? What will happen to those who are laid off, and so on.

In the week and months *after* the layoff typical survivor questions include: Will there be another round of layoffs? Could I be affected? If so, is there anything I can do to enhance my job security? If not, what is the job market like for me? How do I feel about my work (e.g., do I feel more competitive towards co-workers, more distrustful towards management, less intrinsically interested in my job)? What happened to the people who were laid off? Are layoffs taking place at other organizations similar to ours? What does this layoff and/or its handling tell me about the organization, and so on.

In short, the proposed process approach to the study of survivor reactions should focus on these and other pertinent concerns of survivors. Such an approach should consider the impact of one step in the sequence on subsequent ones. In a related vein, the process approach should consider the *cumulative* effects of the various stages on the key psychological states mentioned in Figure 1. For example, in what way do the events before, during, and after the layoff *combine* to affect the survivors' level of job insecurity?

Thus far our discussion of the process of survivors reactions has dealt with fractionating a single episode of layoffs into the "before, during, and after" stages. We took as our starting point the period in time in which the possibility of a layoff was in the air and culminated with the time period shortly after the actual layoff. This analysis, while useful, ignores other possible processes of survivor reactions. For one, future research should consider survivors' postlayoff reactions as they unfold over longer periods of time. For another, it is worth exploring the possible bidirectional process(es) by which survivors' reactions may feed back to influence the "resting point" state of the organization.

Time course of survivor reactions. A question of considerable significance is the longevity of survivor rea tions to layoffs. Most of the studies reported herein are mute on this issue, because they only assessed the short-term impact of the layoffs. Although the field studies (studies IV and VII) explored longer term effects spanning several months, further longitudinal research is an important mandate for future research.

On a related note, it is quite possible that layoffs produce *sequential* effects on survivors over time. Kübler-Ross (1969) and others have noted that the grief process consists of a number of distinct stages. If so, then survivors' reactions to work layoffs may interact with the point in time at which such reactions are assessed. The psychological states of job insecurity, positive inequity, and anger focus on different entities. The job insecure individual's focus of attention is on the *self.* Positive inequity refers to a comparison between the outcomes and inputs of *others* (who were dismissed) *and the self.* Anger reflects an attitude towards the *organization.* It could be that survivors' psychological states progress from being self-referential ("Will I be the next to go?") to comparative ("I feel badly that my co-workers were let go") to organizationally directed ("How could they do this?"). Regardless of the accuracy of this sequential anal ysis, it is both theoretically and practically important to determine the quantitative and qualitative effects of layoffs *over time.*

Bidirectional influences. Figure 1 presents a unidirectional model. Probably more accurate (and definitely more complex) is a conceptual model that includes bidirectional influences between the layoff, psychological states, and outcome variables. For example, survivors' level of productivity may feed back to affect the likelihood of a future layoff (Greenhalgh, 1983). In addition, the psychological states and outcome variables may be reciprocally related. For example, suppose that the layoff elicited job insecurity among survivors, causing them to look for work elsewhere. If the job-hunting process revealed that their alternatives were few, then survivors may come to feel increasingly guilty about the relative plight of their dismissed co-workers and themselves, and possibly angry at the organization for "inflicting" such hardship on themselves and the laid-off employees. This example also suggests that it is *the events* that unfold over time, rather than the mere passage of time itself, that underly the possibly sequential aspect of survivors' reactions.

In summary, much useful information may be unearthed by future research which views layoff survivorship as a process. To reiterate, by advocating a process orientation I do not mean to imply that the previous research discussed in this paper is *inaccurate;* rather, it is being suggested that the prior orientation leads to an *incomplete* analysis of survivors' reactions. Indeed, a more comprehensive understanding of survivors' reactions undoubtedly will need to go beyond survivors' perceptions of equity and stress. For example, Figure 1 implies that layoffs can elicit phenomenologically positive psychological states in survivors (e.g., feeling glad that the organization took long-needed action, feeling relieved that they were not chosen to be laid off). However, our discussion to this point has focused on more negative reactions such as anxiety, guilt, and anger. Perhaps an even greater portion of the variance in survivors' reactions may be explained by a conceptual model that actively investigates positive survivor reactions as mediating variables.

Unit of analysis. The conceptual model that has guided our thinking employs the individual as the unit of analysis. As future research begins to explore the process of layoff survivorship, it is likely (and desirable) that survivors' reactions will be explored at two other, more collective levels of analysis: the group and the entire organization. The decision about the most appropriate unit of analysis for study probably varies across situations, depending upon a host of factors. For example, certain layoffs are targeted at jobs or individuals within a work group. In this instance, the group remains viable, albeit smaller in membership. Other layoffs are targeted at more collective entities (e.g., groups, departments, plants), in which every job and individual within the collective is eliminated. Logically, I would argue that the greater the collectivity of the entity that is being laid off, the more collective should be the survivor unit of analysis.

Regardless of *how* to make the unit of analysis decision, it is clear that we need to learn much about the effects of layoffs on work group processes and outcomes. For example, a basic tenet of the small group literature is that group cohesion and productivity norms interactively affect group performance (e.g., Schachter, Ellertson, McBride, & Gregory, 1951). Groups that have developed the norm to work productively will do more and/or better work than those that have not; moreover, high group cohesiveness amplifies the impact of the group's productivity norm on its performance. To understand survivors' performance at the group level, it thus becomes important to delineate the impact of the layoff on the cohesiveness and/or performance norms of the group. As in our individual-level model, a host of moderating variables must be identified. That is, under some conditions survivors may "pull together," i.e., develop high cohesiveness and productivity norms; under other conditions one can imagine how the layoff could "break the group up," leading to a performance loss.

Other performance-relevant group processes may also be affected by layoffs. For example, the past decade has witnessed considerable research on the "social loafing" phenomenon, i.e., the tendency for group members to work less hard in groups than as individuals (Latané, Williams, & Harkins, 1979). Social loafing occurs primarily on additive tasks, in which group members perceive that others are working on the same task that they are, and that their own individual performance will not be identified. Faced with this anonymity, they diffuse the responsibility of working hard onto their fellow group members and, as a result, work less hard themselves (saying, in effect, "let the other guy do it"). It is possible that layoffs will affect survivors' perceptions of the factors that mediate the social loafing effect. For example, the decreased size of the surviving work group could reduce members' anonymity; if so, then an increase in survivors' work effort could be due, at least in part, to reduced social loafing. In short, future research should attend to the effect of layoffs on within and between-group processes. In order to understand better survivor reactions at the group level, in all likelihood it will be necessary to utilize a conceptual model of group effects that is similar in tone to the individual model offered in the first section of this chapter. That is, layoffs *can* affect group processes, which, in turn, *can* mediate group outcomes (Hackman & Morris, 1975; McGrath, 1964). Moreover, a host of moderator variables, probably drawn from the same five categories mentioned in the individual-level conceptual model, will affect the relationship between layoffs and group processes, and between group processes and outcomes.

Also, as noted above, the effects of layoffs can be subjected to an organizational level of analysis. Most layoffs simply do not entail a quantitative reduction in the workforce; in addition, there are usually a wide variety of organizational restructurings. For example, individuals and work groups might be required to perform different tasks, and strategic groupings and linkages between groups could be altered dramatically as the organization attempts to recover. It is beyond the scope of this paper to offer an organizational-level mediational analysis of the impact of layoffs on survivors. I mention it, however, because it is likely that survivor reactions, at least in part, may be most profitably explained at this macro level of analysis.

Summary. It may be useful to summarize briefly the proposed ways in which future theoretical development on survivors' reactions may proceed, i.e., how might a future conceptual model compare to the one with which we began this program of research? At the outset (see Figure 1) it was suggested that: (a) layoffs can affect several psychological states, (b) the psychological states can affect a variety of outcome variables (i.e., survivors' work behaviors and attitudes), (c) various factors play moderating roles in the potential relationships mentioned in (a) and (b) above, and (d) the literatures on equity theory and organizational stress may help us to predict and explain the impact of the moderator variables.

For the future, I propose the following conceptual model for the study of survivor reactions, the utility of which should be evaluated in light of empirical findings (see Figure 2).

1. Layoffs have the potential to influence not only survivors' individual psychological states, but also group processes and organizational structures.

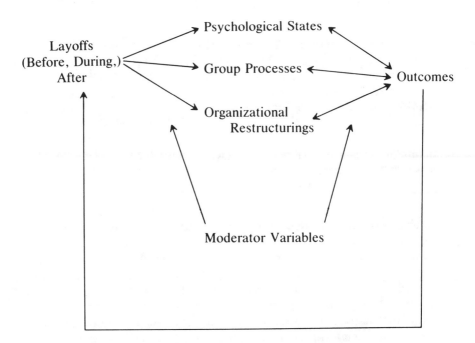

Figure 2. The proposed conceptual model in future research.

2. Changes in survivors' individual psychological states, changes in group processes, and changes in organizational structures have the potential to influence survivors' work behaviors and attitudes.

3. The categories of the moderator variables are identical to those in Figure 1.

4. Theories of group behavior and organizational structure, in addition to individual level models such as equity theory and organizational stress, should help predict and explain the impact of the moderator variables.

Figure 2 differs from Figure 1 in that the former considers the mediators of survivors' reactions at three levels of analysis (individual, group, and organization) rather than one; the conceptual model in Figure 2 also differs from its predecessor in the following respects: (1) greater attention is paid to the fact that the layoff event has a "before," "during," and "after" stage, (2) the relationships between the mediating variables and the outcome variables are reciprocal, (3a) the outcome variables may progress through sequences or stages over time, and (3b) the outcome variables may feed back to affect the "before" and "during" stages of future layoffs.

Towards a Broader Backdrop

The third section of this chapter described the reciprocal relationship between theory and research in the study of survivors; equity theory and stress notions were employed to generate predictions, and the empirical results, in turn, had implications for the theories from which the hypotheses were derived. In a similar but more general vein, theory and research on layoff survivors have implications for several related areas of organizational inquiry. Thus, future researchers of survivors' reactions would be well advised to be attuned to the insights they can offer to the "bigger picture" of organizational behavior. Two such broader backdrops are discussed below: the consequences of organizational exits and the role of culture in organizations.

Consequences of organizational exits.   A considerable portion of organizational psychology deals with employees' attachments to, or exits from, their work organizations (e.g., Mowday, Porter, & Steers, 1982). Accordingly, much research has focused on employee absenteeism and turnover, as exemplars of withdrawal or exit behavior. Virtually all of this research has explored the *antecedents* of employees' exits. Recently, however, there has been growing attention to the much more neglected part of the study of employee withdrawal: the *consequences* of exits and, in particular, their impact on the work behaviors and attitudes of those who remain. Krackhardt and Porter (1985), Mobley (1982), Mowday, et al., (1982), and Staw (1980) have offered theory and/or empirical research on the consequences of turnover, whereas Goodman and Atkin (1984) have studied the impact of employees' absenteeism on their fellow workers.

The research on layoff survivors may ultimately contribute to a more general conceptual analysis of the consequences of organizational exits. Such an analysis would have to delineate the distinctions between the various types of exits; at least three dimensions readily come to mind in comparing layoffs with turnover and absenteeism. First, layoffs differ from turnover (and certain absences) in that the former are involuntary, whereas the latter are voluntary. Implicit in my calling attention to this variable is the notion that the attribution(s) made for the employees' exit may moderate the effect of the exit on those who remain. Layoffs are initiated by the organization; turnover (and certain absences) are initiated by the exiting employee. From perceivers' point of view, this distinction roughly corresponds to the external vs. internal or pawn vs. origin dimension in causal attribution (de Charms, 1968; Kelley, 1973). The various ways in which attributional differences mediate individuals' thoughts, feelings, and behaviors are beyond the scope of this paper. The more general (and important) point is that the meanings of co-workers' exits, and thus their impact on those who stay, may be determined by the latters' causal attribution for the exit, and that layoffs and turnover may elicit very different causal attributions (Steers & Mowday, 1981). The different results produced by the random and merit layoffs in study II are consistent with an attributional analysis of the impact of organizational exits. The random decision rule is external to the laid-off worker; the merit rule, in sharp contrast, implicates the laid-off worker as the cause of his/her dismissal; these two sorts of exits evoked very different survivor reactions.

Second, layoffs (as discussed herein) refer to a *permanent* separation of the employee from his or her work organization. Absenteeism reflects a *temporary* exit. The more transient nature of absenteeism may require those who remain to adjust to their co-workers' periodic presence *or* absence. That adjustment process is likely to be quite different from the one elicited by the permanent absence of laid-off workers.

Third, and possibly building on the first two dimensions, layoffs may differ from the other two types of exits in the extent to which they threaten those who remain. For example, many if not most layoffs probably threaten survivors' job security (to varying degrees); in contrast, the turnover or absenteeism of fellow workers is less likely to arouse job insecurity among those who stay.

The final analysis (of the consequences of organizational exits) may prove that the more generalist approach is untenable. That is, turnover, absenteeism, layoffs, and other types of employee withdrawal behaviors (e.g., firings, early retirements) may be so qualitatively different from one another that they do not lend themselves to a more general conceptualization like the one I am hinting at here. Perhaps. In any event, the present research will at least join a slowly growing movement in the field of organizational psychology to study the consequences as well as the antecedents of employees' separations from the workplace.

Organizational culture.   The past decade has witnessed a resurgence of interest in the "softer" side of management, with emphasis on such constructs as the informal organization, climate, and culture (Peters & Waterman, 1982; Schein, 1986). Although the precise definition of culture is a matter of some debate among organizational scholars, most would probably agree that it refers at least in part to the values and norms that are often quite subtle, but nevertheless very powerful determinants of individual, group, and organization performance.

Research on the effects of layoffs on survivors raises a number of questions that students of organizational culture should find of interest. More specifically, an empirical question that my students and I are in the process of investigating deals with whether the layoff is congruent with the existing corporate culture. Our working hypothesis is that layoffs that are incongruent with the organization's culture are likely to have greater impact on survivors' psychological states than are layoffs that do not violate survivors' culturally generated expectations. That is, culture-incongruent layoffs are likely to amplify whatever negative psychological state survivors happen to be experiencing (i.e., anxiety, anger, guilt) as a result of other situational and dispositional factors mentioned in the first section of this chapter.

Note that culture-incongruent layoffs can come in many forms. In certain organizations the mere existence of a layoff can violate unwritten policies. For example, many workers formerly chose to work in public-sector organizations because of their implicit belief that such employment included job security. In the past decade, however, many public-sector organizations have suffered layoffs, which undoubtedly came as a shock to those laid off as well as the survivors. Moreover, it is even possible for private-sector organizations to experience culture-incongruent layoffs. For example, certain organizations (such as Kodak) have developed paternalistic corporate cultures, in which workers expect to be "taken care of" by their employers (in return, of course, for the employees' commitment to the organization). If and when layoffs do occur in paternalistic organizations, as in the case of Kodak, then survivors are much more apt to be "taken aback" than if the same layoff took place in a less paternalistic organization. In other instances, it could be *the way in which* the organization implements the layoff, in addition to, or instead of, the mere existence of the layoff, that is incongruent with its prevailing culture. For instance, consider the possibility of a paternalistic organization that does not act respectfully towards employees in the process of laying them off, e.g., does not provide ample forewarning in delivering the news, or other tangibles such as severance pay and outplacement counseling.

Moreover, the management of layoffs has more than mere theoretical implications concerning the role of culture in organizations. A practically important point is that the process of managing layoffs gives organizations the opportunity to reinforce the culture that it is trying to achieve (Porter, 1986). Given that the implementation of layoffs is frequently quite painful for all concerned, it is often viewed as a process to be "gotten through," rather than one that provides the organization with a real and important opportunity. Nevertheless, a poorly managed layoff can go a long way towards damaging the existing culture, and thereby have severely negative consequences for its human resource system. For example, a paternalistic organization that implements a culturally incongruent layoff may have difficulty retaining and recruiting valued employees who weight paternalism heavily.

Research on survivors' reactions also incorporates many other issues related to the role of culture in organizations. Recently, there has been considerable interest in employees' "sensemaking" processes within organizations, i.e., the mechanisms through which workers describe and explain their organizational realities (e.g., Louis, 1980). A basic notion is that sensemaking processes are most apt to occur in the face of organizational events that are both important and ambiguous; the layoffs of fellow employees would seem to include both of these attributes. Indeed, a hypothesis that we are in the process of testing is that survivors' perceptions of the layoff (and thus their behavioral and attitudinal reactions to it) are largely governed by their beliefs of the perceptions that significant others (e.g., peers, supervisors) maintain about the event (Salancik & Pfeffer, 1978).

As Porter (1986) has noted, research on layoff survivors may also contribute to the literature on communication processes within organizations. Suppose, for example, that the organization is contemplating, but is still uncertain about, implementing a layoff. What is the most effective way in which to communicate this possibility? Similarly, *when* would it be most prudent to announce that the organization is evaluating the possibility of introducing layoffs? On the one hand, by communicating this information early on the organization may better prepare the workforce for the layoff when it finally occurs. On the other hand, early communication may act as a self-fulfilling prophecy in which the news serves to distract the workforce, decrease productivity, and thus virtually ensure the necessity of the layoff. Obviously, there is no easy answer to the question of the proper timing of communication of the possibility of layoffs. It is possible, however, for future research to address this issue, and, in so doing, provide more general information to scholars interested in communication processes within organizations.

In conclusion, the study of survivors' reactions is replete with opportunities for future research. Some may choose to delineate additional moderators and mediators of the effects of layoffs on survivors. Others may wish to adopt the strategy of viewing layoffs as a series of interlocking processes, as I have hinted at in this final section of the paper. Still others may focus on the practical and managerial implications of this line of research. Regardless of the substance of the questions addressed in future research, it is important for investigators to be sensitive to the possibility that theory and research on survivors' reactions are relevant to a variety of "bigger pictures" in organizational behavior. Consequently, in exploring the effects of layoffs on survivors future researchers forever should consider, how, if at all, their empirical and theoretical efforts inform related areas of organizational studies.

ACKNOWLEDGMENTS

The author expresses sincere thanks to Bob Bies, Larry Cummings, Jerry Greenberg, Charles O'Reilly, and Barry Staw for their insightful comments on an earlier version of the manuscript.

NOTES

1. The results of study I bear a striking resemblance to an earlier study (Notz, Staw, & Cook, 1971), which was conducted in a very different context. The previous experiment explored the effect of (randomly) receiving draft lottery numbers—that made college students more or less likely to be drafted—on the students' attitudes towards troop withdrawal in Vietnam. Interestingly, it was the students whose draft numbers made them *less* likely to be drafted who expressed the greater desire for troop withdrawal. Although the language of equity theory was not employed in the Notz, et al. study, the results, as in experiment 1, suggested that when individuals are *randomly* selected to receive some valued outcome they could experience a sense of dissonance, positive inequity, or lack of deservingness. By expressing a stronger desire for troop withdrawal, those with favorable draft numbers may have attempted to achieve equity through cognitive means (i.e., hoping that all students—regardless of their numbers—would not have to fight in Vietnam).

2. As this chapter went to press, the results of study V were conceptually replicated in a field setting.

3. Even if the layoff evoked only one psychological state, it still could be difficult to predict its impact on survivors. This is due to the possibility that the mediating psychological states and the relevant outcome variables may be related in a nonlinear fashion. For example, if job-insecurity-produced anxiety is moderate, performance should be facilitated; on the other hand, very low or high levels of anxiety should interfere with performance (Yerkes & Dodson, 1908).

REFERENCES

Adams, J.S. (1965). Inequity in social exchange. In L. Berkowitz (Ed.), *Advances in experimental social psychology* (Vol. 2, pp. 267–299). New York: Academic Press.

Adams, J.S., & Rosenbaum, W.B. (1962). The relationship of worker productivity to cognitive dissonance about wage inequities. *Journal of Applied Psychology, 46*, 161–164.

Aronson, E. (1984). *The social animal* (4th ed.) San Francisco: Freeman.

Barton, E. (1986). *Layoffs and effective management.* Paper presented at the Twenty-fifth Academy of Management Convention, Chicago.

Bies, R.J. (1987). The predicament of injustice. The management of moral outrage. In B.M. Staw & L.L. Cummings (Eds.), *Research in Organizational behavior* (Vol. a). Greenwich, CT: JAI Press.

Blonder, M.D. (1976). *Organization repercussions of personnel cutbacks: Effects of layoffs on retained employees.* Unpublished doctoral dissertation, City University of New York.

Brockner, J. (1983). Low self-esteem and behavioral plasticity: Some implications. In L. Wheeler & P.R. Shaver (Eds.), *Review of personality and social psychology* (Vol. 4, pp. 237–271). Beverly Hills, CA: Sage.

Brockner, J., Davy, J., & Carter, C. (1985). Layoffs, self-esteem, and survivor guilt: Motivational, affective, and attitudinal consequences. *Organizational Behavior and Human Decision Processes, 36*, 229–244.

Brockner, J., Greenberg, J., Brockner, A., Bortz, J., Davy, J., & Carter, C. (1986). Layoffs, equity theory, and work performance: Further evidence on the impact of survivor guilt. *Academy of Management Journal, 29*, 373–384.

Brockner, J., Grover, S., & Blonder, M.D. (1987). *Factors predicting survivors' reactions to work layoffs: A field study.* Manuscript under editorial review.

Brockner, J., Grover, S., & O'Malley, M. (1986). *The effects of layoffs, identification with those laid off, and compensation to those laid off on survivors' work performance: A laboratory extension of equity theory.* Manuscript under editorial review.

Brockner, J., O'Malley, M.N., Grover, S., Esaki, N., Glynn, M.A., & Lazarides, S. (1987). *The effects of layoffs, job insecurity, and self-esteem on survivors' work performance and attitudes.* Manuscript under editorial review.

Cobb, S., & Kasl, S.V. (1977). *Termination: The consequences of job loss.* Cincinnati: NIOSH.

Cornfield, D.B. (1983). Chances of layoff in a corporation: A case study. *Administrative Science Quarterly, 28*, 503–520.

de Charms, R.C. (1968). *Personal causation: The internal affective determinants of behavior.* New York: Academic Press.

Deci, E.L. (1975). *Intrinsic motivation.* New York: Plenum.

Deutsch, M. (1985). *Distributive justice: A social-psychological perspective.* New Haven, CT: Yale University Press.

Festinger, L. (1954). A theory of social comparison processes. *Human Relations, 7*, 117–140.

Goodman, P.S., & Atkin, R.S. (1984). Consequences of absenteeism. In P. Goodman (Ed.), *Absenteeism.* San Francisco: Jossey-Bass.

Greenberg, J., & Ornstein, S. (1983). High status job title as compensation for underpayment: A test of equity theory. *Journal of Applied Psychology, 68*, 285–297.

Greenhalgh, L. (1982). Maintaining organizational effectiveness during organizational retrenchment. *Journal of Applied Behavioral Science, 18*, 155–170.

Greenhalgh, L. (1983). Managing the job insecurity crisis. *Human Resources Management, 22*, 431–444.

Greenhalgh, L., & Rosenblatt, Z. (1984). Job insecurity: Toward conceptual clarity. *Academy of Management Review, 9*, 438–448.

Hackman, J.R., & Morris, C.G. (1975). Group tasks, group interaction process, and group performance effectiveness: A review and proposed interpretation. In L. Berkowitz (Ed.), *Advances in experimental social psychology* (Vol. 8, pp. 45–99). New York: Academic Press.

Hackman, J.R., & Oldham, G.R. (1976). Motivation through the design of work: Test of a theory. *Organizational Behavior and Human Performance, 16,* 250–279.

Hershey, R. (1972). Effects of anticipated job loss on employee behavior. *Journal of Applied Psychology, 56,* 273–275.

Hovland, C.I., Lumsdaine, A.A., & Sheffield, F.D. (1949). *Experiments on mass communication.* Princeton, NJ: Princeton University Press.

Ichniowski, C., Brockner, J., & Davy, J. (1987). *Performance of survivors after seniority-based layoffs: A multi-method analysis.* Manuscript under editorial review.

Ilgen, D.R., Fisher, C.D., & Taylor, M.S. (1979). Consequences of individual feedback on behavior in organizations. *Journal of Applied Psychology, 64,* 349–371.

Jahoda, M. (1982). *Employment and unemployment: A social psychological analysis.* New York: Academic Press.

Jick, T. (1985). As the ax falls: Budget cuts and the experience of stress in organizations. In T.A. Beehr and R.S. Bhagat (Eds.), *Human stress and cognition in organizations* (pp. 83–114). New York: Wiley Interscience.

Kelley, H.H. (1973). The processes of causal attribution. *American Psychologist, 28,* 107–128.

Krackhardt, D., & Porter, L.W. (1985). When friends leave: A structural analysis of the relationship between turnover and stayers' attitudes. *Administrative Science Quarterly, 30,* 242–261.

Kübler-Ross, E. (1969). *On death and dying.* New York: Macmillan.

Latané, B., Williams, K., & Harkins, S. (1979). Many hands make light the work: The causes and consequences of social loafing. *Journal of Personality and Social Psychology, 37,* 822–832.

Louis, M.R. (1980). Surprise and sense making: What newcomers experience in entering unfamiliar organizational settings. *Administrative Science Quarterly, 25,* 226–251.

McGrath, J.E. (1964). *Social psychology: A brief introduction.* New York: Holt, Rinehart, & Winston.

McGrath, J. (1976). Stress and behavior in organizations. In M.D. Dunnette (Ed.), *Handbook of industrial and organizational psychology* (pp. 1351–1395). Chicago: Rand-McNally.

McGuire, W.J. (1972). Attitude change: The information-processing paradigm. In C.G. McClintock (Ed.), *Experimental social psychology* (pp. 108–141). New York: Holt, Rinehart, & Winston.

Mobley, W.H. (1982). *Employee turnover: Causes, consequences, and control.* Reading, MA: Addison-Wesley.

Mossholder, K.W., Bedeian, A.G., & Armenakis, A.A. (1982). Group process-work outcome relationships: A note on the moderating impact of self-esteem. *Academy of Management Journal, 25,* 575–585.

Mowday, R.T. (1979). Equity theory predictions of behavior in organizations. In R.M. Steers & L.W. Porter (Eds.), *Motivation and work behavior* (pp. 124–146). New York: McGraw-Hill.

Mowday, R.T., Porter, L.W., & Steers, R.M. (1982). *Employee-organization linkages: The psychology of commitment, absenteeism, and turnover.* New York: Academic Press.

Nadler, D.A., & Tushman, M.L. (1980). A model for diagnosing organizational behavior. *Organizational Dynamics, 9* (2), 35–51.

Notz, W.W., Staw, B.M., & Cook, T.D. (1971). Attitude toward troop withdrawal from Indochina as a function of draft member: Dissonance or self-interest? *Journal of Personality and Social Psychology, 20,* 118–126.

Peters, T.J., & Waterman, R.H. (1982). *In search of excellence*. New York: Harper & Row.

Porter, L.W. (1986). *Discussant's comments for, "The effects of work layoffs on survivors."* Symposium presented at the Twenty-fifth Academy of Management Convention, Chicago.

Salancik, G.R., & Pfeffer, J. (1978). A social information processing approach to job attitudes and task design. *Administrative Science Quarterly, 23*, 224–253.

Schachter, S., Ellertson, N., McBride, D., & Gregory, D. (1951). An experimental study of cohesiveness and productivity. *Human Relations, 4*, 229–238.

Schein, E.H. (1986). *Organizational culture and leadership*. San Francisco: Jossey-Bass.

Sherif, M., Harvey, O.J., White, B.J., Hood, W.E., & Sherif, C.W. (1961). *Intergroup conflict and cooperation: The robber's cave experiment*. Norman: University of Oklahoma Book Exchange.

Shrauger, J.S. (1972). Self-esteem and reactions to being observed by others. *Journal of Personality and Social Psychology, 23*, 192–200.

Staw, B.M. (1980). The consequences of turnover. *Journal of Occupational Behavior, 1*, 253–273.

Staw, B.M., Sandelands, L.E., & Dutton, J.E. (1981). Threat-rigidity effects in organizational behavior. *Administrative Science Quarterly, 26*, 501–524.

Steers, R.M., & Mowday, R.T. (1981). Employee turnover and post-decision accomodation processes. In B.M. Staw & L.L. Cummings (Eds.), *Research in organizational behavior* (Vol. 3, pp. 235–281). Greenwich, CT: JAI Press.

Thomas, K.W. (1976). Conflict and conflict management. In M.D. Dunnette (Ed.), *Handbook of industrial and organizational psychology*, Chicago: Rand McNally.

Yerkes, R.M., & Dodson, J.D. (1908). The relation of strength of stimulus to rapidity of habit formation. *Journal of Comparative Neurological Psychology, 18*, 459–482.

J
A
I

P
R
E
S
S

Work in Organizations

Edited by **Barry M. Staw** and **L.L. Cummings**

CONTENTS: **Motivation Theory Reconsidered,** *Frank J. Landy and Wendy S. Becker.* **Activation Theory and Job Design: Review and Reconceptualization,** *Donald G. Gardner and L.L. Cummings.* **Toward an Integrated Theory of Task Design,** *Ricky W. Griffin.* **Of Art and Work: Aesthetics Experience, and the Psychology of Work Feelings,** *Lloyd E. Sandelands and Georgette C. Buckner.* **The Expression of Emotion in Organizational Life,** *Anat Rafaeli and Robert I. Sutton.* **"Real Feelings": Emotional Expression and Organizational Culture,** *John Van Maanen and Gideon Kunda.* **Work Values and the Conduct of Organizational Behavior,** *Walter R. Nord, Arthur P. Brief, Jennifer M. Atieh, and Elizabeth M. Doherty.*

1990   296 pp.   LC 90-4474   Paper $19.50
ISBN 1-55938-216-3

All articles are reprinted from: **Research in Organizational Behavior,** Edited by **Barry M. Staw,** *School of Business Administration, University of California, Berkeley* and **L.L. Cummings,** *Carlson School of Management, University of Minnesota*

JAI PRESS INC.

55 Old Post Road - No. 2
P.O. Box 1678
Greenwich, Connecticut 06836-1678
Tel: 203-661-7602

8384